MW00987576

HELL WITH THE LID OFF

HELL

with the **LID OFF**

Inside the Fierce Rivalry between the 1970s Oakland RAIDERS and Pittsburgh STEELERS

ED GRUVER and **JIM CAMPBELL**

Foreword by Andy Russell

University of Nebraska Press

LINCOLN

© 2019 by Ed Gruver and Jim Campbell
Foreword © 2019 by the Board of Regents of the
University of Nebraska

All rights reserved
Manufactured in the United States of America

Library of Congress Cataloging-in-Publication Data
Names: Gruver, Ed, 1960– author. | Campbell, Jim,
1937– author.
Title: Hell with the lid off: inside the fierce rivalry between the
1970s Oakland Raiders and Pittsburgh Steelers / Ed Gruver
and Jim Campbell; foreword by Andy Russell.
Description: Lincoln: University of Nebraska Press, [2019]
Identifiers: LCCN 2019010727
ISBN 9781496214676 (cloth: alk. paper)
ISBN 9781496219138 (epub)
ISBN 9781496219145 (mobi)
ISBN 9781496219152 (pdf)
Subjects: LCSH: Oakland Raiders (Football team)—
History—20th century. | Pittsburgh Steelers (Football
team)—History—20th century. | Sports rivalries—United
States—History—20th century.
Classification: LCC GV956.024 G78 2019 |
DDC 796.332/64097309047—dc23
LC record available at https://lccn.loc.gov/2019010727

Set in Arno Pro by Mikala R. Kolander.

Contents

Foreword

After decades of being known as the "Steel City," Pittsburgh was in something of a funk by the end of the 1960s and into the 1970s. The production of steel was down, and unemployment was rising. In general, Pittsburghers were not feeling so good about themselves.

Probably not too many realized it, but things were about to change, and change for the better.

With the hiring of Chuck Noll and the drafting of Joe Greene in 1969, a firm and winning foundation was being laid. The turnaround was more gradual than immediate, but progress was being made.

After years of being "lovable losers," a tag that I know bothered Mr. Art Rooney, we had an 11-3 record in 1972—helped immeasurably by rookie Franco Harris—and won our first championship of any kind, the AFC Central.

Our last regular-season win in San Diego set up a game I'll never forget, a hard-fought, hard-hitting game against a team that became our fiercest rival, the Oakland Raiders. We were up, 6–0, with 1:17 to play, when Raiders QB Ken Stabler "snaked" his way around our right end for a 30-yard touchdown. George Blanda's extra point put us down a point with little time left.

It didn't look good, but we weren't about to give up. Down to fourth and 10, we still thought of Chuck Noll's motto: "Whatever it takes."

What it took was a tremendous collision between Jack Tatum, John "Frenchy" Fuqua, and the football to produce what has been called by NFL Films "the greatest play in NFL history"—Franco's miraculous catch.

The ball, propelled by Tatum's impetus, shot back in Franco's direction, the left flat. He picked it off his shoe tops and headed for the end zone. When Franco got there, back judge Adrian Burk signaled a touchdown, but not many, if any, were sure what had happened. I, like many of my defensive mates, watched in disbelief. Eventually, it was ruled a legal touchdown and became known as "the Immaculate Reception."

It was the start of a Steelers dynasty, even though we lost the AFC Championship narrowly to the Dolphins, who would go on to a perfect 17-0 season. It was also the start of a rivalry with the Raiders that to both Pittsburgh and Oakland is the greatest not only in NFL history but perhaps in sports history as well. After all, what other rivalry routinely resulted in the crowning of a Super Bowl champion? And what other rivalry forced its league to add new rules?

For three straight years, from 1974 to 1976, our AFC Championship Games with the Raiders decided a Super Bowl berth and the eventual Super Bowl champion. Steelers-Raiders games captured the attention and imagination of NFL fans across the nation, from East Coast to West Coast. Our games were violent and the hitting vicious, and we forced the NFL to change the rules of its game, leading to the making of the modern offense-oriented National Football League.

Coach Noll's philosophy was to build through the draft, and we improved markedly in his early years. Perhaps the greatest draft ever was 1974. It yielded four Hall of Famers—Lynn Swann, John Stallworth, Jack Lambert, and Mike Webster. This was also the year Rocky Bleier emerged at running back.

It was the season too when we won the first of our four Super Bowls in six years. It was my distinct pleasure as captain to present the Super Bowl IX game ball to the Chief, Art Rooney—an experience I'll cherish always. Thinking back over the years, the thought of winning a Super Bowl—particularly prior to Chuck's arrival—was something I could never have realistically dreamed of.

The most important game, to my way of thinking, that led to our

Super Bowl era was the 1974 AFC Championship Game that we won in Oakland. Dwight "Mad Dog" White and Ernie "Fats" Holmes shut down the Raiders' left-handed running game behind Pro Football Hall of Famers Gene Upshaw and Art Shell. But what sealed the deal was Jack "Hammer" Ham's late interception. Before the play Stabler came up to the line and actually winked at me. I inferred that he was telling me he was going to throw a game-winning TD pass, as he had done the previous week against Miami. Ham had a different thought. As history shows we won the game and went on to establish the Steelers' first Super Bowl era.

While NFL football was very popular by then, I like to think that our rivalry with the Raiders elevated the game even more.

What the Rooneys meant to all of us can't be overestimated. They truly cared and fostered a family atmosphere and always demonstrated class.

I consider myself fortunate to have played for Chuck Noll, a man I consider the most underappreciated coach in NFL history. Lessons learned from him have helped me as a player and, later in life, in my business career. I'm sure many other Steelers feel the same way.

It's been said that the Steelers gave Pittsburgh a reason for getting back its swagger. But Pittsburgh gave the Steelers something, too. The city embraced us unconditionally. The fact that so many from our era have made Pittsburgh home and have had successful postplaying careers is a testament to the two-way street of affection between a city and its football team.

At times I've reflected on my football journey as akin to the 1967 Sergio Leone spaghetti western *The Good, the Bad, and the Ugly*. I learned from the "bad and the ugly" and relished "the good" and would not trade a minute of any of it.

Jim Campbell was there on the Steelers' sideline throughout our great rivalry with the Raiders and had a front-row seat for everything from the Immaculate Reception to our Super Bowl victories over Minnesota and Dallas. Coupled with Ed Gruver's meticulous research and insightful writing, the inside, behind-the-scenes look this book provides into our rivalry with the Raiders is both entertaining and informative.

Enjoy!

Andy Russell

HELL WITH THE LID OFF

Prologue

Immaculate Reception or Deception?

"Last chance for the Steelers . . ."

In the broadcast booth high above the bright-green Tartan Turf of Three Rivers Stadium, legendary NBC-TV sportscaster Curt Gowdy joined more than fifty thousand fans inside the stadium and millions more watching on television and listening on radio in leaning forward from his seat late in the afternoon on December 23, 1972.

On this day before Christmas Eve wintry skies shrouded the flaring stadium lights. Game-time temperatures for this AFC divisional play-off between Pittsburgh and Oakland peaked at forty-two degrees and were dropping steadily as night approached. The weather had been solemn all day, but Steelers fans had initially seen it as an omen, and a good one at that. To them the skies were not just gray but *steel* gray.

On the Mutual Broadcasting Network Bob Reynolds, teamed with his Detroit Lions broadcast partner Van Patrick, noted at the outset, "Though the skies are overcast, the lights have been on here at Three Rivers Stadium since early this morning. Nonetheless for Pittsburgh fans, of course, the sun is shining brightly."

The reason was simple, Reynolds said. "This is a big day here in Pittsburgh. The Steelers' fans have waited forty long years for this one."

Indeed. There was a time when two-thirds of Pittsburgh's work-force was foreign born. They had arrived on ships from the old country and settled among their own—Italians in the Bloomfield section, Germans on Troy Hill, Poles and Eastern Europeans on the South Side, Galway Irish on the North, Irish in East Liberty—"Sliberty" as it's pronounced by 'Burghers. From Somers Point to Squirrel Hill to Greenfield, Steelers fans rallied behind their young Central Division champions.

Interestingly, and not without irony, a college—or "cawledge" in Pittsburghese—town in Pittsburgh carries the name of the city from which the Steelers' hated rivals hail. Oakland sits a couple of miles away from Sliberty, and while most neighborhoods in Pittsburgh were parochial, Oakland being a college town had outside influences, thanks to its serving as home for the University of Pittsburgh.

Oakland had Forbes Field, where Clemente, Stargell, Maz, and the rest of the Pirates' Pittsburgh Lumber Company played until they joined the Steelers as cotenants in the sparkling new Three Rivers Stadium.

Billy Conn, the light-heavyweight champion who nearly beat the legendary Joe Louis in one of boxing's most famous fights, was a Pittsburgh guy. 'Burghers recall that it was *Cawn*, their favorite *bawxer*, who said that Pittsburgh is the town you can't wait to leave and the town you can't wait to return to. Writer Frank Deford described Pittsburgh as a metropolitan area of more than two million people but one that had the soul of a small town. H. L. Mencken saw something else. Taking note of city skies black with smoke, of streetlights lit nearly all day every day, of the hard, dirty work required in the mills, Mencken said Pittsburgh was "so dreadfully hideous, so intolerably bleak and forlorn that it reduced the whole aspiration of a man to a macabre and depressing joke."

Steel City citizens coughed up the smoke, spit the soot from their lungs, and rinsed the grime from their throats with a shot of Imperial whiskey and an Iron City beer. An Imp and an Iron—it was the favorite boilermaker of the shot-and-a-beer shift workers who stood three deep at their neighborhood bars in the early-morning dawn after leaving the mills.

Pittsburgh was gritty and gloomy, and by the final seconds of the fourth quarter, the figurative sun that shone so brightly for Steelers fans for much of the game had grown as dark as the sooty skyline. With just twenty-two seconds remaining, Pittsburgh trailed 7–6 and faced fourth and 10 from its 40-yard line. The Steelers' chances flickered like a flame in the wind. For their fans the only color left to this suddenly sullen Saturday was provided by the uniforms of the players on the field below—the black and gold of the Steelers and silver and black of the Raiders.

"Hang onto your hats," Pittsburgh Steelers radio announcer Jack Fleming told his listening audience. *"Here come the Steelers out of the huddle, Terry Bradshaw at the controls. Twenty-two seconds remaining..."*

Twenty-two seconds and the Steelers, playing for a berth in the first championship game in franchise history, found themselves trailing after leading much of the afternoon.

Twenty-two seconds and the Raiders would reach their fifth championship game in six seasons. "Commitment to excellence," a franchise slogan, would be realized again.

There were layers to this game that not everyone was aware of. Steelers head coach Chuck Noll and Raiders general managing partner Al Davis had served on the same coaching staff with Sid Gillman's electrifying Chargers in the American Football League a decade prior. Noll and his coaching opposite, John Madden, had been hired as head coaches in 1969, and both began their pro coaching careers in the old AFL. As the final seconds prepared to tick down, Davis chewed his already shortened fingernails, Noll gritted his teeth as was his custom, and Madden ran his thick fingers through his wavy auburn hair. Up in the television booth reserved for the National Broadcasting Company, Gowdy, the venerated voice of NBC Sports and another AFL alum, studied the situation unfolding below.

This was indeed the last chance for the Steelers, and the last chance, too, for Franco's Italian Army, Gerela's Gorillas, and the rest of the Steelers zealots, many of whom, because of the NFL's blackout rule that prevented the game from being televised within a seventy-five-mile radius of the city, had fled to western Pennsylvania steel towns Erie and Meadville and even to Zanesville, Ohio, to watch their beloved Steelers.

It did not seem to be a day of destiny after all. Pittsburgh had pounded out a 6–0 lead behind Roy Gerela field goals from 18 and 29 yards and a Steel Curtain defense just gaining fame. The game had been a tremendous defensive struggle. Fronted by defensive coaches Bud Carson and George Perles, the Steel Curtain shut down Oakland's celebrated "Mad Bomber," quarterback Daryle Lamonica, and his rocket-launching right arm. It was quite a feat, since Lamonica's sixty-five victories since becoming the Raiders' starter in 1967 were the most by any quarterback in pro football. But the Raiders, renowned for their last-minute miracle comebacks, grabbed a sudden and startling lead when Kenny "Snake" Stabler, sent in by Madden to replace an ailing Lamonica, wove 30 yards downfield on a broken play. The Snake didn't stop until he slithered into the Steelers' gold-and-black-painted end zone.

Linebacker Andy Russell's dark features grew darker on the suddenly disconsolate Steelers sideline. He was mad, Russell recalled, that the Steel Curtain had screwed up and let the Raiders score.

To some the letdown seemed to indicate sos—Same Old Steelers. In thirty-one of their previous thirty-nine seasons the Steelers had failed to compile a winning record. The long-awaited turnaround began with the hiring of the no-nonsense Noll in 1969. Pittsburgh then drafted future stars Joe Greene and L. C. Greenwood in '69, Bradshaw and Mel Blount in 1970. The '71 off-season brought the "Elite Eight"—eight eventual Super Bowl starters, including a future Hall of Famer and six Pro Bowlers. Jack Ham, Dwight White, Ernie Holmes, Mike Wagner, Gerry Mullins, Frank Lewis, and Larry Brown constituted Pittsburgh's draft haul in '71, and Glen Edwards was signed as an undrafted free agent. While the 1974 draft class that yielded four Hall of Famers in Mike Webster, Jack Lambert, Lynn Swann, and John Stallworth is considered the gold standard, the '71 draft was particularly important to the Steelers' success. When Pittsburgh reached its first Super Bowl following the 1974 season, each of the Elite Eight started.

The rookie class of '71 helped the Steelers turn the corner, and Harris's arrival in 1972 accelerated their success rate. The big rookie running back set records en route to rushing for 1,055 yards, and Pittsburgh went 11-3 and beat the rival Cleveland Browns to win the AFC Central.

Now, as Fleming reminded his audience, Pittsburgh's offense was facing fourth and 10. It might as well have been fourth and forever. As the white stadium lights reflected off his shiny black helmet, Bradshaw bent low in the Steelers' huddle and licked his fingers.

"Sixty-six Circle Option," he said.

Barry Pearson would be the primary receiver in 66 Circle Option. A rookie, Pearson had been standing near position coach and former American Football League star wideout Lionel Taylor on the Steelers' sideline. Taylor suddenly told Pearson to go in for Ron Shanklin. With the Steelers' season on the brink, the man who had not played a single down all season was being sent into the game. Pearson was given the play by Noll to take in to Bradshaw. It was a play designed to get a first down, to get into Gerela's range to attempt a game-winning field goal.

In the Pittsburgh huddle Harris was thinking, "This is our last play of the year." Franco's backfield mate, the outrageous John "Frenchy" Fuqua, was wishing the Steelers' special season didn't have to end in defeat.

If this was the end, Harris was going to play it all the way out. Unfortunately for him, the play called didn't really involve him at all. His assignment was to stay in and block a linebacker if the Raiders blitzed Bradshaw.

Across the line of scrimmage the Raiders' defense was thinking along with Harris. Linebacker Phil Villapiano, assigned to man-on-man coverage on Harris in Oakland's prevent scheme, heard a teammate exclaim, "No penalties. This game is over!"

Tatum, wearing a scowl behind his half-cage face mask, hissed, "One more time." A ferocious hitter, Tatum would author a book titled *They Call Me Assassin*. His blindside hit on New England's Darryl Stingley in 1978 left Stingley paralyzed for life. With his heavily taped forearms and bristling black mustache, Tatum cut a fearsome figure in a hard-hitting Oakland secondary that took pride in calling itself the "Soul Patrol."

Tatum had broken up two of Pittsburgh's previous three pass plays, and as the Raiders broke the huddle and braced for one final defensive stand, Tatum's partner at safety, George Atkinson, shouted, "We got this game won. . . . All we gotta do is knock the ball down!"

Tatum, however, wasn't thinking knockdown. The Assassin wanted a knockout. "I wanted to smash one more Steeler before the final gun went off," he said.

It had been that kind of game. Tatum said later the very air around Three Rivers Stadium that day seemed to explode from the sonic booms of bone-shattering tackles. Madden thought the violence of the game so visceral that it was like war, football's version of Vietnam.

The Steelers have one more chance, Tatum thought. Do or die.

The design of 66 Circle Option called for wide receiver Al Young to run an out pattern to the left. Fuqua, who would draw single coverage from linebacker Gerald Irons, was to curl over the middle, while tight end John McMakin ran a deep post. With McMakin running a clearing pattern, Pearson, the primary receiver, was to run underneath, about 12 yards, which would put him just past the large, colorful Steelers logo at midfield.

On the Steelers' sideline, Terry Hanratty sneaked a glance at Noll. What the backup quarterback saw in his coach's face convinced him that Noll believed Pittsburgh was going to win.

"He knew something would break," Hanratty said. "It was weird."

Hanratty noted how calmly Noll was calling the pass plays. Noll would say later that leaving the game plan would be a sign of panic.

"And panic," he stated forcefully, "is not in our game plan."

Fleming: *"This crowd is standing . . ."*

Standing and, in many cases, praying. In the upper-level seats in Three Rivers Stadium, Mario Camaioni glanced at his hand siren that had just stopped working. It seemed an ominous sign, considering Pittsburgh's predicament. "All I can do now," Camaioni thought, "is pray."

People were praying outside the stadium as well. Twenty-five miles southwest of the city, Chuck Finder, who grew up to be a Pittsburgh sportswriter, was among those in the blacked-out area. As he listened to the radio broadcast, Finder felt the Steelers' desperation. He did something Jewish boys weren't supposed to do. He rang up "Dial-a-Prayer."

As center Jim Clack snapped the ball into Bradshaw's hands, what transpired over the next seventeen seconds would become sport's version of the Zapruder film. It would also lead to a cottage industry of questions that will remain forever unanswered. It's a play that has given rise to conspiracy theories and taken on religious overtones.

At the snap Bradshaw dropped straight back and saw the Raiders' defense dropping into prevent coverage. Feeling pressure to his left, the Steelers' quarterback rolled to his right. He barely eluded Raiders ends Tony Cline and Horace Jones. Charging from Oakland's left side, Cline collapsed the pocket with a bull rush that drove right tackle Gerry Mullins to the turf. A fourth-round pick out of the University of Miami and the 102nd pick overall in the 1970 draft, Cline nearly made the defensive play of the Raiders' season.

Cline reached out with his right arm over the prone body of Mullins, who was face-down on the ground. Cline was 6 feet 3, and his long wingspan nearly allowed him to succeed in his determined grab at Bradshaw's left sleeve. As it was, Cline clutched air.

Gowdy: *"Bradshaw trying to get away ..."*

A desperate Bradshaw dipped behind his 30-yard line. Jones, who had rushed from the right side, fought off the block of Jon Kolb. Freed from the Steelers' muscular left tackle, Jones closed on Bradshaw. Still rolling right as he retreated, Terry abruptly stopped at his 29.

Like Cline, Jones was not a high draft pick. A product of the University of Louisville, he had been selected in the twelfth round, the 305th pick overall, in the '71 draft. He had played his first season in Oakland at Cline's position, left end, but was switched to the right side for the '72 season.

On this play the fury of Jones's rush forced him to overrun the play as Bradshaw alertly and at the last second took a half step to his left. Jones reacted and reached back toward Bradshaw with an extended right arm.

Viewed from the sidelines, pro football is pure mayhem. The synchronization and precision that fans see from the stands, the spacing they view on their TVs, are destroyed by the sheer speed of the sport. Twenty-one bodies are set in motion with each snap of the ball; the twenty-second, the quarterback, is the one seeking to stay calm amid the fury.

Violence and velocity fill the vacuum that exists just prior to the start of the play. Linemen curse and grunt as they slam bodies into one another. Thickly padded forearms smash into chests; clenched fists find their way to unprotected arms and abdomens; helmets are driven into shoulder pads. There is additional hollering and screaming; Vince Lombardi's championship Green Bay defenses of the 1960s were said to scream like banshees, sending shivers up and down the spines of opposing offenses. Players on both sides call out coded references to what is unfolding on the field.

In the radio booth, Fleming called the frantic, frenzied action:

"Bradshaw running out of the pocket, looking for somebody to throw to . . ."

Harris, who had positioned himself behind Clack to provide extra protection for Bradshaw, looked back and saw his quarterback break containment. Harris immediately headed down the middle of the field as the pocket broke down.

"I knew Brad was in serious trouble," he said. "So I went downfield in case he needed me as an outlet receiver."

As he moved past the line of scrimmage Harris was picked up in man-to-man coverage by Villapiano, who stayed on the rookie's right shoulder. Seeing Bradshaw's snap throw to Fuqua, Harris headed in Frenchy's direction.

"I was always taught to go to the ball," Harris said, "so when he threw it, that's what I did."

Fuqua has always figured that life is all about "ifs." If the pass protection hadn't broken down, if the Raiders' rush hadn't forced Bradshaw to run to Fuqua's left, Terry would have hit Frenchy with a short pass and the fullback would have run out of bounds to set up Gerela's field-goal attempt. Or, he later said, maybe he would have broken a tackle or two and run all the way for a touchdown. Then, joked Frenchy, he would have been on Johnny Carson's *The Tonight Show* as the "first black prince of Pennsylvania."

The precise, intricately drawn designs of the playbook become meaningless when all hell is breaking loose on the field. Football is a game of breakdowns—physical missteps, mental mistakes. Bodies accelerate rapidly, and when a player is operating under the kind of severe pressure inherent in potentially season-ending playoff games, his ability to think clearly becomes paramount.

With Jones clawing at him and Cline lowering his battle-scarred silver helmet as he moved to within a yard of his prey, Bradshaw, who had taken his eyes off his receivers as quarterbacks do when scrambling for their lives, looked up to see whom he could find downfield. All he saw was Fuqua. Bradshaw pumped once and then set his white cleats on the far-right hash mark as he drew his passing arm high above his helmet.

"I was about to get hit," he recalled. "I unloaded it."

Bradshaw buggy-whipped a bullet-like pass to Fuqua, who was at the Raiders' 34. Fuqua was wide open and he knew it. Tatum had taken off on the post pattern, but as Fuqua planted his feet he thought about Tatum. "He's coming. No doubt about it."

Hearing Tatum's cleats pounding on the hard artificial turf confirmed Fuqua's fear. In his mind Frenchy was calling for his quarterback to make the pass. "Bradshaw, throw it!" Fuqua could hear the onrushing Tatum breathing behind him, and each breath was bringing ever closer the man called the "Assassin."

Fuqua knew he and Tatum were running to the same point on the field; he could hear Jack's cleats clomping on the carpeted turf. Frenchy didn't want Tatum to step in front of him, intercept the ball, and run down the sideline, so he prepared to position himself between Tatum and the ball. Fuqua was hustling to get to a point on the field, and Tatum was coming at the same speed to destroy whoever was going to be at that point. Frenchy heard the Assassin approaching; he knew Tatum was one to "knock your crown off." Fuqua didn't consider Jack a dirty player or cheap-shot artist. Tatum wasn't one to grab an opponent's finger in a pileup and dislocate it, as some players did. Jack just hit the hell out of opponents on every play.

On this play, the Frenchman was Tatum's target.

Fleming: *"[Bradshaw] fires downfield . . . And there's a collision!"*

Beneath his white jersey Tatum had an awesome torso. His remarkable muscular development was augmented by regular gym workouts with weights. He was a corded and compact 5 feet 11 and 205 pounds, and because he could also cover 100 yards in ten seconds, Tatum became feared for his explosive hits. He raised his right forearm into Fuqua and laid Frenchy out flat.

Tatum knew Fuqua couldn't catch a helmet in the back and hold onto the ball at the same time, so he blasted into Fuqua with a full head of steam.

George Atkinson was trailing Pearson at the Oakland 32-yard line when he saw Tatum close for the kill shot. Atkinson knew that Tatum, being the aggressive player he was, would go for the knockout blow rather than knock the ball down. It was, Atkinson thought, a big mistake for Oakland. Villapiano thought Tatum had hit Fuqua early, but figured no official would call interference at that point in the game.

Gowdy: *"His pass is broken up by Tatum!"*

Steelers teammates thought the violent collision left Fuqua concussed. Frenchy acknowledged he didn't know where he was or even who he was. He recalled being on the turf and looking skyward when he saw Tatum jumping up and down smiling. While he was still in the air, Tatum's smile suddenly turned to a frown.

Tatum didn't honestly know if the ball hit him. He wasn't worried about the ball at the time. He had just wanted to lay some wood on Fuqua, and he did. Tatum's bone-rattling blow caused the ball to carom into the brittle air.

"The next thing I knew," Harris said, "the ball was coming right to me."

As Bradshaw lay flat on the turf, another Steelers quarterback named Terry—Hanratty—watched the play unfold from the sideline. The former Notre Dame star saw the ball pop high into the air and fly what Hanratty estimated to be seven or eight yards back toward the offense.

Back, in fact, toward Franco. Hanratty, the Golden Domer, had played in the shadow of Notre Dame's Touchdown Jesus in the mid-1960s. As the ball arced toward an onrushing Harris, it seemed to Hanratty to be guided by the hand of God.

Fleming: *"It's caught out of the air . . . The ball is pulled in by Franco Harris!"*

Hanratty saw Harris clutch the ball at the Oakland 42. There was no question in Hanratty's mind that it was a clean catch. Villapiano was stunned. In his mind a "lazy" Franco had "jogged" to the spot. Harris later countered that if he had been as lazy on that play as Villapiano said, then how did he beat Phil to the ball?

A review of black-and-white snapshots of the play's sequence shows Harris and Villapiano in lockstep together at the Raiders' 48, just to the left of the Steelers' logo at midfield. As the ball wobbled back toward them, Franco put on a sudden burst of speed that allowed him to race past Villapiano, reach down, and, with the ball calf high and to his left, grab it in full gallop a split second before it would have touched the Tartan Turf.

The rest has always been a blur to Harris.

"It happened so fast," he said. "It was all reaction. My only thought was to get to the end zone."

Noll, who admitted he did not see the play but could tell from the crowd noise that something good had happened, later gritted his teeth and grinned. "Good things," he said, "come to those who hustle."

The ball could have bounced to a million different places, Villapiano vented, but it went right into Franco's hands. Villapiano was right there with Franco, but after Bradshaw threw the ball Phil headed toward Fuqua to help out in coverage. The ball then ricocheted over his head. Had he stayed where he was, Villapiano lamented, the ball "would have been right to me."

In 1972 the Moody Blues climbed the pop charts with "Nights in White Satin." On this day Harris became a knight in black nylon in the eyes of Steelers fans. Stationed at the 40-yard line, Franco's Army, wearing World War II–style helmets and brandishing Italian flags, chanted, "Run, paisano, run!" Earlier, the Army's "generals" had paraded around Three Rivers Stadium in military trucks to support their generalissimo, Franco. Founded by East Liberty business owners Al Vento and Tony Stagno, the Army protected the Steelers from misfortune by blowing into an Italian horn known as the *corno* and cursed the Raiders with the *malocchio*, "evil eye" in Italian. According to the Army, a last-minute *malocchio* had been cast on the Raiders just prior to Tatum's violent hit on Fuqua and Franco's shoe-top reception.

Fleming: *"Harris is going for a touchdown for Pittsburgh!"*

It was a miracle of a magnitude of which even Smokey Robinson dared not dream. Villapiano attempted to chase Harris but was blocked by McMakin at the 37. "The Magnificent Obstruction," McMakin called it.

Villapiano called it something else. "A clip!" he exclaimed. Otherwise, Villapiano said, he would have made the play, and there would be no Immaculate Reception.

As it was, it was left to defensive back Jimmy Warren, who exulted briefly by flinging both arms skyward when Tatum flattened Fuqua, to try to stop Harris. Warren reacted and took an angle on Harris at the 31. He lunged for Franco at the 11 and got both hands on Harris's jersey, but the 230-pound Franco reached back with his right arm and stiff-armed Warren, sending the smaller man to the ground.

Gowdy: *"Franco Harris grabbed the ball on a deflection! He grabbed it with five seconds to go and scored!"*

An explosion of noise filled Three Rivers Stadium. Steelers right guard Bruce Van Dyke, on the ground after battling Otis Sistrunk in a ferocious hand fight, heard the lusty roar of thousands of fans. Van Dyke hadn't seen the play, but he heard the crowd's reaction and assumed something good had happened.

An ocean of emotion washed over Three Rivers Stadium. Van Dyke got the chills. The Raiders' reaction was much different.

"We got screwed," Villapiano spat. Raiders tight end Raymond Chester said if the Raiders' rage and frustration had been packaged, "it would have been nuclear." Madden, outfitted in a dark jacket, ran toward the closest official and waved his meaty arms and screamed, "No good! No good!" Tatum could hear screaming and cussing coming from both sides.

Field judge Adrian Burk, who had been trailing Harris, initially signaled a touchdown. Burk was no stranger to sensational plays. A former NFL quarterback, he tied a league record when he threw seven TD passes in a game on October 17, 1954, in Philadelphia's 49–21 win over Washington. By strange coincidence, fifteen years later Burk was an NFL official working a game in Minnesota when Vikings quarterback Joe Kapp tied his record by throwing seven TDs against the Baltimore Colts.

Umpire Pat Harder wasn't certain Harris's catch was legal, and neither was the rest of the officiating crew. Like Burk, Harder was a former NFL player well acquainted with sensational moments on the football field. He was part of the Chicago Cardinals' famed "Million Dollar Backfield." Harder was the first NFL player to produce more than one hundred points in three consecutive seasons. He was instrumental in the Cardinals' victory over the Eagles in the 1947 NFL Championship Game and helped lift the Lions to consecutive league titles in 1952–53. As a fullback for the Wisconsin Badgers and a future College Football Hall of Famer, Harder was responsible for the now familiar crowd chant, "Hit 'em again, hit 'em again, harder, harder." As an official Harder was present for two of the more famous games in NFL history—the iconic Ice Bowl in Green Bay in 1967 and the Immaculate Reception five years later.

None of the officials confirmed Burk's call. As the Steelers celebrated in the end zone, as the Raiders raged in protest, and as delirious fans spilled onto the field, referee Fred Swearingen pulled his crew together to discuss what the proper call should be. What ensued was a roughly fifteen-minute delay.

In 1972 NFL Rule 7, Section 5, Article 2, Item 2-c, stated that two receivers could not touch the ball consecutively on the same play. The double-touch rule had been at the heart of a controversial call in Super Bowl V, when Baltimore Colts tight end John Mackey hauled in a game-changing 75-yard TD reception from John Unitas.

Gowdy was doing the NBC-TV broadcast of Super Bowl V and told viewers the play would be brought back because of the NFL rule. But officials ruled that after being touched by Baltimore receiver Eddie Hinton, the ball had grazed the fingertips of Dallas defensive back Mel Renfro, and thus the touchdown was legal. It proved to be a critical call, since the Colts went on to win 16–13 on a last-second field goal by Jim O'Brien.

Amid the melee in Pittsburgh, Swearingen and his six-man crew asked each other: "Did the ball hit Tatum or Fuqua?" Swearingen counted four "I don't knows" and two "I thinks." If the ball hit Tatum, it was a legal catch. If it hit Fuqua, the pass would be ruled incomplete and Harris's touchdown nullified.

Madden and the Raiders tried to help clear the confusion. They pointed an accusing finger at Frenchy and then at Franco. The ball touched two Steelers, the Raiders screamed. The play was illegal. Tatum grabbed Fuqua, who was still sitting on the turf.

"Tell them you touched it!" screamed Tatum, his face contorted in anger. "Tell them you touched it!"

Frenchy, regaining his senses, responded with a high-pitched cackle. The man who claimed to be an ebony reincarnation of a French count, who said he played football just to make enough money to travel back in time to reclaim his castle and resume his life as a playboy soccer player, called it a planned play. Fuqua said he and Franco met in private and dreamed it up but kept it a secret just in case the Raiders had Bradshaw bugged. Maybe, Fuqua mused with a mischievous smile, he sneaked his glass cane onto the field and batted the ball back to Harris. Frenchy said physicists and mathematicians could only guess how that ball bounced as it did. The Count said he knew but insisted the truth would remain Frenchy's "little secret."

Swearingen shoved his way through the crowd and reached Steelers sideline official Jim Boston, who was in charge of security and field conditions. The referee asked for a nearby phone and was led to one of the baseball dugouts, Three Rivers Stadium also serving as home to the Pirates. The referee dialed the NFL's supervisor of officials, Art McNally, who was in the press box.

"He called a conference, which was good to do," McNally said of Swearingen. "You ask them, 'What did you see?' You put it together and you come out and say yes or no."

Except that's not what happened. McNally, who had been appointed the NFL's supervisor of officials in 1968 and officiated more than three thousand football, basketball, and baseball games in a twenty-two-year span, watched from the press box as the officials' conference stretched out and then stretched out even longer.

What, McNally wondered, was the problem?

"Lo and behold," McNally said, "here comes the referee. He's leaving the field."

And proceeded to place a call to McNally in the press box.

"Two of my men say that opposing players touched the ball," Swearingen told McNally.

Swearingen was a man on the spot, but as tumult goes this was nothing compared to what he had been through as a dive-bomber during World War II. Graduating from Ohio University in 1942, he joined the Naval Air Corps that same year and served as a carrier base pilot aboard the uss *Bunker Hill*. Swearingen was decorated ten times, earning the Navy Cross, four distinguished Flying Crosses, four air medals, and the Presidential Citation. Six years after the Immaculate Reception he served as field judge in Super Bowl XIII and once again made a controversial call involving the Steelers. This involved Pittsburgh wide receiver Lynn Swann getting tangled up with Dallas defensive back Benny Barnes. Incidental contact interpretation wasn't in force at the time, and Swearingen penalized Barnes for pass interference. The call kept alive a Steelers touchdown drive, and to this day the Cowboys claim the controversial call aided Pittsburgh in its 35–31 win.

Art Rooney, the Steelers' longtime and much-beloved owner, had already departed the press box in Three Rivers Stadium and was in an elevator heading down to the locker room to console his players; he hadn't seen the Immaculate Reception. Pittsburgh's patriarch, the man called the "Chief" by players and coaches alike, had mashed out his ever-present cigar prior to the fourth-down play, risen slowly from his seat, and nodded when a security guard mentioned next season.

Rooney wanted to get to the locker room and tell his team not to forget what a great season it had. He wanted to talk with his players privately, and to do that he had to get there before the media. Rooney was riding the elevator in silence with six friends, Pirates announcer Bob Prince among them, and was somewhere between the mezzanine and ground levels when Pittsburgh's prayers were answered. Rooney heard the crowd roar even before the elevator doors opened. Still, he didn't believe it even when a delirious security guard told him what had happened.

Rooney's son Dan remained in the press box and overheard McNally's conversation with Swearingen. The league's supervisor of officials kept telling his referee, "Call what you saw." The Raiders have maintained that Swearingen pleaded for more security for his crew if he called the pass incomplete. Raiders executive Al LoCasale said, perhaps only half-jokingly, that Swearingen asked how many cops could escort the officials out of the stadium if they didn't rule the play a Pittsburgh touchdown.

Told the number was just six, Swearingen raised his arms to signal a score. "That's six for Pittsburgh!"

Dan Rooney insists that story isn't true. So does McNally.

"That's a lot of baloney," McNally stated.

Nor did anyone in the broadcast booth use the video recorders to study the play for Swearingen's benefit. In its game story, the story in the *New York Times* began with the following falsehood:

"Television helped decide a pro football game today, the cameras re-enforcing a decision made on the field by a referee about a 60-yard touchdown play that won the game for the Pittsburgh Steelers over the Oakland Raiders. . . . Art McNally, the National Football League's supervisor of officials, had access to the instant replay on television. . . . Score one for man's technology, in this case camera and film. The play was probably a first for football because of the conformation by television."

Truth is, NBC cameras couldn't determine clearly on their televised replays if the ball had hit Tatum, Fuqua, or both men. Villapiano, who said he has studied the play on film from six different angles, still can't say for certain what happened.

McNally insists he never looked at a replay in the press box, instant replay not being a part of officiating in 1972. He also said he didn't tell Swearingen what call to make. McNally said he heard Swearingen tell him that two of his crew believed the ball had been touched by Tatum; everything was good to go.

"Okay, you're fine," McNally told Swearingen. "Go ahead and go."

Seeing Swearingen hang up the phone, Boston asked, "What do we got?"

"We got a touchdown."

Returning to the Raiders' sideline, a disgusted Madden shoved his hands deep into the pockets on the backs of his pants. A few feet away Raiders running back Pete Banaszak hung his head in despair and fought back tears. Backfield mate Marv Hubbard was so broken up and disappointed by the defeat that he would think seriously about quitting football. A sideline photographer snapped a photo of Madden and his players framed by the stadium scoreboard flashing an ironic "Merry Christmas" in bright, bold letters. Despite his protests, all Madden received was the dugout telephone used by Swearingen. The Raiders' coach later turned it into a trophy in his home.

What bothered Madden about that game and what still bothers him to this day is this: If it was a touchdown, why didn't the officials call it a touchdown right away? If Swearingen didn't know it was a touchdown when it happened, how did he know it was a touchdown after he went and talked on the telephone?

Sprinting back onto the field, Swearingen raised both arms to signal a score. He also seemed to be pointing to the source of the miracle, a theme picked up by Gowdy in the NBC television broadcast booth.

Gowdy: *"You talk about Christmas miracles. Here's the miracle of all miracles . . ."*

Within hours this "miracle of all miracles" that had occurred just hours before Christmas Eve came to be known as the Immaculate Reception. The name is credited to Steelers fan Michael Ord, who thought it up while celebrating the victory in a Pittsburgh bar. With Christmas Eve fast approaching, Ord hushed the crowded tavern and asked fellow patrons to join him in a toast to the "Feast of the Immaculate Reception."

Sharon Levosky, Ord's girlfriend at the time, phoned Myron Cope and told the Steelers' sportscaster he should use the phrase on his evening show on WTAE-TV. Cope pondered for some fifteen seconds whether the term was tasteless. On his show he introduced the phrase and then issued a hasty disclaimer: "I accept neither credit, nor should you hold the moniker to be impious . . ."

Decades later Cope claimed to have examined frame by frame a film taken of the play by a WTAE cameraman. The film was never aired and was destroyed in 1997. But Cope said the film clearly showed Bradshaw's pass striking Tatum on his right shoulder pad.

More than forty years later irate Raiders and Raider Nation aren't buying it. Truth is, they never will. To them the play remains the Immaculate Deception and will always be so. Tatum defended his decision to go for the knockout rather than the deflection by stating he was simply trying to knock the ball loose from Fuqua. "I touched the man, not the ball," he said.

In Oakland's morgue-like locker room, the Raiders struggled to find the right words. Stabler couldn't accept it. It didn't seem fair, he drawled in his southern accent. "What an awful way to lose a game."

Madden and Davis were just as disconsolate. Counting the preseason, the Raiders had played twenty-one games to get to that moment. Fourth down. One play. Then the ball bounces off one man's chest into another man's arms, and it's all over. No tomorrow.

"I'm telling you," Madden said. "This will hurt for a long, long time."

Bay Area football fans weren't done suffering this day. The NFL's late-afternoon game featured the defending Super Bowl champion Dallas Cowboys at the San Francisco 49ers in an NFC divisional playoff contest. Bay Area fans found balm for the Raiders' disappointing defeat as the 49ers forged a 28–13 lead late in the third quarter in Candlestick Park. Shockingly, the Cowboys rallied behind Roger Staubach in the fourth quarter. The game winner—62 Wing Sideline—resembled 66 Circle Option in that Staubach, liked Bradshaw, had to find a secondary receiver, in this case flanker Ron Sellers. Also, the score came in the final minute, with fifty-two seconds remaining, and broke the hearts of Bay Area fans for the second time that day.

Small wonder that Saturday, December 23, 1972, was called Black Saturday by a Bay Area newspaper.

Fuqua has made part of his living since that day retelling his story on the banquet circuit. LoCasale said he heard that Fuqua started talking about the play in the postgame but was told, presumably by Steelers officials, to "shut up."

Fuqua did chide those who asked about the collision with Tatum. "Damn, that sucker really hit me!" he exclaimed. "I didn't know where the hell I was or even who I was, and you're asking me about the ball?" As to who actually touched the ball, all Frenchy will say is that the play was "immaculate."

Whatever name Harris's last-second score goes by, it is recognized as the most famous play in NFL history. Pearson calls it the defining moment of Steelers history, and Van Dyke declares it to be the Steelers' destiny. To Hanratty it's the most memorable moment in sports; Russell calls it the quintessential moment. Harris said that one play altered the course of the Steelers franchise. Lovable losers no more, Pittsburgh was suddenly a team that could stand toe-to-toe with anyone, even Davis's self-styled "bad asses"—the rebellious, renegade Raiders.

Noll agreed. The man who would win four Super Bowls always cited the Immaculate Reception as his favorite Steelers memory, smiling at the mere mention of it. "This was a sign," he said of Franco's play, "that this was a team of destiny."

What that single play also served to do was spark what for five years was the most ferocious and fiercely fought rivalry in sports history.

When a sports rivalry reaches all the way to the United States Supreme Court, it's a rivalry without peer. From 1972 to 1977 the Steelers and Raiders played ten times; five of those games were in the postseason, and three straight decided the AFC Championship and the eventual Super Bowl champion. Their games became so vicious, so violent, that the league was forced to adopt rule changes to stop the strangleholds that dominating defenses were putting on the offenses of their day. The more liberated rules aided aerial games and led to the making of the modern NFL.

The Raiders-Steelers series was defined by memorable plays and events, not all of them limited to the football field. It escalated from soap opera to blood feud and served as a fertile breeding ground for many of the game's greatest stars. An astounding twenty-six future Pro Football Hall of Famers were involved in the Pittsburgh-Oakland turf wars in the seventies, and from the smoldering embers of the Immacu-late Reception there emerged a rivalry so heated, so fiery, that its blast furnace–like intensity stirred memories of James Parton's description of Pittsburgh—"the Smoky City"—as "hell with the lid taken off!"

In a 2012 *Sports Illustrated* poll more than eighty-seven thousand people named the Immaculate Reception the most famous play in NFL history. NFL Films has also called it the most famous touch-down in league history. It may be the play that had the most impact.

Historians and fans can argue it was Alan "the Horse" Ameche's 1-yard touchdown gallop in the gathering darkness inside Yankee Sta-dium in the 1958 sudden-death overtime championship game, Bart Starr's quarterback sneak on the frozen Lambeau Field in the 1967 "Ice Bowl," Roger Staubach's "Hail Mary" in Minnesota in 1975, "the Catch" by Dwight Clark in 1981, "the Music City Miracle" in 2000, or the "Tuck Rule" call in a New England snowstorm in the 2001 playoffs. All iconic moments, but none ignited a white-hot rivalry that would come to involve some of pro football's greatest legends and most colorful players and rabid fans: the "Mad Bomber" and the "Snake" staring down the Steel Curtain; Franco's Italian Army and Gerela's Gorillas versus Raider Nation; a graceful Swann and a "Mad Stork"; "Mean" Joe and a feared "Assassin"; Silver and Black and the Terrible Towel; rugged running backs Rocky Bleier, a Vietnam War hero, and his Raiders counterparts Pete Banaszak, Marv Hubbard, and Mark van Eeghen; Hall of Fame centers Jim Otto of Oakland and Pitts-burgh's Mike Webster; receivers with a gift of grab—Swann and Stall-worth and Raiders Fred Biletnikoff, Cliff Branch, and Dave Casper; Hall of Fame cornerbacks Mel Blount and Willie Brown; a patriarch in Rooney and a rebel in Davis.

It was a rivalry that reached from East Coast to West Coast and caused celebrities to take sides. Frank Sinatra was inducted as a one-star general in Franco's Italian Army; James Garner was a regular fix-ture on the Raiders' sideline.

From 1972 to 1976 Pittsburgh versus Oakland was arguably the most physical rivalry in NFL history, born out of a play that had never hap-pened before and could never happen again.

"I've played football since the second grade and nothing like that ever happened," Bradshaw said of the play that ignited a blood feud. "It'll never happen again."

"I was damn lucky," Harris said, but Noll thought there was more to Pittsburgh's victory than just luck. "We never gave up," Noll stated, "and that was the story of our year."

The Immaculate Reception not only launched the Steelers' dynasty and the NFL's greatest rivalry of the super seventies, but also helped forge the NFL's current policy of allowing sold-out games to be televised in their local markets. The latter came about because of the discontent among Steelers fans over the fact that the AFC playoff versus Oakland and the AFC Championship Game against Miami were not televised in Pittsburgh. Steelers fans fled Pittsburgh on game day and drove to nearby cities such as Wheeling, West Virginia, and Steubenville, Ohio, where hotels picked up the broadcasts from a Cleveland station.

All of this led to Pennsylvania lawmakers being among the leaders of a battle to force the league to change its TV policy. Beginning with the 1973 season, NFL games that are sold out seventy-two hours prior to kickoff are televised in their local market.

The year 1972 proved pivotal in Pittsburgh history, a roller coaster of emotional extremes. In September Pirates legend Roberto Clemente recorded his three thousandth career hit. In October the reigning world champion Pirates lost the National League Championship Series to Cincinnati on a wild pitch in the bottom of the ninth inning of the fifth and deciding game. In December came the Immaculate Reception. On the final day of the year Pittsburgh lost the AFC Championship to Miami in the afternoon, and on that New Year's Eve night the city suffered the loss of Clemente in an airplane crash while on a humanitarian mission.

Following Pittsburgh's victory over Oakland, Fuqua emerged from the Steelers' locker room wearing red knickers, a velour sports jacket flecked with tiny stars, star-peppered patent-leather shoes, and matching socks. Frenchy had a reputation for being something of a flake, and he flashed a new outfit for each winning game. One outfit that gained notoriety had goldfish inside his clear plastic heels.

He declared one of the stars in the outfit he wore following the Immaculate Reception to be the Steelers' lucky star. Maybe, mused the Count, all of them are lucky stars. Frenchy strutted to Franco's locker, where Harris, whom Fuqua sometimes called "Stallion"— short for "Italian Stallion," Franco being part Italian and part black— was pulling on a necktie.

Flashing a broad smile, Fuqua told Harris he looked . . . "immaculate."

Jim Campbell: Sideline access gave me an up-close-and-personal view of the game—the sights, smells, and sounds of what was going on out on the gridiron. In this case the gridiron was the new Tartan Turf that served as the playing field for both the Pirates and the Steelers.

My association with the Steelers began in September 1969, when I moved to Pittsburgh. Years prior to the move I had done freelance research on the early NFL Drafts, particularly the first (1936) "player selection meeting."

The NFL office described their info on the first draft as "sketchy, at best." It was. Their draft list for '36 had only the player's last name, his position, his college, and what team had chosen him. In a letter from Don Weiss, executive vice president and NFL commissioner Peter Rozelle's right-hand man, Weiss stated, "We can in no way vouch for the listing we are sending you as the actual order in which the member NFL teams drafted."

With much correspondence with the players named and viewing what probably was miles of microfilm, I was able to verify the order as accurate, add first names of players, and determine if the draftee actually played in the NFL and with whom. I shared this annotated information with the league office and was then asked to "verify" subsequent drafts through 1942—the time the NFL kept more accurate and complete records of its drafts. I sent the fleshed-out data to NFL teams (including the Steelers) whose histories went back that far.

Ed Kiely, Steelers public relations director, was at least familiar with my name and work when I called his office upon arriving in the Steel City. When I asked about any part-time positions for the season, which was already in the exhibition phase, he said, "Sorry, Jim, but we've filled them all for this season. Perhaps next year." Slightly disappointed, I became a spectator for the Steelers' 1969 season, hopeful of landing something for the 1970 season.

As the '70 season approached I placed several calls to publicity director Joe Gordon, who sounded encouraging as he said, "Give me your number. I'll get back to you." About a week before the preseason began, Joe called and offered me the opportunity that changed my career path, and perhaps my life. "We can use you on the sidelines on game days. You'll have a two-way [radio] to the press box and relay information on specific penalties and injuries," he informed me.

Timing was critical on penalties—it had to be called up to the press box before the next play in order for public address announcer Ray Downey to inform the in-stadium fans. Commissioner Rozelle's thinking was: "If those watching at home for free had this information, then those buying $20 tickets [the average price of an NFL ticket at the time] should also know." Injury reports weren't so time sensitive. That information was not announced over the PA; it was more for media only.

My two-way radio had a cord that seemed as though it was the length of the Tartan Turf field at Three Rivers Stadium. And perhaps it was. I had to roam the length of the field to gather the data. There were also the "TV guys" with their ponderous cables. If we cooperated and looked out for each other, there was no problem. If we were less vigilant, cables and wires got crossed and tangled, limiting the mobility of both parties. TV guys seemed to think theirs was the first and only priority—and maybe theirs was. But more than once I had to not so subtly remind a TV production person, "Hey, this was a game long before it became a TV show, so let's watch where we're going with our lines." It seemed to work for a while.

As is well documented, the Steelers of 1969 won their opening game at Pitt Stadium over the Detroit Lions 16–13 and then lost the rest—1-13 in Chuck Noll's first season, but there was a glimmer or two of hope. Joe Greene was a force. Terry Hanratty was a vast improvement over Dick Shiner and Kent Nix at quarterback. And the 1-13 record, after a coin flip with the Chicago Bears, produced Terry Bradshaw as the first overall draft choice of 1970.

During the preseason Bradshaw's athletic ability was clearly evident—the arm, the strength, the running ability. The regular season was a rude awakening for the blond rookie from Louisiana Tech, though. In the opening game the Houston Oilers, with wily veteran Charley Johnson quarterbacking, showed the young Steelers the stark difference between preseason and regular-season NFL football. Johnson's "clinic" produced a 19–7 victory.

However, as the season progressed, so did the Black and Gold. Pittsburgh finished with an improved 5-9 record.

Then came the 1971 draft. While a few years later the 1974 draft would produce four Pro Football Hall of Fame inductees—Lynn Swann, Jack Lambert, John Stallworth, and Mike Webster—it was the '71 draft that contributed mightily to the core of the Steelers' 1970s Super Bowl dynasty. As noted elsewhere, wide receiver Frank Lewis, linebacker Jack Ham, guard Gerry "Moon" Mullins, defensive end Dwight "Mad Dog" White, tight end (later offensive tackle) Larry Brown, defensive tackle Ernie "Fats" Holmes, and safeties Mike Wagner and free agent Glen "Pine" Edwards were all starters in the Steelers' first Super Bowl, SB IX, an unexpected, by some, victory over the veteran and seasoned Minnesota Vikings, 16–6, at Tulane Stadium in New Orleans. Labor difficulties delayed the opening of the Louisiana Superdome, which was to be the site of the game.

However, the Super Bowl would have to wait. The 1971 season produced only slight improvement—6-8. But there was one incident, a minor one, that stuck with me through the years. In midweek I bumped into Charlie Sumner, defensive backfield coach, in the hallway of Three Rivers before the Steelers were to take on the Colts—a team from which Chuck Noll was only two years removed as defensive coach. I asked the personable Sumner what that was going to be like, going up against a defense that was basically unchanged from when Noll was coaching it. Charlie gave me a wry smile and said, "It's gonna be like playin' in a freakin' mirror." The more talented Colts won that encounter, 34–21.

Much of the quality of the 1971 draft was a direct reflection on scout Bill Nunn Jr. Nunn joined the Steelers in 1967 as a part-time scout at the behest of Dan Rooney and became a full-time scout in 1969, when Noll was hired as head coach. Nunn, whose father, Bill Sr., was sports editor of the *Pittsburgh Courier*, an influential African American newspaper with a national circulation of four hundred thousand, had been picking a black All-America team since 1950. His knowledge of and rapport with the historically black colleges of the South gave him an advantage over most other scouts. Of the '71 rookie class, Lewis, White, Holmes, and Edwards were all from little-known and seldom-visited (by NFL scouts) schools.

Prior to his affiliation with the Steelers, Nunn tipped off Los Angeles to David "Deacon" Jones, an unheralded defensive end from Mississippi Vocational College, via South Carolina State. He also touted tackle Roosevelt Brown of Morgan State to the New York Giants. Both are enshrined in the Pro Football Hall of Fame.

When Franco Harris arrived in 1972, things really took off. The Rookie of the Year from Penn State made an immediate impact. There were those who thought the 235-pound running back could also have been the AFC or NFL most valuable player.

How he got to Pittsburgh speaks volumes about two men—Art Rooney Jr. and Chuck Noll. Noll had his mind set on drafting Robert Newhouse, a sturdy running back out of the University of Houston. Rooney lobbied for Harris, who was not much of a practice player and, although he was eclipsed by the considerable shadow of Lydell Mitchell at Penn State, was a stellar performer "when the lights went on." Noll was eventually swayed, Harris was drafted, and the rest, as they say, is well-documented history.

With Harris providing an explosive ground game and Bradshaw maturing, the Steelers won their first championship of any kind in their nearly four decades of existence. The 24–2 road victory over the San Diego Chargers led to a date with destiny.

The next week Pittsburgh and I were ready for the city's first-ever NFL playoff game, if you can overlook a game in 1947 when the Steelers and Philadelphia Eagles tied atop the Eastern Division and had a game, played at Forbes Field, to decide who would face the Chicago Cardinals in the NFL Championship. Earlier in that season the Eagles prevailed 21–0. Behind Steve Van Buren and friends, they repeated the same margin of victory in the playoff game.

When the Steelers hosted the Raiders, winners of the AFC West with a 10-3-1 record, it was like a new era. I don't recall much of a different feeling. It was all new, so it was just another important home game. The hoopla that now accompanies any postseason game of any sort was missing. No special uniforms, no patches to mark the occasion, no helmet decals, nothing.

I took my place at the mouth of the tunnel for the pregame introductions, lining up the starters. Shrouded in the mists of time is whether it was the Steelers' offense or defense, but it coincided with my sending the players onto the Three Rivers field with the announcements of public address announcer Ray Downey (pronounced "Donnie" by true Pittsburghers).

The game started out as expected. Low scoring, hard hitting, back and forth. Pittsburgh got on the scoreboard first—and second. Two field goals by Roy Gerela put the Steelers in the lead, 6–0. Along with nearly everyone else in the stadium, I'm thinking, "One touchdown can wipe out that lead." Not that I didn't have faith in the near-impregnable Joe Greene–led Steel Curtain defense, but reality is reality.

After two interceptions Raiders coach John Madden substituted for Lamonica, but not for the next man up, ageless George Blanda, but third-year veteran Ken "the Snake" Stabler, a crafty left-hander.

Nevertheless, inside of two minutes the Steelers still clung to that 6–0 lead. It was at this point the drama began to unfold.

Defensive end Dwight White got dinged and had to come out. His replacement was rookie Craig Hanneman. The Oregon State product was something of an eccentric. His persona was fittingly that of a lumberjack. His nickname was "Cope," short for Copenhagen. He dipped smokeless tobacco considerably before Dallas Cowboy Walt Garrison was hawking the product on TV and calling for "just a 'peench' between your cheek and gum."

On the first play Hanneman got hooked inside. Stabler slithered outside to his left and didn't stop running until he got to the end zone

31 yards later. Blanda's successful PAT made the score 7–6 in favor of the Silver and Black.

Like the rest of the capacity crowd, I had a sinking feeling. If it took more than fifty-eight minutes to score six points, how would the Steelers score a field goal or touchdown in fewer than two minutes?

Then a thought occurred to me: Preston Pearson! The Illinois basketball player turned NFL running back was awaiting Blanda's kickoff. Maybe he could take it to the house, as they say these days. He got decent yardage to the 40 before being stopped, but not enough to assure Gerela of a shot at a reasonable field goal.

Bradshaw and the offense took the field. I was standing in my customary place on the Steelers' sideline between special teamer Rocky Bleier and center Ray Mansfield, who by that time was splitting playing time with young Jim Clack. Mansfield would start and play the first quarter, Clack would come in for the second, Mansfield again in the third, and Clack would finish the game.

All too soon the Steelers got down to the fateful fourth down with very little time left. Tatum sandwiched two pass breakups between an overthrow to Ron Shanklin. A play was sent in from the sideline—66 Circle Option. It was an intermediate route to rookie Barry Pearson. Clack snapped, and Bradshaw then eluded the rush and fired the ball downfield. As I like to say, when recounting the events of the day, "the ball, Frenchy Fuqua, and Jack Tatum all simultaneously intersected with history."

The result was a ball rebounding back toward its point of origin. From his shoe tops Franco Harris scooped up the ball and raced to the end zone. Raiders linebacker Phil Villapiano can spin the story any way he wants, but it had to be Tatum who supplied the impetus to the ball, making Franco's catch legal under the existing NFL rules. (Had it not been the hard-hitting Tatum last touching the ball, it would not have rebounded as sharply and taken as low a trajectory in the direction that it did.) To my way of thinking, if, as Tatum said, the ball was off Fuqua's hands, the velocity of Bradshaw's throw would have the ball traveling farther downfield, not ricocheting (like a speeding bullet) toward Franco.

Some twenty-five years later, a professor emeritus of physics at Carnegie Mellon University, John Fetkovich, conducted a conclusive experiment, which left little doubt that Tatum was the final force behind the rebounding ball. He slowed down the game film, checked it frame by frame, applied all kinds of laws of physics, and came to the same conclusion I did years before.

As to Franco, he said, "I was off to the left, but when I saw what was happening, I remembered my Penn State training, 'always go toward the ball,' and did just that."

The loquacious Villapiano claims—often and vociferously—that tight end John McMakin's block on the Raiders' linebacker was a clip. Game film tells a different story. McMakin's head is clearly visible to the side, thus negating Villapiano's claim of being "blocked in the back." It takes another leap of faith to assume Villapiano would have been able to tackle the galloping Harris before reaching the goal line. Another factor: Harris caught the ball deep enough that had he taken any forward steps, the ball would have been within reasonable distance of a successful Gerela field goal. And there was time for that.

Some question whether Franco got the ball before it hit the ground. The most often shown footage doesn't show exactly how close the ball is to the ground when Franco gains possession. However, other NFL Films footage, seldom seen, clearly shows Franco scooping the ball out of the air well before it would have touched the artificial turf.

As this was happening Mansfield and I turned to each other and simultaneously said, "I saw it, but I don't believe it." Then the import of the moment hit Mansfield. "Hey, we better get down to the end zone and get in the pictures." This is the same "Ol' Ranger," Mansfield's nickname, a tribute to his storytelling prowess, who said to young Jim Clack a week earlier in San Diego as the Steelers clinched their first division title, "Hey, kid, you wanna be famous? Grab Chuck's other leg."

The resulting photo, Clack and Mansfield carrying head coach Chuck Noll off the Jack Murphy Stadium field, was used to exemplify Steelers success until the franchise started winning Super Bowls and other photos came into existence.

Somewhere in the expansive and dusty vaults of NFL Films there is footage of Mansfield, helmet in hand, sideline cape flapping in the breeze, running down the sideline, stopping and looking back every so often to make sure the cameras got his best side.

I guess my fifteen seconds of fame came via a sideline shot that showed a somewhat out-of-focus, younger, darker-haired me smiling from ear to ear behind a beaming Noll. Who said he never smiled?

To be sure, it was chaotic after Raiders defensive back Jimmy Warren failed to tackle or knock Franco out of bounds on Franco's 42-yard jaunt to the end zone. No one was sure what exactly happened, but the celebration, at least on the Steelers' side, had begun. Madden and his players protested vehemently, but to no avail.

After referee Fred Swearingen made a trip to what was in baseball season the Pirates' dugout phone to consult upstairs with head of officials Art McNally, the official signal of a touchdown was given, and all hell really broke loose. Swearingen had interpreted Rule 7, Section 5, Article 2, Item 2-c, of the Official NFL Rules as Harris's scoop being legal.

It hadn't been christened "the Immaculate Reception" just yet, but Franco's miraculous catch was nevertheless celebrated. Bradshaw was mobbed, robbed of his chinstrap. Other Steelers were also recipients of back slapping and shoulder pounding. The field was littered with Steelers faithful and others who had vaulted onto the Tartan Turf to become part of Pittsburgh football history.

Madden, for whom I have the utmost respect, proclaimed that "Swearingen never even signaled 'touchdown.'" Not to quibble with the Hall of Fame coach, but game film clearly shows referee Swearingen, both arms raised, signaling a touchdown. To this day Madden contends, "No matter how many times I see the play, I'm not sure what happened." And Fuqua says he knows but will take that knowledge to his grave.

Before the game Gordon gave me a pass to go into the Raiders' locker room "to get quotes" after the game. Joe told me I didn't need to ask any questions, just take down what was answered to others' questions. Sounded simple enough—before the game.

I did venture into the Raiders' stunned and basically silent locker

room. I recall seeing very few members of the media. They were probably all over in the more jubilant Steelers' dressing quarters. I can't
say any questions were asked. The players were nonexistent, assistant
coaches nowhere to be seen. It was a scene of utter dejection.

I vividly recall a despondent and silent Madden sitting on a stool
in front of a near-empty locker just staring into it and running his fingers through his tousled hair, perhaps even a cigarette in hand.

About that time Wayne Valley, one of the Raiders' minority owners, came into the room and solemnly said as he put his large hand on
Madden's shoulder, "John, you deserved better." If Madden responded,
it was only a grunt. I had sympathy for the Raiders' coach. The loss
was obviously gut-wrenching. My later contact with him was always
pleasant, but I did avoid mentioning anything about the Immaculate Reception.

A bit of irony: Thinking the cause was lost, Mr. Rooney left his box
sometime before the climactic play. He wanted to be in the locker room
to console and congratulate the players on an outstanding season.
While riding down in the stadium elevator, the Chief heard the tremendous noise that accompanied Franco's mad dash and was unaware
of what just happened. The man who suffered through four decades
of futility missed the shining moment. He soon found out what the
shouting was about.

I left the Raiders' quarters and found Gordon. When I told him I
had no significant quotes of any type, he simply said, "That's fine. The
story isn't really about the Raiders today."

Maybe not, but the Steelers-Raiders story was far from over. It was,
in fact, just getting started.

1

Steelers a Work of Art

He was the "Chief," the cigar-chomping, bespectacled, and beloved boss of the Pittsburgh Steelers who, for his first forty years as an owner, was the league's most lovable loser.

Small-time politician, big-time gambler, folk hero, and, ultimately, creator of a football dynasty to rival any in NFL history, Arthur Joseph Rooney Sr. was all of these things.

The Pittsburgh patriarch was also something more, according to those who knew him.

Byron "Whizzer" White, a future U.S. Supreme Court justice who was paid a then princely sum of $15,800 to play for Rooney's Pittsburgh team in 1938, thought the Chief a "man's man," the finest person White had ever known. To White, Rooney was an engaging fellow, a fellow one could trust.

To famed sportscaster Howard Cosell, the Rooneys were the people he most respected in sports ownership. They were the finest people, Cosell said, people of integrity and character.

Pro Football Hall of Fame head coach Don Shula had mixed emotions when his Miami Dolphins played Pittsburgh in the 1972 AFC Championship Game. Not only did he have great respect for Steelers head coach Chuck Noll, Shula's former assistant with the Balti-

more Colts, but Don also greatly admired Art Rooney. Shula had
more respect for Mr. Rooney, he said, than any other NFL owner.
He considered Art a tremendous human being.

"You talk about goodness and you begin with Art Rooney,"
Shula said. "You talk about generosity and once again you start
with Art Rooney."

When Rooney was honored with induction in Pro Football's Hall
of Fame in 1964, Vince Johnson of the *Pittsburgh Post-Gazette* said the
Steelers' owner had achieved the "inscrutable dignity of a philosopher."

Art's son Dan said the philosophy was simple: Treat everybody
the way you'd like to be treated. Give them the benefit of the doubt,
but never let anyone mistake kindness for weakness. It was, Dan
once said, the Golden Rule with a little bit of Pittsburgh's hard-edged
North Side mixed in.

Art Rooney Sr. wasn't the first member of the Steelers organization to be inducted into the Hall of Fame, and that was perfectly
fine for a man who preferred his players and coaches get the credit
for the team's success. Rooney was "Chief," but he liked to be in the
background, away from the bright glare of the spotlight.

When the Steelers won their first Super Bowl in January 1975,
veteran linebacker Andy Russell noticed the Steelers' owner standing in the recesses of the champagne-lathered locker room. Russell
thought Mr. Rooney, with his ever-present stogie and thick shock of
white hair, looked like an onlooker, and he made Art go up onstage
to receive the Lombardi Trophy.

"Chief, come up," Russell told his boss. "It's your team."

Russell saw it as a sweet moment for an amazing man. Rooney
routinely braved the elements—cold, rain, snow—to watch his team
practice. When practice ended, the Chief would be in the locker
room, talking with his players.

"It was like a family," Russell remembered.

Steelers safety Mike Wagner said watching Mr. Rooney accepting the team's first Lombardi Trophy following Super Bowl IX was
the highlight of that January day. The Chief was known as the good-
guy owner, a wonderful man. He sought to connect with his players

in a personal way, and he did so by always having something good to say and showing interest in his players' lives.

Rooney's players knew the number of years the Steelers had been a losing team. They knew, too, that the move to bring in Dan Rooney to run the Steelers' day-to-day business and the hiring of Chuck Noll as head coach were great moves. But at the end of the day, Wagner said, it was all about the Chief. The Steelers were his dream, his vision.

To fully understand what Franco Harris's Immaculate Reception meant to the Rooney family, the Steelers organization, and their fans, it's important to know Art's history and the history of his team and their community.

Art understood Pittsburgh, understood the people who lived and worked in the shadows of the steel mills. He often said that he once had a steel job. "For half a day," he said. "I never went back to collect my pay."

The great-grandson of immigrants James and Mary Rooney, who fled Ireland during the potato famine in the 1840s and moved to Montreal, Art's philosophical wisdom was won in "the Ward," a rugged section of the North Side near Exposition Park. He was of Welsh-Irish descent; the Rooney name in Gaelic is Ruanaidh. His father, Dan Sr., a saloonkeeper, was Welsh; his mother, Margaret, Irish.

Born in Wales, Dan was two years old when the family returned to Canada. In 1884 they moved again, this time to Pittsburgh. Dan opened a saloon in Coulter, a coal town in the Monongahela Valley, and it was there he met and married a coal miner's daughter, Margaret "Maggie" Murray.

Art was born on January 27, 1901, in Coulter, and the family took up residence on the North Side in 1913. Purchasing a three-story building on the corner of Corey Street and General Robinson Street, Dan ran a saloon and café on the first floor, while the family resided upstairs. Their house sat just a block from Exposition Park, which had been home to Honus Wagner and the Pittsburgh Pirates baseball club until 1909.

A product of St. Peter's Parochial School and Duquesne University Prep School, Art was a standout multisport athlete who played football and baseball and was a boxer. He was sought after by Notre

Dame football and Boston Red Sox baseball and was named to the 1920 U.S. Olympic boxing team, though he didn't participate in the Games. He studied at Indiana (Pennsylvania) Normal School, now Indiana University of Pennsylvania, and spent his final year at Georgetown University on an athletic scholarship.

Art was Amateur Athletic Union welterweight champion in 1918 and played Minor League Baseball from 1920 to 1925 for the Flint, Michigan, Vehicles and Wheeling, West Virginia, Stogies. In 1925 he was Wheeling's player-manager and as an outfielder appeared in the most games (106) in the Middle Atlantic League, scored the most runs (109), collected the most hits (143), and led the league in steals (58). His .369 batting average was the second highest in the league; his brother Dan was third at .359.

Art loved baseball and would later state he was a better baseball fan than football fan. From time to time he helped support a Negro League baseball team, the great Homestead Grays. Located in Homestead, adjacent to Pittsburgh, the Grays were founded by Cumberland "Cum" Posey and during their existence featured twelve future Hall of Fame inductees, including Josh Gibson, James "Cool Papa" Bell, Oscar Charleston, Martin Dihigo, Judy Johnson, Buck Leonard, et al.

An arm injury cut short Art's promising baseball career, but he continued his involvement in athletics by playing for several semipro football teams. As a teenager he founded the Hope-Harvey Football Club, an enterprise he later claimed was, in a small way, the start of the Steelers.

Art and younger brothers Dan and Jim helped Hope-Harvey win Western Pennsylvania Senior Independent Football Conference titles in the early 1930s. Hope-Harvey was renamed Majestic Radio after gaining a sponsor and was then renamed a second time the James P. Rooneys to promote Jim's run for the state legislature. Along with the Rooneys the team was composed largely of local college players from the University of Pittsburgh, Carnegie Tech, and Duquesne.

In 1931 Art married Kathleen McNulty, and the couple would have five children—Dan, Art Jr., Tim, John, and Pat, the latter two being twins. They purchased a house on North Lincoln Avenue for $5,000, a three-story redbrick Victorian on Pittsburgh's North Side. Their new home had twelve rooms, high ceilings, and a backyard large enough for a fast-growing family. The boys would water their yard until it was muddy enough for trench warfare. In winters Art Sr. would place boards around the blacktop out front and hose it down so it could freeze over and host hockey games.

Deeply religious, Art Sr. kept for some forty years a weathered red leather-bound prayer book whose pages had yellowed from age and constant use. The book contained a prayer card with Art's marking in pen; the Chief kept a strict count of his devotions. The words in Art Sr.'s prayer book were crucial to the code that the Chief lived by. He went to Catholic Mass every morning, prayed the rosary, and treated everyone with respect.

When the Steelers moved into Three Rivers Stadium, Art Sr. had equipment manager Tony Parisi keep a hidden statue of the Virgin Mary in the Pittsburgh locker room with a lid on it for holy water. Over the years the Chief would sprinkle the holy water in the Steelers' locker room. Parisi eventually gave the Virgin Mary statue to Art Jr., and when the Steelers moved to Heinz Field, Art Jr. sprinkled the statue's holy water into the carpet of the Steelers' new locker room.

Along with his religious beliefs, Art Sr. had one other code: if you wanted to smoke, the tobacco better come from a cigar. The Chief favored fine cigars the same way he favored French provincial furniture, Buick cars, and baseball on the radio. For the most part, Art Sr. did not care about material possessions. He would tell his sons, "The more you own, the less freedom you have."

Art taught his sons not to be what he called "big shots." It's why the Chief drove Buicks his while life, and it's why he scolded his son John for buying a Lincoln and why Tim Rooney kept the Rolls-Royce he purchased hidden from his father. The only degree of vanity his sons ever saw in their father was his brushing lanolin cream into his hair; it was as much a daily ritual as morning Mass, praying the rosary, and smoking a cigar. Appearances mattered to the Chief; he wanted to keep his thick head of hair, which he did. He also kept his clothes neat and his shoes so shiny they could have served as reflective mirrors.

Like a lot of people, Art's life changed dramatically in the watershed year of 1933. In Art's case it was change for the better, despite the country being in the depths of the Great Depression.

The repeal of Pennsylvania's restrictive blue laws had begun in 1931 when the Philadelphia A's successfully challenged a law declaring the illegality of organized sports competitions on Sundays. Because NFL teams scheduled games on Sundays to avoid conflicting with college football games played on Saturdays, Philadelphia Eagles cofounder and co-owner Bert Bell helped convince Pennsylvania governor Gifford Pinchot in 1933 to introduce a bill to the state legislature deprecating blue laws. The bill passed that April, allowing the Eagles to play on Sundays, and became law on November 7.

Anticipating the repeal of the blue laws, Art applied for a franchise, and his request was granted on May 19. Pulling together $2,500 during the Great Depression—an amount equal to $46,000 in modern money—Rooney purchased the Pittsburgh Professional Football Club, Inc., on July 8, 1933. In deference to their baseball club landlords at Forbes Field, the NFL's newest team was named the Pirates.

Art Sr. was the proud owner of a fledgling pro football team, but his passions were still racing, boxing, and baseball. In the summer of 1937 he stopped at Yonkers Raceway and made enough money to fund a follow-up trip to Sarasota. It was here that he earned a reputation as one of the country's top handicappers. With his friend Tim Mara, the owner of the New York football Giants, serving as his bookmaker, Art won a small fortune.

The Chief watched races in his typical fashion—cigar in hand and displaying little emotion whether he won or lost. Yet on this occasion he was so grateful he told Tim he would name his newborn third son after him. Tim Rooney's daughter, Kathleen, married Chris Mara, one of Tim Mara's grandsons. The couple produced two granddaughters who became movie actors—Kate Mara and Patricia "Rooney" Mara.

Pittsburgh's city flag was the inspiration for the fledgling franchise's first uniforms. Gold with black stripes and adorned with the city's crest, they were functional as well as aesthetic. The black stripes were felt overlays, and as such helped ball carriers hold the football more securely.

The Pirates were paced by their player-coach, Forrest Douds. A local legend, Douds was born in nearby Rochester in Beaver County and was a three-time All-America tackle at Washington & Jefferson College in suburban Washington, Pennsylvania. He was All-Pro in the NFL in 1930 for the Providence Steam Roller, which in 1928 was the first New England team to win an NFL title.

The Pirates' inaugural game was a 23–2 loss to the New York Giants before a crowd of twenty thousand. The fans, Rooney thought, didn't get their money's worth. They did one week later, when Pittsburgh earned its first win, a 14–13 final over the Chicago Cardinals. The Pirates finished 3-6-2 in 1933 but made history by being progressive. Pittsburgh tackle Ray Kemp became the first black man to play NFL football for Pittsburgh and one of just two African Americans in the league at that time, the other being Joe Lillard of the Cardinals.

The Pirates' total attendance for their five home games in their first season was fifty-seven thousand. The gap in popularity between the NFL and college football at that time is illustrated by the fact that the Pitt-Duquesne game that fall drew sixty thousand fans.

Declining to retain Douds as head coach—he remained a player for the Pirates for two more seasons—Rooney looked to lure Heartley "Hunk" Anderson, who had recently stepped down as head coach at Notre Dame, and then Earle "Greasy" Neale. Both turned down their offer in favor of coaching jobs at North Carolina State and Yale University, respectively. In 1947–49 Neale would coach the Philadelphia Eagles to three straight Eastern Conference titles and in 1948–49 consecutive NFL Championships.

In 1934 Rooney turned his attention to the legendary Red Grange, who had recently retired as a player. Grange spurned Rooney's offer in favor of being an assistant coach with the Chicago Bears. In 1936 Pittsburgh earned its first nonlosing season, going 6-6 under coach Joe Bach. Bach was a former Duquesne coach and one of Notre Dame's "Seven Mules" who paved a path for the famed "Four Horsemen." Rooney then made what he later called a mistake when he let Bach go to Niagara University. Rooney would later muse, behind his ever-present cloud of cigar smoke, that if Bach had stayed in

Pittsburgh, the organization might have won championships long before the 1970s.

Bach wasn't a racetrack man like Rooney, but his successor, Johnny "Blood" McNally, was. Rooney, by his admission, was at racetracks all the time. Problem was, Johnny Blood was usually there with him. Rooney told the *Pittsburgh Post-Gazette* that Blood was one of the few coaches who never worried about his players; his players worried about him, Blood being a playboy. A former player for the Pirates and a colorful character, Blood was a fan favorite, and Rooney hired him in part to boost ticket sales.

Pittsburgh suffered severe growing pains in the franchise's early years. Their first seven seasons saw them burn through five head coaches while winning just twenty-two games. Forbes Field was home, but competition with baseball and college football forced Rooney to take his team to nearby cities Johnstown, Latrobe, and Youngstown, as well as Louisville and New Orleans, in attempts to generate fan interest. Rooney said that the biggest thrill in those days wasn't in winning on Sunday but in meeting the club's payroll on Monday.

In 1938 the Steelers signed their first star player, Whizzer White. He led the league in rushing that year and was considered by Rooney to have given as much of himself as any athlete who ever lived. Teams traveled by train in that era, and while most players occupied themselves playing cards, Rooney would see White reading books. Rooney would later say he figured they were law books. As a Supreme Court justice in future years, White became one of the NFL's more illustrious alums.

To represent and pay tribute to the heritage of steel-town Pittsburgh, Rooney adopted the name "Steelers" in 1940. Two years later the Steelers, aimed by head coach Walt Kiesling and triggered by rookie rushing leader "Bullet" Bill Dudley, secured the first winning season in franchise history. Dudley joined the armed forces the following year as the nation engaged in World War II. Depleted wartime rosters caused Rooney to merge his Steelers with the Eagles in 1943—the team becoming known as the Steagles—and in 1944 the Steelers merged with the Chicago Cardinals (Card-Pitt).

Throughout the Steelers' struggles, Rooney hid his disappointment behind an unruffled exterior. Still, his inner fires were well banked. "Nobody," he said, "feels any worse than I do about losing."

In 1946 Rooney named legendary Pitt boss Jock Sutherland head coach. Dudley returned from the war, and the future Pro Football Hall of Famer earned the NFL's Most Valuable Player honors after leading the league in rushing, interceptions, and punt returns. Rooney considered Dudley the best all-around football player he'd ever seen; he compared Dudley to Jimmy Brown on offense and Dick "Night Train" Lane on defense. Philadelphia's Earle "Greasy" Neale and his New York Giants coaching counterpart, Steve Owens, imposed fines on their quarterbacks if they dared call a pass play in Dudley's territory. Despite their successful partnership, Dudley and Sutherland had their problems. Bullet Bill, Rooney said, preferred to play his game rather than Sutherland's.

Despite the discord the Steelers went 8-4 in 1947 and shared the Eastern Division title. Playing in their first postseason game, the Steelers lost to the Eagles 21–0 in the Eastern Division playoff. The Steelers organization was shocked the following spring when Sutherland died suddenly of a brain tumor while on a scouting trip.

John Michelosen succeeded Sutherland as head coach and went 20-26-2 from 1948 to 1951. The carousel of coaches continued with the rehiring of former bosses Bach in 1952 and Kiesling in 1954. In 1952 the Steelers became the last NFL team to abandon the single wing and adopt the T formation; in 1957 Pittsburgh's Lowell Perry became the league's first African American assistant coach. Lowell's playing career ended when New York Giants star defensive tackle Rosey Grier broke his pelvis. Rooney kept him on as a coach and paid his law school tuition. Perry never forgot the kindness, and he went on to hold high posts with Chrysler and in the federal government.

The 1957 season was also Buddy Parker's first as Steelers head coach. Parker brought an impressive coaching pedigree to Pittsburgh. From 1952 to 1954 he led the Detroit Lions to three consecutive NFL Championship Games and back-to-back titles in 1952–53. Parker had worn out his welcome with the Lions at, of all things, a banquet prior to the 1957 season. "When you get to a situation where you can't handle football players, it's time to get out—and that's what I'm doing tonight," Parker told his stunned audience. "I'm through with football in Detroit."

But he was not through with football. Steelers fans were frantic to bring a successful coach to the 'Burgh. Rooney, however, stood fast in his support of Kiesling.

A loss to the rival Cleveland Browns in the second exhibition game forced Rooney's hand. *Pittsburgh Post-Gazette* sports editor Al Abrams fanned the flames of discontent when he predicted Pittsburgh fans would have precious little to look forward to in 1957. The Steelers' ground game, Abrams observed, was all but nonexistent, and the passing numbers were more impressive on paper than on the field.

With Parker still available, Rooney made the move and installed the former Lion king as head coach of the Steelers. Parker immediately impressed Pittsburgh fans with an example of the power of positive thinking that would have done Dr. Norman Vincent Peale proud: "I am coming to Pittsburgh with one objective—to give the Steelers a winner."

Parker acquired QB Earl Morrall from San Francisco, and the former 49er struck gold in his debut performance, throwing three touchdowns in a victory over Washington at Forbes Field. Parker guided Pittsburgh to a 6-6 record, the first of five nonlosing seasons in his eight-year reign.

The Steelers' slow start in the 1958 season prompted fast action from Parker. Bombed by the Browns in Week Two, Parker's thoughts raced to the Motor City. His former championship QB, Bobby Layne, was in limbo due to having lost his starting job to Tobin Rote the previous season following an injury at season's end. Rote had stepped in and led the Lions to an NFL Championship win over Cleveland.

The colorful, cocky Layne was a forerunner to 1960s NFL stars Joe Namath and Joe Kapp. Layne was a swashbuckling figure; former NFL player and future coach Mike Holovak thought Layne ran his teams like Morgan the Pirate. "Sometimes," Holovak said, "you would swear [Layne's teams] were playing for gold doubloons instead of money."

But Layne was no longer the main man in Motown and was thus expendable. Parker contacted Detroit head coach George Wilson, and on October 7 Pittsburgh fans awoke to the wild news that Layne was their new QB. Morrall was dealt to Detroit, and Parker delivered a parting shot. "I don't think Morrall is a top flight quarterback," he said. "He may be in the future. But he isn't right now. Layne will help us immensely. We've got our running game going and we've got good receivers. With the addition of Layne we might get back in the race."

Layne flew from the Motor City to the Steel City on the morning of October 8 and was met at the airport by Dan Rooney. On their journey to the Steelers' practice grounds Layne peppered Rooney with questions. Bobby asked about the players, the coaches, and the city. Dan Rooney was impressed. From the time Layne's foot hit the ground at South Park, Dan Rooney thought, Bobby Layne was in charge.

The irrepressible Layne shrugged off concerns about his injury (a fractured right ankle) in much the same fashion he shrugged off would-be tacklers. He assured reporters he would play in Sunday's game against the rival Eagles. Layne also expressed his enthusiasm for playing for Parker, saying he hoped he would do as well for Buddy in Pittsburgh as he had in Detroit.

Layne impressed in practice. His passes—be they 10 yards or 50—were on target. Layne's confidence spread quickly to his teammates. Parker felt the same surge of confidence from his swashbuckling signal caller, telling reporters he believed the Steelers were ready to start winning.

The Steelers did win, Layne leading the way in a victory over Norm Van Brocklin, "Concrete" Charlie Bednarik, and the Eagles. Abrams's story the next day captured the new excitement in the Steel City:

> Just as Dr. Raymond K. Parker prescribed, the only tonic the ailing Pittsburgh Steelers needed was a top-notch quarterback to steer them.
>
> Blond Bobby Layne, a 31-year-old grizzled veteran of the pro wars, supplied that tonic at the stadium yesterday afternoon. The transformation of the Steelers from a sick team into a powerful, fast moving, hard hitting aggregation was positively amazing.

With Layne at the controls, Rooney U. stomped the slightly favored Philadelphia Eagles 24–3 to rack up their first win after two losses.

Layne led the aerial assault, Tom Tracy and Tank Younger ground out yards, and lineman Ernie Stautner steeled the defense to help Pittsburgh improve to 7-4-1. The high point in Pittsburgh for Parker and Layne came in 1962. The Steelers battled Sam Huff, Frank Gifford, and the star-studded New York Giants and Jim Brown's Cleveland Browns for the Eastern Division title. Pittsburgh eventually placed second to the Giants, but their 9-5 record earned them the right to play Parker and Layne's former team, Detroit, in the Playoff Bowl in Miami.

Fronted by Alex Karras, Roger Brown, Joe Schmidt, Night Train Lane, and Dick LeBeau, Detroit's defense was one of the best of its era, and the Lions rode it to a 17–10 postseason win over Pittsburgh.

One of the mainstays of Rooney's Steelers in the 1950s and '60s was Stautner. Born in Germany and a product of East Greenbush, New York, and later the United States Marine Corps during World War II, the 6-foot-1, 235-pound Stautner was an undersize defensive tackle even for his era. What he lacked in size, however, he made up for with toughness and technique. His Hall of Fame biography states in part that he "excelled in a land of giants."

Also in a land of Giants, as Stautner's Steelers warred with New York—as well as Cleveland and Philadelphia—to be beasts of the East.

A nine-time Pro Bowl selection and four-time All-Star in his fourteen-year career, Stautner made Steelers history on October 25, 1964, when he became the first to have his number (70) retired by the team. Since then only Joe Greene has had his number (75) retired by the Steelers.

Baltimore Colts Hall of Fame offensive tackle/guard Jim Parker's trench warfare with Stautner was so ferocious that Parker thought Stautner otherworldly. Ernie, Parker said, was too strong to be human. Stautner missed just six games in his NFL career, and that was only because he was sidelined with fractures of his hands, nose, ribs, and shoulder.

Dick Modzelewski, a defensive lineman for the Redskins, Steelers, Giants, and Browns at that time, thought if a team could field four Stautners up front, it would have a championship team. Fueled by Stautner, Pittsburgh's defenses were physical and ferocious. Their offense, however, was often inept. Twice in that era the Steelers' top rushers failed to score a single TD.

Heeding Horace Greeley's advice to go west, Rooney in 1966 looked to the Western Conference and hired former Green Bay Packers assistant coach and Vince Lombardi protégé Bill Austin as head coach. Austin played offensive line for the Giants in the 1940s and '50s and was a Pro Bowl guard in 1964 and a member of the Giants' 1956 NFL Championship team.

After playing under Lombardi, who was the Giants' offensive coordinator in the 1950s, Austin became Lombardi's offensive line coach in Green Bay when Vince took over the Packers in 1959. For the next six seasons Austin helped coach the famed Packer Power Sweep, the NFL's signature play of the '60s. During Austin's time as a Green Bay assistant the Packers powered their way to three Western Division titles and NFL Championship Game victories over the Giants in 1961–62.

Austin coached the Los Angeles Rams' offensive line in 1965 and then led the Steelers through the 1968 season. Unable to repeat the remarkable rebuilding job Lombardi had engineered in Green Bay and George Allen was undergoing in Los Angeles, Austin went 11-28-3 in Pittsburgh.

Austin's failure seemed to be another case of SOS — Same Old Steelers. The franchise that was marked by failure was treated as something of a joke compared with its baseball counterparts, the Pirates. The Bucs won the World Series in stunning fashion over the lordly New York Yankees in October 1960 and were building toward another run that would see Roberto Clemente, Willie Stargell, Manny Sanguillen, and Co. win the National League East in 1970 and the World Series in 1971.

The Steelers, meanwhile, were known mostly for cutting a young QB named Johnny Unitas in training camp and losing out on another future Hall of Famer in middle linebacker Dick Butkus when they dealt their first-round pick in the 1965 draft to the Chicago Bears.

Few knew it at the time, but the fortunes of the Steelers franchise were about to change. On January 27, 1969—Art's sixty-eighth birthday—the Steelers made the coaching hire of a lifetime when they named Chuck Noll their new field boss. Many thought at the time the Steelers had botched it yet again. Pittsburgh's first choice had been Penn State's Joe Paterno, who had just led the Nittany Lions to an undefeated season and an Orange Bowl victory. Paterno initially accepted the offer to become the Steelers' coach but then changed his mind. That opened the door for Noll.

Noll was a little-known assistant for the Baltimore Colts, a defensive backs coach whose secondary had just been shredded by Namath and the New York Jets in their shocking 16–7 upset victory in Super Bowl III.

Noll's first meeting with Dan Rooney came the day after what many still consider the greatest upset in pro football history. The Steelers were impressed that on that Monday morning following Super Sunday Noll displayed none of the bitterness that the NFL was feeling after falling to an AFL team. He instead dealt with the business at hand and displayed depth of knowledge about the Steelers organization and its players. Noll liked what he saw in the Steelers; the biggest challenge was purging the negativism that was rampant among the players following so many losing seasons.

Noll spoke with a cool detachment that impressed the Steelers executive. Dan Rooney remembered Noll being totally logical in his points about the Steelers and knowing a great deal about their players. Rooney liked Noll's overall decorum as well as his knowledge of the organization and his concepts on putting the pro game together. "[Noll] had his own ideas on every facet of being head coach," Dan recalled, "how players should be handled, how things should be run."

Along with working under Don Shula in Baltimore, Noll had also coached for Sid Gillman in Los Angeles and San Diego. The Chargers' fast-break offense symbolized the fledgling AFL's emphasis on offense, but under Noll and Jack Faulkner the Chargers also fielded the West Coast's original "Fearsome Foursome." The Chargers' front line of "Big Cat" Ernie Ladd, Earl Faison, Bill Hudson, and Ron Nery predated the LA Rams' famous foursome of Rosey Grier, Deacon Jones, Merlin Olsen, and Lamar Lundy.

Noll continued to focus on defense in building the Steelers, Pittsburgh using its top pick in 1969 on defensive tackle "Mean" Joe Greene of North Texas State.

It was a solid pick, fitting since Art Sr. had a well-earned reputation as one of the nation's best gamblers. In 1935 the Chief accompanied former lightweight champion Tony Canzoneri to Saratoga. The bull-shouldered Canzoneri, as much a fixture on Broadway as Jack Dempsey's Restaurant, won titles in three divisions and is a member of the International Boxing Hall of Fame.

Rooney placed a bet and headed to the men's room. The porter began talking football with the Steelers owner, and Rooney missed the race. Minutes later he was told his horse had won. Rooney thanked him and continued speaking with the porter. The casual conversation was surprising, considering Rooney had just won $50,000 in the depths of the Great Depression.

Fast-forward to the hiring of Noll in 1969, and the days of Art Rooney leaving anything to chance were about to become a thing of the past.

Jim Campbell: During one of my visits to Three Rivers early in the 1970 season, Joe Gordon introduced me to Mr. Rooney, who by this time had given over much of the day-to-day operation of the ball club to sons Dan and Art Jr. (a.k.a. Artie). Shaking Mr. Rooney's hand can only be described as a thrill. As I got to know him better, like anyone who met him, I regarded him as close to a saint as I would ever meet on earth.

To say he was known affectionately as "the Chief" is an understatement. He was respected, revered, and even loved by anyone who had even the slightest contact with him, as well as countless others who only know of him.

Never was a man as important so unassuming and down-to-earth. Devoid of ego, he genuinely cared about you, always asking about yourself and your family.

When we'd pass each other in the lobby or hallways of Three Rivers or on the practice field during my first days with the team, we'd always exchange greetings. I can't say positively whether he called me by name. With those heavy glasses, the lenses of which were often described as "thick as the bottom of a Coke bottle," I wasn't sure how clearly he saw me.

One day I was visiting Gordon in his office, but Joe had temporarily left the room to attend to another of his myriad duties. Gordon mastered multitasking before it became a twenty-first-century buzzword. He'd hunch his left shoulder to cradle the phone to his ear, leaving both hands to take notes or type a press release or ad copy, and still carry on a conversation with a visitor.

With Joe gone, I was perusing a game program with my back to the office door, when I heard a familiar voice ask, "What's new, Jim?" Not knowing for certain if the Chief really knew who I was—remember those Coke-bottle glasses—I expected that Jim Boston (a front-office worker) had somehow entered Joe's office. When there was no answer to Mr. Rooney's greeting, I turned around. No Jim Boston. It was Art Rooney all by himself. I returned his greeting and assured him not much was new, and we made small talk about the upcoming game.

After Mr. Rooney moved on, it dawned on me: Jim, the Chief really does know who you are. To this day, I remember the satisfying feeling of recognition, but I still lack the words to fully describe what it meant to me.

When Joe returned, I told him about my close encounter of the meaningful kind. He said, knowingly, "Don't let the Coke bottles fool you. The Chief doesn't miss much."

One way Art Rooney endeared himself to his players and other men he came in contact with was to hand out cigars as though they were pieces of penny candy. At the time when many cigar smokers were investing in five- or six-cent Marsh Wheelings, William Penns, or Hav-a-Tampas, the Chief was passing out dollar Bances Aristocrats. They may not compete with today's twenty-dollar Cubans, but in the early seventies they were welcomed by Terry Bradshaw, Joe Greene, trainer Ralph Berlin, and others.

As a nonsmoker, especially of cigars, I never had the pleasure, but I was on more than one occasion the beneficiary of another of Mr. Rooney's random acts of kindness—personally handwritten postcards.

One of Art's best friends—it seemed anyone who met him felt like one—was James A. Farley. Jim Farley was a New York politician, a "kingmaker," to use the political term of the day, and U.S. postmaster general during Franklin D. Roosevelt's first two terms as president. Farley advised Mr. Rooney, "Always carry a bunch of stamped post-cards and a pen and use both quite often." Art took Jim's advice to heart. In fact, it was the most frequent way he reached out to touch someone. The ones I received most often were that year's team picture and always included "Best to you and yours," simply signed, "Art."

While Rocky Bleier was recovering from his Vietnam War wounds in a Japanese hospital in 1969, he got one of the Chief's trademark cards. Mr. Rooney had written, "Get well, Rock. We need you. The team's not doing so well. Best, Art."

Shortly after I arrived in Pittsburgh, a local TV station aired a documentary on Art Rooney titled *The Prez*. There was a time when the Steelers president was referred to as such, but when I began my association with the franchise, he was almost universally referred to as "the Chief." That moniker was hung on him by his sons, who were great fans of the *Superman* TV show. Clark Kent's boss at the *Daily Planet*, Perry White, was called "the Chief" by his staff.

Mike Collier is a name not often associated with the Steelers' early dynasty, but he is part of the lore surrounding Art Rooney. The running back from Morgan State was a fine kickoff returner in 1975, his only season with the ball club. One day at practice, Art got a little too close to the action and was leveled by the 205-pound Collier, who was aghast at knocking over the owner of the franchise. In typical and gracious fashion, the Chief, perhaps lifting a line from a B movie, said, "Thanks, Mike. I needed that." And that's all there was to it.

Without being a pest, I would try to soak up as much NFL history from Mr. Rooney as I could. One time he gave his assessment of current players versus old-timers. I remember it almost verbatim. He said, "There were guys then who couldn't play now. And there are guys now who couldn't play then. But the guys who were good then would be good now. And the guys who are good now would be good then." Think about it.

One of those who the Chief thought could play in any era was a favorite of his—and mine. Johnny Blood (McNally). Blood played for and coached Pittsburgh in the late 1930s. It was Blood's insistent pursuit of Byron "Whizzer" White that landed the future U.S. Supreme Court associate justice with the Steelers in 1938.

Blood was a character in the truest sense of the word. He became known was "the Vagabond Halfback" in his playing days with the Green Bay Packers, when a lack of funds forced him to jump a slow-moving freight train hobo style to arrive at the Packers' training camp. League president Joe F. Carr thought Vagabond Halfback sounded better and looked better in print than "Hobo Halfback," as Blood was initially known.

Although more recent publications may list him as John "Blood" McNally (full name John Victor McNally), he adopted "Johnny Blood" as something of an alias more so than a nickname and was known far and wide as such. He even signed his contracts and legal documents as Johnny Blood and never referred himself anything but that—except when he was being playful and might sign a letter as J. Victim McNally or Johnny the Blood.

I first met Johnny at the 1973 Pro Football Hall of Fame induction weekend in Canton, Ohio. He and other members of the Hall's charter class were invited back for a tenth anniversary celebration. Blood and I became fast friends, and long after Saturday night's official events were concluded, he and I and a few other HOF staffers found ourselves in a hospitality suite until the wee small hours of the morning. He regaled us with tales of the NFL's pioneer days, sometimes called "the rag days," while we all consumed more adult beverages than prudent.

As time flew by, we asked Blood if he shouldn't be headed back to his room and his wife, whom he referred to as Katherine the Great or Sweet Meat. Blood, who never married until his midfifties, opined, "I think marriage should be a five-year contract. We've been married six. So, you might say I'm playing out my option." While Johnny admitted he and Katherine "had their moments—calling the tanks up to the border," they remained married until his death in 1985.

One such "border" moment was about six on the morning in question. Johnny either didn't have or lost his room key, but he did remember the room number. So we assisted him to his room and awakened a sleeping Katherine. It wouldn't be overstating it to say she was less than pleased with her spouse's arrival and condition.

Later that Sunday morning I happened to be at the hotel as guests of "Football's Greatest Weekend" were checking out and heard Katherine tell the desk clerk, "When that son of a bitch Johnny Blood sobers up, which should be about Tuesday, you can put his ass on a plane and send him any-damn-where you want."

After moving to Canton, whenever I called Joe Gordon, I'd always inquire about Mr. Rooney. He was in his seventies then. Joe would usually say that he mostly had his good days, along with a few that weren't so good. This always reminded me of one day when I was at a Steelers practice when a youngster ran up to the Chief shouting, "Grandpa! Grandpa!" Art looked at the tyke and inquired, "Are you Jackie or Joey?"

I thought to myself, "Uh-oh, the Chief's losing it. He doesn't even recognize his own grandson." I guess I must have expressed myself aloud, because Richie Easton (Mr. Rooney's longtime driver and close friend) said, "Well, he has thirty-four grandkids." As I thought about how I might have reacted in a similar situation, a sense of relief came over me—the Chief was still the Chief.

Being around the Steelers organization, there were several things I observed that reflected the influence of Art Rooney. Perhaps most indicative was the virtual absence of his name or photograph in the team's annual media guide. Only once, and in small type, was his name mentioned—listed as president in the team directory of front-office officials. No full-page picture, no five- or seven-page biography that some team owners featured in their own media publications.

While other teams, if they had one, would show Super Bowl trophies (no matter how far in the past they were won) and team slogans (such as "Commitment to Excellence"), for years the cover of the Steelers' guide was a picture of only their black helmet with whoever's white number on front (for example, Joe Greene's No. 75 in 1975) coincided with that particular year.

After the Steelers' victory in Super Bowl IX in New Orleans, their first, the Steelers' receptionist answered all phone calls, "Good morning, Super Bowl champion Pittsburgh Steelers." The Chief was one of those calling in on Monday morning and was greeted thusly. When his Tuesday call was answered in a similar manner, he said, "That was okay yesterday, but we don't need to do that anymore."

Early on, I naively thought all front offices were run like the Steelers. Then I took a position with NFL Properties in Los Angeles and was exposed to the Georgia Frontiere–led LA Rams. Talk about night and day . . .

More than once, when I would cross paths with Dan or Artie Rooney, I would tell them, "You guys spoiled me. Nobody does it like the Steelers." They'd usually just smile and say nothing.

Several years before, there was a controversial incident with another team or team owner that involved the release or firing of a longtime employee. I recall discussing it with Joe Gordon and Joe saying, "I thank God daily that I work for the Rooneys." That is a good summation of the feelings of anyone even remotely associated with the family enterprise.

In the eyes of Art Rooney, all were equal. Mention is made elsewhere how he shared Cuban cigars with members of the Three Rivers grounds crew. Sometimes he would invite members of the crew to dine with him and visiting dignitaries in the Stadium Club. On one such occasion he asked Ralph Giampaola to join Curt Gowdy and him. Giampaola was overwhelmed by the Chief's magnanimity. He said, "Mr. Rooney introduced me as 'Ralph Giampaola, a member of our organization.' Not 'a member of our grounds crew.' For all Mr. Gowdy knew, I coulda been a vice president. I felt ten feet tall. What a fine, fine gentleman."

It was once written of Mr. Rooney, "What he did for the NFL is well documented. What he did anonymously for others may never be fully known." Two concrete examples are known, if not well publicized.

Lowell Perry was an All-American from Michigan and a Steelers rookie in 1956. He got off to great start. As a receiver, punt, and kickoff returner, he was a budding star. That is, until he caught a pass against the New York Football Giants. As he made his way deftly downfield, he was hit simultaneously by huge Roosevelt "Rosey" Grier and Bill Svoboda. There was a sickening sound as Perry suffered a crushed pelvis and dislocated hip.

Perry spent thirteen weeks in a Pittsburgh hospital, visited almost daily by Mr. Rooney. When Perry fully recovered, Mr. Rooney paid his Duquesne School of Law tuition and later brought Perry back to the team as an end coach. Perry later had a long and successful career with the Chrysler Corporation and held a high-ranking position in President Gerald R. Ford's administration.

Al Young was a wide receiver with the Steelers in the early 1970s. He long suffered from high blood pressure, and when he could no longer play because of his condition, the Steelers honored his contract and latter signed him to a scouting position.

Sadly, Mr. Rooney suffered a stroke at his Three Rivers office on August 17, 1988, and was taken to Mercy Hospital. He seemed to rally but slipped into a coma and died on Thursday, August 25. On Friday more than five thousand people paid tribute to this great man, filing through St. Peter's Roman Catholic Church on Pittsburgh's North Side.

The next day driving into the city, I noticed all flags at half-staff. I was fortunate enough to be among the 1,200 mourners filling St. Peter's to capacity for Mr. Rooney's funeral. Several hundred others viewed via close-circuit TV in a church basement social hall. The gathering was like a who's who. Not only Steelers players past and present, but key NFL people and others from many walks of life. The tributes were heartfelt and emotional.

I can only echo what Justice White some years earlier said: "Art Rooney is the finest person I've ever known."

After Mr. Rooney's death, the low-key tradition continued. A small, discreet "AJR" patch was sewn on the players' jerseys for just the 1988 season. By contrast, a certain midwestern team still incorporates its late founder's initials into the left sleeve of their jerseys more than three decades after that owner's passing.

Darth Raider and the Mad Bomber

If the Dallas Cowboys of the 1970s were America's Team, the Oakland Raiders were America's Most Wanted.

The Cowboys were clean-cut and corporate-like in comportment and appearance, computer complex in their game strategies. The Raiders were renegades, rebels, but with a cause. Like their baseball counterparts in Oakland, Charlie Finley's famed "Mustache Gang," the Raiders looked, as A's star Gene Tenace said of his squad, like a biker gang on a three-day bender.

The face of the Cowboys franchise was head coach Tom Landry, whose calm, controlled demeanor was as much the iconic sideline picture he presented on game days as was his fedora, bright-blue blazer, crisp white shirt, and patterned necktie. Raiders coach John Madden, by contrast, wore blousy shirts unbuttoned at the neck and bellowed at officials, "Hey, throw the damn flag!" Madden was described by one observer as resembling an "unmade waterbed."

Quarterback Roger Staubach was called "Captain America," and the bright-blue star Dallas wore on its helmet could have been part of the original Captain America's costume. Raiders QB Kenny Stabler, by sharp contrast, was nicknamed "the Snake," and his ferocious teammates had monikers such as "Big Ben," "Assassin," and "Dr. Death." It was all perfectly fitting for a squad whose swashbuckling logo bore the visage of a pirate—his head covered by a silvery Raiders helmet, his right eye covered by a black patch—and a pair of crossed swords. The Raiders' logo was reportedly a rendition of Randolph Scott, a square-jawed actor who was an action hero and leading man in movies and had a significant role in the pirate movie *Captain Kidd*.

These were the original Darth Raiders, and the outlaws of Oakland took their cue from their emperor, Al Davis. If the Cowboys were known for their blue stars, the Raiders could have been known for the Death Star made famous in the 1970s by George Lucas and *Star Wars*. Gonzo journalist Hunter S. Thompson took it a step further, stating that Al Davis made Darth Vader "look like a wimp."

Davis declared, in his oft-parodied Brooklyn accent, that his *Raid-iz* would "rather be feared than respected," and the man who spent his adult life in football as a scout, assistant coach, head coach, general managing partner, and owner created a culture in Oakland unlike any other in pro football history. From the opening kickoff to the final gun, Oakland's opponents were going to get hit, stated George Atkinson, an All-Pro safety for the Raiders from 1968 to 1977. They were going to get hit hard, and they were going to get hit often.

The Raiders wanted to leave opponents with the conviction that football isn't a contact sport; it's a collision sport, as Vince Lombardi often stated. And that's what Oakland did, Atkinson said. The Raiders created collisions.

Atkinson's partner at safety was Jack Tatum, also known as the Assassin. A huge hitter for Woody Hayes's Ohio State Buckeyes squads that won a national championship in 1968 and fell just shy of national titles in 1969 and again in '70, Tatum found the Raider Way to his liking when Davis drafted him in 1971.

It was appealing to Tatum that once he became a Raider he was going to go out on the field and destroy opponents. Oakland was going to hit opponents and intimidate them, said Tatum, who liked to believe that his best hits bordered on "felonious assault."

Oakland linebacker Phil Villapiano said he and his mates hit as hard as they could because that was the "Raider Way."

The Raider Way was established in the late 1960s when they began winning league and division championships in the American Football League. The more Oakland won, the more prominent and feared its image became. Villapiano said some teams would lie down and let the Raiders beat them. Opponents, he opined, were afraid of the image.

The Silver and Black's bullying led to a mystique that left the rest of the league wary. Like those who faced the Philadelphia Flyers' brutally physical Broad Street Bullies teams in the 1970s, opponents of the Silver and Black knew what awaited them on game day.

Kansas City head coach Hank Stram hated seeing those silver and black uniforms on game days in the Oakland Coliseum. Miami Dolphins wide receiver Nat Moore said players were aware of the Raiders' mystique and knew going into games that they were going to get hit hard. The key question, Moore stated, was simple: Were you going to get hit fairly, or was it going to be a cheap shot?

New England Patriots star tight end Russ Francis thought some of the Raiders were outstanding athletes but that other members of Oakland's outfit weren't very good. The latter, Francis stated, were intimidating types who tried to hurt people. Joe Namath believed opponents knew they were playing a rough football team in the Raiders. The New York Jets' Hall of Fame quarterback adopted his half-cage face mask—notable in an era of single- and double-bar looks—late in 1967 after his cheekbone was smashed by the clubbing fists of 6-foot-5, 270-pound Raiders lineman Ike Lassiter. Some of the Raiders, Namath asserted, kicked and bit and hit you in the back of the helmet. The proof, he insisted, was in the game films.

Davis was as distinct in his appearance as his Raiders were in their play. He wore his hair slicked back and mirrored his team's colors by wearing black suits with silver ties and, in his later years, black or white satin running suits. His office was styled in similar fashion. When hulking defensive lineman John Matuszak was cut by the Washington Redskins and signed by the Raiders in 1976, an assistant led him into Al's office. What the self-styled "Tooz" saw was quintessential Raider. Everything in Davis's domain was silver and black. Black walls, black couch, black telephone, silver drapes, silver carpet, sil-

ver chairs. Seated behind a big black desk was Davis, who looked to
Tooz as if he had just stepped out of the fifties: hair slicked back in a
pompadour, a ducktail creeping down his neck.

Davis maintained that the fire that burns brightest in the Raiders
organization is the will to win. His most oft-repeated creeds—"Just
win, baby!" and "Commitment to Excellence"—reflected beliefs that
Davis grew up with.

Houston Oilers original owner Bud Adams, one of the eight founding members of the AFL's "Foolish Club," said Davis was a football
man whose entire life revolved around the sport he loved. "He worked
his way up through the ranks and had a knowledge of all phases of the
game," Adams said. "That experience aided him as an owner."

Along with the Bengals' Paul Brown, Davis was the only other owner
in the NFL in the seventies who had been a pro head coach. Because
of that experience Al did things other NFL owners didn't dream of
doing. He studied film, scouted players, and constantly worked the
phones in search of trades. Davis made it a point to always be at the
Raiders' full-contact practices on Wednesdays and Thursdays and in
some weeks the practice before the game. He kept a low profile on
the practice field, standing alone on the distant sideline or beneath a
goalpost. But his players and coaches always knew he was there. Davis
had a presence, and he had something else—a deep love for his team.
He amazed his players by knowing the name of every one of them,
even during training camp, when there were dozens of rookies and
free agents trying to make the team.

On some NFL teams players might see the owner three or four times
the entire season. Because their roots are in other businesses they rely
on others when faced with football decisions. Matuszak said some
owners didn't know Red Grange from red wine; they thought Bronko
Nagurski was some kind of tropical disease. Not so with Davis. Al's
greatest love, besides his wife, Carol, and their family, was his Raiders.

Adams believed Davis differed from other owners because of his
background. Al was an AFL guy who helped push the rebel league
forward. Like Pittsburgh patriarch Art Rooney Sr., Davis is one of
the most important figures in pro football history. He proved to be

a pivotal figure in hastening the historic merger between the upstart AFL and established NFL.

Like his beloved AFL, Davis was a rebel with a cause—a renegade coach, commissioner, and owner who bucked NFL authority for more than three decades. He is the only executive in pro football history to be an assistant coach, head coach, commissioner, general manager, and owner.

Unlike Rooney, Davis did not prefer being in the background. Al was an out-in-front, in-your-face Type A personality. When a reporter asked a young Davis how he would adjust to California's laid-back lifestyle, the former Brooklyn street kid bristled. "Adjust?" Davis said, spitting out the word as if it were ashes in his mouth. "You don't adjust. You dominate."

Davis dominated because for him football was not just his sport, not just his profession, but his life. The tough-minded coach and owner of the Oakland Raiders transformed a failing franchise and turned it into one of the more iconic in all of sports.

"When you think of Al Davis," Madden said, "he gave his whole life to football. He's done nothing else." Madden would tell Davis, "You've got to do something." But Davis never hunted, fished, or played golf. Al's job, his profession, his free time, Madden said, was football.

Born on July 4, 1929, in Brockton, Massachusetts, to Rose Kirschenbaum Davis and Louis Davis, Al was an Independence Day baby whose life would come to reflect the fiery passion and free thinking that marked the origins of his holiday birthday. His father found employment in several fields, garment manufacturing among them. Louis, Rose, and sons Al and older brother Jerry, who was born in 1925, moved to a rented sixth-floor walkup off Utica Avenue in Brooklyn, New York, in 1934.

Al's father supported him in anything he did as long as he didn't back down from a confrontation. One of Al's heroes was fellow Brockton native Rocky Marciano. Prior to big fights the Rock would refrain from shaving for a few days in order to look scruffy and foreboding. Davis would do the same years later when the Raiders had a big game.

Childhood friends of Al thought him more of a talker than a fighter.

He was drawn to basketball and gained a reputation for hard play. Davis was a backup at Erasmus Hall High School, a public school located on Flatbush Avenue. The school proved to be a spawning ground for people who would become famous in sport and entertainment. NFL Hall of Fame quarterback Sid Luckman of the Chicago Bears preceded Al at Erasmus and was a lifelong hero to Davis. Barbra Streisand is also a graduate of Erasmus Hall. While Davis didn't gain much playing time, he did study the coaching techniques of Al Badain, a man whom Davis would credit for teaching him much about coaching.

Davis graduated from Erasmus in 1947 and enrolled at Wittenberg College in Springfield, Ohio. He spent a semester there, focusing on baseball, and then transferred to Syracuse University. Davis tried out for numerous sports but was relegated to backup status on the junior varsity baseball team.

He transferred to Hartwick College in Oneonta, New York, before soon returning to Syracuse. Failing to make the varsity basketball team, Davis threw himself into studying football strategy. He hung around the team's practices taking notes so often that he was asked to leave by a suspicious coaching staff. Undeterred, Davis attended classes in football strategy, courses taught by coaches and normally taken by players only. He earned a degree in English and developed deep interests in literature and jazz as well as military and political history. The latter became a lifelong fascination, so much so that in the years ahead, after taking over the Oakland organization, every Raiders itinerary would contain the words "We go to war!"

Davis's six decades in football began in 1950 when he graduated with a bachelor of arts degree in English and was named line coach at Adelphi College in New York. He had been pursuing both a master's degree and a position as an assistant football coach in order to jump-start his career. While pursing a job Al would introduce himself as "Davis from Syracuse." Some thought the deception—George Davis was a star halfback for the Orangemen—intentional. Al was turned down at Hofstra and initially at Adelphi, but he sought out Adelphi's president and was hired as freshman football coach.

Davis's student deferral ended when he earned his master's degree in 1952 and he was inducted into the U.S. Army. He was assigned head football coach at Fort Belvoir, Virginia. Military teams at the time were stocked with college stars, and Davis helped build a national power service team. Yet his methods for securing former college and pro players drafted into the military raised eyebrows and suspicions in equal amounts and very nearly led to a congressional investigation.

In 1953 Davis coached Fort Belvoir to an 8-2-1 record and just missed earning a berth in the Poinsettia Bowl following a season-ending loss to Quantico Marine Base.

During his time in the army Davis sold scouting information on his players to NFL teams. Among those contacting Al at the time was the Los Angeles Rams' public relations specialist Pete Rozelle. Since Rozelle would not pay for information, Davis did not provide him any scouting reports. Their personal feud would continue for the next several decades and result in several lawsuits.

When most of Davis's team was sent to Korea, Al remained at Fort Belvoir until he was discharged in 1954. The twenty-four-year-old Davis gained his first pro football job, serving as a scout for Baltimore Colts head coach Weeb Ewbank. The next two years saw him serving as line coach and chief recruiter at the Citadel. From 1957 to 1959 Davis joined Don Clark's staff as line coach at the University of Southern California. He persuaded Clark to implement a blocking scheme described by a former Trojan player as a "hit 'em and hit 'em again double block." Davis is credited with helping turn around the Trojans, USC going 8-2 in 1959.

Davis returned to pro football in 1960, but not with the NFL. Lamar Hunt and seven other owners who would become known as "the Foolish Club" had started the American Football League, and Davis was hired by new Los Angeles Chargers head coach Sid Gillman as an assistant coach.

With an offensive armada that would eventually feature Tobin Rote and John Hadl at quarterback, Paul Lowe and Keith Lincoln in the backfield, Lance Alworth at receiver, and Ron Mix at tackle, the Chargers' electrifying, quick-striking attack symbolized the exciting, wide-open style of the fledgling AFL. "The stopwatch never lies," Davis stated. "Speed kills but absolute speed kills absolutely."

Helping coach the Charger defense was Chuck Noll, a former Cleveland Browns lineman under legendary Paul Brown. Noll, who would build a Steelers squad to rival Davis's Raiders for AFC supremacy in the seventies, had been a messenger guard for Otto Graham and blocked for Jim Brown. Under Gillman Noll bossed a Charger front that featured stars in Earl Faison and Ernie "Big Cat" Ladd.

Davis was instrumental in the Chargers winning two Western Division Championships in their first three years and playing for the AFL title in 1960 and again in '61.

Gillman knew his cocky young assistant was headed for bigger things. "There isn't a doubt in Al Davis's mind that right now he's the smartest guy in the game," Gillman said at the time. "He isn't, but he will be pretty damned soon."

In January 1963 Davis was named head coach of the Oakland Raiders. The Raiders had gone 1-13 in 1962 and won a combined three games in the two seasons prior to Davis taking over. Oakland played its home games in Frank Youell Field, a high school–size complex named after a local undertaker.

At age thirty-three Davis was the youngest man in pro football at the time to combine the demanding dual positions of head coach and general manager. Still, he had fourteen years of coaching experience and was called by *Sports Illustrated* a "young coaching genius." *Scholastic Coach* magazine said Davis owned the "most inventive mind in the country."

San Francisco coaching legend Bill Walsh, who borrowed Gillman's concepts and popularized them as the famed "West Coast Offense" the 49ers used to succeed Noll's Steelers as the NFL's dominant dynasty, called Davis a "truly great coach" and one of the greatest coaches he had ever observed. Had Al chosen to remain in coaching, Walsh stated, he would be considered one of the greatest coaches of all time.

In 1963 Davis coached the Raiders to the greatest turnaround in pro football history. Oakland is the only team in pro football to improve its record by nine wins in one season while playing a fourteen-game schedule. "The fire that burns brightest in the Raiders organization," Davis stated, "is the will to win."

The Raiders served notice of their turnaround from the start. Two-touchdown underdogs to the host Houston Oilers in the regular-season opener, Oakland won 24–13. Davis and Company returned to the West Coast the following week for their home opener and blitzed East Division contender Buffalo, 35–17. Four straight losses followed before the Raiders ripped off eight straight wins to close their campaign. Oakland finished 10-4 and second in the West by one game to Gillman's Chargers, whom Oakland defeated twice during the regular season. The Raiders' historic turnaround led to Davis being named Pro Football's Coach of the Year.

As he remade their record, Davis also remade the Raiders' image. As a boy in Brooklyn Davis was fascinated by Red Blaik's undefeated national champion Army squads that featured game-breaking stars in fullback Felix "Doc" Blanchard (Mr. Inside) and halfback Glenn Davis (Mr. Outside). Al saw the Black Knights of the Hudson, as Blaik's teams were known, charge the field in their black jerseys and invoke fear in their opponents. He believed Army's uniforms made their players look larger than they were and thus made them appear more intimidating to opponents.

Those memories were still fresh in Al's mind when he joined the Raiders. He changed Oakland's uniforms from black-and-gold secondhand relics from the University of the Pacific to a new silver-and-black scheme whose design resembled his beloved Black Knights of the Hudson.

At the same time he adopted the sartorial splendor of Army's football teams, Davis built the Oakland offense to combine the power of the New York Yankees' "Bronx Bombers" that had boasted Lou Gehrig, Joe DiMaggio, Bill Dickey, Yogi Berra, Mickey Mantle, Roger Maris, et al. and the speed of the Brooklyn Dodgers' "Boys of Summer" squads featuring the fleet Jackie Robinson. It was Davis's dream to combine the elements of Yankee power and Dodger speed in one dynamic team.

Taking over in Oakland, Davis turned his fantasy into reality. He remodeled the Raiders along the lines of the champion Charger teams he had helped Gillman build. Oakland's offense would have the same kind of strong-arm quarterback, swift receivers, and large linemen to pass block and pull out on sweeps and toss plays. The Raiders' defense would feature a front four that could pressure the quarterback and cornerbacks who covered receivers man-to-man.

While pro football has always had a maxim of "Take what the defense gives you," Davis installed a new motto with the Raiders: "We take what we want."

Stretching the field vertically with the deep passing game of quarterbacks Tom Flores and Cotton Davidson and end Art Powell and horizontally with the wide running game of Clem Daniels, the Raiders scored 363 points and averaged just under 26 points per game to rank second in the AFL. The vertical passing game Davis had learned from Gillman, his mentor, became a Raiders trademark. The wide-open offensive scheme with its long bombs to a bevy of speedy receivers was the signature strike of the Oakland offense. Davis didn't hesitate sending the swift Daniels out of the backfield on deep patterns, where he enjoyed mismatches with linebackers trying desperately to keep up. Oakland also employed an "East" formation that saw two receivers lined up on one side of the field, one in the slot position and the other wide. The formation forced mismatches, as safeties sought to cover the speedy slot receiver all over the field.

The Raiders became feared for an ultra-aggressive defense featuring a physically imposing front that punished quarterbacks and "bump-and-run" coverage by hard-hitting defensive backs. Davis changed defenses nearly every week, giving his linebackers the freedom to freelance and his secondary free rein to hunt down receivers.

From the start Davis infused the Raiders organization with his commitment to excellence. More than just a motto, the phrase became as much a mind-set within the organization as "Pride and Poise" and "Just win, baby." Despite the Raiders' struggles, banners proclaiming "Commitment to Excellence" would come to occupy prominent places in Oakland's home stadium on game days. "I had a dream," Davis said once, "to build the finest organization in sports."

Davis's commitment to excellence caused him to make changes

beyond the field. Players were traded or cut, front-office personnel fired. Team offices had been located in an open mezzanine overlooking downtown Oakland; Davis moved them to a more private location. Within four years of his arrival the Raiders moved from tiny Frank Youell Field, whose capacity was fifteen thousand, to the new Oakland–Alameda County Coliseum, which housed more than sixty-three thousand. "We want to win," Davis once said. "Raiders fans deserve it. Raiders players deserve it. . . . You have to win and you have to win with a vision. That's our passion."

Davis's other key moves involved front-office personnel. Scotty Stirling, a Raiders beat writer for the *Oakland Tribune*, was named the team's new public relations director. Ron Wolf was hired as director of scouting, and Al LoCasale, who would become known as "Little Al" to Davis's "Big Al," was selected as executive assistant.

LoCasale's handling of the organization's day-to-day operations allowed Davis to focus on football. Wolf was a former intelligence officer stationed at Checkpoint Charlie in Berlin and was working for *Sports Illustrated* when Davis hired him. Wolf built the Raiders' scouting system and later pulled off one of the great coups in NFL history when as general manager of the Packers he acquired an unknown quarterback named Brett Favre.

Davis's professional passion was the Raiders, but while he knew everything about everyone connected with his team, few knew much about him. Ken Stabler said Davis made sure no one got to know him very well. It was apparent, Snake said, that people were afraid of Al. None of the Raiders wanted to mess with the man whose name was on their paychecks.

Stabler said that Davis promoted the image of him being a street thug from Brooklyn; that's why Big Al dressed in black-and-white or black-and-silver suits like the crime bosses in old gangster movies. Some claimed Davis donned the silver-and-black schemes because he was color-blind, but Stabler believed it was because Big Al liked the Raiders' colors and the tough look. Halfback Pete Banaszak jokingly told teammates he was willing to bet that even Davis's pajamas had the Raiders' logo on them. Wide receiver Fred Biletnikoff agreed, stating that Davis loved the Raiders' pirate and his eye patch. "Al would wear an eye patch," Banaszak said, "if it wouldn't ruin his peripheral vision."

Like many football men, Davis always believed someone was spying on his team. When Biletnikoff joined the Raiders in 1965, one of the veterans told him he had once seen Al throw a rock at an airplane that flew over the practice field, the reason being that Davis thought it a spy plane. Davis didn't like intruders at practice. He once sent a ball boy to shoo away kids who were watching the Raiders work out.

Secrecy and mystery surrounded Davis and his Raiders. Big Al hid his eyes behind sunglasses; Snake thought the shades made Davis look like the *Spy vs. Spy* cartoon character.

Davis was enthralled with physical size in his players, and Raiders players thought Al tried to make himself look bigger by padding the shoulders in his suits. Davis denied wearing padded suits, and the Raiders would see their boss pumping iron in the weight room so he could, Stabler said, stop wearing those padded jackets that he denied wearing.

Davis's Raiders continued to play big, claiming another second-place finish behind Gillman's Chargers in 1965. Davis then turned the coaching reins over to John Rauch.

In April 1966 AFL owners sought a new league commissioner to replace the retiring Joe Foss. A World War II fighter ace in the Pacific theater, Foss had piloted the AFL through its formative years. By the midsixties league owners were seeking more aggressive leadership.

Buffalo Bills owner Ralph Wilson considered Davis a "coaching genius and astute administrator." Wilson's fellow AFL owners, embroiled in a bitter bidding war with the NFL for players, implored Davis to accept their offer to be point man in negotiations. Knowing that being named commissioner would effectively end his days as a coach, Davis, with Oakland co-owner Wayne Valley's approval, accepted the job on April 8. "History will dictate what my legacy is," Davis said later. "And 'maverick' is fine, because I am."

Madden would say that the things people criticized Al for were really the things they should have praised him for. Davis had his own ideas, Madden said, and many of them were contrarian. When people said, "Let's do it the way we've always done it," Davis would say, "Hey, wait a minute, let's look at this. Maybe there's another way."

By the midpoint of the decade the six-year-old AFL was making great strides in gaining equality with the forty-six-year-old NFL. The fledgling league was expanding, and new franchises would soon be added in Miami and Cincinnati. A multimillion-dollar contract with NBC in 1964 secured the league's future, and state-of-the-art stadiums were being built in Houston, New York, San Diego, and Oakland. New and aggressive leadership had helped save the New York and Oakland franchises, and AFL teams were winning some of the signing wars with the NFL and securing much of the top talent emerging from the colleges. Alabama quarterback Joe Namath, USC Heisman Trophy–winning running back Mike Garrett, glue-fingered Florida State receiver Fred Biletnikoff, and bruising Ohio State running back Matt Snell all chose the renegade AFL over the established NFL.

Fronted by the Chiefs' superb talent scout Lloyd Wells, the AFL brought black colleges out from the shadows. Future stars Buck Buchanan and Willie Brown were products of the AFL being more proactive than the NFL in signing athletes from black southern schools.

The AFL had fewer teams but more players from black colleges. The reason was twofold: Some NFL teams, the Washington Redskins foremost among them, maintained a quota for the number of black athletes on their roster. Unlike Redskins boss George Preston Marshall, AFL owners had no such quotas. Their only interest was in signing the best available talent, regardless of skin color.

Davis was very active in civil rights. He refused to allow his Raiders teams to play in any city where black and white players had to stay in segregated hotels. In time he became the first NFL owner to hire an African American head coach and the second to hire a Latino head coach. Davis also fought for gender equality; he was the first NFL owner to hire a female chief executive in 1997 when Amy Trask was hired.

The second reason is that NFL rosters in the early and mid-1960s were more fully stocked with veteran players. The AFL started from scratch in 1960 and spent its formative years filling its rosters with black athletes, as well as former NFL players Lenny Dawson, George Blanda, Ben Davidson, Tobin Rote, Jack Kemp, et al. and Canadian Football League players Cookie Gilchrist, Babe Parilli, Gino Cappelletti, Wray Carlton, Tom Flores, and Ernie Warlick.

AFL owners were not unanimous in how to deal with the NFL. Some owners, like Lamar Hunt, wanted peace. Others, like new Jets owner Sonny Werblin, a show-business impresario, believed the addition of Namath and Snell and the added attraction of sparkling new Shea Stadium meant the up-and-coming Jets could compete with the aging, declining Giants.

As the AFL's maverick new commissioner, Davis's plan of attack mirrored his play calling as the Raiders' head coach. He would go for the quick strike, the big score. The two warring leagues fought for draft choices but had an unwritten rule of not going after the other league's established players. The Giants broke this rule when they signed Buffalo placekicker Pete Gogolak. Davis responded by targeting the NFL's star quarterbacks, namely, the Los Angeles Rams' Roman Gabriel and John Brodie of the San Francisco 49ers.

"You don't have to love him," Wayne Valley said of Davis. "Just turn him loose." Once Davis was turned loose, the AFL's signings of Gabriel and Brodie sent shock waves along the corridors of power in the NFL. Even staunch NFL leaders like Green Bay Packers head coach and general manager Vince Lombardi, who detested all things AFL, reacted. The Packer strongman put out feelers to pry All-League center Jim Otto, "Mr. AFL" and a native of Wausau, Wisconsin, away from the Raiders. With future Hall of Fame center Jim Ringo having been dealt to Philadelphia at his own request, the NFL champion Packers were in need of a new linchpin for their formidable offensive line.

Thoughts of escalating a bidding war that would result in red ink for some of the less secure franchises frightened owners on both sides. Cooler heads prevailed, and AFL founder and Kansas City Chiefs owner Lamar Hunt and Dallas Cowboys president Tex Schramm entered into secret negotiations to bring peace to pro football.

Two months after Davis was named AFL commissioner, Hunt and Dallas Cowboys vice president of player personnel Gil Brandt agreed to a peace treaty. The historic agreement was announced to a stunned sports world on June 8, eight weeks to the day after Davis had been named commissioner. Davis's aggressive tactics and all-out pursuit of NFL stars Gabriel, Brodie, Chicago Bears tight end Mike Ditka, Green Bay "Golden Boy" Paul Hornung, et al. caused him to be acclaimed as a driving force in the merger between the warring leagues.

Davis did not approve of the negotiated settlement. He believed AFL owners had named him commissioner to win the war with the NFL. He came to realize they had used him only to bring the NFL to the negotiating table. Generals win the war, Davis would say, but the politicos, the politicians, make the peace. Confident he could have beaten his old acquaintance Rozelle, now the NFL commissioner, and the older league, Davis came to consider the AFL owners' peace plan a "sellout." He would compare the AFL-NFL merger to Yalta, the 1945 Crimea Conference in which U.S. president Franklin Roosevelt and British prime minister Winston Churchill are said by critics to have sold out Eastern Europe to Soviet dictator Joseph Stalin.

Davis did not appreciate AFL owners agreeing to million-dollar indemnities to be paid to their NFL rivals. He had also believed he would be commissioner of the merged leagues. When Rozelle was named instead and the post of AFL commissioner abolished, Davis's dislike for the NFL boss intensified. Davis could have remained AFL president until the leagues merged in 1970, but he refused the lame-duck post. Milt Woodard, who had served as assistant commissioner under Foss, accepted the position, and Davis returned to the Raiders.

He formed A. D. Football, Inc., a holding company, and joined Valley and Ed McGah as one of the team's three general managers. Davis owned a 10 percent share of the team and was named head of football operations. The Raiders moved into the new Oakland Coliseum in 1966 and hired a young assistant coach named Bill Walsh to help coach the offense. Walsh worked in Oakland just one season, but he called the exposure to the Raiders' system the biggest influence on his career. He knew that Davis's system emanated from Gillman's system and that Sid's system emanated from Clark Shaughnessy's system. Walsh would later modify the Raiders' system into the pro-

gressive system he ran in Cincinnati with the Bengals from 1968 to
1975 and to the West Coast schemes he perfected with the San Francisco 49ers from 1979 to 1988.

Walsh said he learned more football from one season in Oakland
than he would have if he had spent ten years somewhere else. Gillman's
system was a fully dimensional approach. Taken to Oakland, it used
every conceivable blocking combination, and where most teams might
have three or four pass patterns for the halfback, the Raiders had twenty.

Davis put this advanced offense into the hands of one of the more
dynamic young quarterbacks in pro football when he traded for Buffalo's backup quarterback, Daryle Lamonica, prior to the 1967 season.

A California native, Lamonica was a four-sport letterman in high
school and had turned down a baseball contract from the Chicago
Cubs to play quarterback at Notre Dame. A three-year starter with the
Fighting Irish, Lamonica was drafted by both the Bills and the Packers
in 1963. His initial inclination was to sign with the Packers, who had
drafted him in the twelfth round, while the Bills had selected him in
the twenty-fourth round. But the presence of All-Pro QB Bart Starr,
who had just led Green Bay to its second straight NFL Championship, convinced Lamonica to sign with Buffalo. He backed up Kemp
so successfully that he was nicknamed the "Fireman" for his ability
to rescue the Bills when Kemp was hurt or ineffective.

Lamonica was introduced to the hazards of pro football in a game
against San Diego in his 1963 rookie season. The massive Ladd bore
down on Lamonica, his long arms obscuring Daryle's vision. Bending down a bit, Lamonica whipped a sidearm pass that went beneath
Ladd's huge arms and was good for a completion. Just as he got the
pass away Lamonica was hit by Ladd. Hoping to avoid having Ladd's
320 pounds collapse on top of him, Lamonica grabbed him by his jersey and managed to fall on top of him instead. Ernie picked up Daryle with one huge hand and set him back on his feet.

"Real good play, kid," grinned Ladd, a genial giant.

Born on July 17, 1941, in Fresno, California, Lamonica was the son
of Sam and Vera Lamonica. Big and physical even as a youth, Lamonica played fullback his first two years at Clovis High School in

San Joaquin Valley. He was switched to quarterback by his coach, Lloyd Leest, who took note of the ease in which Daryle threw the ball. Because his team needed a quarterback, Leest installed Lamonica at the position. Daryle developed quickly, improving himself in a variety of ways, including jumping rope for footwork and punching a speed bag for hand-eye coordination.

Lamonica's father was a rancher, the family owning twenty acres of fruit trees. Daryle spent part of his youth picking peaches and apricots from dawn to dusk. At age six he was stricken with polio and at thirteen endured a sleeping sickness. By the time he reached his teens, Lamonica had grown stronger and was on his way to reaching physical maturity.

When he was in high school Lamonica was named by his father the foreman of the family ranch. Daryle still found time for athletics. In baseball he was a solid infielder with home run power. The Chicago Cubs took notice and offered him $40,000 to turn pro. Lamonica wanted to take the money, but Sam and Vera convinced him to go to college. Daryle eventually agreed. He could see the sense of getting an education, and he also wanted to continue playing football.

Receiving a number of scholarship offers, Lamonica chose Notre Dame. To him, just hearing the Fighting Irish fight song—"Cheer, cheer for old Notre Dame!"—got to him. Notre Dame's spirit was in his blood, Lamonica said, and would be there forever.

Lamonica arrived in South Bend, Indiana, at a time when the Fighting Irish were struggling under Joe Kuharich. At the time, Kuharich was the only coach in Notre Dame football history to have a losing record. Hoping to wake the echoes, Lamonica was instead used sparingly and was overshadowed nationally by Heisman Trophy winner Terry Baker of Oregon State and All-America QB George Mira of Miami.

Given little chance of making it in pro football, Lamonica served notice with a spectacular performance in the East-West Shrine Game in San Francisco's Kezar Stadium. Completing twenty of twenty-eight passes for 349 yards and driving his team 85 yards to victory in the final two minutes, Lamonica was a unanimous Most Valuable Player selection.

Backing up starting quarterback and future congressman Jack Kemp, Lamonica helped the Bills to an AFL-record four straight postseason appearances, a remarkable achievement in an era when only division winners reached the playoffs. The Bills were, in fact, the only team in pro football in the 1960s to make four consecutive trips to the post-season. Lamonica and the 1964–65 Bills joined George Blanda and the 1960–61 Houston Oilers as the only AFL teams to win back-to-back league championships. The 1964–66 Bills, 1960–62 Oilers, 1963–65 Chargers, and 1967–69 Raiders are the only AFL teams to claim three consecutive division titles. From 1963 to 1969, the span of his AFL career, Lamonica made the postseason every year and was a part of every AFL title game from 1964 to 1969, a remarkable run of six straight championship contests. Counting the 1970 merger season, Lamonica reached the playoffs his first eight years in pro football and played in seven straight league or conference championships.

Davis coveted the strong-armed Lamonica, the "Mad Bomber" who averaged almost 9 yards per attempt in the Bills' first title-winning season in '64. "If we could just get that big kid away from Buffalo," Davis would muse.

On March 14, 1967, the first day of the college draft, Davis finally did get that big kid away from Buffalo. Dealing QB Tom Flores, split end Art Powell, and a second-round draft choice to the Bills for Lamonica, split end Glenn Bass, and two draft picks (third and fifth rounds), Davis engineered one of the most one-sided deals ever in pro football as he landed the player who gave the Raiders their identity on offense.

The twenty-five-year-old Lamonica was grateful that Bills boss Lou Saban hadn't thrown him to pro football's wolves but had instead brought him along slowly and allowed him time to study AFL defenses. Daryle had developed during what he called his "four-year education" in Buffalo. But he was stunned at the trade. Daryle said he had spoken the day before the deal with Ralph Wilson and was told by the Bills' founder and owner that he would have a chance to unseat Kemp at quarterback. There was no talk of a trade, and Lamonica was returning home from a hunting trip the following day when he learned he had been dealt to Oakland.

Daryle drove to Oakland the next day and immediately circled the Raiders' game at Buffalo on his calendar. Lamonica was grateful to Davis for having the faith to trade for him and to Rauch for having the faith to play him. Lamonica always had self-confidence and believed all he needed was the opportunity to prove himself.

Rauch put Lamonica at the wheel of the offense, and Daryle initially struggled with the new system, calling the wrong plays and throwing to the wrong spots. Oakland's offense was more complex but also more explosive than Buffalo's. Davis's scheme had a play for every situation, so play calling was more wide open than that of the buttoned-up Bills. The Raiders used their backs as receivers more, and their tight end was another receiving option, as opposed to being a third tackle, as was sometimes the case in the Bills' system.

Studying playbooks and game films, Lamonica had expected going into his first Raiders camp that he would need a month or so to adjust to his new teammates and new system. One critical change Lamonica had to make was the depth of his drop in the pocket. It had to be deeper than in Buffalo because Oakland's patterns broke later. Lamonica thought the patterns looked jumbled until he saw receivers running free after making their break. He had to discipline himself not to get itchy and step up in the pocket to throw. He learned to hold back until the last second before firing his pass.

Raiders veterans helped Lamonica learn the new system. At first he stuck to basic plays, calling simpler patterns and throwing to the first receiver on virtually every play, even if it meant forcing the pass. Still, Lamonica was big enough and strong enough to turn even broken plays into positive gains. On one play Lamonica forgot the call he had made in the huddle, but rather than audible to a new play he took the center's snap, kept the ball, and ran around end for an 18-yard gain.

Lamonica impressed his Raiders teammates. Defensive tackle Tom Keating had played alongside Lamonica in Buffalo and knew what Daryle could do. When the Raiders made the trade and reunited the two, Keating was confident Lamonica could help the Raiders. "He could really throw the ball," Keating said. That said, Keating didn't know if anyone believed Lamonica would play as well as he eventually did.

Blanda, acquired from the Oilers as a placekicker and backup QB, believed Lamonica had the strongest arm in football and more confidence than any quarterback he'd ever known. Banaszak said Lamonica was the boss in the huddle. Try to talk when Daryle's calling a play, Banaszak said, and Lamonica would tell them to keep quiet. Lamonica knew that while every receiver thinks he's open, it was up to him to decide where the openings were.

Some teammates considered Lamonica a loner, but as a quarterback and team leader Daryle didn't believe in getting too close to other players. He reasoned that it would be difficult to chew out a friend if he had to. If teammates thought him distant, he was okay with that; Lamonica wanted respect, not popularity.

The Mad Bomber's big arm was a perfect fit for the Raiders' big-play mentality. He could throw a football 50 yards with a flick of his wrist. He excelled on deep out, corner, and post patterns. Lamonica would tell reporters he was thinking of the end zone all the time. His first season in Oakland saw Lamonica firebomb defenses for 3,228 yards and a league-leading thirty touchdowns, and he was named AFL MVP.

Gene Upshaw, a Raiders rookie in 1967, noticed how Lamonica would begin windmilling his arm in the locker room and in the tunnel going down to the field. "He couldn't wait to start throwing the ball," according to Upshaw.

The Raiders soon discovered what Keating already knew. Lamonica had a great arm and threw beautiful passes. When Daryle threw deep passes in practice, it was like future fellow Oakland great Reggie Jackson hammering home runs in batting practice—the rest of the team just stopped and watch.

Lamonica, Upshaw once recalled, could really throw the bomb. And because he could, Daryle fitted perfectly with Davis's desire to build the ultimate deep passing game. "Al believed in the vertical passing game," Lamonica remembered. "That's what we did. We threw the ball downfield."

The Raiders would rather complete a 15-yard pass, even it took three attempts, than three 5-yarders. Through its use of formations and motion, Oakland's offense could dictate to opposing defenses.

Lamonica was the perfect quarterback for an era when most teams used man coverages, leaving defensive backs to cover the Raiders' speedy and savvy receivers all over the field. Oakland believed any of its receivers could get open in one-on-one coverage, and Raiders pass patterns used all their receivers all over the field.

"Ever since I began playing football," Lamonica said, "I've always believed that I was meant to lead." In 1967 he led the Raiders to their first division title and league championship.

Davis's dealing for Lamonica had changed the fortunes of the Raiders organization. Oakland's ferocious defense, meanwhile, became known in 1967 as the "Eleven Angry Men," thanks to Larry Felser. The Buffalo sportswriter penned a line that read, "The Raiders play defense like eleven angry men," after Bills QB Jack Kemp was sacked eleven times in a 24–20 loss in Week Five. Felser's inspired prose was a play on the 1957 courtroom drama 12 Angry Men, starring Henry Fonda and Lee J. Cobb. Bob Valli, Raiders beat writer for the Oakland Tribune, liked the moniker so much he popularized it by using it in virtually every story he wrote for the rest of the season.

Whatever nickname it went by, Oakland's destructive defense played with Al's admonitions ringing in its ears ("The quarterback must go down, and he must go down hard!") and set a pro football record with sixty-seven sacks as the Raiders won an AFL-record thirteen games in the '67 regular season. Facing the Oilers' league-leading defense and ground-gobbling offense in the AFL title game on New Year's Eve, Lamonica and the Eleven Angry Men led Oakland to a 40–7 romp and a berth in Super Bowl II.

Davis was thrilled to be facing the great Green Bay Packers and fellow New Yorker Vince Lombardi in the big game. "Imagine," he said, "the lil' ol' Raiders on the same field as the Green Bay Packers . . ."

Ironically for Lamonica, Oakland's opponent in the Miami Orange Bowl had drafted Daryle four years earlier. Lamonica threw for two touchdowns, but Oakland was overwhelmed, 33–14, in Lombardi's final game as Packers coach.

An avid outdoorsman whose love of hunting dates back to his childhood days when he accompanied his parents on rabbit hunts around their ranch, Lamonica preferred the quiet life in his Alameda apartment, enjoying his stereo and listening to jazz and classical music, reading, and planning his hunting adventures. He wasn't outspoken like Namath, didn't wear mod clothes, and kept his dark hair short in an age of hippies. Lamonica was a big-game hunter, be it hunting big game on an African safari or hunting big-game victories in the Oakland Coliseum.

To increase the possibility of the latter, Davis continued to add talent via trades and drafts, and the Raiders from 1967 to 1969 became the first pro football team to win at least twelve games in three straight seasons. Oakland went 37-4-1 during that span, the best record of any team in pro football. The Raiders' AFL Championship losses in 1968 and '69 came from the Jets and Chiefs, respectively, and both went on to beat the NFL champion in Super Bowl upsets.

Following a late 27–23 loss to the Jets in windswept Shea Stadium in the 1968 AFL title game, Davis replaced Rauch with Raiders defensive assistant John Madden. "I saw greatness in John, and he lived up to it," Davis said. "I also saw a tremendous competitor who loved to win. John is a standard bearer, someone that players, coaches, fans and the Raider Nation can all look up to. One of his great virtues, the fire that burned brightest in him, was his love and passion for football, which was seldom ever equaled."

Oakland went on to win Western titles in '69, '70, and '72. The latter year marked not only a return to glory for the Raiders, who in 1971 had missed the playoffs for the first time since '66; it also marked a watershed year for Davis. While Valley was attending the tragedy-marred Summer Olympics in Munich, Davis revised the partnership agreement. The new draft established him as the Raiders' general managing partner.

A stunned Valley sued to overturn the agreement when he returned Stateside. But since McGah had also signed the agreement—meaning two of the three general partners had voted in favor of the new draft—it was binding under California partnership law.

Al Davis's control of the Raiders was now absolute.

Jim Campbell: There's no question Al Davis was an outstanding inno-
vator and forward thinker. One incident left me duly impressed with
the man many called "the Genius."

In 1964 the Oakland Raiders made Don Green, a running quarterback from Susquehanna University (my alma mater), their fifth-
round draft choice. For personal reasons Green left the Raiders' camp
after only about a week.

When I met Davis in 1974 at Football's Greatest Weekend, as the
induction weekend at the Pro Football Hall of Fame in Canton, Ohio,
is called, I introduced myself—"Mr. Davis, I'm Jim Campbell from
Susquehanna University . . ." Before I could say anything further, Davis
stopped in midhandshake, flashed that Cheshire-cat smile, and said,
"You know Don Green could have made our ball club. Don't you?"
This was a full decade after the fact—a midround draft choice, who
spent hardly any time in their training camp.

Considering how long this was before modern scouting combines
and how truly unsophisticated college scouting was in the mid-1960s,
this was a tribute to the thoroughness of Davis's player-personnel
efforts. At the time Susquehanna was a private, liberal arts, Lutheran-
affiliated school of considerably fewer than one thousand in enroll-
ment. It played in a conference that included Ursinus, Haverford,
Swarthmore, and Dickinson—not exactly traditional powers, or football factories.

The Raiders' organization man sent to Selinsgrove to sign Green
was Gordon "Scotty" Stirling. Stirling stayed at the only viable hotel
in town—the Hotel Governor Snyder. The "Gov's" bar also doubled
as the student watering hole. With several days to kill before attempt-
ing to sign "Greenie"—the Susquehanna Crusaders QB was also the
seventeenth draft choice of the Baltimore Colts—and not much to
do, Stirling logged a lot of hours at the college hangout.

I got to know the personable Stirling quite well, and in the course
of our frequent conversations Scotty revealed why the Oakland team
colors became silver and black when Al (as everyone called Davis)
took over as head coach and general manager in 1963. The team's colors had been black and gold during their first unremarkable three

seasons. Scotty said, "Al's color-blind, but the shades he sees best are black, white, and gray or silver. That's also why he always wears the white or black, trimmed in silver, jump suits and tracksuits."

Before most of the pro football world knew much, if anything, of Al Davis, Stirling allowed that "Al does things differently. He's got his own ideas and convictions on how to do things. He's almost obsessed with speed, and he'll take a chance on players who 'don't fit the mold' or ones who may come with some baggage." As the Davis era unfolded, these maverick methods would become more evident to the rest of pro football.

These idiosyncrasies of Davis would eventually become the Raider Way. In trying to fulfill my duties as a sideline worker at Steelers home games by getting specific injury reports from a visiting team's trainer, I dealt with the Raiders' longtime trainer George Anderson, who was with the organization from 1960 to 1994. Anderson was always cordial in answering my inquiries as to a player's injury, but like most associated with the Oakland club he really didn't divulge much. Nothing specific, such as "a left knee strain," simply "a leg injury," or "he just got his bell rung." The tighter the game, the tighter the Raiders' collective lips.

The say-nothing policy carried over to the team's requisite weekly press releases. All other teams would provide their statistics, player status, milestones, and so forth. The Raiders' handouts and mailings were notorious for lack of information; there was nothing dealing with the Raiders.

The Raiders had no PR person for many years. In fact, the front-office staff was probably the smallest in pro football. Al LoCasale, whose title was administrative assistant, wore many hats with the Raiders. While no name or contact information was included in the press releases, it was undoubtedly the work of "Little Al," who stood 5 feet 4 on a good day.

A typical Raiders release of the 1970s would trumpet the virtues of the upcoming opponent. If the Raiders were playing the Kansas City Chiefs, the Raiders' release would sing the praises of Lenny Dawson (whom Davis always addressed as "Len-id"), Bobby Bell, Buck

Buchanan, Willie Lanier, Otis Taylor, or Emmett Thomas—as if the Kansas City media didn't know they were stellar performers.

The same weekend that I first met Davis I was seated behind him in the stands at the July 27 annual AFC-NFL Pro Football Hall of Fame game—Buffalo Bills versus St. Louis Cardinals. The Fawcett Stadium press box was too small to hold all of the NFL types and writers attending the game, so Davis and his companion were seated among the general public.

Davis's companion was Jimmy "the Greek" Snyder. It was Snyder, a fixture on CBS's Sunday-morning pregame show *The NFL Today* and Las Vegas oddsmaker, who gave Davis a gaudy onyx, diamond, and platinum "AL" bracelet, which the Raiders' owner wore daily until his death.

The odd couple didn't talk much but did pass brief notes back and forth. Inquiring minds wanted to know, so I saw the content of some of the notes. One note Snyder passed to Davis simply said, "Bubba's knee is shot," Bubba being Bubba Smith, acquired by Davis from the Baltimore Colts after a serious knee injury. Smith, truly a force to be reckoned with before the injury, played the 1974 season with Oakland, was shrewdly traded to the Houston Oilers in 1975, and was out of football and off to Hollywood one year later. Davis's reply was succinct and accurate: "You're so right."

Davis's pregame behavior further solidified his maverick image. Many owners were on the field long before kickoff. They would visit with the opposing owner, coaches, and even a player or two. But what I observed of Davis, always attired in the ubiquitous high-end white tracksuit, was decidedly different. He interacted just briefly with Raiders personnel and never with anyone from Pittsburgh, even though he and Chuck Noll served three years together (1960–62) on Sid Gillman's Los Angeles/San Diego Chargers staff.

Davis trained his eyes only on Steelers players as they warmed up and went through their pregame drills and rituals. Sometimes he crossed over to "between the white lines," taking what I assumed were copious mental notes on Pittsburgh players and tactics. He never said a word, just observed. Perhaps it was only a coincidence, but Warren

Bankston, a Steelers fullback from Louisiana State University, went from the Steelers to the Raiders, and Steelers assistant Charlie Sumner later found himself on the Raiders coaching staff.

During pregame warm-ups there is an unwritten rule: the field is divided into two halves, with the 50-yard line as the territorial divider. Ninety-nine percent of NFL personnel strictly observed the rule and line of demarcation. Al Davis was an exception. More than once, I observed him as far inside Steelers "territory" as the 35-yard line. Occasionally, an errant (?) pass would zing a little close to Davis's ear. Could Terry Hanratty, a noted prankster, have been sending Big Al a message?

Davis reveled in being "the Evil Genius." If, as a visiting team, you thought he had your locker room bugged, that was fine with him. A classic bit of pro football lore involves the Raiders and Chargers in the early 1970s. The Chargers, coached by Harland Svare, were in Oakland for a road game. Coach Svare had his team gathered for final pregame instructions before they were to take the field. Suddenly, there was a banging noise emanating from a steam pipe or an air duct or vent. Svare stopped his pregame talk in midsentence, looked up at the offending vent or pipe, shook his first, and uttered, "Damn you, Al Davis!" Mind games were a vital part of Davis's bag of tricks.

Davis's persuasiveness was legendary. This applied to job seeking, college recruiting, and NFL free agency. I had this verified to me during a casual sideline conversation with Paul Maguire, who was several years into his postplaying career as an analyst for NBC.

Knowing Maguire was something of a free spirit, I asked him, "How did a swingin' dude from Youngstown, Ohio, like you end up at a tightly run military school such as the Citadel?" Maguire looked at me, tilted his head, and muttered, "That SOB [only Maguire didn't use the accepted abbreviation] Al Davis." He needn't have elaborated further. Nevertheless, Maguire began his pro career as a member of the Chargers, on whose staff Davis served. Undoubtedly, with Davis's influence the Chargers made Maguire a draft choice in 1960.

Angelo Coia, a Philadelphia prep star (what would be called a "five-star recruit" in today's lexicon), also matriculated at the Citadel briefly. But when Davis beat the posse out of Charleston, South

Carolina, and landed in Los Angeles at the University of Southern California, Coia also made the trip to the coast and completed his collegiate career as a Trojan.

Coia was drafted in 1960 by both the Chicago Bears of the NFL and the New York Titans of the AFL. Coia, a speedy wideout, cast his lot with Papa Bear George Halas. After Angelo's playing career, Davis, always considered a mentor by Coia, hired him as a scout.

While I was working at Bucknell University in the 1990s, Coia would occasionally visit the Lewisburg, Pennsylvania, campus to view film and tape of Bison potential pros. He also confirmed that it was Davis's power of persuasion that got him to the Citadel and USC. His regard for Davis, it is safe to say, was considerably higher than that of Maguire.

Another example of Big Al's outside-the-box thinking was 1967 tenth-round draft choice Richard Sligh, a defensive tackle from North Carolina Central. Sligh had the numbers that made Davis salivate—an even 7 feet in height and a solid 300 pounds. This was at a time when many defensive linemen weighed about 250 pounds.

No doubt Davis saw Sligh as an antidote to Kansas City's behemoth offensive linemen like Ed Budde and Jim Tyrer. There was only one complication: Sligh just wasn't much of a football player. After appearing in only eight games, mostly on special teams as a potential field-goal and point-after kick blocker, Sligh became a member of the Oakland Raiders Alumni Association.

While Davis hit on many transactions—Daryle Lamonica, Art Powell, and Willie Brown to name a few, and other acquisitions such as Lyle Alzado, John "the Tooz" Matuszak, and Ted Hendricks—he missed on others. Mike McCoy, a giant defensive tackle out of Notre Dame, was a force with the Green Bay Packers but, like Bubba Smith, was damaged goods when signed by the Raiders. McCoy became a member of the New York Giants after two rather ordinary seasons in Oakland.

Another Davis deal that didn't exactly pay huge dividends was getting all-star cornerback Monte Jackson from the Los Angeles Rams. Mention of the deal is made if for no other reason than comic relief. The move was commonly referred to as the "Lawrence Welk" trade.

The defensive back, who never really panned out as a Raider, cost the team "a one, and a two, and a three [draft choices]."

To those not citizens of Raider Nation, it seems as though the Raider Way was composed of equal parts bullying, chicanery, psychology, intimidation, mystique, trash talking, braggadocio, and anything else perceived to give the Silver and Black an edge or an advantage. Mixed with an ample supply of talent, this made the Raiders a formidable opponent.

In the mid-1970s it was customary for the home team to host a "conference" party the night before the AFC or NFC Championship Game. Thus, on Saturday, January 3, 1976, the Steelers organization entertained local and league dignitaries at the Allegheny Club of Three Rivers Stadium.

The night was cold, rainy, icy, and windy and portended a less than ideal playing field for the next day's game. But that Saturday night was festive—drinks, hors d'oeuvres, and tales from the NFL trenches. My wife and I attended, along with local politicians, industrialists, and NFL representatives.

Across the room I spied Art Rooney Sr. talking with Stan Musial—the St. Louis Cardinals baseball Hall of Famer was a native of nearby Donora, Pennsylvania, and something of a lifelong Steelers fan. Having never met Musial, this was too good of an opportunity to pass up. I excused myself and dropped in on Messrs. Rooney and Musial. Both were very genial, and after a few exchanges I went back to my stranded and understanding wife.

In my absence she had struck up a conversation with a red-haired young man, probably in his early twenties. She introduced me to "Mark Davis." Never having really outgrown my smart-aleck stage, I flippantly replied, "Oh, Al's boy." Well, it turned out that was exactly who Mark Davis is. We chatted briefly about the next day's game but nothing too deep. Given the time line, Mark was probably still pursuing his undergraduate degree at California State University–Chico. He seemed only moderately interested in pro football generally or the Raiders specifically.

I'm not sure if it was coincidence or just Al Davis's way of ingratiating himself to a higher-up, but when Mark was born during Al's tenure at the Citadel, the president of the "West Point of the South" (a term also used by Virginia Military Institute) was World War II general Mark W. Clark.

Regardless of one's opinion of Al Davis, no one can deny the loyalty he instilled in anyone who was part of his *Raid-iz*. There is no better example of this than the fact that nine Raiders Pro Football Hall of Fame inductees all chose Davis as their presenter at their induction ceremony.

3

Raider Nation, Franco's Army, and Knowledge Noll

Dan Conners was on the Oakland Raiders' sideline when Franco Harris snared the deflected football from the steel-gray sky.

The irony for Conners is that the final play of the 1972 AFC playoff in Pittsburgh was Oakland's only defensive play that day in which the veteran middle linebacker did not take part. Had Conners been on the field, he believes the Immaculate Deception, as Raiders fans remember the play, would not have happened. The reason, Conners thought, is that where Harris caught the ball in the middle of the field is the same spot where the Raiders' veteran would have positioned himself.

Conners holds a special place in Raiders history. He was the first Oakland draft pick Al Davis ever signed. An old school–style player from St. Mary's in western Pennsylvania, Conners was not the first player Davis drafted in Oakland. That honor went to Arizona State running back Tony Lorick in the 1964 American Football League draft. In that draft, which was held amid somber surroundings on November 30, 1963—eight days after President Kennedy's assassination—Davis took Lorick with the seventh pick. Lorick had also been selected by the Baltimore Colts and decided to sign with the established league.

Conners, the Raiders' second-round selection and the fifteenth pick overall, had also been chosen in the NFL's fifth round by the

Chicago Bears. Believing the Bears were not as interested in signing him as the Raiders were, Conners went with Oakland. While playing at the University of Miami in Florida, Conners had been impressed that a Raiders scout in South Florida had checked on him constantly.

Over the next decade, Conners was there for the Silver and Black's pivotal moments. He was there when the Raiders moved from Frank Youell Field to the glittering new Oakland–Alameda County Coliseum in 1966. He was there for the Raiders' AFL Championship season in 1967 and a Super Bowl II showdown with Vince Lombardi's lordly Green Bay Packers. He was there for the famous *Heidi* Game against Joe Namath and the New York Jets in 1968 and for the AFL title-game duels with Namath and the Jets in '68 and Len Dawson and the Kansas City Chiefs in 1969. And Conners was there for the historic merger with the NFL in 1970 and the AFC Championship Game against the legendary Johnny Unitas and the Colts in the Baltimore dirt bowl known as Memorial Stadium.

The amazing thing is that Conners was there for these signature events despite getting in Davis's face his rookie season. One season after finishing 10-4 in the greatest single-season turnaround in pro football history, the Raiders went 5-7-2. Before packing his car for the long ride home to Pennsylvania, Conners, who had appeared in five games his rookie season, approached Davis. "You said I was going to play!" Conners screamed at his coach. "I hate this. I hate you!"

Rather than retaliate with his own harsh words, Davis was so impressed by his rookie's passion that he responded by grabbing Conners by the shoulders, looking him in the eye, and then hugging him. "I love you, kid," Davis said.

Conners had been a hands-in-the-dirt defensive tackle in college, but the Raiders converted him to middle linebacker. They would do the same in future years with Conners' successors at inside linebacker—Monte Johnson and then Matt Millen.

Conners was part of a new wave of players Davis brought in to rebuild the Raiders. In 1964 Conners, defensive end Ben Davidson, and receiver Bill Miller joined the team; in 1965 the new arrivals were receiver Fred Biletnikoff, defensive back Kent McLoughan, linebacker

Gus Otto, and offensive tackles Harry Schuh and Bob Svihus; in 1967 quarterback Daryle Lamonica and future Hall of Famers in cornerback Willie Brown, kicker-quarterback George Blanda, and offensive guard Gene Upshaw.

Tom Flores, an Oakland quarterback in 1966 and teammate of Conners before becoming an opponent when Flores played for the Bills and then the Chiefs, considers Conners one of the smartest linebackers in Raiders history. Conners was quick rather than fast, and while he was physically strong, his biggest strength was his knowledge of the game and ability to be in the right place at the right time. Raiders teammates and coaches thought Conners was always there to make an interception, recover a fumble, or cause a fumble.

It was great having a playmaker like Conners as a teammate, Flores thought. But it was a pain to play against him. The Oilers found that out in the 1967 AFL Championship Game played on a sunny New Year's Eve in Oakland. Houston mounted a drive into Raiders territory early in a scoreless game when Conners forced and recovered a fumble by tight end Alvin Reed. The aggressive play helped set a tone for a defense that wouldn't surrender a point until Oakland owned a 30–0 lead in the fourth quarter.

As the middle linebacker in Oakland's defense, Conners was the linchpin for a unit whose ferocious style led to their "Eleven Angry Men" moniker. He remains one of the great defensive playmakers in Raiders history.

Ken Stabler said that while Conners wasn't really big and didn't have a lot of range, he was smart and an overachiever. On top of that, Conners was a team leader who could calm down volatile teammates on the field and take younger players like fellow linebacker Phil Villapiano under his wing off the field. "Dan was the kind of guy," said Stabler, "who could handle the linemen and linebackers who got too emotional in games and wanted to maim people."

In his pro career Conners played in 141 regular-season games and hauled in 15 interceptions for 232 return yards and 3 touchdowns and recovered 16 fumbles for 112 yards and 2 TDs. "He was always around the ball," Stabler said, and it's this playmaking ability that Conners believes would have allowed him to be in position to prevent Harris from making the Immaculate Reception.

As it was, Oakland made plenty of plays during the 1972 season. Davis and John Madden continued to rebuild the Raiders, showing a knack for finding fresh talent and easing aside established but aging veterans. Tony Cline, Horace Jones, Otis Sistrunk, and Art Thoms were young guns starting on the defensive line, taking the place of Davidson, Tom Keating, and Carleton Oates. Outside linebackers Villapiano and Gerald Irons were new faces flanking Conners. In the secondary young safeties George Atkinson and Jack Tatum joined veteran cornerbacks Willie Brown and Nemiah Wilson.

Continuing his rise as one of the AFC's top young running backs, Marv Hubbard hammered out 1,100 yards on the ground to lead the Raiders' rushing attack. But the flashy new addition to the offense was world-class sprinter Cliff Branch, a rookie who gave Lamonica, a.k.a. the Mad Bomber, a new deep threat and gave the special teams a boost as a punt returner.

Branch was a game changer, a home run hitter for a team that wanted to stretch the field and favored a vertical passing game. He didn't catch a high volume of passes—he topped out with sixty receptions in 1974 and averaged thirty-six catches per season—but for a team that wanted to throw the deep ball, Branch was the perfect deep threat.

Branch was a blazer; he was also a trailblazer by wearing uniform number 21 in an era when NFL wide receivers routinely wore numbers in the 80s. Like Houston's Ken Burrough, who wore oo, and Philadelphia's Harold Carmichael (17), Branch's 21 gave him immediate recognition and would prove iconic.

Like contemporary Lynn Swann, who would join the Steelers in '74, Branch was a smallish but stylish receiver whose consistency helped lead to championships. Because of his speed Branch intimidated the defenders of his day. Al Davis said Branch was the Raider that opposing defenses feared most; indeed, Branch's burning speed often left cornerbacks in cliff-hanging mode.

Breakaway speed calls for double coverage, and the 5-foot-11, 170-pound Branch forced defenses into special assignments. A sprinter at the University of Colorado, Branch set a world indoor record of 9.3 in the 100-yard dash and twice ran 9.2 outdoors.

Branch was quick, and equally quick to impress teammates. Running the 100, Branch may have looked to teammates such as Tatum like he was coasting. But once Branch got a step on the defender, the gap quickly widened to 10 yards, and he was en route to six points. Tatum noticed that Branch had more than great speed; he also excelled in running pass routes and had courage as well as intelligence. Because he had the ability to turn a 5-yard catch into a 90-yard touchdown, Branch was dangerous from any spot on the field.

Branch had qualified for the Olympic Trials his senior year in college, but after being drafted by the Raiders he opted for the NFL. "We drafted him mainly as a return man," Madden said. "But I've always felt that any player who can get open can be taught to catch a pass. Hands can be developed."

Branch's hands developed via a strong work ethic. He spent hours at his home squeezing Silly Putty to strengthen his grip and played pool and Ping-Pong to improve his hand and eye coordination. He also played tennis because he knew it would be good for his legs and would benefit him when he had to make quick breaks when running routes.

Branch called his greatest physical attribute, his speed, a "God-given grace." He developed it with the aid of others dating back to junior high coach Oliver Brown. Brown worked on Branch's running technique, and when Branch headed to Worthing High, Brown went with him and continued to work with him. Their hard work paid off. Branch became the first Texas high school athlete to run the 100 in 9.3, and he did so twice.

On gridiron highways in the NFL, speed can kill. But to be successful over the long run, Branch knew he needed to be more than a winged Mercury. He wouldn't make it in pro football running fly patterns downfield all day; he would have to learn how to run routes, how to play off a defender, and how to hang onto the ball when taking a big hit. Branch asked teammate George Atkinson, one of the more aggressive defenders in the NFL, about "hearing footsteps," and Atkinson's advice left an impression. "Clifford, you know that defensive man is going to hit you whether you catch the ball or not.

He's going to hit you because you're there. But you're responsible for the ball. That's what they're paying you for. So you've got to catch it."

Branch's clutch 19-yard catch helped key a last-minute 21–19 victory over neighboring San Diego during the 1972 season. The win was the fourth in a six-game streak that gave Oakland a 10-3-1 record and returned the Raiders to the top of their division. The streak started with a 20–14 win in Cincinnati and continued with a 37–20 victory in icy Denver that saw Biletnikoff haul in two Lamonica touchdown passes en route to his second straight AFC receiving title. The streak climaxed with a 26–3 thumping of rival Kansas City in Week Eleven and a 24–16 Monday-night handling of the Joe Namath–led Jets in the penultimate week of the regular season.

The victory over the Chiefs on a near-perfect sun-soaked Sunday proved particularly sweet for the Raiders. Oakland's division rivalry with Kansas City dates back to their AFL years and ranks as the most ferocious in AFL history and one of the fiercest in pro football history. From 1966 to 1969 the Raiders or Chiefs represented the West in the AFL title game, and it was Kansas City and Oakland that carried the AFL's banner into battle with the NFL's Green Bay Packers in Super Bowls I and II, respectively. The Raiders romped past the Chiefs 41–6 in a Western Division Championship Game in 1968, but Kansas City returned the favor by beating Oakland in the 1969 AFL title game. The Raiders won the West for the fourth straight season in 1970; Kansas City claimed the crown in '71.

Late in the '72 season Oakland and Kansas City were again battling for supremacy in their division when they met on November 26 in the Coliseum. The Chiefs had handled the Raiders 27–14 before a record crowd of eighty-two thousand in their new Arrowhead Stadium three weeks prior, but Oakland at 6-3-1 still maintained an edge over the 5-5 Chiefs as the season entered its stretch run.

The Daryle Lamonica–Len Dawson quarterback duel, the Raiders' silver-and-black uniforms and the Chiefs' cherry-red pants and helmets, stirred memories of big games past and served notice that this was the latest incarnation of one of the game's great rivalries. More than fifty-four thousand fans found their way to the Coliseum for the rematch with the Chiefs, many of them listening to legendary Raiders radio announcer Bill King calling the key plays:

"Lamonica throws for Biletnikoff . . . Touchdown, Raiders! Fred caught that ball after quite a physical battle with Marsalis in the right corner of the end zone."

The intensity of the physical battles between the Raiders and Chiefs was exemplified by Biletnikoff's catching the 14-yard touchdown pass from Lamonica that made it 16–3 in the second quarter and then running to where defensive back Jim Marsalis stood in the end zone and spiking the ball with emphasis at his feet.

Lamonica all but put the game away later in the second quarter when, with Oakland operating out of a two tight-end alignment, he found tight end Raymond Chester wide open for a 19-yard strike that made it 23–3 at the break.

King: *"Back goes Daryle to pass. He's looking for Smith but instead goes down the middle to Chester . . . Touchdown, Raiders! Holy Toledo! What a nice call!"*

Hubbard, Charlie Smith, Clarence Davis, and Pete Banaszak combined for a Raiders record sixteen rushing first downs. Rolling on Highway 78 (left tackle Art Shell) and Highway 63 (left guard Gene Upshaw), the Raiders ran fifty-three times for 255 yards. Oakland's defense limited KC quarterbacks Dawson and Mike Livingston to a combined ten completions while intercepting three passes.

One week later Oakland clinched its fifth division title in six years. Raiders fans followed their team to sun-drenched San Diego, where they watched another incredible late-game comeback and listened to King call the division-clinching plays:

"[John] Hadl throws deep to the end zone . . . Intercepted by Dan Conners! It was a deflection, hit into the air by Willie Brown, and Conners came down with the pass!

"Lamonica back, throws down the middle . . . Branch at the 20, tripped up, keeps going, reverses to the 15, dances down to the 9-yard line! First and goal to go Raiders! One minute, thirty seconds to go! Hang onto your hats!

"Lamonica gives to Smith, sending him to the left . . . He's at the 5, he's at the 2 . . . Touchdown, Raiders!"

After beating the Chargers, the Raiders had a Monday-night matchup with New York in the Coliseum. Broadway Joe and the Mad Bomber launched a combined sixty-three passes in a retro shoot-out that stirred memories of AFL classics. At 7-5 the Jets and head coach Weeb Ewbank needed a victory to remain in contention for a wild-card berth in the playoffs. The Raiders, riding an 8-3-1 record, were on their way to their fifth Western Division title.

Howard Cosell declared in ABC's *Monday Night Football* pregame show that the Jets' hopes "ride on Joe Willie Namath." Broadway Joe versus the Mad Bomber attracted the largest television audience in the history of *Monday Night Football* to that point.

The expected shoot-out between the former AFL gunslingers materialized, and the game lived up to its hype. Filling the night sky with footballs, Namath and Lamonica aired it out for a combined 605 yards and three touchdowns.

Playing with a sore throat and chills, Namath nonetheless gunned forty-six passes into the teeth of the Raiders' self-styled "Soul Patrol" secondary. He completed twenty-five for 403 yards and a touchdown but was picked off twice.

One of those was an end-zone pick by Jack Tatum. The Raiders' safety respected the Jets' superstar QB formerly known as Lord Fu Manchu for his leadership and facial hair. Tatum was aware of Namath's impact on the game; he knew Namath's name was synonymous with quarterbacking and that Broadway Joe had offered the game many exciting moments, including becoming the first pro quarterback to throw for more than 4,000 yards in a season in 1967 and one year later guaranteeing a victory over the eighteen-point favorite Baltimore Colts in Super Bowl III and delivering the AFL its first championship win over the NFL.

But Tatum also felt that, contrary to popular belief, Broadway Joe did not do a good job of reading pass coverages. Tatum thought that at times, Joe Willie White Shoe's decisions defied all logic. Jack knew Namath had a quick, strong release and the ability to set up quickly, despite crystal-fragile knees. But he believed Broadway Joe forced passes rather than seek a secondary target. Despite everything Namath did for the sport, Tatum rated him as just a fair quarterback.

Broadway Joe was more than fair against the Raiders on this night. His 49-yard scoring pass to Rich Caster gave New York a 7–3 lead in the first quarter, and he led the Jets to a pair of Bobby Howfield field goals in the second quarter for a 13–10 advantage at halftime.

Lamonica rallied the Raiders by throwing for 202 yards, 39 of them coming on his second-quarter bomb to Biletnikoff that brought praise from the ABC crew.

Frank Gifford: *"Lamonica going to the air to Biletnikoff, and he's open!"*

Don Meredith: *"That was a throw right on the money! The Mad Bomber really unleashed that one, and Biletnikoff never broke stride!"*

Lamonica's touchdown pass to Biletnikoff made it 10–7 Oakland, and Charlie Smith's 1-yard touchdown run returned the lead to the Raiders in the third quarter. Namath cut New York's deficit to 17–16 by guiding the Jets to another Howfield field goal. Lamonica clinched the win in the fourth, connecting with Raymond Chester for a 68-yard score on a third-and-1 play fake.

Gifford: *"Lamonica switches up and Chester's wide open!"*

Cosell: *"Great call!"*

The loss doomed the Jets' drive to return to the postseason for the first time since repeating as the AFL's Eastern Division champion in 1969. Yet Madden was so impressed with Namath's performance that he made it a point to seek him out and congratulate him personally.

Eliminating former AFL playoff foes Kansas City and New York from the postseason left Oakland primed for the playoffs. Their first-round game with the Central Division champion Steelers provided the Raiders with an opportunity to even another old score, Pittsburgh having dealt Oakland a 34–28 defeat in the season opener.

Raiders fans geared up for the contest. Stabler saw them as his kind of people, hardworking, blue-collar folks who arrived at the Oakland Coliseum hours before kickoff. They partied in the lots where they parked their recreational vehicles of every size and shape. Wearing black Raiders hats and shirts and waving silver-and-black Raiders pennants, fans would pull out their barbecue grills, well-stocked coolers, television sets, tables, and chairs and drink their beverage of choice from Raiders mugs.

Raiders players usually lingered in their locker room on game days to let the traffic thin out. Yet when they finally left and headed for their cars in the parking lot, they had to move through dozens of parties still going on. Stabler enjoyed this time with the fans, talking football, signing autographs, and accepting the free food and drink thrust upon them.

Stabler saw Raiders fans as another "special team" for Oakland during the game. Fans in the lower right-hand bleacher seats of the Coliseum sat directly behind the visiting team's bench. They were tough people, bikers and longshoremen among them. They showed up for games wearing wild outfits and made it a point to harass the opposition any way they could. Opposing players hated and feared Oakland's bleacher fans; they were pelted in the back with a variety of objects. Enemy players learned to wear their helmets on the sideline. Kansas City running back Ed Podolak said that playing in the Coliseum was as tough as playing the Raiders themselves.

Raider Nation was accustomed to playoff fever; Steel City fans were not. Enamored with their team's drive to their first title of any kind, Steelers faithful adopted players of their own. There was Franco's Italian Army, whose membership included Frank Sinatra, and Gerela's Gorillas, whose idol was placekicker Roy Gerela; Frenchy's Foreign Legion, started in honor of Frenchy Fuqua; Bradshaw's Brigade for Terry Bradshaw; Dobre Shunka (Good Ham) for Jack Ham; Russell's Raiders for Andy Russell; and, in time, Lambert's Lunatics for Jack Lambert; Rocky and the Flying Squirrels for Rocky Bleier; Webster's Warriors for Mike Webster; and Shell's Bombers for Donnie Shell.

Harris was the catalyst for the club's rise to prominence. The rookie fullback rushed for 1,055 yards, had twenty-one receptions, scored eleven touchdowns, and was the NFL's Offensive Rookie of the Year. With Harris running over and around defenders and Bradshaw strong-arming the competition, the Steelers scored a team-record 343 points.

The Steelers started the season on uneven footing, splitting their first four games. Pittsburgh opened with a 34–28 win over Oakland on a bright, beautiful afternoon in Three Rivers Stadium. The Steelers sprinted to leads of 17–0 in the first quarter and 27–7 in the third. Lamonica led a late comeback by bombing the Steelers' secondary for eight completions in ten attempts and throwing for 172 yards and two touchdowns in relief of Stabler. But the deficit was too great, Pittsburgh having pirated three Stabler passes and registered two sacks and two fumble recoveries to forge a 34–28 win.

The Steelers lost two of their next three, but turned it around beginning in Week Five with a 24–7 home win over Houston. Five straight victories followed, including a gritty 16–7 win in Week Nine over a Kansas City squad that was defending Western Division champions and in the hunt to repeat. Hank Stram's squad still boasted many of its famous Super Bowl IV stars—Dawson, Otis Taylor, Buck Buchanan, Curley Culp, Bobby Bell, Willie Lanier, and Emmitt Thomas—and their meeting with the Steelers resulted in a hard-hitting contest between two physical and famous clubs.

The victory over Kansas City was followed by a late 26–24 loss at rival Cleveland. It was a disappointing defeat for the young Steelers but not a devastating one. Pittsburgh rallied the next week to beat NFC contender Minnesota and then met the Browns beneath slate-gray skies on December 3 in a bitter battle to claim control of the Central Division.

Steelers fan clubs headed into Three Rivers Stadium in full force; the Steelers themselves were in full fury. Cleveland had captured six straight, including a comeback win over Pittsburgh just two weeks prior on the muddy turf of Municipal Stadium. The Browns were unbeaten on the road, the Steelers undefeated at home. Something would give on this day.

Jack Fleming and Myron Cope made the calls on Steelers radio:

Fleming: *"This crowd is in a frenzy . . ."*

With a title at stake, Cleveland's defense keyed on Harris, who was seeking his sixth straight 100-yard rushing day, a mark that would tie the record set by Browns Hall of Famer Jim Brown. While the Browns focused on Franco, the Steel Curtain keyed on Leroy Kelly, the great Cleveland ball carrier.

Gerela's 36-yard field goal climaxed Pittsburgh's first series and gave the Steelers a lead they never relinquished. With Kelly and backfield mate Bo Scott held to a combined 71 yards rushing and quarterback Mike Phipps limited to just 1 yard passing in the first half and 59 for the game, the Steelers seized physical control of the game. Pittsburgh punished the Browns with a grinding ground game, and with offensive lineman Gerry Mullins lined up as a second tight end in one of the Steelers' favorite formations, Harris headed to his right in the second quarter and squeezed in from a yard out despite being bearhugged by linebacker Dale Lindsey to make it 10–0.

Fleming: *"Handoff to Harris. Hits off the right side. He's in for the touchdown!"*

With the scoreboard imploring the Steelers to "Beat the Browns" and celebrity Soupy Sales in the packed stadium, Pittsburgh forced a turnover in the third quarter when Ernie Holmes stripped the ball from Kelly and Andy Russell recovered. From the Browns' 11-yard line several plays later, Franco followed guard Bruce Van Dyke and tackle Jon Kolb to the goal line, where he muscled past linebacker Billy Andrews for a 17–0 lead late in the third.

Fleming: *"Handoff to Franco. Big hole over the left side. He drives over the 5 and in the end zone for a touchdown!"*

Cope: *"He plowed his way into the end zone! Franco can really put on that power!"*

The Steelers effectively buried the Browns on the second play of the fourth quarter. Bradshaw rifled a seam pass to rookie tight end John McMakin, who got behind Lindsey and romped untouched for his first pro touchdown, a 78-yard score that made it 24–0.

Fleming: *"Terry will throw. Pulled in beautifully. John McMakin, he's going all the way! Boy, did he gallop!"*

Cope: *"McMakin made a nifty catch and then turned on a lot of speed!"*

A pair of Gerela field goals closed the scoring at 30–0. With the outcome not in doubt, the only thing left to be decided was whether Harris would tie Brown's NFL record. The scoreboard flashed "Let's Go Franco," but he needed 35 yards to reach 100 with less than nine minutes remaining. With Bradshaw handing to Harris on virtually every down, Franco fueled a drive that elapsed eight minutes. He bulled through the middle of the defense for the yards that gave him 102 on twenty carries.

Fleming: *"The crowd standing . . . Handoff to Franco. He drives through. He has it! He ties the NFL record!"*

The Steel Curtain registered four sacks and three turnovers and did not allow the Cleveland offense to advance past midfield for the entire second half en route to recording Pittsburgh's first shutout in nine seasons and its first blanking of the Browns.

Pittsburgh pounded out a 9–3 win at Houston in the penultimate week of the regular season, a victory that left a host of Steelers struggling to stand tall. Mullins slumped on a bench, inhaling oxygen through a thin green tube as he dealt with both a concussion and the flu. Line mates Kolb, Van Dyke, Jim Clack, and Ray Mansfield were likewise suffering. Kolb was fighting the flu; Van Dyke suffered a torn calf muscle early in the game and joined the previously injured Sam Davis on the bench; Clack wrenched a leg, and Mansfield was also hobbling. Bradshaw dislocated a finger, and backup QB Joe Gilliam suffered a leg injury, as did receiver Ron Shanklin. Defensive end L. C. Greenwood was sidelined with a leg injury, and *his* backup, Craig Hanneman, played the first half before his knee gave way. Defensive end Dwight White had to be dragged from the field, only to return because, as he said, "there wasn't anybody else."

So the Steelers, all "spit and grit and adhesive tape," as Phil Musick wrote in the *Pittsburgh Press* the next day, "gutted" out a win that was a "tribute to tenacity."

As his players straggled to see team trainer Ralph Berlin, Chuck Noll paid tribute to that tribute to tenacity, telling reporters "We had guys out there bleeding . . . gutting it out."

Working behind a wounded offensive line, Harris gouged out enough yards to become the sixth rookie in history to gain 1,000 yards in a season.

Setting Steelers single-season records for field goals (27) and points (113), Gerela provided the margin of victory with 3 field goals, and the Steel Curtain crashed down on the Oilers' offense. Joe Greene wore out a pair of Houston guards, while fellow defensive tackle rookie Steve Furness contributed to a unit that in the second half held Houston to 26 yards on 27 plays.

Playing one of the great games of his Hall of Fame career, Greene provided relentless pressure on QB Dan Pastorini. Greene also blocked a field goal, forced a fumble, and recovered the ball to set up a Steelers score.

If the injured Steelers were, as Musick called them, "the Gang That Couldn't Walk Straight," they had still managed to take one step closer to the title.

The following week saw the Steelers wing westward to San Diego with an opportunity to wrap up their division. Veteran linebacker Andy Russell, a member of the struggling Steelers of the late sixties, had a feeling of "impending doom." Ray Mansfield remembered all those years when the Steelers blew games they could have won and felt sick thinking about it.

Earlier in the day the Browns had beaten the Jets in the frozen sunshine inside wind-whipped Shea Stadium, thus making mandatory a win or tie if the Steelers were to claim the crown.

San Diego buried Bradshaw for an early safety, but that was all the points the Chargers would score, as the Steel Curtain did not surrender a touchdown for the seventh time that season.

The Steelers went on to score three unanswered touchdowns in a 24–2 victory. Noll was given a ride off the darkening field on the shoulders of Clack and Mansfield. Art Rooney, the seventy-one-year-old owner, was given the game ball by Russell, the Steel Curtain's captain. "This," a smiling Rooney told his team days before Christmas, "is the best gift I've ever received."

The Steelers' owner told reporters the division title was the high point of his forty years with the organization. He said he knew his team would win a title if he lived long enough, but half-jokingly remarked that he was beginning to worry as his birthdays piled up. Rooney said he knew early in the '72 season this would be the year. He thought the Steelers had the division's best team in '71 but believed Pittsburgh's players didn't yet realize how good they were.

They knew in '72. The Steelers were growing up, and the hard-running Harris provided another big piece to Pittsburgh's puzzle. He led the league in 100-yard games in '72 with seven and averaged 5.6 yards per carry. Heady stuff for a guy who had an outstanding career at Penn State but was overshadowed by backfield mate Lydell Mitchell. Noll wanted to bypass Harris in the 1972 NFL Draft and go with University of Houston running back Robert Newhouse. Steelers brass, however, favored Franco's unique combination of size and power, and Pittsburgh, drafting thirteenth in the first round, picked Harris.

Newhouse, a native son of Texas, was taken by the Dallas Cowboys in the second with the thirty-fifth pick overall. Newhouse and Harris would help lead their respective teams to Super Bowl showdowns following the 1975 and '78 seasons.

Dick Hoak, Pittsburgh's backfield coach and a former Steelers running back in the 1960s, said that along with Harris's size and skill, there were other intangibles the Steelers liked in their big back. Hoak considered Harris one of the hardest workers the Steelers had. But it went beyond that, Hoak added. Franco had great vision. Maybe Harris didn't really see everything, Hoak said, but Franco seemed to sense things.

The son of an African American soldier and Italian war bride, Harris acknowledged that his natural running style was the product of long hours of hard work. It made him feel better to know he was working for something rather than thinking it was just going to come on its own. Harris knew that most of the time, when you work for something, it pays off.

In the offensive huddle Harris would look in the faces of his linemen—Clack and Kolb, Mansfield and Mullins, Davis and Van Dyke. It was a tremendous thrill for him to share his accomplishments with them. After all, he reasoned, the linemen open the holes. The Steelers' offensive line, Harris felt, was tremendous.

Bradshaw thought Harris the most unselfish superstar he ever played with. Russell considered Harris a clutch runner. When the Steelers needed 4 yards for a first down, Franco would find a way to get it. Russell had played against Jim Brown, and he thought Harris was like Brown in that he could combine power with elusive qualities.

A vivid illustration of this was Franco's electrifying run in Cleveland in 1972, which saw him toss defensive back Thom Darden aside on an off-tackle slant and streak 75 yards through slick mud for a score.

Mansfield didn't understand why people criticized Harris for stopping and stuttering on some of his runs. The Steelers had an off-tackle play called "18 Straight" and one to the opposite side of the line labeled "19 Straight." Sometimes, Mansfield said, Harris ran 19 Straight, and it wound up looking like 18 Straight. Mansfield said it was testament to Franco's ability to find the hole and then turn on the speed. Franco was fast, Mansfield said, and there were many times when Harris simply outran smaller and supposedly speedier defensive backs.

Linebacker Jack Ham said that because Harris was so consistently good, the constant factor in the Steelers' offense became their ground game. "In bad weather, in good weather, in wind, whatever," Ham said, "you could always count on Harris and our running game."

"Franco," Greene said, "was a key man on our club. We were coming on every year, getting closer and closer to the right combination. All we needed was that catalyst and Franco was it . . . He was just what we needed."

Beginning in his rookie season in '72 Harris rushed for at least 1,000 yards eight times and was selected to nine straight Pro Bowls. From 1972 to 1984 Franco forged a Hall of Fame career by rushing for 12,120 yards and 91 touchdowns.

Harris let his numbers speak for themselves, but others weren't so shy. Dallas defender D. D. Lewis, who played opposite Franco in Super Bowls X and XIII, noted that while Harris was 230 pounds in his prime, he could stop and accelerate better than anyone outside of Lewis's teammate Tony Dorsett, a much smaller man than Franco. Harris, Lewis said, could run east and west, stop abruptly, and then cut north and south. Franco's fullback size and halfback moves made for a devastating combination and left coaches of his day desperately seeking ways to defend against him.

Dallas Cowboys assistant coach Ernie Stautner, a Hall of Fame defensive tackle with the Steelers in the 1950s and '60s and a man who tried in two Super Bowls to serve up schemes to stop Harris, thought

Franco had tremendous balance for a big back. Harris would be running toward the hole he's supposed to go, Stautner stated, and if the hole was closed, he'd stop, change directions quickly, find another hole, and go through it.

Defensive mastermind George Allen thought Harris a strong, determined, hardworking athlete who played with consistency. Allen considered Harris an "intelligent and inventive player." While Franco's Immaculate Reception was memorable, Allen was just as impressed with a play Harris made in a Monday-night game against his Washington Redskins. Ron McDole recovered a Steelers fumble and was headed for a touchdown when he was stopped by a Steeler who had run all the way across the field to tackle him. The Steel Curtain stopped the Redskins and won the game. Allen made it a point to watch the game film and identify the player who tackled McDole. It was Harris.

The Raiders respected Harris. Tatum thought Franco one of the most gifted athletes in the NFL, a big back with great power and breakaway speed.

Greene was Noll's first pick, the cornerstone of the dynasty the Steelers were building, and even Mean Joe considered Harris the guy who made it all happen. Prior to Franco's arrival, Noll's Steelers did not have a winning season. With Harris in black and gold, the Steelers became consistent winners. Greene echoed Art Rooney's comments that the Steelers didn't have a lot of confidence prior to Harris's arrival in Pittsburgh. But Franco lifted the entire team.

Harris lifted an entire city on his shoulders in the playoffs against the Raiders, pulling the ball from a ghostly gray sky in the final seconds and scoring the most miraculous of touchdowns two days before Christmas. "A miracle, that's what it was," said Bob Adams, a Steelers veteran who had spent the season on the taxi squad.

The Steelers had their miracle. They also had a date with the undefeated Miami Dolphins. The Dolphins, the first NFL team to go 14-0 in the regular season, had barely survived the upset-minded Browns 20–14 in a Christmas Eve playoff.

The Steelers' rallying cry for the AFC title game had been provided some forty-five minutes after their victory over Oakland. It came in a telegram and read: "The following is an order, Attack, Attack, Attack, Attack."

It was signed Colonel Francis Sinatra (of Franco's Italian Army).

For a time the following Sunday afternoon, it seemed the miracle of Three Rivers Stadium would be repeated. The Steelers gained an early lead when Bradshaw's fumble was recovered—miraculously, it seemed—by Mullins in the end zone for a 7–0 lead.

The Steelers visibly sagged when Dolphin punter Larry Seiple ran for a critical first down on a fake punt. Noll said later that it was like the Steelers were waiting for something like that to happen. The thing that a winning team does, he stated, is counter adversity. "Something like that [Seiple] play shouldn't matter because the game is played for 60 minutes and you have to keep playing," Noll said. "Things have a way of evening out and you can still get the things done."

Trailing Miami 21–10 in the fourth quarter following touchdowns by the Dolphins' celebrated "Butch and Sundance" backfield duo of Larry Csonka and Jim Kiick—ironically, Kiick's father played for the Steelers in the 1940s—Bradshaw returned from a shoulder injury suffered in the first half and buggy-whipped Pittsburgh 71 yards in four plays. His 12-yard touchdown toss to wideout Al Young, who made a brilliant one-handed grab, brought the Steelers to within four points.

The Steel Curtain got the ball back twice for the offense, but the stunning run of good fortune that resulted in eight straight victories at Three Rivers finally ran out. The Steelers' two late drives ended with Miami's complex zone defense pilfering two Bradshaw passes. December 31, 1972, in Pittsburgh—an unseasonably warm day in the northeast—turned out to be the Day of the Dolphins.

The defeat was disappointing but not disastrous. No less an authority than Vince Lombardi stated as early as 1969 that something special was brewing in the Steel City. "Chuck Noll is building one hell of a football team up in Pittsburgh," Lombardi stated. "I look for the Steelers to be the team of the future. Just remember I said that."

Lombardi was well aware of Noll's capabilities, though the two coaching legends had squared off just once as head coaches. On October 26, 1969, Lombardi, in his first and only season as Washington

Redskins head coach, claimed a 14–7 win at Pittsburgh in Noll's first year as Steelers boss.

The two men shared some similarities as players, both serving as offensive linemen. Lombardi was a member of Fordham University's celebrated "Seven Blocks of Granite" offensive line. Noll was a messenger guard for the dean of modern coaches, Paul Brown, with the Cleveland Browns. Noll felt demeaned by Brown's use of him as a messenger to relay plays to quarterback Otto Graham and disliked the practice so much that as Steelers coach, he trusted his quarterbacks to call their own plays.

As coaches Noll and Lombardi were different types of leaders. Noll was notoriously shy, so much so that his contributions to the Steelers' success have been too often overlooked. He was known as "Emperor Chaz," a moniker given him by Cope; "Knowledge Noll" by his defensive players on the Baltimore Colts; and the "Pope." The latter came during his college years at the University of Dayton, a Roman Catholic institution. Teammates knew that when Noll, who rarely made mistakes on the field and had an infallible grasp of the game, talked technique, he spoke without fear of contradiction—*ex cathedra*, as it's said in Vatican City.

Noll was a quiet teacher whose best-known phrase was "Whatever it takes." Some Steelers would long for Noll to give Lombardi-like speeches, but it wasn't in Noll's makeup. Noll did share Lombardi's traits as a disciplinarian and an excellent teacher. Like Lombardi, Noll favored fundamentals. "Champions are champions not because they do anything extraordinary," Noll said, "but because they do the ordinary things better than anybody else."

Noll called it "winning the battle of the hitting." A defensive force like Joe Greene, Noll said, didn't run around blockers; he ran right through them. "That," Noll stated with emphasis, "is basic."

Don Shula thought Noll's Steelers as basic and subtle as "a punch in the mouth." It was the perfect brand of football for a city whose steel mills and shot-and-a-beer lifestyle left little room for subtlety. Like Noll's Steelers, the people of Pittsburgh championed a blue-collar work ethic. They worked from dawn to dusk every day to keep the

mills that make up the heavy industrial complex of the Golden Triangle and the plants that produce railroad cars and huge electronic
generators churning. The steel- and mill workers weren't doing anything glamorous or extraordinary; they were just doing the ordinary,
everyday things better than anyone else. Noll said that winning, be it
on the football field or off, was a matter of doing the "ordinary things
better than anyone else does them, day in and day out."

Struggling and striving to win their daily battles and earn a living
amid the fiery blast furnaces belching black smoke, sooty and tired at
the end of a long workweek, Pittsburgh's steelworkers wouldn't support fancy football on Sundays. Neither would Noll. He once picked
up a book written by retired wide receiver Lance Rentzel, read the
introduction in which the former Dallas Cowboy proclaimed the pres-
sures of modern football an almost overwhelming burden, and dis-
missed it as "pure bull." Years later, when Dick Vermeil stepped down
as Eagles head coach and claimed he was burned out, Noll had other
thoughts. "Burnout," he bluntly stated, "is bull."

Noll's no-nonsense approach stemmed from a life spent accumulat-
ing facts. He had a great curiosity about many things, topics as diverse
as trap blocking and scuba diving. His curiosity led him to become
a renaissance man. Members of the Steelers' front office believed he
was a better photographer than the professionals they employed.

Noll learned to fly his own plane to cut down travel time to the
family condominium in Florida. He was a patron of the Pittsburgh
Symphony and loved classical music. He leaned toward the masters—
Bach, Beethoven, Mozart. Noll discussed string quartets—the Russian
Borodin Quartet, the Budapest String Quartet, the modern Julliard
String Quartet—in as much detail as he did the Raiders' defense. He
was a wine connoisseur and gourmet cook and spent most of his free
time with his wife, Marianne, and son, Chris. Noll's interest in snor-
keling stemmed from his desire to find an activity he and his then
teenage son could enjoy.

Steelers players called Noll "Jazzy Chaz." Cornerback J. T. Thomas
thought Noll a down-to-earth, fun guy. Defensive end Dwight White
was one of the funniest men Thomas had ever known, a guy who

always had something to say. White was very quick-witted, and he would say something to Noll, and Noll would go right back at him.

Unlike many coaches, Noll refused to allow football to consume or define him. He had a lifelong zeal to discover new things, be it a fine wine, restaurant, or an island in the Caribbean. During the season he devoured how-to books, and his diverse interests kept his mind fresh and invigorated him during the grind of a long campaign. He was not so caught up in football that he didn't have room for others. He was a surrogate father for his widowed sister's children and stuck by his players when they faced problems.

Russell said Noll had a warmer personality than many might have believed. Greene agreed and said that while Noll never hugged or embraced his players, he still loved his players; he just wasn't one for showing emotion.

Russell thought Noll exceptionally fair and applied discipline only when it really counted. Noll had no embargoes on beards and mod clothes, witness Frenchy Fuqua's clear elevated heels that housed live goldfish. A manager at a hotel frequented by NFL teams described Noll's Steelers as the "lousiest looking" and "worst dressed." Under Noll Pittsburgh's players had freedom of speech, and Noll did not get upset when one of his players would pop off publicly about an opponent being inferior to the Steelers. "All I ever tell my players," Noll once remarked, "is that they might have to suffer the consequences for what they say."

Russell thought Noll had a knack for getting every player to play his best and did so by conveying the point that it isn't what you did for the team a year ago or even in the previous game that counts. What counts is what you can do for the team today or in the next game.

Greene considers Noll the ultimate leader. He said Noll had truth and belief in what he said, and over time those things Noll said about winning games and being a solid citizen were validated. To Greene, having Noll as head coach made all the difference in his playing career in Pittsburgh. When the Steelers went 1-13 in his first year, Greene said it was hard to put his belief in Noll. When nothing positive is happening, Greene was one of the guys who said what the Steelers were doing wasn't working. Noll never panicked, never changed his approach, and around 1971, Greene's third year in Pittsburgh, he began to see that if the Steelers continued to bring in better players and followed Noll's teaching, they would win. If they didn't do what Noll said, they would lose. Greene became a believer in Chuck Noll. He saw the consistency in him, and it was clear to Greene that Noll was coaching the team the right way.

His Colts players called him "Knowledge Noll," but he was not a know-it-all in an obnoxious sense. He was low key, rarely acted on impulse, and took an approach to football and life that was based on logic.

Noll's attitude toward work ethic and education began early in life. Born not far from Pittsburgh, in Cleveland, Ohio, Noll was the youngest child of William and Katherine Noll. William was a butcher who was frequently out of work due to Parkinson's disease; Katherine worked as a florist. Their family home was the same one Katherine had grown up in amid a melting pot of races and religions. Growing up in a neighborhood with a large African American population likely accounts for Noll's supporting a substantial inclusion of black athletes in the American Football League of the 1960s and on his Steelers squads of the 1970s.

At Benedictine High School Noll excelled in the classroom and on the field. He graduated 28th in a class of 252, earned All-State honors in football, and was named to the All–Catholic Universe Bulletin team. A running back, he moved to the offensive line and played guard when a team need arose.

Noll's emphasis on education early in life would lead him as coach of the Steelers to seek players who studied practical subjects in college. "I didn't want to pick guys," he explained, "who just took wood shop or some other easy course they could breeze through to play football."

Noll looked to continue his academic and athletic careers at Notre Dame but suffered an epileptic seizure during a practice prior to his freshman year. Fighting Irish coach Frank Leahy didn't want the risk of Noll playing in South Bend, so Chuck accepted a football scholarship from the University of Dayton. Noll saw time as a lineman and linebacker and was named co-captain.

Drafted by the Browns in the twenty-first round in 1953, Noll was part of a team that played in the NFL Championship Game in each of his first three seasons. Cleveland won NFL titles in 1954 and '55, and Noll supplemented his small salary with the Browns by selling insurance and serving as a substitute teacher.

Teaching became a Noll trademark, and much of what he taught about pro football came from his close association with the game's masters—Paul Brown, Sid Gillman, Don Shula. He learned from each but copied none. Copy someone, Noll reasoned, and you wind up doing a second-rate job because that's what a copy is—a second-rate imitation.

Noll broke into coaching as an assistant coach with Gillman and the Chargers of the fledgling American Football League in 1960 and said once he was exposed to more football in six years than he would have been in double that time at most other places. As a defensive coordinator who also coached the line and secondary, Noll helped the Chargers claim five Western Division titles in six seasons. Based in Los Angeles and then in San Diego, the Chargers played in five league championship games and won the 1963 title with a team many consider the best of the AFL's early years and the first to draw serious comparison with the NFL's best.

Noll coached a Chargers front that included stars in Ernie "Big Cat" Ladd and Earl Faison and was California's first "Fearsome Foursome," predating by several years the LA Rams' famous quartet, which included Hall of Famers David "Deacon" Jones and Merlin Olsen. Ladd said Noll had a "great way of teaching" and called him the best teacher he ever played under.

Noll and Al Davis, a coaching assistant and scout, both worked under Gillman at the same time, and much of what they learned would be used to build the Steelers and Raiders into AFC powerhouses in the 1970s. "Sid was one of the prime researchers in the game and had a great deal of time to bring all of the concepts and ideas to the fore," Noll said.

Gillman thought Noll "a natural" as a coach. "He had a great way with the players," said Gillman, noting that Noll corrected players in a soft-spoken way so as not to embarrass the player but still served to get the message across. "He was a low-key guy," Gillman recalled, "and that's how he coached."

Noll's approach to coaching was to show players how to get things done. "We teach techniques," he once stated, "and the function is then reduced to a habit."

Moving from the AFL to the NFL and coaching the defensive secondary in Baltimore from 1966 to 1968, Noll learned from Shula about organization and the importance of attitudes. Shula, who was so impressed with Noll's coaching capabilities that he recommended him to Art Rooney Sr. when the Steelers were seeking a head coach, watched how Noll would explain to Colt defensive backs how to do things and write up the technique. Shula said Noll was one of the first coaches he was around who wrote up in great detail all of the techniques used by the players—how to backpedal at the snap of the ball and how to position yourself on the receiver. "He was like a classroom teacher," Shula said.

From Al Davis to John Madden to Jack Tatum, the Raiders respected Noll as well. Tatum thought Noll a great coach whose greatest asset was his vision. Noll, Tatum believed, had an ability to look into the future and picture what a young player would look like years later. Noll's vision, Tatum said, was always three or four years into the future. The result, Tatum added, was that the Steelers became two or three deep at almost every position, and every draft seemed to land two or three more blue chippers.

Lombardi stated as early as 1969 that Noll was building something special in Pittsburgh. What Noll eventually built wit.h the Steelers would rival the dynasty Lombardi built with the Packers a decade earlier.

Jim Campbell: After a 2-11-1 season in 1968, Bill Austin was fired as the Steelers' head coach. With the Patriots (still known as Boston) and the Steelers both looking for new leadership, rumors circulated that the coordinators of the Super Bowl III teams would be the prime candidates to fill two of several N F L and A F L openings—Clive Rush, offensive coordinator of the Jets, and Chuck Noll, defensive backfield coach of the Colts. With Joe Namath and the Jets upsetting a highly favored Colts team, Boston seemingly won the coaching sweepstakes in signing Rush. Pittsburgh was left with Noll. What a break!

Following extensive film study, Noll knew he wasn't blessed with much playing talent. In fact, he was quoted as saying to his players, "You've lost a lot of games, and the reason is you aren't very good."

Not all Steelers were stiffs, though. A nucleus to build on was there, however thin. Linebacker Andy Russell, center Ray Mansfield, defensive end Ben McGee, wide receiver Roy Jefferson, tackle John Brown, guards Sam Davis and Bruce Van Dyke, and running back Dick Hoak had talent. They, along with new acquisitions, contributed in the early years of Noll's long and successful tenure, but only veterans Russell and Mansfield lasted to bask in the Super Bowl glory later.

Russell was one of the first to experience first hand Noll's attention to detail. Russell, a Pro Bowler before Noll's arrival in 1969, admitted to being "overly aggressive" and "a bit of a freelancer." Andy said, after meeting with Noll for the first time, "He had looked at film and suggested a change in how I lined up. 'Move your right foot two inches to the right, and one inch back.' Talk about football being a game of inches . . ."

Gradually, Noll and the scouting department (Art Rooney Jr., Dick Haley, and Bill Nunn Jr.) added key pieces. Along with Joe Greene in 1969 came defensive end L. C. Greenwood, quarterback Terry Hanratty, and offensive tackle Jon Kolb. In 1970, of course, it was Terry Bradshaw. His talent, worthy of being the overall No. 1 choice, was immediately evident.

Looking at Hanratty's rifle arm, I could see a vast improvement over incumbents Dick Shiner and Kent Nix. Seeing Bradshaw's rocket arm a year later was truly amazing. Also added in 1970—a year that saw Pittsburgh improve from 1-13 to 5-9—were wide receivers Ron Shanklin, Jon Staggers, and Dave Smith as well as future H O F cornerback Mel Blount.

Jack Butler, a fine defensive back for the Steelers in the 1950s (he was finally inducted into the Pro Football Hall of Fame in 2012), was an integral part of the Steelers' success, although he was not an official member of the Steelers' scouting department. Jack, an early proponent of computer use, was director of the BLESTO-V scouting combine. He was quartered in his native Pittsburgh, but his player evaluations were given to all combine members—Bears, Lions, Eagles, Steelers, Vikings. He was a no-nonsense guy and devoted to his profession.

It was a pleasure meeting Jack in 1969, when I arrived in Pittsburgh. As mentioned, he was an All-Pro defensive back, but he also had the speed and hands to sometimes play offensive end. When his career was ended after a brutal collision with Eagles tight end Pete Retzlaff, Butler trailed only Emlen Tunnell in career interceptions—fifty-two to Tunnell's seventy-nine. Jack almost lost his leg as a result of the horrific knee injury, and when I met him a decade later he always walked with a limp—and sometimes a cane.

Jack estimated once that he "must have scouted at least seventy-five thousand players." Because of my early research on the NFL Drafts, he and I had numerous discussions on players and player evaluation. Jack said, "I believe players are everywhere. If you can play well, we'll find you. That's why we scout the junior colleges. Hell, I'd like to scout even the college club teams."

One of our discussions was about late-round draft choices as compared to undrafted free agents. I asked, "Are nondrafted free agents as good as the late-rounders?" In his always matter-of-fact way, Jack replied, "No, the late-rounders are as bad as free agents." Another time I asked, "How do scouts miss on someone like Harold Lucas?" Lucas was a 286-pound All-America defensive lineman at Michigan State. He was drafted in the second round by the St. Louis Cardinals in 1966. He never played a down in the NFL. Never one to sugarcoat anything, Jack stated, "We [BLESTO] never had him rated very high. He simply didn't have the abilities to play well in the NFL, despite his All-America mention."

Jack was also chagrined when Mike Wagner turned out to be such an outstanding player. The hard-hitting safety from Western Illinois was taken in the eleventh round by the Steelers in 1971 and quickly developed into a Pro Bowler. Butler was as put out about someone being rated fairly low who turned out to be a great player as he would have been to have rated someone high and have that player turn into a bust. He said, "We strive for accuracy. We look to be right on. We don't want low guys being good or high guys being bad. Get it right!" This is not to say that Jack wasn't pleased with how well Wagner's career turned out. He just didn't like to see such a wide gap between a player's rating and his career results.

Only slight improvement was seen in 1971 (6-8), but the foundation was expanding, and unlike his predecessors Noll was implementing his philosophy—"Build through the draft." Draftees that year included wide receiver Frank Lewis, linebacker Jack Ham, running back Steve Davis, tackle/guard Gerry "Moon" Mullins, defensive end Dwight White, tight end Larry Brown, defensive end Craig Hanneman, defensive tackle Ernie Holmes, and Wagner.

Then came the breakout season of 1972, starting with the draft. Franco Harris, thanks to the lobbying of Art Rooney Jr., was No. 1, followed by offensive tackle Gordon Gravelle, tight end John McMakin, linebacker Ed Bradley, defensive lineman Steve Furness, and quarterback Joe Gilliam.

I attended the 1971 and 1972 drafts as a quasi representative of the Steelers. I recall a conversation with Pro Football Hall of Fame linebacker Sam Huff after Pittsburgh took Franco in the first round. Huff was playing for Vince Lombardi and the Redskins in 1969 and doing some informal scouting. He said, "I was looking at some Penn State film [it was Franco's sophomore year at PSU], getting a fix on one of their linebackers—probably Dennis Onkotz—when I couldn't help but notice Franco. He was fast. He was big. He ran smart and he ran over people. I told Vince about him, but mentioned that he was half-Italian and half–African American. Vince snorted and said, 'He's probably half a football player, too.'" Lombardi passed away before Franco was draft eligible, but Sam intimated that Lombardi wasn't much interested at the time in the college sophomore. Sam then shook his head, saying, "One of Vince's few misreads. You [the Steelers] are getting a good one." Just how good would soon become evident. While Franco possessed vast talent, Al Young may have discovered the secret of Harris's success. Said Young, "I never saw anyone work harder. Franco was always the last to leave the practice field."

The NFL Draft in the early seventies was seventeen rounds, down from a peak of thirty rounds in 1959. Scouting was just beginning to take on the sophistication of later years, and some teams were still drafting out of a rolled-up back-pocket copy of *Street & Smith's Football Annual*. It was becoming evident that the excellent rapport that Bill Nunn built up over the years with historically black colleges in the South was paying off: Mel Blount (Southern), Ernie Holmes (Texas Southern), L. C. Greenwood (Arkansas AM&N, now Arkansas–Pine Bluff), Frank Lewis (Grambling), Steve Davis (Delaware State), Mel Holmes (North Carolina A&T), and Al Young (South Carolina State). Nunn was so thorough and dedicated in his scouting that he often attended after-game dances just to see which of the giant linemen he was scouting were "light on their feet."

Franco was the talk of training camp, and there was an overall air of optimism about the team. SOS (Same Old Steelers) seemed to no longer apply. The infusion of new talent had the city buzzing with Steelers talk. No longer were neighborhood bars, purveyors of "Imp and Iron" (a shot of bottom-shelf Imperial blended whiskey and an Iron City beer chaser), filled with "curbstone coaches" advocating the sale of the team by the Rooneys or that the Steelers needed a more rah-rah coach than the low-keyed, magisterial Chuck Noll. The Black and Gold bandwagon was rolling right along, and the seats were filling up quickly.

An indicator as to how much the fans bought in to the new, winning Steelers was the signage—mostly of the bedsheet variety—that began appearing at Three Rivers Stadium. The first, and most prominent, was "Franco's Italian Army," a large banner sporting the colors of the Italian national flag—green, white, and red. Two ultra-Steelers fans— Tony Stagno and Al Vento—hatched the contagious idea. Accompanying that was another, "Run, Paisano, Run!" Later the Army would enlist the services of Frank Sinatra as "generalissimo." Almost any Steeler of any consequence had a fan club and an appropriate banner draped from the superstructure of Three Rivers. There were signs for "Rocky's Flying Squirrels," "Kolb's Kowboys," "Russell's Raiders," "Lambert's Lunatics," and "Dobre Shunka" for Jack Ham, but perhaps second only to Franco's Army was the sign announcing "Gerela's Gorillas." Not only was there a considerable number of season-ticket holders behind the sign, but the titular head of the group, Bob Bubanic, came every week dressed in a gorilla suit worthy of the original *King Kong* movie. It was quite a testimony to his endurance and heat tolerance during preseason and early-season games. Not bad for a kicker who was claimed early in the preseason from the Oilers for the one-hundred-dollar waiver fee.

About this time, a large professional-looking "Steel Curtain" banner appeared. Greene, Greenwood, Holmes, and White were easily recognized, giving credence to the artistic ability of the sign's creator.

As the team jelled, especially the defense, the fans became more rabid. I doubt any unit up until that time was more appreciated than the Steel Curtain defense. The noise as the unit came off the field was deafening and sustained. I can only describe it—from the sideline down on the stadium floor—as sending shock waves through the air. Standing on the sideline as a smiling Joe Greene or Dwight White led the defense off the field after a three-and-out was something resembling an electrical shock wave that would play tricks on my ears. It was a totally unique experience—paradoxically, one that would be played out over and over again.

After the 1972 preseason, there was cause for optimism. The defense was maturing, Bradshaw was about to start his third season, and Noll's "build through the draft" was seemingly paying dividends. Franco emerged as a candidate for rookie of the year. The Steel Curtain was proving to be made of stainless (as in scoreless) steel. In Weeks Five through Fourteen, Pittsburgh compiled a 9-1 record. In the midst of the streak I remember thinking, "Damn, these guys are good, and as young as they are they are only going to get better—and stay good. We're looking at a long run of good football." As minor as my role was, I wanted to remain a part of it. Because of that, when I got my full-time NFL-related position (historian at the Pro Football Hall of

Fame) in 1972, I continued to drive the one hundred miles from Canton to Pittsburgh on game days.

Looking back, Noll accomplished much with what seems now—in the days of coaching staffs with twenty-plus assistants—like a small staff. Just nine assistants, and two of them were flexibility coach Paul "Red" Uram and strength coach Lou Riecke. Position coaches were Bud Carson (a man Noll had never met until he interviewed and hired him at the time of their first meeting), defensive coordinator; George Perles, defensive line; Vito "Babe" Parilli, quarterbacks; Lionel Taylor, receivers; Dick Hoak, running backs; Bob Fry, offensive line; and Charlie Sumner, defensive backs.

Taylor, the first African American assistant in the NFL, was a well-respected coach. He was famous for helping receivers, who couldn't make the Steelers' roster, get opportunities with other teams. He was certainly worthy of a head-coaching job, which he never got, although he did come close to being tapped by the Los Angeles Rams in the 1980s. I once heard Taylor tell a young group of receivers in his understated way, "You've got the easiest job in the NFL. Just be alone when the ball gets there and catch it."

Against Kansas City the defense was pitching a shutout, but the Chiefs led 7–0 at the half by virtue of Jim Kearney's 65-yard "pick six." Sometime in the second half I noticed "the look." It's hard to describe, but Franco showed equal parts determination, urgency, and whatever other word you'd like to throw in to illustrate a man on a mission. After stalking the sideline he threw off his cape, joined the offense in taking the field, and quickly ripped off a 17-yard run that saw him leave three frustrated Chiefs in his wake. Later, after three Gerela field goals put the Steelers up 9–7, Harris sealed the deal with a 7-yard TD blast to end the scoring at 16–7. The defensive line that day was the storied Steel Curtain—Greene, Greenwood, White, Holmes, with veteran Ben McGee rotating in occasionally in place of Holmes. Chiefs quarterback Lenny Dawson spent the day fleeing for his life. The Pittsburgh defensive backs bottled up his receivers all day. It wasn't until late in the third quarter that All-Pro Otis Taylor made his first catch.

Cleveland, along with Cincinnati, was still in contention in the AFC

Central. Pittsburgh hadn't won in Cleveland since 1964, and that wasn't going to change. In venerable Municipal Stadium, the Browns prevailed 26–24 on Don Cockroft's 26-yard field goal with eight seconds left. A 75-yard touchdown run by Franco wasn't enough to pull it out.

The Steelers rebounded by scoring twice late to defeat the Minnesota Vikings 23–10 after being tied 10–10 in the fourth quarter. It was at this game that my sideline duties became more difficult. I usually got injury reports from the visiting team's trainer, but when I introduced myself to Vikings trainer Fred Zamberletti, he told me head coach Bud Grant was the only one authorized to give out that information. When I confirmed that with Grant, he said, "That's right. I'm the one." Fine, again. Only problem was Grant would never let me get close enough to him to find out what a player's injury was.

The win over the Vikings set up a return match with the Browns—this time in the friendlier confines of Three Rivers. It was a mismatch. Pittsburgh 30, Cleveland 0. The only scoring chance the Brownies had was a missed 37-yard field goal attempt by Cockroft. As I was wont to do sometimes, I offered commentary from the sideline. On a play where Leroy Kelly was run out of bounds for a loss by Jack Ham, I ventured, "Nobody home today, Leroy." The HOF runner just gave me a "who-the-hell-are-you?" look and went back to the huddle.

It was earlier in the season, perhaps after the Steelers' loss to the Browns in Cleveland, when Dick Gallagher, the director of the Pro Football HOF, general manager of the Bills' AFL Championship teams of the mid-'60s, and an original Paul Brown assistant in 1946, said, "I think the Steelers made a big mistake. With that defense, if they would have taken Mike Phipps instead of Bradshaw they'd be in a Super Bowl soon." Well, even NFL lifers can be wrong. Minus sack yardage, Phipps dented the Steel Curtain for 27 passing yards and subsequently never got to the Super Bowl, unless he bought a ticket.

With the issue no longer in doubt, the Steelers' main focus was getting Franco his customary 100 yards for the game. In the fourth quarter he was at 65 yards, as someone noticed (probably Joe Gordon calling down from the press box). Bradshaw, who called his own plays, then fed the ball to the rookie until he reached 102 yards on the day. This tied the immortal Jim Brown's NFL record of six consecutive 100-yard games. As I recall, there was no celebration of any kind. Just another day at the office.

The next game against the Oilers in Houston's Astrodome was one for the ages. A victory would clinch at least a tie for the Central Division title. What happened on the field was something I'd never seen before or since. Gerela and Skip Butler traded field goals, knotting the score at 3–3 when the halftime gun sounded. Yes, they were still using blank-firing pistols to mark the end of each half. Gerela added two more field goals to make the score 9–3. Then Bradshaw dislocated a finger on his throwing hand and was replaced by rookie Joe Gilliam.

The Steel Curtain was solid all day, but the hard fact was that an Oiler touchdown could put the Steelers behind 10–9. It appeared to me that Joe Greene said, "Guys, jump on my back. I'll take you home." What he single-handedly did to Houston quarterback Dan Pastorini should happen only to your worst enemy. Mean Joe was truly mean! He sacked the Oilers' signal caller five times, blocked a field goal, forced a fumble, and recovered it. Later, Andy Russell said, "He [Greene] came into the huddle and said, 'I'm taking the ball away from 'em on this play!' The next thing I know, I hear a big bang as Joe smacked [running back Fred] Willis for a 12-yard loss, knocking the ball loose, and recovering it."

I was mesmerized. Before the Immaculate Reception game, I mentioned my amazement to Ray Mansfield, my sideline buddy. Mansfield said, "I couldn't believe what I was seeing. Pastorini didn't have a chance. We all knew Joe was a force of nature, but this was above and beyond." Later that day, December 23, 1972, Mansfield again had trouble believing his eyes.

The Steelers prepped for the end-of-the-season game in balmy Palm Springs. The finale was against the Chargers. It was at this time that Frank Sinatra was made generalissimo of Franco's Italian Army. Ol' Blue Eyes posed in an army helmet with the rookie sensation.

The actual game, except for a first-quarter Chargers safety, was a shutout. "Sticks" Anderson—his arms and legs resembled pipe cleaners—intercepted John Hadl early on, setting up Franco's touchdown. It was the first of seven takeaways. Ham recovered a fumble and made an interception. Mel Blount also picked off Hadl. When the final gun sounded it was 24–2, and the Steelers had their first championship of any kind in their forty-year history.

Not one to miss a historic moment, Mansfield said to young offensive lineman Jim Clack, "Hey, kid, you wanna be famous? Grab Chuck's other leg." At the final gun a photograph was taken of Mansfield and Clack, each with a leg, carrying a jubilant Chuck Noll out of Jack Murphy Stadium. Until the Steelers started winning Super Bowls it was the photo used to symbolize the success of the Steelers.

"Clickety" Clack's rise from the taxi squad to stellar and versatile offensive lineman is remarkable. As noted, he was a 217-pound free-agent defensive tackle from Wake Forest. He spent inordinate amounts of time in the weight room bulking up, but that wasn't the only key to his success. A very bright and personable young man, Clack mentioned to me that he read and practiced what was written in Maxwell Maltz's popular 1960s self-help book, *Psycho-Cybernetics*. The book advocated meditation, positive thinking, and visualization of success. For Clack it worked very well, as attested to by his multiple Pro Bowl selections.

My recollection of the '72 AFC Championship Game against Miami was how unseasonably warm the weather was. Pittsburgh had had snow earlier in the week, but by Saturday it was downright balmy. A lasting impression was how Don Shula and his staff came dressed for really winter weather—turtlenecks and parkas. They would later change to lighter jackets.

Earl Morrall was the story of the year. As he did for Shula in Baltimore in 1968 when Johnny Unitas went down, Morrall stepped in and stepped up when Bob Griese had his ankle broken in Week Five versus San Diego. Morrall was more than adequate, but Larry Csonka and Mercury Morris helped tremendously by each rushing for 1,000 yards.

I felt good about the Steelers' chances, once I switched my focus from Franco's miracle to the upcoming championship.

The game began well. On Miami's opening drive, safety Glen Edwards intercepted and returned the ball to close to midfield. Franco carried seven times for 35 yards. On a third-and-2 from Miami's 3-yard line, Bradshaw skirted his left end. To say he was upended by Jake Scott would be putting it mildly. He landed in the end zone on his head, having been flipped by Scott, and fumbled. The alert "Moon" Mullins was there to recover and score a touchdown.

Shortly afterward, I got a call from Gordon from the press box, "What's wrong with Brad?" I went to trainer Ralph Berlin with Joe's request. He said, "Tell Joe he's disoriented." I relayed Ralph's diagnosis. Apparently, Joe was looking for something more specific. "Disoriented? I know a thousand people who are disoriented." Regardless, Bradshaw would not return until midway through the fourth quarter.

Next came the first game changer. I can still see it in my mind. Larry Seiple was back to punt—only he didn't. The Steelers' special teamers violated the first and cardinal rule of punt rushing: MAKE SURE HE KICKS THE BALL! Seiple, also an occasional tight end, saw the Steelers peel back to block for the return. I can still see Seiple following Rocky Bleier and Steve Furness and others as though they were blocking for him. He showed the patience of a running back setting up his "blockers" as the Steelers' sideline was screaming to tackle Seiple. Barry Pearson ended Seiple's run by knocking him out of bounds deep in the red zone. But the damage was done. Morrall connected with Csonka in the left flat for a 9-yard touchdown to even the score at 7–7.

The offense was now under the direction of Hanratty, who was much more than adequate. He quickly hit Shanklin and McMakin for 22 and 24 yards, respectively, and fed Frenchy Fuqua on a draw play for another 24 yards. The Notre Damer had the Steelers in scoring position, but instead of a touchdown, Gerela's 14-yard field goal gave the home team a 10–7 lead.

Shula made a move that would prove to be another game changer; he inserted Griese for Morrall. Surgically, Griese, who appeared to me to be amazingly nimble coming back from a broken ankle, dissected the Steelers' secondary on a 52-yard post pattern to future HOFer Paul Warfield on his first passing attempt. I got a sinking feeling, even though the elusive wideout didn't score. Russell took the blame on that play, saying, "I was supposed to close off the inside. I simply didn't do it." It was one of the few mistakes the meticulous Russell ever made on a football field. Ham then intercepted Griese, but an offside penalty nullified the pick. The sinking feeling just sank a little lower. Kiick completed the 80-yard drive with a 2-yard touchdown run. Miami was up 14–10, its first lead of the day.

As the third quarter wound down, Seiple slightly shanked a punt— only 33 yards—that gave the Steelers the ball at the Miami 48. The offense, now directed by Hanratty, failed to convert on third down. Gerela's 48-yard field goal attempt was blocked. Griese engineered a 49-yard drive, mostly on runs, before Kiick went in from the 3.

Bradshaw came back in but showed little signs of being "disoriented"—at least for now. Hitting Larry Brown, Al Young, and Ron Shanklin on consecutive passes, he had Pittsburgh at the Miami 12. On the next play Young made a spectacular one-handed grab in traffic and burst into the end zone. The score was 21–17, with plenty of time left. Hope again resurfaced. But the last two drives ended in interceptions.

I was naturally disappointed, as were all Steelers and their fans, but for me it was well after the game that it sank in that the Steelers were just one game and four points away from the Super Bowl. Fortunately, in the near future the empty feeling would be replaced by pure elation.

Mean Joe, Marv, and Madden

He never thought he deserved to be called "Mean."

The nickname came into vogue during Joe Greene's sophomore year at North Texas State. The team wore green, and because Greene and the defense was playing well they were called the Mean Green. Joe being named Greene, the moniker rubbed off on him.

When he signed autographs in his early years with the Steelers, the future Pro Football Hall of Fame defensive tackle would sign Joe Greene, leaving off the Mean.

The way Greene saw it, he did the best he could on every down and played hard on every play. "But," he would quickly add, "I'm not mean." Sometimes he talked to opposing quarterbacks when he got to them during games, but it was never mean. "Don't bother to run the draw," Greene would tell the flustered QB, "because I'm going to be sitting right there in the hole waiting for it."

Greene respected offensive lineman but never believed any of them should ever beat a defensive lineman man on man. Some offensive lineman sought to beat their defensive counterparts with quickness, some with strength. Greene never studied the man who would be opposite him. The leader of the Steel Curtain defense would wait to see what his opponent was trying to do when the game started, and Greene would react. "I do what I have to do," he would say.

Steelers offensive linemen found this out firsthand in team scrimmages. After being the first pick in new head coach Chuck Noll's first draft in 1969, Greene held out before signing. He was considered the cornerstone for what the Steelers were trying to build, and the contract holdout angered some of the team's veterans. Center Ray Mansfield and guard Bruce Van Dyke looked forward to teaching the rookie a lesson or two. A couple of days of dealing with Greene in practice left Mansfield and Van Dyke wishing they'd never met Mean Joe.

In the Steelers' Oklahoma drill, which pitted an offensive lineman and a defensive lineman in a one-on-one drill, Greene beat a couple of Pittsburgh linemen, rested, and then faced Gordon Gravelle. Gravelle had earned high praise earlier in the day for putting L. C. Greenwood on his back in the same drill.

Working against Greene, a straining, grunting, groaning Gravelle held him out. When someone stated at the training table following practice that Gravelle had beaten Greene in the Oklahoma drill, the O-lineman responded. "Joe didn't try," Gravelle said, and guard-tackle Gerry Mullins stated with emphasis that when Greene does try, he "does what he wants." Mullins was Greene's roommate on road trips, and he spelled out some of the reasons for his 6-foot-4, 260-pound roomie's success in beating the blocks of opponents. Greene's hands were so big, Mullins said, that when the heel of them hit the shoulder pads on his initial charge, one would think he was pushing them back. It was at that moment that Greene's fingers grabbed beneath the back of the pads and pulled the opposing lineman forward.

Mansfield, who would earn an NFL Blocker of the Year Award, believed there wasn't an offensive lineman in the league who could handle Greene one-on-one. That Greene seemed to win every battle wasn't infuriating, Mansfield said. It was frightening.

Even more frightening to opposing teams. Cleveland Browns center Bob DeMarco had three of his teeth shattered by Greene. Greene admitted to once trying to twist the helmeted head of someone who was holding him. Losing a game to the Eagles, Greene grabbed the football before the center could snap it, fired it into the second tier of stands at Veterans Stadium, and stomped off the field.

Steelers linebacker Andy Russell remembered the crowd being eerily silent at Greene's rage. Russell thought Joe seemed to be saying, "If we're not going to play right, we're not going to play at all."

Russell considered Greene the most intimidating man in football. If Mean Joe saw someone taking a cheap shot at a Steeler, Russell believed Greene was liable to do anything. "The sight of that," said Russell, "would strike fear in anyone."

Greene was a winner, which made his rookie season in Pittsburgh such a difficult one. The Steelers went 1-13 in 1969, and Greene found it tough to adjust. "It's like a nightmare," he said at the time. "Everything goes against us and there's nothing we can do."

Greene took out his frustrations on opponents. A pair of forearm shivers against Minnesota Vikings linemen cost Pittsburgh 30 yards in penalties. The first forearm was retaliation against the Vikings' Jim Vellone, who had hit Greene from behind. Greene, who couldn't stand being pushed around, told Vellone, "I'm gonna get you."

Vellone said after the game he would take a punch from Greene any time if it meant getting Mean Joe ejected. Vellone thought his teammate Alan Page the best rookie defensive tackle he had ever seen. But after playing Pittsburgh, Vellone said Greene could "do things Page couldn't do."

Hall of Fame defensive tackle Buck Buchanan saw Greene up close when Kansas City played Pittsburgh in 1971 and '72. To Buchanan, Greene was a tackle who had the pass-rushing attributes of those who played on the perimeter. And, he added, Greene was kind of nasty. "They didn't call him 'Mean Joe' for nothing," Buchanan said.

Torgy Torgeson, an NFL player and later a coach, said Greene was the guy who made the Steel Curtain go. Greene was quick and strong, he said, and hard to handle. Greene relished the role he played in Pittsburgh's defense. "I'm the glue," he said. "I keep it together."

Pittsburgh employed Greene in a unique fashion, lining him up in an angle between the center and right guard. The alignment caused problems for blocking schemes, which struggled to deal with Greene's quickness off the ball and his immense strength.

Greene had memorable battles with Miami Dolphins Hall of Fame center Jim Langer at a time when the Steelers and Dolphins were dueling for AFC supremacy. As great as Langer was, he said he never thought in terms of "handling" Greene. Langer didn't even allow himself to think of knocking Mean Joe down. "All you hope to do," Langer said, "is neutralize him so he can't jam up the play."

Greene said that going after the ball carrier was like playing the kid game King of the Mountain. When Greene got to the ball carrier, he figured he was on top of the mountain, particularly if his victim was the enemy quarterback. "He's the brains of the team," Greene said. "I learned a long time ago that if you killed the head the body would die."

Greene wasn't always devoted to football. Growing up in Temple, Texas, he quit the sport the first time he tried out for it in the eighth grade because they didn't give him a full uniform. Greene gained confidence in his ability as a 203-pound high school freshman. By his sophomore year he was a 235-pound middle linebacker. He weighed 250 his senior season, and his reputation was just as outsize.

Greene had the reputation of being the dirtiest ballplayer to come out of Temple. He acknowledged that when his team was losing, he'd act the fool. He grew up with a loving mother but without a father and wondered if having a dad would have given him more stability. For a time he was more round than tall; he was timid and shy and was picked on and ridiculed.

Greene took out his aggressions on the football field. He got the reputation of being a bully. Greene knew he wasn't; he was exacting revenge for being teased. He once recalled being kicked out of every game his sophomore season and nine more his junior year. He ran over a few officials, sometimes intentionally, he said. Following a loss on his high school's home field, Greene went to a diner and encountered the team that had won. The opposing quarterback was enjoying an ice cream cone. Greene took the cone and smeared it all over the quarterback's face. Later that night he charged the front door of the opposing team's bus after being hit in the chest with a soda bottle thrown by one of the players. As Greene forced his way in through the front door, opposing players scampered out the back.

Greene ran amok during his high school days. The same lack

of discipline was evident to scouts who visited North Texas State. "Puts on weight, tendency to loaf," one scout said. Another opined that while Greene was physically gifted, he used his ability only in spurts. The final line in the Steelers' 1969 scouting file on Greene questioned taking him in the first round, "as he could turn out to be a big dog."

Greene instead became the Steelers' top dog, the cornerstone of one of sports' greatest dynasties. Opponents saw him as mean, nasty, and intimidating—a big man who threw his weight around fiercely. Sometimes he could be reckless and take himself out of plays. But Greene also made tremendous plays that turned games around. He was inconsistent at times, given to playing some ordinary games. But Greene's ordinary games were better than outstanding games by other players. Mean Joe was one of the few defensive linemen who could dominate for four quarters. He was a powerful player on a powerhouse team, and he was always up for the big games. "Greene," George Allen said, "was the one who scared you the most."

Greene's coach at North Texas State called his defensive star a "fort on foot." In Pittsburgh the fort fronted what became known as the Steel Curtain.

Greene had all the physical tools to be successful in the NFL. He also had vision, a quality he considered more valuable than all the others. He could see what was happening on every play, could see where the blocks were coming from and where the ball was going. His biggest handicap was his tendency to guess. Early in his pro career Greene said that when he got into the game, he didn't always have time to think about what he ought to be doing. Monty Stickles, a former All-America at Notre Dame and an NFL tight end from 1960 to 1968 before becoming a Raiders color analyst on KGO Radio, noted during a Steelers-Raiders game that while Greene was a very active tackle, his aggressive style sometimes took him out of the play.

Greene credits Noll for curing him of his tendency to play a guessing game with opposing offenses. When Greene guessed right he turned into a tornado that tore up everything in his path. Noll convinced Greene that guesswork meant he would be right only half the time. Do the job you're supposed to do, Noll told him, and let his teammates do their jobs.

When they didn't Greene let them hear it. Russell recalled Greene growing angry when an opponent had success against the Steelers' defense. "Andy," Greene thundered, "what're *you* going to do?"

Greene got just as excited on the sidelines. He would approach Noll and say, "What's the quarterback doing?" and then approach wide receivers coach Lionel Taylor and say, "What're the receivers doing?" Russell said Greene was such a great player that he thought everyone could play better if they only tried harder. Greene pulled himself from a game in '73 and stalked out of a team meeting in '74, upset with what he saw as his teammates' lack of fervor.

The Steelers needed all the fervor and fight they could muster in 1973, the AFC Central featuring the tightest division race in the NFL.

Pittsburgh started the season 4-0, outscoring Detroit, Cleveland, Houston, and San Diego by a combined 131–44. While the Steelers' offense averaged 33 points the first four weeks, the Steel Curtain surrendered an average of just 11 points per contest. Ernie Holmes helped limit future Hall of Fame running back Leroy Kelly and Cleveland without a touchdown in Week Two. Against the Chargers the Steelers held fading legend Johnny Unitas without a point until Pittsburgh led by 38.

Week Five saw the first of two showdown games with rival Cincinnati. Aided by a young offensive genius named Bill Walsh, a Cincinnati assistant from 1968 to 1975, the Bengals dented the Steel Curtain for four Horst Muhlmann field goals in a 19–7 win. In the rematch Noll and defensive lieutenants George Perles and Bud Carson were ready for Walsh's schemes, and safety Mike Wagner intercepted three Ken Anderson aerials in a 20–13 win.

Steelers defensive captain Andy Russell said Walsh's offenses flustered Carson. Walsh remembered a game in which Anderson completed twenty of twenty-two passes, including an NFL-record sixteen straight. "We cut up the great Steelers defense," Walsh said, "and soundly defeated them."

Russell recalled Carson worrying all week prior to games against Walsh and the Bengals. Walsh's offense would show the Steel Curtain four, sometimes five, formations before Anderson snapped the ball. That Walsh wouldn't hold still long enough for the defense to audible to the most effective set frustrated Carson, Perles, and Woody Widenhofer and left them agonizing over their defensive plan. They came up with a counter to Walsh's multiple presnap sets by changing their defenses every time the offense set up differently.

Carson required the Steelers to check off several defenses in a matter of seconds. Russell doubted whether any team before or since has ever executed such a complicated scheme. Walsh was amazed years later when Russell revealed Carson's strategy. He realized then just how intelligent the Steel Curtain was, individually and as a unit.

The Steelers opened November with a Monday-night hosting of the reigning NFC champion Washington Redskins. The Steel Curtain limited Larry Brown to 54 yards on the ground, and Wagner's big hit on Brown at the goal line led to a 21–16 win.

The following Sunday in Oakland, the Steel Curtain stepped to the fore in the highly anticipated rematch with the Raiders. Pittsburgh's defense intercepted Daryle Lamonica four times, two of those picks coming from defensive end Dwight White. White's interception at the Oakland 36 set up a Steelers score, Terry Hanratty hitting Ron Shanklin from 14 yards out. George Blanda's 40-yard field goal as time ran out in the first half reduced the Raiders' deficit to 7–3, but the Steelers increased their lead to 14–3 on Franco Harris's 1-yard scoring run. Franco's score was set up by Wagner's recovery of a fumble by Raiders running back Charlie Smith at the Oakland 8-yard line. Smith had lost the ball after being blasted by Greene.

Cornerback Mel Blount's end-zone pick protected the lead after Lamonica drove Oakland to the Steelers' 2-yard line. Gerela's 17-yard field goal early in the fourth made it 17–3. With five minutes left Lamonica found Fred Biletnikoff through the rain to bring Oakland to within 17–9. But a wild snap from center on the extra-point attempt sealed the deal.

Throughout the afternoon Raiders guard Gene Upshaw had a running physical and verbal battle with former Oakland teammate and Steelers defensive tackle Tom Keating. The Raiders had dealt Keating to the Steelers in the offseason, and Ken Stabler, among others, found it interesting to watch Keating and Upshaw engaging in trench warfare. "Tom seems to know when you're going to pull, when you're going to pass block," Snake told Upshaw. "We practiced against one another for six years," Upshaw responded. "This is homecoming for him."

When Upshaw grabbed Keating's jersey on one play, Keating cussed him. Upshaw cussed back, and when he turned away Keating cuffed him in the back of the helmet. On the next play Upshaw punched Keating in the mouth. The two jawed at each other and had to be separated by Otto. "It was an emotional thing," Upshaw said. "Keats went all out and I respect him. We're still friends."

When a writer noted that the Steelers had given Keating a game ball for his performance against Upshaw, Gene shrugged. "I don't mind them giving him the game ball," he said. "I just wish we hadn't given them the game."

The muddy Oakland Coliseum sod hadn't slowed Keating or the Steel Curtain, which forced five turnovers. Oakland's offense produced 395 yards and twenty-six first downs to Pittsburgh's 194 yards and eight first downs, but the Steelers walked away with the win. "They can outrush us and outpass us," Noll said, "as long as we outscore them."

Greene knocked Stabler from the game on the second play of the second quarter, Mean Joe falling on the Snake's left knee as Kenny threw an incomplete pass. Stabler thought he probably could have gone back in, but since the Steelers' pass rush was forcing him to roll out and scramble, not by design but by necessity, he didn't believe he could continue to do that against what he considered the best pass rush in the league.

The week after the Steelers game, Raiders trainer George Anderson designed and built a lightweight brace for Stabler's left knee. It was two pieces of aluminum hinged on each side, with padding underneath and secured by Velcro. The brace provided solid support, particularly on hits to the side of the knee. Anderson called it a "Knee-Stablerizer," and it worked so well for Snake that the Raiders' trainer sold the brace to college teams.

The Steelers were hobbled too, yet despite injuries to key players, the Pittsburgh offense kept posting points. Harris missed the early part of the season with a bad knee, and Terry Bradshaw was injured in midseason. Hanratty, too, went down and eventually out with injuries. By the time Franco returned to the lineup, Frenchy Fuqua went out with a broken collarbone.

Fortunately for Pittsburgh, the Steel Curtain continued to shine as Greene, Greenwood, Russell, Wagner, and Jack Ham all put forth All-Pro performances.

Owning an 8-2 record, the Steelers led the Browns and Bengals in the Central and were on track to win a second straight division title. The next two weeks saw Pittsburgh play two of the more thrilling games of the '73 season. The Steelers dropped both decisions—a 21–16 final in the cold mud in Cleveland and a wild 30–26 Monday-night loss in Miami.

Browns coach Nick Skorich said prior to the resumption of the turnpike tournament that while his team had to head to the river to play in Three Rivers Stadium, the Steelers had to come to the lake in Cleveland. By game day heavy rains had turned cloud-shrouded Municipal Stadium into a swamp that was only slightly less watery than Lake Erie.

Pittsburgh was seeking its first win in Cleveland since 1964, and the tone for this November 25 collision between two of pro football's most bitter rivals was set on Hanratty's first pass, which turned out to be the former Notre Dame star's last pass of the day. Dropping back on the dirt infield on the Steelers' opening series, Hanratty threaded a pass through three defenders to tight end John McMakin. Belted by Browns defensive tackle Jerry Sherk, Hanratty tried to break his fall but landed heavily on his right arm. He headed for the sideline with a severely sprained wrist.

Taking Hanratty's place was Joe Willie Gillie, as Gilliam called himself. He found Shanklin with his first throw and then spotted Shanklin in the end zone with his second pass for a 7–0 lead. The Steel Curtain keyed on Kelly, but the Browns, relying on their reserve backfield of Bo Scott and Greg Pruitt, battled to a 14–10 lead.

The second half saw Steelers running back Preston Pearson pierce the Browns' "Rubber Band" defense and the Steel Curtain slam down on QB Mike Phipps. Pittsburgh forged a 16–14 lead late in the fourth quarter, but Phipps eluded blitzing safety Glen Edwards and found Pruitt for a 43-yard gain. Nine Steelers missed tackles on one of the most remarkable plays of the season. One play later Pruitt proved he could do it, sweeping left from 19 yards out for the winning score.

The 21–16 final brought the Browns to within a half game of the first-place Steelers with three games to go. Eight days later on December 3, a mild Monday night in Miami, the Steelers played their second riveting game in as many weeks.

ABC's Frank Gifford welcomed a national viewing audience to the Orange Bowl:

"We have a game here tonight, a critical game . . ."

Seeking to tie the 1967–68 Oakland Raiders' record for most wins in a two-year span with twenty-five, the Dolphins dominated early. Safety Dick Anderson stepped in front of a Gilliam pass on the opening series and returned it 27 yards for a quick 7–0 lead. Accompanied by the waving of thousands of white handkerchiefs by self-proclaimed Dol-fans, Garo Yepremian followed with a pair of field goals to make it 13–0. Miami upped its advantage to 20–0 in the first quarter on a 2-yard pass from Bob Griese to Jim Mandich.

Anderson's second pick-six covered 38 yards and put Miami up 27–0 in the second quarter. An exchange of field goals between Yepremian and Gerela made it 30–3 at the half. Anderson's four interceptions tied an NFL record, a record he reached in the first half. The second half belonged to the Steelers. Bradshaw's two touchdown passes highlighted a furious rally which saw Pittsburgh score twenty-three unanswered points.

For those who favored line play, the matchup between Miami's awesome offensive line and Pittsburgh's Steel Curtain was fascinating and one of the highlights of the evening. Greene battled guard Larry Little and center Jim Langer in matchups of Hall of Famers. Ernie Holmes hand-fought guard Bob Kuechenberg, and on the outside

Dwight White dueled Wayne Moore and L. C. Greenwood worked against Norm Evans.

Howard Cosell watched Mean Joe and Mad Dog get to Griese early and told ABC viewers, "That's what's going to have to hold Pittsburgh in there tonight, that defense."

Color analyst "Dandy" Don Meredith agreed. "That Pittsburgh defense doesn't really give anybody room to breathe. They're on [offenses] all the time."

This collision of two dynasties took a physical toll. The Steelers lost linebacker Andy Russell to an injury; Mel Blount sidelined Mercury Morris with a bruising hit.

Pittsburgh posted wins in its final two games to finish tied with Cincinnati atop the division. Because the Bengals boasted a better record within the conference, the title went to the old master, Paul Brown, rather than his prized pupil, Noll.

Losing three of their final five games left the Steelers with little momentum heading into the first round of the AFC playoffs opposite Oakland. Yet the Raiders had also struggled. After opening with a 24–16 loss at eventual NFC champion Minnesota, the Raiders met Miami before what was then the largest crowd (74,121) ever to watch a pro football game in the Bay Area. Oakland dealt the Dolphins a 12–7 defeat, ending Miami's record regular-season win streak at eighteen games. But Oakland's high-octane offense was sputtering, and after failing to score a touchdown in its first three games and dropping a 16–3 decision at hated rival Kansas City, head coach John Madden made the switch and benched the Mad Bomber for the Snake, southpaw Ken Stabler.

A precision passer who thrived on strategic gains, Stabler was suited to running the ball-control offense favored by Madden, a former offensive linemen. The Raiders' recipe for success resided in the fierce blocking of center Jim Otto, guard Gene Upshaw, and tackle Art Shell; a strong runner in Marv Hubbard, the heir to Hewritt Dixon in the Oakland offense; and a sure-handed receiver like Stickum-slathered Fred Biletnikoff.

Just as Greene was a symbol of strength for the Steelers' defense, the bullish Hubbard personified the power of the Raiders' ground game. At 6 feet 1 and 225 pounds, Hubbard by his own reckoning was a "human bowling ball." He gouged out 1,100 yards rushing in 1972 and was considered by some in the Bay Area as the "Joe Rudi of pro football." Rudi was the quiet, productive left fielder for the Raiders' fellow rebels of Oakland, the Swingin' A's.

While they shared similarities in their steady performances, Hubbard and Rudi differed personality-wise. Rudi avoided saying anything that could be considered controversial. Hubbard was bold and brash. He thought the rebels of Oakland should speak their minds and state openly that they were going to beat their opponent if that's what they believed.

Hubbard thought that people needed to realize the NFL is entertainment. Players put on a good game for the fans, and what they said was an extension of the entertainment. Hubbard knew why players didn't pop off to the press. It took a big man to do so, since he would have to eat his words if he was wrong. Hubbard would point to Joe Namath, who guaranteed a Jets victory over the heavily favored Baltimore Colts in Super Bowl III. Like Namath, Hubbard rarely held his tongue. In 1972 he told the press the week before the Raiders met the rival Chiefs that Oakland would win. "When we go to Kansas City," he said, "we're going to kick some rears."

Hubbard remembered arriving at Arrowhead Stadium and seeing fans cheering on the Chiefs to shut Hubbard up. Snarling and snorting, Hubbard took the fight to Willie Lanier, Bobby Bell, Curley Culp, and Company. Lanier thought no one came at Kansas City harder than Hubbard, who got mad at Chiefs defenders when they tackled him.

The Raiders would break their huddle, and Hubbard would yell at Lanier, "I'm coming right at you, Willie!" Because the play was going exactly where Hubbard told Lanier it would go, Stabler would scream at Hubbard, "Shut up, Marv!"

Hubbard ran so hard he broke his helmets and shattered his shoulder pads. His determination was born of desperation. Considering himself a big, slow runner, he had to get by on extra effort. If he had great ability, he said, he would have gone to Notre Dame, USC, or

Ohio State rather than Colgate. If he was a star, he added, he wouldn't have been drafted in the eleventh round as a tight end, wouldn't have been cut by the Raiders, and wouldn't have gone to Denver and been cut by the Broncos.

He wouldn't have ended up in the Continental League, where guys were playing for twenty-five dollars a game. When Hubbard rejoined the Raiders in 1969 he had bulked up and was packing 230 pounds on his frame. As blue collar as the Bay Area, Hubbard became a fan favorite in the Coliseum. He scored a touchdown in Oakland's mud-caked humbling of Houston in the 1969 AFL playoffs and helped crush Kansas City in the Coliseum to clinch the 1970 division title.

Hubbard hammered his way to a team-high 903 yards and six scores in 1973 and made the December cover of *Sports Illustrated* following Oakland's victory over Kansas City. Despite the high-gloss treatment, Hubbard deflected praise to Oakland's offensive linemen. The Raiders, he said, had big, strong people up front who physically beat down their opposition.

The Raiders sought to dominate with man-on-man football. They looked to beat the man opposite them at the point of attack, proving in the pits that they were stronger and tougher. Hubbard played his role to the hilt, wearing lineman's pads as he powered from tackle to tackle on Oakland's signature running plays, "68 and 69 Boom Man." Hubbard would follow his halfback into the hole at a hard gallop, a fullback who was the size of a middle linebacker plunging into holes ripped open by the Raiders' rugged line.

To prepare himself for the physical pounding, Hubbard not only wore a lineman's oversize shoulder pads, thigh pads, and kneepads, but also stuffed cardboard liners into his socks to protect his shins and wore heavy leather shoes with round safety heels. His silver-and-black battle-scarred helmet was guaranteed by the manufacturer to withstand 200 g's of force. In time Hubbard would break twelve of those helmets.

Hubbard identified with the Raiders' no-frills attack. Growing up in Red House, a small upper Appalachian town in western New York, Hubbard was raised amid poverty. It was a depressed area, he said, where some people lived in dirt-floor shacks. Hubbard attended a one-room school until the seventh grade. He excelled in the classroom, skipping a grade in high school and attending Colgate University on an academic scholarship.

Few runners had more impact on their team's success in the early 1970s than Hubbard. Replacing Hewritt Dixon as the power gear in Oakland's freewheeling offense, Hubbard led the Raiders in rushing every season from 1971 to 1974. He trucked his way to a 4.8 yards per carry and close to 1,000 yards every year, despite the fact that he owned neither speed nor slick moves and was fronting the Raiders' straight-ahead running game.

A mid-November slump saw Oakland fall to Pittsburgh and Cleveland and fight to stave off surprising Denver. In late October the Raiders and Broncos battled to a 23–23 tie in Denver in a memorable Monday-night game in Mile High Stadium.

Entering the season's stretch run the Raiders rallied for three straight wins, including a rout of the Chiefs on Oakland's sodden turf. The Coliseum sod was in notoriously bad condition in 1973; for a second straight year the A's had pushed their postseason into mid-October en route to repeating as world champions. When Hubbard rumbled through the left side for a 31-yard touchdown run, it was the first time all season a back had covered more than 20 yards on a run in the Coliseum.

Hubbard led all rushers with 115 yards in the victory over Kansas City, and the Raiders entered the final game one half game ahead of Denver. Oakland won the showdown with the Broncos, and the Raiders had their sixth division title in seven seasons.

Oakland's division title put them in the playoffs for the sixth time in Madden's seven seasons with the team. He had joined the Raiders in 1967 as linebackers coach under John Rauch. Madden and fellow future coaching legend Bill Walsh missed working together on the same Raiders staff by one season, Walsh leaving Oakland following the 1966 season.

Madden helped coach the Raiders to a 13-1 mark in 1967, the best record in pro football and the greatest in AFL history. Oakland's defense that season set a league record for sacks with sixty-seven, and the Raiders romped to their first division title. Oakland overwhelmed Houston 40–7 in the AFL Championship Game, giving Madden an opportunity to coach against Green Bay legend Vince Lombardi in Super Bowl II.

The Raiders cruised past Kansas City in a Western Division playoff in 1968 to repeat as champions and advance to their second straight AFL title game. Oakland dropped a 27–23 decision to the Jets in cold, windswept Shea Stadium, and New York went on to make sports history in Super Bowl III.

The game marked the final one as Raiders head coach for Rauch, who resigned to become boss of the Buffalo Bills. Al Davis made Madden the youngest head coach in pro football, the thirty-two-year-old taking the reins of a Raiders team loaded with some of the game's greatest talent.

In his first season as head coach Madden led Oakland to its third consecutive Western title in 1969 and the AFL's best record at 12-1-1. The Raiders handled Houston in the rain-soaked Oakland Coliseum to earn a playoff rematch with rival Kansas City. The game marked the final AFL Championship showdown due to the impending merger with the NFL and matched the rebel league's representatives from Super Bowls I and II.

The Chiefs earned a 17–7 victory and the right to carry the AFL banner into the final Super Bowl with the NFL. Kansas City manhandled Minnesota, forever squaring the AFL-NFL Super Bowl series at two wins apiece.

Madden took the Raiders to a Western Division title in 1970 and a muddy playoff win over a young Miami Dolphins squad led by new head coach Don Shula. In the AFC title game in Baltimore, Unitas paced the Colts to a 27–17 win. The following season Oakland missed the playoffs for the first time since 1966, but Madden and Company rebounded in '72 to reclaim the Western crown.

Madden cut a distinctive figure on the field. Yet if Big John was disheveled in his appearance, he was not disorganized in his approach. He may not have worn a business suit, but he was an organization man nonetheless. Despite being a mountain of a man at 6 feet 4 and 260 pounds, Madden worked in the even larger—figuratively, at least— shadow of Al Davis.

Yet Davis claimed the only credit he should receive in the Raiders' success under Madden was his hiring John away from San Diego State in 1967 and naming him head coach in 1969. "He is one of the best and one of the brightest," Davis said once, "and he has done it himself."

Madden was indeed one of the best and brightest in the NFL ranks. He had more than seventy head-coaching victories before turning forty. In his first seven seasons his record stood at 70-21-7. Shula and Bud Grant were the only NFL coaches with more wins in that span, and no coach had fewer losses than Madden. Oakland won six Western titles and played in five AFL/AFC Championship Games, losing to the eventual Super Bowl winner each time.

Madden credited Davis for being the biggest influence on his coaching career. Madden was thirty-one years old with zero pro coaching experience when Davis hired him to be the first linebackers coach in Raiders history. "It took a lot of guts for him to hire me," Madden said. "It would have been much easier to get someone with more coaching experience."

Madden soon found out that Davis didn't always do things the easy way; Al wanted to do things the right way. "Without him having the confidence and hiring me," Madden said, "I just don't know what might have happened."

Madden's working relationship with Davis changed over the years. Initially, Davis would okay the game plans and suggest improvements. On game days he would leave it up to Madden to make decisions.

Change came midway through Madden's first season. Facing Rauch, his former boss, Madden coached Oakland to a 50–21 win. Davis called a press conference shortly thereafter to proclaim the changing dynamic in the Raiders organization. "My role has changed since he's been head coach from giving direction to giving assistance," Davis stated. "I am no more important than the lowest assistant coach today. Madden is in full control of the troops. Rauch never had such authority here. Madden doesn't need my help or advice; Rauch, on the other hand, did."

Madden's road to being Raiders head coach was filled with enough plot twists and surprises to fill a Grisham novel. A good small-college offensive tackle for California Poly at San Luis Obispo, Madden was taken by Philadelphia in the twenty-first round of the 1959 draft. In training camp he suffered a knee injury that required surgery and resulted in his pro playing career ending before it could even begin.

Rehabilitation on his knee required Madden to arrive in the training room for taping ahead of other players. It proved to be the best thing that could have happened to Madden, for it allowed him to spend time studying game film with future Hall of Fame quarterback Norm Van Brocklin, who was also there early every morning to watch film.

Learning the pro game from the celebrated Dutchman's viewpoint marked a new beginning for Madden. As a player he knew his assignment but didn't pay attention to the big picture. Watching film with the veteran Van Brocklin allowed Madden to really learn football. Van Brocklin would run the film back and forth several times, talking about what he was seeing. Madden wasn't always certain the Dutchman was talking to him or just talking out loud, but it didn't matter. Madden was learning either way.

Van Brocklin believed coaches must make the best use of their best players. He would watch an opposing defense and think how Eagle flanker Tommy McDonald could best run a post pattern against it. McDonald ran the best post pattern in the NFL at that time, but the Dutchman wasn't satisfied with just running the post. He wanted his best player to run it the best way possible. Bobby Walston was a ball-control receiver, so Van Brocklin sought ways to run hook-and-out patterns for 12–15 yard gains.

Madden watched Van Brocklin study ways of getting bread-and-butter running back Billy Barnes some straight-ahead gains and how to get outside running room for Clarence Peaks, who excelled on toss sweeps. Van Brocklin wanted to take advantage of everything his players did well. Offense, Van Brocklin told Madden, was nothing more than getting your players to do the things they could do best and finding ways to put them in that position.

In the mid-1960s Madden learned from another great offensive mind when he coached with Don Coryell at San Diego State. Madden also learned from Lombardi and Paul "Bear" Bryant, spending hours at lectures they delivered at coaching clinics. Lombardi, Madden recalled, spent an entire day breaking down one play—his famed Packers Power Sweep. He listened to Bryant lecture for three hours, and while Madden didn't learn anything new about football he enjoyed hearing the Bear's personal philosophy about the sport.

Madden took what he learned from offensive minds and applied it to defense. In his three years as San Diego State defensive coordinator, the Aztecs went 27-4 and surrendered just 263 points in thirty-one games. In his first coaching stop prior to San Diego State he was at Hancock Junior College in Santa Maria, California, spending two years as an assistant while earning his master's degree at nearby San Luis Obispo. Madden was named head coach in 1962 and went 8-1 the following season to attract the attention of Coryell assistant Tom Bass. Madden brought with him a wide-tackle-six defense that he favored. Coryell preferred the 3-4 defense. Madden studied both and settled on variations of each, using overshifting alignments that Coryell considered well thought out.

Under Madden San Diego State's "kamikaze" defense found favor with fans because they played, as one observed stated, "maniac football." Coryell gave Madden control of the defense, and for three seasons it matched the Aztecs' high-octane offense. At the end of the 1966 season Madden was being talked about as the top prospect for the Utah State head-coaching position. His career path took a sudden change when Davis, in San Diego to visit Aztec QB Don Horn, met Madden. The two talked, and Madden made a favorable impression with his knowledge, enthusiasm, and strong rapport with his players. When Davis went looking for assistant coaches a year later, Madden came to mind. "At that time I wasn't thinking of him as a future head coach of the Raiders," Davis said. "But I knew that if he came with us he could help us."

Prior to Madden's arrival Raiders assistants Tom Dahms and Charlie Sumner had been coaching the defensive line and defensive backs and splitting responsibilities for the linebackers. When Madden took

over as linebackers coach, he inherited a solid corps that included starters Dan Conners, Bill Laskey, and Gus Otto. As impressed as Madden was with them, they were equally impressed with him. Laskey
said the linebackers had not expected a newcomer to the pro game
to be so knowledgeable.

Raiders players responded to Madden's dedication and enthusiasm. Veterans like Jim Otto, knowing that pro football is an emotional
game, liked the raw emotion Madden showed on the practice field.
"That really rubbed off on people," Otto said.

The John Madden that a generation of football fans came to know
for his "Boom!" and "Whap!" and Telestrator drawings alongside Pat
Summerall is the same guy who ran their film meetings. His enthusiasm was the same then as it would be a decade later on TV broadcasts.

Madden never doubted he would succeed as Raiders head coach.
"I just started going forward," he said, "and never looked back."

Entering the 1973 playoff rematch with Pittsburgh, Madden was
seeking a similarly successful outcome with the Steelers. The Raiders took the field in the Oakland Coliseum on Saturday, December
22, looking to overcome the Steelers and a field made sloppy by rain
the day before. Pittsburgh placekicker Roy Gerela, the conference's
leading scorer with 123 points, recalled what the Coliseum turf had
been like when Pittsburgh won there on November 11. "You have to
be careful when you put your foot down because of the loose sod,
ruts and bumps," he said.

Franco Harris had few reservations. "When you're going for the
big Super Bowl money you don't care about what kind of field you're
playing on," he said. "I'd play on water if I had to."

Harris had seemingly walked on water with his miraculous catch
and score the previous December. "We've been lucky to win some
games over Oakland," Terry Bradshaw admitted.

The Raiders were intent on ruling out any more miracles. "A fluke
won't beat us this time," Upshaw stated.

Pittsburgh had overcome injuries to Bradshaw, Hanratty, Harris,
Fuqua, and others to finish 10-4 and earn a playoff berth. Along the way
the Steelers scored a then team-record 347 points and allowed just 210.

Though the Steelers were a wild-card team, they owned a better record than the Raiders, who rode a four-game win streak into the playoffs and looked overpowering at times, despite winning the West with a 9-4-1 record. Plus, Pittsburgh had outlasted Oakland in each of their three previous meetings.

Still, Stabler, the AFC's leading passer with a 63 percent completion rate, predicted that the Raiders had "a lot of football ahead of us."

Hubbard, who led the Raiders in rushing, thought the playoff rematch would be decided by "who gets the breaks." That would seem to be the Steelers, whose thirty-seven interceptions led the NFL. "They create turnovers," Oakland All-Pro cornerback Willie Brown acknowledged, yet it was the Raiders who ranked first in the AFC in defense as well as offense.

Since they closed the regular season in San Francisco, the Steelers stayed on the West Coast, in Palm Springs. Following practice, Greene spoke of the urgency of winning in the postseason. "You approach all games to win," he said. "But if you don't win a playoff game, you go home."

The playoffs started early Saturday afternoon with the NFL on CBS, Don Criqui doing the voice-over for the classic opening theme "Confidence," also known as the "Walter Mitty March" because it served as the show-stopping end to act 1 of the 1964 Broadway play *The Secret Life of Walter Mitty*. Jack Whitaker and Wayne Walker called the action as the Vikings, spurred by Carl Eller's fiery halftime speech, ended the Redskins' reign as NFC champions by scoring seventeen points in the fourth quarter to claim a dramatic 27–20 comeback win in the frozen sunshine of Minnesota's Metropolitan Stadium.

In sun-soaked Oakland later that afternoon NBC viewers saw the equally classic montage of action footage and Kevin Gavin's driving jazz beat that was a staple of the NFL on NBC in the 1970s. Play-by-play announcer Jim Simpson and color analyst Kyle Rote were in the broadcast booth as the Raiders, resplendent in their black jerseys with the silver numerals, opened the scoring with an 82-yard touchdown drive that started with a personal foul by safety Glen Edwards on Raiders receiver Mike Siani.

Oakland set a tone from the outset, its offensive line seizing control of the scrimmage line. Hubbard swept left for 20 yards, and Clarence Davis drove for 9 more on a third-and-8 trap play. On the sixteenth play of an 82-yard drive, Hubbard plowed in from the 1 behind Upshaw and Shell to cap a nearly ten -minute marathon march.

Al Wester provided the call on the Mutual Radio Network:

"Third and goal for the Raiders . . . Here's the Snake, Kenny Stabler, hands under the center, the snap . . . Hubbard with the football, cracks into the end zone! Touchdown, Oakland! Beautiful block by Upshaw!"

The Raiders were physically dominant up front. With Jim Otto as its linchpin, the line of guards Gene Upshaw and George Buehler and tackles Art Shell and Bob Brown was outmuscling and outhustling the Steel Curtain.

Wester's broadcast partner, color analyst Monty Stickles, noted Oakland's early dominance in the trenches.

"Here's something you don't usually see against Pittsburgh. Pittsburgh may give up one or two first downs on a drive but never this many [6]. This is really unique."

Otto was the original Raider, old "Double Zero," Mr. AFL. He reported to the Raiders' first training camp in 1960 as a 6-foot-2, 217-pound center, one of a hundred or so hopefuls at Santa Cruz. The undersize Otto not only made the team, but was also Oakland's only starting center for the next fifteen seasons. He was also the AFL's only All-Star center in its ten-year existence and played in thirteen AFL All-Star or NFL Pro Bowl games.

Not that it was easy for the Wisconsin native and University of Miami product. He was a two-way force for the Hurricanes, playing center and middle linebacker, earning more notoriety at the latter. He had big games against Tulane and Navy, intercepting passes and making numerous unassisted tackles. The Packers and 49ers showed interest, but Otto's lack of size—he played college ball at 205 pounds—and shoulder injuries scared many teams away. Otto was drafted by Minnesota, signed by Houston, and sent to Oakland.

He became fiercely loyal to his new team, Otto said, the first time he pulled on the Raiders' helmet. Feeling he had something to prove,

Otto hit the weights hard, supplemented his diet with high-protein drinks and beer, and bulked up to 240 pounds. He knew the Raiders and the AFL were fledglings compared to the NFL, but Otto kept his barometer high. He looked at the best centers in the NFL—Green Bay's Jim Ringo and Philadelphia's Chuck Bednarik—and believed he was going to be as good as they were.

Otto also believed the AFL was going to be better than the NFL, and it was this belief that kept him loyal to the Raiders when NFL teams came calling and tried to convince him to jump leagues. "The NFL was knocking at my door," he said. "They knocked every year until the merger but I wouldn't [switch leagues]. I had faith in the Raiders."

Otto wore No. 50 his first year in the league and in the first game of 1961. His nickname among teammates was "Ott," which sounded like "Ought," or zero. Oakland equipment man Frank Hinek called AFL commissioner Joe Foss and asked permission to give Otto the number 00.

Otto was okay with it as well, and Double-O became his trademark in Oakland. So, too, did a double-bar face mask that was unusual for a lineman. Otto excelled at his position in part due to diligent film study. He ignored what he did well and asked coaches to rerun his mistakes several times as he strove for perfection. "When I had a problem," he said, "I wanted to see it over and over again until I figured out how I was going to correct it."

Shaken up in 1963, Otto took himself out of the game only to discover new head coach Al Davis waiting for him on the sideline. "When I was with the Chargers," Davis told Otto, "we felt if we could get you out of the game the rest of the team would quit because you are the leader of this team."

Otto got the message and never again took himself out of a game, despite the fact he had numerous knee surgeries over the course of his career and constant stingers in his neck. From 1960 to 1974 Otto played in 210 consecutive games, overcoming several broken noses, broken ribs, a broken jaw, and a few broken fingers, and traced his durability to what Davis had told him. "What Al said to me became indelibly etched in my mind," he said. "I took a beating sometimes but I stayed in the game."

It meant enduring pain and blood, injuries and surgeries, but since Otto was a team captain, he didn't want to disappoint Davis, his Raiders teammates, his family, or the fans. "I was a football player," he said, "and I wanted to play."

So did his linemates. The media at the time regularly reported that the Raiders ran predominantly to their left side because Stabler was a southpaw. Oakland did run left even without the tight end set to that side, but it wasn't because the Snake was left-handed. "We had Shell and Upshaw over there," Stabler said, "and they buried people."

Shell and Upshaw, Highways 78 and 63, respectively, played alongside each other at left tackle and left guard. Together with Otto they've gone from the Oakland Coliseum to Canton, Ohio, reunited for all time in the Pro Football Hall of Fame. The Raiders of the 1970s join the Packers of the 1960s as offensive lines that featured three Hall of Famers. The strength of Green Bay's line was its right side, where Ringo, guard Jerry Kramer, and tackle Forrest Gregg resided. If Green Bay featured the greatest right side of an offensive line, Oakland owned the most dominant left side.

It didn't start that way for the Raiders. When Upshaw was picked by Oakland in the opening round of the first AFL-NFL combined draft in 1967, Raiders fans wondered who Gene Upshaw was.

Davis knew all about Upshaw, and knew he could not only fill a hole in Oakland's offensive line, but at 6 feet 5, 255 pounds, he could also match up physically with 6-foot-7, 274-pound defensive tackle Buck Buchanan of rival Kansas City. "I figured if Buchanan was going to play for the Chiefs for the next 10 years," Davis said, "we better get some big guy who could handle him. Some thought we were crazy but look who was on the other side of the line. I wanted to go to sleep at that position for about 10 years."

So the Raiders took Upshaw, and over the next several years he and Buchanan battled in high-profile trench warfare worth the price of admission. In an era of short fireplug-type guards who had low centers of gravity, Upshaw was among the first of a new breed of linemen.

Upshaw, however, didn't want to be play guard when he was drafted and didn't want to play for the Raiders. "He thought we were renegades," Davis said.

A product of Robstown, Texas, Upshaw was a multisport star who preferred baseball and track. He was 5 feet 10, 180 pounds at graduation, but he bulked up at Texas A&I. He rotated among three positions on the line and was named National Association of Intercollegiate Athletes All-America his senior season.

Upshaw earned a starting role his rookie season in Oakland and excelled on a play that was a Raiders staple, the sweep around the left side. "That's my play," he said.

Wide receivers want to catch long touchdown passes, defensive tackles want to break through and sack the quarterback, but Upshaw's satisfaction came from pulling to lead on the sweep. He knew the success of the play came down to just him and the defensive back. "If I get him clean, we're going to make a big gain," he said. "If I miss him we don't get a yard."

Upshaw made more plays than he missed, helping lead the Raiders to the AFL Championship in 1967 and a berth in Super Bowl II. He was named All-AFL, All-AFC, or All-NFL his first six seasons, a span that saw Oakland win five Western Division titles and appear in four straight league or conference championship games.

Larry Little, a contemporary who starred at guard for the Miami Dolphins, said Upshaw always seemed to rise to the top in big games. One of the reasons Upshaw was so successful, Little stated, was his great speed.

Upshaw prided himself on his speed, and his pride was easily offended. Prior to a special Western Conference playoff game against the Chiefs in 1968, Upshaw stood at the center of the Oakland Coliseum floor for the coin toss. Kansas City won the toss, and coach Hank Stram deferred to his defense. Upshaw couldn't believe the Chiefs would challenge the Raiders' offense. "You'll regret this," he told KC middle linebacker Willie Lanier and then yelled the same to Stram. Returning to the Raiders' sideline, Upshaw told teammates, "Buckle up your chinstraps. We've just been insulted."

Oakland proceeded to pound KC, 41–6.

Pounding opponents became a trademark of the Raiders' line. The 6-foot-5, 290-pound Art Shell matched Upshaw in bulk and durability, the pair playing side by side in more than 200 games. Shell's 207 games played for the Raiders trailed only Otto and Upshaw.

Shell grew up in a housing project in Charleston, South Carolina. His father worked at a paper mill, and his mother passed away from heart problems when Art was just fifteen. The oldest of five children, Art cooked dinner, cleaned the house, and washed clothes for his three brothers and one sister while his father worked in the mill. Shell took care of business on the football field as well, starring for Bonds-Wilson High and gaining a scholarship to Maryland State–Eastern Shore. He became a four-year, two-way starter and earned Little All-America honors his senior season.

Shell was also a three-year starting center on his college basketball team, and his size and agility impressed the Raiders enough that they selected him in the 1968 draft. Playing with what he called "controlled aggression," Shell exploded off the scrimmage line.

Baltimore Colts line coach John Sandusky described Shell as a knock-'em-dead player. "He came off the ball and would get into you." Madden called Shell a quiet leader who commanded respect by being a great player.

The 1973 season was the first of six straight seasons that Shell earned All-AFC honors, and he and Upshaw made the Raiders' weak-side run work so well that right tackle Bob Brown and right guard George Buehler had to complain to get plays run their way. "Can I please get a few plays run to my side?" Brown would ask Stabler in a booming voice. The Snake looked at the man mountain confronting him and merely nodded. Buehler rarely complained, mainly because, as Stabler said, George's mind tended to drift during games. Someone would have to slap him, Stabler stated, to get his attention.

Late in a close game when the Oakland offense was trying to figure out what play to call, Buehler looked at Pete Banaszak and asked, "Where'd you get those shoes?" Banaszak, not believing what he was hearing, blurted, "What?" "I was just thinking of where you got those shoes," Buehler said. Banaszak promptly slapped Buehler's helmet.

Buehler, like Upshaw, was strong, smart, and a great pulling guard. Like the rest of the Raiders' line he was, as Stabler described him, "a huge slab of a man." Buehler weighed 270, and Brown tipped the scales at nearly 300 while standing 6 feet 5, prompting one opponent to tell Stabler, "You guys have a big offensive line!"

Brown was the biggest, and meanest. He wrapped his massive forearms from wrists to elbows, the tape covering hard molded plastic. Stabler said it was like Brown carried two clubs. When defensive ends head-slapped him, Brown responded with body punches, "right in the solar plexus," Stabler noted.

Brown was the only offensive linemen Stabler ever heard say that he wanted to punish defensive ends. Brown's game was based on an attack formula. He used a "Two-Hand Rip-Up" to attack soft spots like the spleen, liver, and solar plexus.

Former Colts center Dick Szymanski said Brown could be too aggressive. "He always wanted to kick the [crap] out of you."

Brown did not disagree. "I'm about as fancy as a 16-pound sledgehammer," he said. "From the opening kickoff on, I beat on people."

Brown also beat on goalposts. On Brown's first day of Raiders training camp, he lined up in his stance in front of a wooden goalpost and shattered it with a forearm smash. "Can you believe that?" a startled Stabler asked Banaszak. "Breaking a damn goalpost with his forearm!"

Brown's enormous strength was testament to his weight-lifting regimen. Brown pumped iron everywhere he went, including the Raiders' dining hall. He was an ambidextrous eater, lifting his fork with one massive hand while lifting weights with the other. "Dumbbells," Stabler noted, "looked like cuff links in Bob's hands."

Brown played in six Pro Bowls and earned acclaim from all sides. Dolphins coach Don Shula called Brown "a great football player." Madden called Brown the "most devastating football player I've ever seen."

In their 1973 playoff game Brown and Oakland's offensive line handled the Steel Curtain on the opening drive to set a tone, and the rest of the Raiders followed suit. Linebacker Phil Villapiano had the first of three interceptions of Bradshaw when he hauled in a pass deflected by defensive tackle Otis Sistrunk near the end of the first quarter. The turnover put the ball at the Oakland 40, and Stabler spotted Siani for 21 yards. Banaszak blasted for 12 yards on two carries, bringing Blanda on to boot a 25-yard field goal to put Pittsburgh in a 10–0 hole.

Noll said before the game that the Steelers wouldn't do anything drastically different from what they had done all season, but as Al Wester pointed out in calling the game on radio, Pittsburgh's style of play this day was not their accustomed approached.

Wester: *"The Steelers normally like to stay on the ground. The problem today is they're putting the ball up in the air on first and second down, which is not their style of play. Consequently, that great Raiders defense has stymied Pittsburgh."*

Their white jerseys brightened by the California sun, the Steelers sliced Oakland's lead to 10–7 at halftime when Bradshaw tossed a 4-yard touchdown pass to Barry Pearson with 1:56 remaining.

Wester: *"Bradshaw sprints out to the right. He throws . . . A great pass into the very edge of the end zone. Barry Pearson got his shoulders and one foot over the goal line, and that was enough for the score!"*

The Raiders argued that Pearson had been ridden out of bounds by Willie Brown before scoring, and replays indicated as much. Officials overruled Oakland, saying Pearson had broken the plane of the end zone.

As the fifty-four thousand crammed into the Coliseum roared their approval, the Raiders dominated the first half in the stat sheet if not on the scoreboard, and they started the third quarter just as strong. Stabler's strategic passing twice guided Oakland into scoring position, and Blanda's field goals of 31 and 22 yards increased Oakland's advantage to 16–7.

With tempers flaring on both sides, Bradshaw looked to rally the Steelers but was intercepted by Brown, who tipped a pass intended for Preston Pearson in the left flat and sped down the sideline for a 54-yard score.

Wester: *"Bradshaw was throwing for Preston Pearson rolling out of the backfield. Willie Brown cut in front, took the football at the midfield stripe, and he goes for the touchdown! Oakland has broken this game open!"*

Stickles: *"Brown read the pattern beautifully. He had flat coverage, and as Pearson came out of the backfield he cut in front of him, tipped it like a basketball, and ran it in!"*

Brown's interception on the play of the day was a testament to his intelligence and skill. On the previous play he had followed Barry Pearson on a pattern that drew him away from the flat area. On the next play, reading the ball and not the man, Brown jumped Preston Pearson's route in the flat and made a great grab of Bradshaw's slightly underthrown pass. "I was reading the quarterback and I knew he was going after the halfback with the pass," Brown said. "I decided to go after the ball."

"Bradshaw was supposed to pre-read the coverage and he didn't," Noll said. "It was the turning point of the game as far as we were concerned."

Madden agreed: "If you're looking for a turning point, the interception was a play that forced Pittsburgh to play a little different game and open up. I don't like to single out any play but that did force them to change their approach."

The score put Oakland up 23–7 late in the third, and Bradshaw, forced to throw on nearly every down, sailed a pass deep down the middle that was intercepted by safety George Atkinson, who was patrolling the area like Bill North patrolled center field for the A's. Charlie Smith swept left for 40 yards, and Blanda followed with a 10-yard field goal early in the fourth.

Bradshaw engineered a 68-yard scoring drive capped by his 26-yard TD pass to Lewis. Coming with nine minutes to go the score gave Steelers fans hope of another miracle. But Oakland controlled the ball for much of the remaining time, and in the final seconds Hubbard closed the scoring the same way he had started it, muscling in from the 1 to make it 33–14.

Wester: *"First and goal for the Raiders. Hubbard dives over the middle. Touchdown, Oakland! This is a shocking defeat for the Pittsburgh Steelers."*

"We didn't have our frenzy," Greene said. "They had it. They beat the hell out of us."

Harris, the miracle man who was the focal point of the fired-up Raiders defense, was limited to 29 yards on ten carries. Bradshaw threw for 167 yards and missed the services of Shanklin, the Steelers' leading receiver who was out with an injury.

Stabler punctured Pittsburgh's pass defense, completing fourteen of seventeen passes. Oakland's thirty-three points were the most the Steelers surrendered all season. "We thought that in the second half we could come out and turn it around," said Noll. "But they took the ball and just blew us out of there. Their offensive line beat the heck out of us. They came off the ball and blew us out."

"Oakland just wanted it more than we wanted it," said Bradshaw. Of Brown's pick-six, Bradshaw said he "just didn't read the rotation right."

Tom Keating, a former Raider, praised Stabler. "He had a super day," Keating said. "Everything he did was right."

Pittsburgh defensive back John Rowser said Stabler benefited from the Steelers changing their coverages. "We were playing a different defense than usual," Rowser said. "We used mainly a straight zone and we usually mix up man to man. But [Stabler] executed real well."

The Snake played it as cool in the postgame as he had on the field. "I'm not concerned with my play other than that we won," he said. "I don't think Pittsburgh beat us before. I think we beat ourselves."

Madden insisted the Raiders weren't looking for revenge. "There was no grudge motive in this game," he stated.

Maybe not. But the Steelers-Raiders rivalry was about to enter a white-hot state.

Jim Campbell: Joe Greene is arguably the most dominant personality of the Steelers-Raiders rivalry. No one left a more indelible mark on the heated contests of the 1970s than the larger-than-life Pittsburgh defensive tackle.

By refusing to stand and sing his college alma mater as a rookie at the Steelers' training-camp dining table, as had been an NFL custom for decades, Joe Greene changed the culture of the Steelers. This didn't sit well with some veteran Steelers. But Joe's performance in the Oklahoma drill—"rag-dolling" vets Mansfield and Van Dyke—ended any thought of confronting the strong-willed rookie. Greene quickly became the Steelers' leader, inspirational and otherwise.

Around the practice field and even in pregame activities, Joe was anything but mean. He was actually jovial on many occasions and mostly lighthearted. I never joked that much with him—too many other things for me to do—and I figured Joe had some pregame things to attend to.

But one incident sticks out. During a week in the '71 season, I was in a Pittsburgh equivalent of what would now be a Dollar General or Dollar Tree store and noticed a stocking cap in the Steelers' black-and-gold team colors. With the season approaching the colder phase, I decided to shell out a buck, or whatever, and purchase the knit cap. At the time the Steelers and most other NFL teams (this was before the NFL got into marketing to the public all the "sideline gear" so prevalent today) wore simple navy-surplus dark-blue knitted "watch caps."

I wore my newly purchased headgear to the Steelers' game that Sunday. It was a little nippy. The Steelers took the field for pregame warm-ups in their team-issued navy watch caps. Joe spied my colorful cap, came over, and said, "Hey, man, trade you caps." Who was I to say no to Mean Joe Greene? The exchange was made, and Joe had the most colorful stocking cap of all the Steelers.

Enter Chuck Noll.

Noll was a stickler for many things, and he could see how Joe having a colorful hat and the rest of the team wearing the bland navy-blue watch caps might not be the best thing for team unity. So, by the next home game all Steelers were provided the black-and-gold stocking caps. I never found out, nor did I ask, if the new fashion statement caps came from the same discount store as mine, but the Steelers were uniformly uniform for pregame warm-ups and on the sideline during the game. As Andy Russell said, "No detail is too small for Chuck to pay attention to."

Another encounter with Joe also centered on cold weather. It was a late-season game, and Pittsburgh was experiencing typical December weather, cold and blustery. As was my wont, I was huddled close to the fire barrel—they actually burned wood in fifty-five-gallon drums on the sidelines for warmth. During the time the offense was on the field, I was showing the effects of the day's weather. Dwight White leaned in and said, "Man, you look cold." I replied, "Man, I am cold. I could use a little Annie Green Springs right about now."

A little edification for those who aren't wine connoisseurs. Annie Green Springs was one of those buck-a-bottle pop wines of the time. Not as popular as Boone's Farm, but with what I thought was a much classier label.

Greene rubbed his hands over the open flame and inquired, "Country Cherry or Berry Frost?"

I remember saying to myself, "If Annie Green Springs is good enough for Joe Greene to at least be familiar with, it's good enough for me."

Being around the practice field, at training camp, before and during games, in the Steelers locker room, it was easy to see Joe Greene was the Steelers' main man. He was never a boisterous presence, but the team looked to him for direction. He set the tone.

On the field it was easy to see his skill and intensity. It was also easy to see his lighter side. When things were going well Joe would flash a 10,000-watt smile. When Fats Holmes and he would stuff an opposing center, along with the guards, and clog the middle of the line, the smile was ear-to-ear. Coming off the field after a three-and-out, more of the same.

Joe had his serious moments, too. If the Steelers were behind, which wasn't often, he wasn't above asking, "What's going on?"

As much of a leader as Greene was, the other members of the Steel Curtain were equally important—Dwight White, L. C. Greenwood, and Ernie Holmes. Holmes was especially interesting to me, somewhat of an enigma—quiet, introspective, and, at times, intimidating in appearance. Although nicknamed "Fats" for most of his life, to me he was just a solidly built 6 feet 3, 260 pounds. Partnering with the others, Holmes was most effective in shutting down opposing offenses. There were many times when he was the equal of Greene and occasionally even surpassed Greene. I heard Noll tell a writer, "If you don't think Ernie Holmes is a force, look at the guy across from him at the end of the game—if the guy makes it to the end of the game."

Later in his career Ernie shaved his scalp in the form of an arrowhead. He contended that it kept him "pointed in the right direction," which I assumed was where the quarterback was located. He once registered at least one sack in six consecutive games, a Steelers record that stood for years.

Greene came to the Steelers as a foundation to build upon and proved to be that and more during his Pro Football Hall of Fame career. Although some in the general public may not have been aware of Mean Joe until his critically acclaimed Coca-Cola commercial of 1979, Steelers faithful knew how much Joe meant to the team from the start. The commercial, where he throws his game jersey to a youngster who offered him his Coke, is considered a classic.

The spot opens with a limping Greene entering a postgame stadium tunnel. A small boy offers Joe his Coke, which he promptly drains. The kid starts to walk away, when Greene says, "Hey, kid, here," and throws him the jersey.

Years later Joe recalled, "I can't tell you how many Cokes I've been offered over the years." He also related how the many takes of the one-minute spot required him to consume bottle after bottle of the soft drink. "Oh, at least a case. That's a lot of carbonation in one day." Joe also said they were going to use a can of Coke at first, "but my large hands made it look too small." The producers settled on a sixteen-ounce bottle for the actual commercial.

Noll was once offered $100,000 to have his signature on a Hershey bar. He turned it down, saying, "Let the players do these things." With a different attitude we may have seen Noll in an American Express commercial rather than other NFL coaches.

After the magical 1972 season, I was looking forward with much anticipation toward 1973. I was living full-time in Canton, working at the Pro Football Hall of Fame, but still making the two-hundred-mile round trip to the 'Burgh on game days.

Despite injuries, the Steelers broke from the gate like Secretariat, a horse that won thoroughbred racing's coveted Triple Crown that year.

One of the games won was 26–14 victory over the Jets. Namath was sidelined by one of his many post–SB III injuries. I was part of a pregame group that Joe Willie was entertaining with tales of the Big Apple. Having felt that the New York press made him out to be more than he actually was, I was prepared to not really like Joe that much. But in truth he was a charming personality—as he remains today. He was amazingly humble, kept his ego in check, and seemed like the kind of guy you would want to have a beer with—or a Johnnie Walker Red.

I got a real kick when a typical Western PA–type yelled from the front row of the stands at Three Rivers, "Hey, Namath, c'mere!" Joe looked up, went over, and accepted a box of cookies that Namath's mother, Rose, had entrusted the guy to give to Joe. Joe Willie seemed quite pleased.

The next week Hanratty helped the Steelers send the Bengals back to Cincinnati with their collective tail between their legs. He hit Ronnie Shanklin with a 51-yard touchdown that broke the ice in a game that had featured only scoring by Gerela and the Bengals' Horst Muhlmann. I always felt Hanratty was more than an average NFL backup. A prankster of the first order, he had a firm grasp of Noll's offense. Maybe even more than Noll had, perhaps.

Once in a skull session Noll took great care to draw up a play on the blackboard. After explaining the play in great detail, Noll asked, "Any questions?"

Hanratty volunteered, "Yeah, it won't work."

Noll: "Whattya you mean?"

Hanratty then pointed out a flaw that would doom the play's success. Noll, exasperated, said, "Why didn't you tell me?"

The Rat simply said, "You didn't ask me!"

This was just one example of Hanratty's let's-keep-it-loose approach to NFL football. It was never life or death to the Notre Dame graduate.

By this time in his career L. C. Greenwood, nicknamed "Hollywood Bags" (for reasons mostly unknown), was wearing gold football shoes.

For the Washington game on Monday night, Greene, Ernie Holmes, and Dwight White also donned "golden slippers."

While most associate the Super Bowl–era Steelers receiving exploits with HOFers Lynn Swann and John Stallworth, mention should be made of Barry Pearson, Ronnie Shanklin, Frank Lewis, and even Dave Smith. Not on a plane with Swann and Stallworth, they were important contributors to the cause and symbolically held the fort until the HOFers arrived in 1974. Pearson, a heady pattern runner from Northwestern, was the designated receiver on Franco's Immaculate Reception before Bradshaw launched the fateful toss toward Frenchy Fuqua—and Jack Tatum.

Continuing the rivalry in Oakland, Harris and Hanratty paced the victory over the home-standing Raiders, 17–9. As usual the defense contributed mightily. The secondary, outstanding all season, gave up a meaningless Lamonica-to-Biletnikoff TD late in the game, but it was purely cosmetic for the Raiders.

By this point in the season, interceptions seemed to me to be almost a given. On the whole the Steelers picked off thirty-seven passes in the fourteen-game season. Strong safety Mike Wagner led the team with eight. Long-forgotten John Rowser had six, as did Glen "Pine" Edwards. Ironically, HOFer Mel Blount had only four of the three-dozen-plus INTs. But teams were wisely avoiding his side of the field.

It was on to the playoffs, but by virtue of a lesser conference record, the Steelers were second fiddle to the Bengals, although both finished the season at 10-4. As a wild card the Steelers would face an encore with the Raiders.

Because the Steelers were already on the West Coast and would be playing in Oakland, they decided to stay out West and spend the week practicing in Palm Springs, a lush desert resort a hundred miles from Los Angeles. Probably not the most ideal setting for what would be an intense, hard-hitting football game.

Having beaten the Raiders earlier, in Oakland with Hanratty in place of Bradshaw, I felt confident. Sure, the game was a road game, but that was not a concern. Hadn't the Steelers won in Oakland earlier? Like all of Pittsburgh and western Pennsylvania, I was used to a Steelers victory. Why would today be any different?

The offense, led by Bradshaw this time, was as sluggish as it was in the earlier regular-season victory over the Silver and Black. Offensively, nothing much was happening for Pittsburgh in the first quarter, as Oakland jumped out to a 10–0 lead. Marv Hubbard blasted into the end zone on a 1-yard smash, and ageless George Blanda kicked a 25-yard field goal.

Kenny Stabler was at his "snakey-est," ending the day at fourteen for seventeen. Unlike the earlier game, when the Steelers' offense was rather pedestrian, the defense was not producing the multiple turnovers of before—no interceptions, no forced fumbles.

In a later conversation center Ray Mansfield, also long snapper of placekicks, told me that the Raiders would send in deflated footballs for field goals and extra points. Remember, this was when home teams furnished all game balls and before visiting teams could bring their own footballs to road games. That changed in 2006. The Ol' Ranger said, "The press reported that the balls had 'Go, Raiders' written on the laces in addition to being underinflated. I can tell you that what was written on the laces was a lot more X-rated than that. Some of the suggestions were physically impossible to perform, if you know what I mean."

Hubbard was one against whom it was tough to hold any animosity. I admired his toughness and sheer power. He was a force with or without the football. A power runner, he was also a formidable blocker—and a true character.

I was fortunate enough to encounter him later at several NFL alumni golf tournaments. He loved the game and was a fixture at many charitable tourneys over the years. In 1975 Oakland A's player Sal Bando and he won the American Airlines Golf Classic, which featured pro football and Major League Baseball players.

In conversation with Hubbard, he would remind you of his love of music. At the height of his playing career he recorded several what he called "jock rock" songs—"Fullbacks Ain't Supposed to Cry," "Country Boogie," and "Legend in His Own Mind." Although his recordings never made the Billboard 100, they were well received, and Hubbard continued to play clubs and other events. Teammates said he enjoyed nothing more than sitting on his front porch telling "NFL war stories" while strumming his guitar.

It wasn't as important then, or at least it wasn't spoken of in such reverential terms as it is today, but NFL teams were always concerned with protecting the quarterback's blind side—a pass rush coming from the offense's left side (for a right-handed quarterback). In more recent times there is a true significance attached to the left offensive-tackle position.

To give the Mad Bomber, Lamonica, time to throw deep and successfully, the Raiders' left side of the offensive line had to be awesome. Including center Jim Otto, guard Gene Upshaw, and tackle Art Shell, it was nearly impenetrable. Appropriately, all three are enshrined in the Pro Football Hall of Fame after long and storied careers. Like all Raiders HOF inductees, the trio chose Al Davis as their presenter.

After Stabler replaced Lamonica, these road-grader operatives continued to pay huge dividends for the Raiders. The transformation was seamless. With Stabler at the helm the team became " left-handed." That is, most running plays went left—while right-handed teams, the vast majority of NFL ball clubs, ran to the right. Seeing the giant linemen leading a power back like Hubbard, or later Mark van Eeghen, had to be a fearsome sight for a linebacker and even worse for a cornerback or safety whose job was to "fill," or, stated another way, sacrifice one's body to take out the lead blockers. Much of the Raiders' rushing yardage was piled up running left. Bob "Boomer" Brown, the right tackle, functioned as a left tackle would in a right-handed offense. He was the one who had the Snake's blind side.

Jim Otto was a fascinating character to me. At the inception of the AFL, he was a 200-pound center from the University of Miami. Through the years he worked to increase his weight to a more realistic 256. The thing that fascinated me most about "Double Zero," his jersey number, was his helmet. To say it was battle scarred would be an understatement. You could practically determine the Raiders' schedule from the smudges of opponents' paint on it—and gouges taken out of it.

You could also say the same thing about the loyal Raider himself. He endured many injuries and surgeries to keep up his iron-man streak.

One season in the mid-'70s, Biletnikoff's name was misspelled on the back of his jersey and remained so for the entire season. When a National Football League Properties publication featured a realistic illustration of the Raiders' wideout, Al LoCasale called to upbraid the NFLP art director for publishing "such a travesty of a painting." When it was explained that the actual jersey had the misspelling, Little Al replied, "That shouldn't matter."

Until the NFL cracked down on Stickum, Slippery Fred, as did other Raiders, slathered the gummy substance on his socks, on his legs, on his arms, and mostly on his sure hands. More than once I heard a Steelers defender complain about the condition of a ball after the HOFer made a catch. Defensive back Lester Hayes was another adherent of the adhesive.

But the Raiders receiver who really scared me was Clifford Branch. Signs at Oakland's home field read like a CHPs (California Highway Patrol) warning: "Speed Kills, No. 21." Branch, a legitimate track star, gathered in 501 passes in his career, averaging 17.3 yards per catch. It was Branch who caught a late-game pass in the 1975 AFC Championship Game deep in Steelers territory that frightened me most. Had he been able to slither out of bounds to stop the clock, who knows if the Raiders could have turned a 16–10 Steelers victory into a 17–16 Raiders win with a touchdown on a final play or two? As it was time ran out. I don't think in my time on the sidelines I've ever experienced a longer ten seconds.

It was about this time that Pittsburgh fans really got behind their team. For years the Steelers were known as "lovable losers." Now the Steelers were winning consistently and were fully embraced. While it was possible for me to get my buddies end-zone seats for three dollars—yes, that was the general admission price—in 1970, '71, and '72, it became impossible to score those tickets for 1973. Seeing the Steelers at Three Rivers was the thing to do and the place to be.

To say the fans were enthusiastic may be doing them a disservice. They were more than that. The noise level was deafening. The loyalty just poured out of the stands. The aforementioned signs—it seemed every Steeler was adopted by some group and a banner was hung—were ubiquitous. Hardly a space in the stadium was left unadorned.

In the days before the NFL found "revenue streams," the fans fashioned their own Steelers regalia and banners. They came early and they stayed late. They cheered long and loud. They were into it, as the saying went.

With Steelers tickets hard to come by for home games, it was nothing to see busload after busload of fans disembark at Cleveland's Municipal Stadium when the Steelers played the Browns. The cavernous lakefront stadium rocked with as many, if not more, Steelers fans than Browns fans. Sometimes the action in the stands was as intense as the action on the field. "Take the bus and leave the driving to us" was an open invitation for the traveling Steelers fans to sample the healing waters of the Iron City and Duquesne brewing companies.

Steelers fans were not shy about putting their money where their mouths were. Taking the Steelers, "Stillers" to the true native Pittsburghers, and giving the points in a bet was a ritual. As Mansfield once said, "It's not whether you win or lose, it's if you cover the spread."

The truth of this was driven home to me one time when the Steelers were winning, but not by enough to cover. They had the ball and were driving, but it was late and Noll was more interested in chewing up clock than whether some fan from McKees Rocks was going to collect from his bookie. A Gerela field goal or a touchdown would have won most bets.

As Bradshaw was milking the clock with the Steelers in field-goal range, one fan was at the front-row railing exhorting the head coach to kick a field goal. When the offense kept moving the ball and showing no signs of calling on Gerela, said fan became quite emotional. In language unbefitting a Sunday, he told Noll what he thought of his coaching methods. Unfazed and probably unhearing, Noll kept Gerela on the sideline.

The clock wound down. The Steelers won. And Mr. Fanatic Fan really went off on Noll. He was very passionate and negative in his critique of a coach who would go on to win four Super Bowls and become enshrined in the Pro Football Hall of Fame the minute he was eligible.

As disappointing as the 1973 wild card loss to the Raiders was, many of us were optimistic about the Steelers' chances for the 1974 season. As it would play out, the optimism wasn't misplaced.

5

Steelers Feel a Draft in '74

The Steelers' road to Super Bowl IX didn't start with their Week One blanking of the Baltimore Colts, 30–0, in Pittsburgh.

It started several months before on January 29–30 in the NFL Draft, when the Steelers' brain trust of head coach Chuck Noll, Art Rooney Jr., personnel director Dick Haley, coaches, and scouts came together at Three Rivers Stadium and selected four future Hall of Famers in wide receivers Lynn Swann and John Stallworth, center Mike Webster, and middle linebacker Jack Lambert.

It's considered by most the greatest draft in pro football history, surpassing the 1958 Green Bay Packer draft that yielded future Hall of Famers in running back Jim Taylor, linebacker Ray Nitschke, guard Jerry Kramer, and All-Pro linebacker Dan Currie.

The Steelers selected four future Canton enshrines in the first five rounds. As amazing as that is, consider that only one player not picked by Pittsburgh in the draft that year—Notre Dame tight end Dave Casper, chosen by rival Oakland with the 45th overall pick—would join the Steelers' Fab Four in Canton.

Pittsburgh chose USC's Swann in the first round with the 21st overall pick; Kent State's Lambert in the second round at No. 46; Alabama A&M's Stallworth in the fourth round at No. 82; and Wisconsin's Webster in the fifth round at No. 125.

The graceful Swann, inducted in Canton in 2001, would star for the Steelers through 1982, earning All-Pro honors three times and being named MVP of Super Bowl X, the first wideout to receive the honor. One year later Raiders receiver Fred Biletnikoff followed in Swann's footsteps by being named MVP of Super Bowl XI.

Lambert, named to the Hall in 1990, played for Pittsburgh through 1984 and was an eight-time All-Pro. Lambert was the league's Defensive Rookie of the Year in 1974 and a two-time NFL Defensive Player of the Year. Thinner than the all-time-great linebackers who preceded him—Nitschke, Sam Huff, Joe Schmidt, Dick Butkus, Nick Buoniconti, and Willie Lanier—Lambert quickly established himself as one of football's most ferocious players.

The elegant Stallworth, selected by the Hall in 2002, was a member of the Steelers' roster through 1987. He retired as the team's all-time leader in touchdown catches with sixty-three and receiving yards with 8,723.

Webster, considered by some the greatest center in NFL history, was enshrined in Canton in 1997. His muscular arms and short sleeves popularized a look modern NFL players have adopted. Iron Mike started 150 consecutive games from 1976 to 1986 and was a seven-time All-Pro.

Each of the four earned four Super Bowl rings with the Steelers. Yet the irony of the Steelers' storied draft is how close Pittsburgh came to missing out on its Canton quartet.

There had hardly been any disagreement inside the Steelers' inner circle on their plan of attack on draft day. Noll was seeking offensive weapons in general, receivers in particular. Since the Steel Curtain defense was, in Noll's words, "pretty good," the plan was to bolster the offense.

Noll favored Stallworth and felt him worthy of a first-round pick. But John was a big fish from a little pond, having played at a small black southern school in Alabama A&M. Swann was a Southern Cal star whose skill and charisma captivated fans from coast to coast and captured the attention of NFL scouts and coaches. Everyone was in agreement that Swann would become a star in the NFL and was a bona fide first-round pick.

Not everyone thought the same of Stallworth, and it was to the Steelers' benefit that Stallworth was used in the Senior Bowl as a defensive back and not at his natural position. There was game film of Stallworth that showed his skills, and the Steelers had the lone copy. They were supposed to pass it on, but it never left the Steelers' headquarters.

Noll wasn't thrilled with Swann's 4.65 in the 40. The Steelers' brain trust had arguments about Swann. They believed he was a great player, but his speed was suspect. The BLESTO-V scouting service would later record Swann at 4.59 a few days before the draft, and while Steelers team president Dan Rooney said that broke the tie as far as he was concerned, Pittsburgh's internal debate continued on draft day and nearly caused them to lose their first-round pick.

The Steelers' discord continued while they were on the clock. As time ticked away on the Steelers' allotted fifteen-minute window, Dallas appeared poised to pass Pittsburgh in the draft selection. The Cowboys filled out an index card and headed to the podium at the Americana Hotel in New York City to hand it in. The card contained the name Lynn Swann.

With Steelers scouts having convinced Noll that Swann would be gone if they didn't draft him in the first round and that Stallworth would still be on the board in the fourth round, Pittsburgh announced its decision with just five seconds to spare.

Had the Steelers deliberated any longer or selected Stallworth in the first round, Swann would have worn the Cowboys' royal blue and silver rather than Pittsburgh's black and gold. A delicious irony, considering the levitating leaps and clutch circus catches Swann burned the 'Boys with in Super Bowls X and XIII.

The Steelers' selecting Swann before the Cowboys could have provided an early flash point in the Pittsburgh-Dallas Super Bowl rivalry that served as one of the highlights of the decade.

Credit in convincing Noll to wait on Stallworth went in large part to club scout Bill Nunn, former sports editor of the *Pittsburgh Courier* who joined the Steelers in the late 1960s and was considered one of the league's top talent evaluators.

While working for the *Courier*, a nationally circulated African Amer-

ican newspaper, Nunn developed a solid rapport with football personnel at small black colleges. Like Lloyd Wells, whose scouting of
black schools in the 1960s had led to the American Football League's
Kansas City Chiefs winning the 1970 Super Bowl with a largely African American roster, Nunn found some of Pittsburgh's top talent at
such schools—defensive end L. C. Greenwood of Arkansas A&M,
defensive tackle Ernie Holmes from Texas Southern, and Stallworth.

While Nunn convinced a skeptical Noll that Stallworth would
remain beneath the radar, Pittsburgh went after another hidden gem
that scout Tim Rooney discovered by accident.

In August 1973 Rooney, seeking the offensive firepower Noll coveted, headed to Kent State to scout a speedy receiver named Gerald
Tinker. Kent State is not far from Pittsburgh, and the Steelers long
enjoyed a friendly relationship with the university's coaches and scouts.
As Rooney chatted with coach Don James, who decades later earned
a share of the 1991 national championship as head coach at Washington and also mentored Nick Saban, he took James's advice to take a
courtesy look at a tall, skinny-legged linebacker.

It was a muddy day, and the players were practicing in a cinder
parking lot. While the rest of the team was going half-speed, Lambert hurled himself at a running back. When Lambert stood up, he
was picking cinders from his arms. The more Rooney watched Lambert in practice, the more the 6-foot-4, 190-pounder impressed him.
If Lambert could put on weight, Rooney figured his toughness would
put him over the top.

Rooney gave Lambert good grades in his scouting report; he thought
Jack's intangibles incredible. Steelers linebackers coach Woody Widenhofer believed Lambert would be a solid special-teams player while
he gained experience. Despite reticence from the rest of the organization, Pittsburgh picked Lambert in the second round.

The Steelers sat silent through the third round, Pittsburgh having
traded its pick to Oakland the previous year for defensive tackle Tom
Keating. Keating had been a mainstay on the Raiders' feared defense
of the late 1960s; he was pivotal in Oakland winning the 1967 AFL
Championship and, despite a painful injury that caused his ankle to

swell to near softball size, put forth a courageous effort in Super Bowl II against Kramer.

Noll figured the experienced Keating would be a good fit for the Steel Curtain, and while it was against his better judgment to surrender draft picks and potential for someone else's castoffs, he pulled the trigger on the deal for Keating. The move didn't work out, and Keating lasted just one season in Pittsburgh.

Thanks to a trade with New England, Pittsburgh had two picks in the fourth round. Noll got his man when the Steelers chose Stallworth, and they also drafted defensive back Jimmy Allen, who played for four seasons in Pittsburgh before being dealt to Detroit.

When Round Five arrived the Steelers selected Webster from their wish list. Noll, a former offensive lineman for Cleveland, loved what he saw in a guy whose smallish size caused some scouts to downgrade him. Webster stood 6 feet 1 and weighed 230 pounds, but Steelers scouts saw him beating bigger men in Big 10 games. Noll watched Webster handle a much larger defensive tackle in the East-West game. Little did anyone know that Webster's dedication to weight lifting and strength training would set a standard.

Almost forgotten in the Steelers' historic draft haul were the freeagent signings that followed the next afternoon. On January 30 Pittsburgh signed free agents Donnie Shell, who would become a starting safety, and Randy Grossman, a contributor at tight end. Both would win four Super Bowls with the Steelers.

When Noll arrived in Pittsburgh in 1969 he was, by his own admission, surprised the Steelers had a first-class organization. Their talent department was improving, Art Rooney Jr. participating in the BLESTO scouting system while also devoting his time to supervising scouting and player procurement. Beginning in 1969 the Steelers drafted players with great promise. They didn't draft to fill a position but rather to select the best possible athlete, even if it meant picking a player for a position that was already stocked.

It didn't matter if the Steelers needed someone at a particular position, Noll once explained. Teams made mistakes in the draft when they panicked and said, "We don't have someone at this position." Then

they drafted a player not as good as someone else, and the other player
makes All-Pro on another team. Pittsburgh's philosophy for drafting
is that when it got to a point where there was no particular standout,
then Noll and the brain trust drafted by position. "But we'll always
find a spot for a guy with size, speed, and physical ability," Noll said.
"If we can upgrade the team at any spot, we're going to help ourselves."

Noll said there were no great secrets to the Steelers' success in the
draft, but he did acknowledge that luck played a role. Drafting a player
is nothing more than guessing what he will do in a different element.
The Steelers sought to leave no stone unturned in getting information to make a sound decision. Noll knew, however, that in the end
all NFL teams are basically taking someone else's word about a player.

Pittsburgh felt it unrealistic to grade more than 150 players, an
amount that covered the first five or six rounds of the draft. They
gathered as much information as possible about the player from his
collegiate career, while also placing great importance on their performance in bowl games and all-star games. The Steelers saw the latter as an opportunity to remove some of the uncertainty about how
a player adapts from moving from a familiar situation to an unfamil-
iar one with new teammates.

When the Steelers drafted Greene in 1969, he was considered by
most the best defensive lineman in college football. The Steelers were
also interested in quarterback Terry Hanratty, a Pittsburgh native who
starred at Notre Dame. Noll, hired the day before the draft, wanted to
take Greene No. 1, believing they could draft Hanratty in a later round.
The Steelers reasoned that they needed the immediate help that Greene
would bring more than they needed a quarterback. One Pittsburgh
newspaper chided the pick with a headline that read: "Joe Who?"

Noll, however, was proved right. Hanratty was still available in the
second round, and the Steelers selected him, and then drafted Terry
Bradshaw the following year. Following years saw the Steelers select
Harris, J. T. Thomas, and Swann in the first round. By 1975 only four
players on Pittsburgh's Super Bowl roster had not been drafted by the
team or signed as free-agent rookies.

Pittsburgh was not against trading for talent; Frenchy Fuqua and

Bobby Walden had been dealt for. When Noll was hired in Pittsburgh other teams tried to trade for the few good players Pittsburgh had in return for second-line players. Noll would tell them that they were asking for a starter in return for a backup, and their response was, "Our backups could start for Pittsburgh."

Noll would trade quality for quality, particularly if Pittsburgh was loaded at a given position, or he would deal a second-line player for someone who wasn't quality at the moment but had the potential to be. The latter was always a consideration for positions where Pittsburgh might not have had a quality player at the time.

Talent wasn't a concern for the Steelers' class of '74. But there was one more fact, now almost forgotten, that helped speed their progress. NFL veterans went on strike during that summer, meaning that for several critical weeks the rookies had Pittsburgh's training camp at St.. Vincent College to themselves. Noll cited the work the rookies got done during that time as critical to their being able to help the team as quickly as they did.

The class of '74 got acquainted quickly. A nutcracker drill matched Webster opposite Lambert. Because he's essentially going on the offensive, the defensive man has the edge in the blitz-pickup exercise. Some expected Lambert to win out against Webster, but Iron Mike handled Lambert in the first collision and then did it again. It wasn't that Lambert was bad, Art Rooney Jr. reflected. It's just that Jack was trying to get past a fellow future Hall of Famer. Watching the drill, Steelers writer Phil Musick asked Rooney Jr., "What little old lady told you about that linebacker?"

It seemed a legitimate question, considering that for several decades the Steelers had struggled to make the right personnel moves. Pittsburgh had parted ways with young quarterbacks named John Unitas and Len Dawson and had declined to draft a running back named Jim Brown. The Steelers reached their nadir in 1963 when they went the first seven rounds of the draft without a pick because they had dealt them away; two years later Pittsburgh surrendered five of its first six picks.

That changed with Noll's arrival and the Steelers' relationship with the Pittsburgh-based BLESTO service, headed by former Pittsburgh defensive back Jack Butler. Following years of futility, it was finally Pittsburgh's turn to get the hot hand in picking players. The rest of the NFL would spend much of the decade getting caught in the Steelers' draft.

The Raiders had their own gang of four in the '74 draft. Opting for offense Oakland chose Florida A&M tackle Henry Lawrence, Casper in the second, Colgate running back Mark van Eeghen in the third, and Ohio State wideout Morris Bradshaw in Round Four.

It didn't take long for the foursome to have optimum impact in Oakland. Van Eeghen became a starter a year later, Casper in '76. Lawrence joined the starting rotation in '77, and by '78 Bradshaw gave the Raiders four starters from their '74 draft. Each earned a Super Bowl ring with Oakland in '76, and Bradshaw, Lawrence, and van Eeghen claimed a second ring in '80. Lawrence picked up a third ring as a starter on the Raiders '83 title team that relocated to Los Angeles following the '81 season.

Casper, called the "Ghost" after the cartoon character, was a five-time Pro Bowler and First-Team All-Pro following his Hall of Fame career at Notre Dame. Named to the NFL's 1970s All-Decade team, he figured prominently in two of the most famous plays in NFL history.

The first occurred in the 1977 Christmas Eve playoff classic in Baltimore. Facing the Eastern Division champion Baltimore Colts in Memorial Stadium, the reigning Super Bowl champion Raiders needed a miracle to force overtime. Oakland got it in the form of Casper's over-the-shoulder Willie Mays–style catch of a Kenny Stabler pass. Called the "Ghost to the Post," the spectacular catch resulted in a 42-yard gain that set up the Raiders' game-tying field goal that forced overtime. Casper's 10-yard touchdown catch in the second overtime gave Oakland a 37–31 win in what was the longest game in NFL history to that point.

On September 10 of the following season the Ghost reappeared to again save the Raiders. Trailing AFC West rival San Diego 20–14 with just ten seconds remaining in the game, Stabler dropped the ball as he was about to be sacked. Running back Pete Banaszak recovered the apparent fumble at the Chargers' 12 but then dropped the ball. As the ball continued to roll forward Casper kicked it forward at the

5-yard line and fell on it in the end zone to tie the game. The point-
after attempt gave Oakland a stunning 21–20 comeback win despite
San Diego's protests that Stabler had flicked the ball forward for an
incomplete pass.

Stabler, Banaszak, and Casper acknowledged later that they had
deliberately fumbled or batted the ball toward the end zone. The play
caused the NFL to institute a rules change, making it illegal for the
teammate of a ball carrier to advance the ball following a fumble on
fourth down or in the final two minutes of regulation.

Casper was cut from the same cloth as contemporaries Jackie Smith,
Kellen Winslow, and Ozzie Newsome in that he was a tight end who
was a deep threat. Predecessors at the position like John Mackey, Mike
Ditka, and Ron Kramer excelled at taking short passes and converting them into long gains by rumbling through secondaries like run-
away trucks. Casper wasn't fast, but he was smart and knew how to
read coverages.

A converted offensive lineman at Notre Dame, Casper would catch
378 passes and score fifty-two touchdowns over his eleven-year NFL
career. Charlie Sanders, an All-Pro tight end with Detroit in the 1970s,
thought Casper a great fit for the Raiders. "He was unbelievable,"
Sanders said. "Sometimes a tight end fits a system and he did that
with the Raiders."

Casper could do it all at the tight-end position. He was blessed not
only with a big body but also with agility and speed. He blocked well
and had good hands, hauling in nearly every pass thrown in his direction. He would play in five straight Pro Bowls from 1976 to 1980 and
had forty-eight receptions or more in each of those seasons. A big-
play threat, Casper had ten touchdowns in 1976 and nine in '78. "He's
so big and wide that not only can defenders not get around him to the
ball, sometimes they can't see it coming," Madden said. "It would be
fair to say he's one of the best blocking tight ends in football."

Casper was one of several new offensive weapons the Raiders
unveiled for the 1974 season. Van Eeghen, a 223-pound power back,
followed in the Raiders' tradition of hard-running fullbacks Hewritt
Dixon and Marv Hubbard. Like Hubbard, van Eeghen was an alum

of Colgate. Van Eeghen led the Raiders in rushing five straight seasons and was a thousand-yard back three straight years from 1976 to
1978. By the time he left the Raiders in 1982, van Eeghen had made his
mark—he was the franchise's all-time leading rusher with 5,907 yards.

Helping lead the way for Raiders runners was Lawrence, a 272-
pound right tackle who teamed with left tackle Art Shell to give the
Raiders two of the biggest and most talented tackles in the NFL. Lawrence became a fixture in the starting lineup in 1977 and gained Pro
Bowl honors in 1983 and '84.

Bradshaw, the former Buckeye, was a speedy receiver who would
play in 104 games for the Raiders from 1974 to 1981. Bradshaw teamed
with Cliff Branch to give the Raiders the vertical passing game coveted by Davis.

Bradshaw's most memorable moment for the Silver and Black, however, came in retirement. In the fall of 2015 he lit the torch in honor of
the departed Davis prior to the Raiders' hosting of the Arizona Cardinals in a preseason contest.

Unlike the Steelers, the Raiders did not belong to BLESTO. At the
time Oakland and Cincinnati were the only NFL teams that did not
belong to any scouting combine.

There were no great mysteries in the Raiders' scouting and drafting process. Davis excelled as an evaluator of talent, and Madden was
in agreement with Al on how players would be used. Oakland wanted
players who could contribute for a long period of time. The Raiders
looked for long-range solidity, not momentary contributors. They
picked players with the idea that they would be wearing silver and
black for eight to ten seasons. A player might not play much in his
first or second season, but the Raiders didn't want players who would
live or die on whether they played full-time as a rookie.

Perfect examples of this Raiders philosophy were found in future
Hall of Famers Kenny Stabler and Art Shell. Stabler didn't start for
his first five seasons, Shell his first two. But they made contributions
in other ways.

Oakland did not subscribe to the "best athlete" theory in drafting.
Madden knew a player could be great in college but questioned how

long that player's talent would last. He didn't want guys who were drafted at their peak and lost their edge a season or two into their pro career. "There is one key point about picking the so-called great athlete," Madden said. "It doesn't mean a thing if he doesn't perform with the team in mind." He had seen players who were great physical specimens and played a mean game of one-on-one basketball. "But in a game," Madden said, "they don't always work out."

Oakland also didn't draft for a specific need. Madden and Davis wouldn't, for example, draft a right offensive tackle just because they felt they needed a right offensive tackle. They believed that if they went into a draft with a preconceived notion of what they had to have, there might not be a first-round pick who was really worthy of being a first-round pick. But because they felt they had to fill a position, they drafted the player in the first round regardless. To avoid this, the Raiders resisted drafting for need.

Offensive tackle John Vella was a prime example of Oakland's philosophy. When Vella was selected in the second round in '72, the Raiders had two standout tackles in Shell and Bob Brown. Vella did not play regularly for the next two seasons, but when Brown left, Vella was there to take his place. He knew the Raiders' system and had enough experience to be effective.

It was the same situation with Stabler. When he was drafted, Raiders QB Daryle Lamonica was MVP of the AFL. In time Stabler replaced Lamonica and became a star. Oakland's strategy was to always have a backup ready so there's no need to panic to find a replacement. Monte Johnson, who took over at middle linebacker for Dan Conners in 1975, had been a backup defensive lineman behind Outland Trophy winners Rich Glover and Larry Jacobson at Nebraska. He never starred at Nebraska, but his play as a backup linebacker for the Raiders in 1974 helped him be ready to replace Conners.

The Raiders believed so strongly in drafting objectively rather than for need that they would not pick a player with the notion that he would replace a particular player in two or three seasons. The player drafted would eventually play the position for which he was picked, but the decision to make him a starter would be made without pressure. This philosophy of drafting players to initially be backups allowed Oakland to maintain a team balanced with a constant flow of veterans and young players.

If there was a need for an immediate starter due to injury, the Raiders would elevate a backup or trade for a quality player. Defensive linemen Otis Sistrunk and Bubba Smith were examples of the latter.

Mostly, the Raiders sought to stock their roster with players who came from winning backgrounds in college. It was an unwritten rule in Oakland's drafts, and it resulted in Davis and Madden selecting players like Stabler (Alabama), Vella and halfback Clarence Davis (USC), Casper (Notre Dame) and fellow tight end Bob Moore (Stanford), Johnson (Nebraska), defensive backs Jack Tatum (Ohio State), and fellow Buckeye Neal Colzie.

Davis and Madden didn't neglect players from smaller schools. The left side of their O-line was manned by all-time greats Upshaw (Texas A&I) and Shell (Maryland State–Eastern Shore). Sistrunk, a fixture on Oakland's defensive front, didn't even play college football.

The Raiders didn't rely on computer readouts when drafting; they leaned on logic and common sense. They chose punter Ray Guy in the first round in 1973 and used him as a special-teams weapon. Madden and Davis also drafted for speed. All else could be taught, but a player either had speed or didn't. The Raiders didn't just want speed on offense; they wanted their defensive backs to be quick and sacrificed size on the defensive line for swiftness.

The Steelers and Raiders differed in strategy when it came to drafting, but the results were much the same. The Steelers felt that once they became a contender, if they could draft three impact players per year it was a great turnover. Prior to Pittsburgh's 1973 season, author Roy Blount Jr. penned an inside look at the Steelers titled *Three Bricks Shy of a Load*. The Steelers found those three bricks and more in '74, and so did the Raiders. That put Pittsburgh and Oakland on a collision course with reigning champion Miami for AFC supremacy.

The Raiders' road to the conference title game began on a manic Monday night before a national television audience in Buffalo. It was the fifth straight year the Silver and Black opened their regular season on the road. Stabler had signed a future pact with the World Football League, but the stylish southpaw didn't let that stop him from slicing and dicing NFL defenses.

In Orchard Park Raiders defensive tackle Art Thoms's 29-yard TD off a fumble recovery marked the second of three lead changes in a wild fourth quarter. But Buffalo rallied for a wild 21–20 win on a 13-yard pass from Joe Ferguson to Ahmad Rashad.

The reigning Western Division champions returned home and, despite having just five days to prepare for Kansas City, romped past the Chiefs 27–7. Amid brilliant sunshine in the Coliseum, Stabler threaded a pass through two defenders to Mike Siani for one score, and Pete Banaszak blasted through the middle for 20 yards and another touchdown. Linebacker Monte Johnson stormed into the Chiefs' backfield for one of four Raiders sacks and then stole a pass for one of five Oakland interceptions. Casper's second TD catch capped the victory and sparked a nine-game win streak.

The Raiders returned east to rematch with rival Pittsburgh in a late-afternoon game played under leaden skies. Just minutes into the 4:00 p.m. kickoff the skies opened up, and a heavy downpour descended on Three Rivers Stadium. Steelers radio announcer Jack Fleming told listeners that the "wrong kind of cloud just drifted over the stadium."

With the rain illuminated by the flaring stadium lights, the Raiders recorded the game's first big play, Ron Smith's 46-yard punt return setting Oakland up at the Steelers' 28-yard line. On first down Clarence Davis slanted behind Shell for three yards, and Stabler followed with a first-down strike to Fred Biletnikoff at the 13. Hubbard rumbled to the 4-yard line and fumbled, but Cliff Branch covered it. Hubbard followed Shell and Upshaw on a slant left and carried to the 1.

Fleming: *"Here's Stabler rolling out to the right, and he's going to go in for the touchdown! Grabbing him at the 2-yard line was L. C. Greenwood, but it was too late, as Stabler hobbled into the end zone on a rollout play to the right. That was a big thing for Oakland, quieting this crowd down and getting the Steelers in a hole from the very start."*

Using the same game plan from the previous season's playoff win in Oakland, the Raiders pounded Pittsburgh with their ground game.

Hubbard slammed for 96 yards and Davis for 63 as the Raiders ran 47 times for 177 yards.

Defensively, big Bubba Smith crashed in on Steelers starting quarterback "Jefferson Street" Joe Gilliam and sacked him for a 20-yard loss. Thoms and Sistrunk combined for another sack, as Pittsburgh was held scoreless for the first time in 132 games.

The Steelers had opportunities. With the rain blowing in sheets late in the first quarter, Fuqua's apparent touchdown run was negated by a holding penalty. Roy Gerela's follow-up 36-yard field goal attempt was wide. Fuqua was playing for Franco Harris, who started the game but was sidelined by a slight ankle sprain.

Early in the second quarter, George Atkinson's interception in Steelers' territory, and his return inside the 20-yard line set up Oakland's second touchdown.

Fleming: *"Gilliam is very deep, looking, throwing under pressure, intercepted! Intercepting was George Atkinson, and Oakland is right back in scoring position."*

Myron Cope, Fleming's color analyst, credited Bubba Smith for forcing the turnover.

Cope: *"Big pressure on Gilliam from Bubba Smith, who roared in on him, slipped aside a blocker, and belted Joe just as he let the ball go."*

On the next play, Stabler found Branch from 19 yards out to increase Oakland's lead.

Fleming: *"Stabler, back to pass, has lots of time, spots his receiver. Touchdown, Oakland! Hitting Cliff Branch in the end zone, and the Raiders lead 13 to nothing."*

Cope: *"When a quarterback has all that time and you're trying to stay with a 9.2 sprinter, which is what Branch is, it's a tough proposition."*

George Blanda, who had recently celebrated his forty-seventh birthday, booted the extra point and followed with a 35-yard field goal to make it 17–0 at halftime, the score standing up to the final gun. Branch, having replaced the injured Siani in the starting lineup, would go on to pace the Raiders in receptions in 1974 with 60 catches for a league-high 1,092 yards and 13 touchdowns.

Putting forth perhaps its finest effort of the season, the Oakland defense pitched its lone shutout of the season and its first since a 42–0 victory over the visiting Giants in Week Eight of the '73 campaign. The Raiders limited Gilliam and Terry Bradshaw to a combined 9 completions in 33 attempts, picking off three passes and surrendering just 117 yards through the air.

At home against Cincinnati, Oakland fell behind late and was forced to mount a desperate drive minus time-outs and huddles. Stabler's clutch passes to Biletnikoff, Moore, and Siani moved the ball to the Bengals' 2-yard line. With thirteen seconds left Raiders announcer Bill King made the decisive call on KNBR 68:

"What a critical situation here . . . Stabler under center, gives the ball to Smith . . . Smith running wide to the right . . . Touchdown, Oakland!"

The Raiders' 30–27 comeback win sent them to San Francisco on a high note. Hubbard churned over the Candlestick Park AstroTurf for 117 yards and one TD, and Branch burned cornerback Bruce Taylor on a 64-yard score.

"Taylor didn't get burned," King excitedly told listeners. "He got absolutely enveloped in a conflagration!"

Trailing 24–14 in the third quarter Banaszak bulled into the end zone from a yard out, Atkinson's fumble recovery led to a Stabler-to-Casper score, and Harold Hart's 40-yard fumble return on a punt completed the Raiders' San Francisco treat, 35–24.

In Week Nine in Oakland Smith and Gerald Irons helped shut down surging Detroit, which was riding a win streak of its own. Altie Taylor, Charlie Sanders, and the rest of the Lion offense was tamed, Conners pilfered two passes, and Hubbard helped lead a ground attack that amassed 284 yards and three TDs. Branch had two TD catches in a 35–13 romp.

The Raiders then had a rare and intriguing encounter with the Dallas Cowboys in *Monday Night Football*'s first Saturday-night game in what was the regular-season finale for both teams.

Prior to the season some saw the Cowboys-Raiders collision in the Coliseum as a possible Super Bowl preview. Dallas and Oakland had come close to meeting in the Super Bowl on several occasions. On New Year's Eve 1967 the Raiders romped past Houston in the

AFL title game, but Dallas endured a late loss to Green Bay in the fabled Ice Bowl.

In 1970 the Cowboys claimed the NFC crown with a win over San Francisco in the 49ers' final game at Kezar Stadium, but the Raiders fell to Baltimore in the AFC Championship. Dallas returned to the Super Bowl in the 1971 season, but Oakland suffered an off year and failed to make the playoffs for the first time in five seasons.

In 1973 Oakland and Dallas both lost their respective conference title games by identical 27–10 finals, the Cowboys dropping a decision in Texas Stadium to Minnesota and the Raiders bowing to Miami in the Orange Bowl.

The December 14 matchup was the first regular-season meeting between America's Team and America's Most Wanted. In 1972 they faced off in their first preseason game, Dallas earning a 16–10 decision. The Raiders rebounded to win four straight in the preseason series from 1973 to 1976.

Cowboys-Raiders Super Bowls in the years from 1967 to 1973 could have been classics. Certainly, the story lines were there. From 1967 to 1969 Dallas-Oakland would have matched two of the premier powerhouse teams in the warring NFL and AFL.

By the time the Cowboys took the Coliseum turf on a cool, drizzly night they were out of the playoff picture for the first time since 1965. Despite the fact they would be, as Pittsburgh-area native Perry Como famously sang, home for the holidays, the Cowboys were the hottest team in football heading into Oakland. It led to a playoff-like atmosphere in the sold-out Coliseum as Stabler and Roger Staubach dueled in their first and only regular-season matchup.

If Staubach was Captain America, Stabler was Captain Comeback. Madden called Stabler as good a quarterback as he's ever seen in a two-minute drill. The list of the Snake's slippery escapes is a lengthy one. In the 1972 playoffs he gave the Raiders the lead against Pittsburgh with an improbable 30-yard touchdown run with 1:13 left. He defeated the Dolphins in the '74 playoffs in the "Sea of Hands" game. In '75 Stabler beat the Redskins and Falcons in overtime games. In '76 Stabler stunned the Steelers in the season opener and put it to the Patriots in the final minute of their playoff game; in '78 the Snake stunned San Diego with the "Holy Roller."

If Snake was a Holy Roller on Sunday afternoons, he was a Holy Terror on Saturday nights. He was said to study game plans by the blinking lights of a jukebox. He was a throwback to Bobby Layne, ironically enough a former Steeler as well as Lion. The pair once played together in a celebrity golf tournament. Layne grabbed Stabler in the lobby of the hotel and told him, "C'mon, Lefty. We've got to warm up." Layne took Stabler to the bar, even though it was eight in the morning.

Stabler may have considered himself to be in the minor leagues when compared to Layne as a party guy, but the Snake was held to high standards in Oakland. He was said to carouse with a woman named "Wonderfully Wicked Wanda." Stories circulated in Oakland Coliseum parking lots prior to kickoff that Snake had been seen partying into the dawn hours in Oakland and Alameda, Concord and Pleasanton.

Stabler had been the hero his entire athletic life, from Foley, Alabama, to the University of Alabama to the Oakland Raiders. He arrived in Oakland as a skinny, 6-foot-2, 170-pounder, but lifting weights and drinking beer boosted his weight to a solid 215. His Layne-like persona made him beloved by teammates; he was the Easy Rider from the "Redneck Riviera," the Gulf Coast of Alabama. He had a fondness for beer, blondes, and speedboats. Snake described himself as a man of "big pickup trucks, fat belt buckles and a few laughs." He danced more than one night away amid neon lights and closed down more than one honky-tonk. Madden said Stabler liked to live wild and would let loose now and then, but was too much of a competitor to let outside influences affect his performance on game days.

Competitive as he was, Stabler was also athletic enough to have turned down a baseball offer from the Houston Astros. Crimson Tide legendary coach Paul "Bear" Bryant called Stabler the "best passer I ever had." He said this just three years after having coached Joe Namath. In three seasons with Bryant, Stabler led the Tide to a 30-2-1 record. As a sophomore in 1965 he led the Tide to an 11-0 record and the national championship. He earned All-America honors in 1966 as Alabama went undefeated again but finished behind once-tied Notre

Dame and Michigan State in the national rankings. Stabler played in three major bowl games—the Cotton, Orange, and Sugar—and was named MVP of the latter.

Snake was the star, and like the Cars, he let the good times roll. "I was always getting into some kind of trouble," he once said. "Nothing serious, more like mischief."

He earned his nickname, "Snake," when he ran a punt back for a touchdown in junior high. "When I got back on the bench the coach said, 'You move like a snake,'" Stabler recalled. "Everybody called me that." Bryant helped popularize the moniker when he said following a game at Alabama that the elusive Stabler was "harder to get ahold of than a river snake."

Stabler was just as elusive off the field. He was a free spirit who by his own recollection had been his own boss since he was fifteen years old. His father was loose, and he never kept tight reins on Kenny. He told his son, "Do what you want to do as long as you don't hurt anybody. . . . Go out and learn. Go ahead, fall on your face, but always get back up."

In college Snake had a 1962 Chevrolet that he called "one of those super sports jobs, with the four speeds and the loud pipes." Stabler and his friends took to drag racing on beaches and were locked up by the police. Bryant had to send one of his assistants, Jimmy Sharpe, to bring Snake back to the university.

When Stabler injured his knee his junior season at Alabama his coaches told him to lay off a year, work with the younger quarterbacks, and come back fully recovered. He enjoyed himself, cutting classes and missing practices. The Snake was a charmer as well; his senior season he convinced a Chevrolet dealer in Tuscaloosa to sell him a new Corvette, despite not putting any money down. Stabler told the dealer he would pay for the car with his first pro contract. The Snake wrecked the Corvette before any money was exchanged. "Son, you're crazy," Bryant told him. "You've gone and lost your mind."

Stabler eventually lost his patience after being drafted by the Raiders in the second round in 1968 and riding the bench behind Lamonica and Blanda through 1971. Madden had seen it as an ideal situation.

1. The most famous play in NFL history is under way as Oakland's self-styled "Assassin"—safety Jack Tatum—hammers Frenchy Fuqua and sends the football flying into the air. Raiders linebacker Gerald Irons looks to give chase on the Tartan Turf of Three Rivers Stadium. Credit: Pittsburgh Steelers.

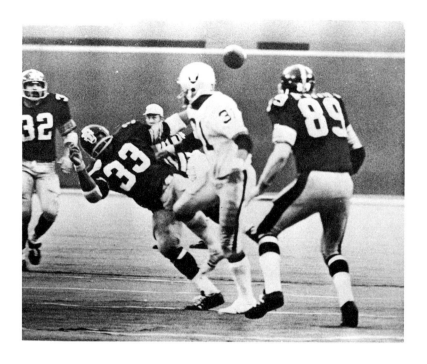

2. Raiders hard-hitting safety Jack Tatum flattens Steelers halfback Frenchy Fuqua on the Immaculate Reception play, sending the ball ricocheting into the air and into the waiting hands of rookie fullback Franco Harris (32) just before it would have hit the carpeted floor of Three Rivers Stadium. Tight end John McMakin (89) moves in. Credit: Pittsburgh Steelers.

3. Christmas came two days early to Steelers Hall of Fame fullback Franco Harris, who stiff-arms Raiders defensive back Jimmy Warren en route to the end zone on the final leg of the famed Immaculate Reception at Three Rivers Stadium in an AFC playoff game on December 23, 1972. Credit: Pittsburgh Steelers.

4. Jim Campbell of the Steelers stands with Hall of Fame wide receiver Lynn Swann during pregame introductions at Three Rivers Stadium. Credit: Tony Tomsic.

5. Jim Campbell of the Steelers meets with Pittsburgh owner Art Rooney (*left*) and writer Steve Cassady prior to Super Bowl XIV in the Rose Bowl in Pasadena. Credit: Tony Tomsic.

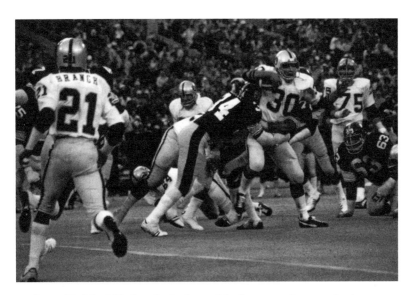

6. All-Pros filled the field when the Steelers and Raiders met in the 1970s. Steelers linebacker Andy Russell collides with Raiders fullback Marv Hubbard in Three Rivers Stadium. Wide receiver Cliff Branch closes in. Credit: Pittsburgh Steelers.

7. Raiders Hall of Fame QB Kenny "Snake" Stabler gets off a pass despite pressure applied by Steelers defensive end L. C. Greenwood in the Oakland Coliseum. Moving in is Oakland guard George Buehler. Credit: Pittsburgh Steelers.

8. Raiders halfback Clarence Davis grounds out yardage before being brought down by Steelers defensive tackle Ernie Holmes (63) and safety Mike Wagner (23). Pittsburgh Hall of Fame defensive tackle Joe Greene (75) and Oakland guard George Buehler (64) survey the play. Credit: Pittsburgh Steelers.

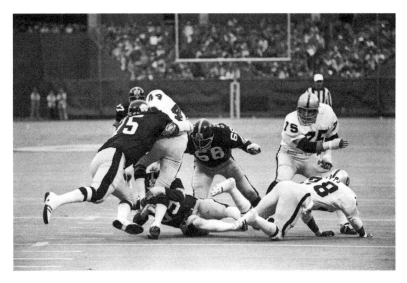

9. Steelers Hall of Fame defensive tackle Joe Greene (75) rides down Raiders fullback Marv Hubbard with help from defensive end L. C. Greenwood and linebacker Jack Ham in Three Rivers Stadium. Credit: Pittsburgh Steelers.

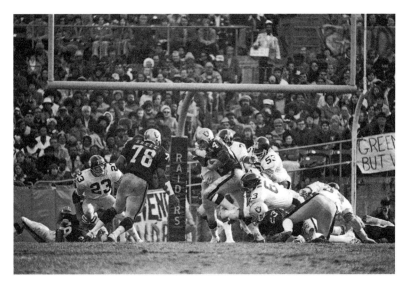

10. Oakland fullback Marv Hubbard pounds out yardage against Pittsburgh's Steel Curtain members Ernie Holmes (63), Joe Greene (75), and Henry Davis (53) in the Oakland Coliseum. Raiders Hall of Fame left tackle Art Shell (78) and Steelers safety Mike Wagner move in. Credit: Pittsburgh Steelers.

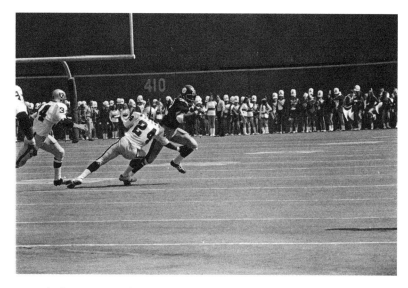

11. With Three Rivers Stadium serving as a backdrop, Pittsburgh fullback Franco Harris veers outside and looks to elude Oakland Hall of Fame cornerback Willie Brown (24) and linebacker Gus Otto. Credit: Pittsburgh Steelers.

12. Raiders power back Marv Hubbard fights for yardage against Pittsburgh's Henry Davis (53), Dwight White (78), and Ben McGee (60) in Three Rivers Stadium. Credit: Pittsburgh Steelers.

13. Steelers Hall of Famer Terry Bradshaw runs a QB keeper against the Raiders' defense in Three Rivers Stadium. Credit: Pittsburgh Steelers.

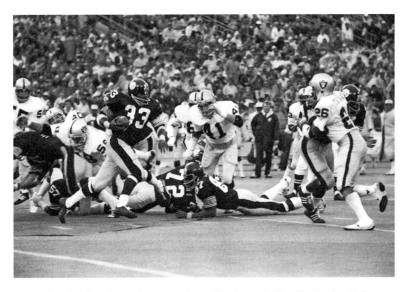

14. Pittsburgh halfback Frenchy Fuqua flows off tackle as Oakland linebacker Phil Villapiano (41) and cornerback Skip "Dr. Death" Thomas (26) move in at Three Rivers Stadium. Credit: Pittsburgh Steelers.

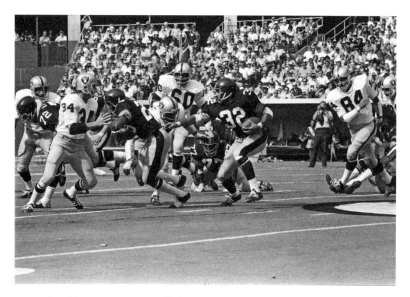

15. Steelers fullback Franco Harris (32) looks for running room as Raiders linebacker Gus Otto (34) sheds a block at Three Rivers Stadium. Credit: Pittsburgh Steelers.

16. Jim Campbell meets with Steelers wide receiver Frank Lewis during pregame introductions at Three Rivers Stadium. Credit: Tony Tomsic.

17. Steelers defensive tackle Mean Joe Greene grounds Oakland's "Mad Bomber," QB Daryle Lamonica, at Three Rivers Stadium. Credit: Pittsburgh Steelers.

18. Hall of Fame owner Art Rooney of the Steelers remains a revered figure in NFL history. Jim Campbell states, "Not only was Mr. Rooney a benefactor to the NFL, but behind the scenes he was a benefactor to fellow human beings." Credit: Pittsburgh Steelers/Mike Fabus.

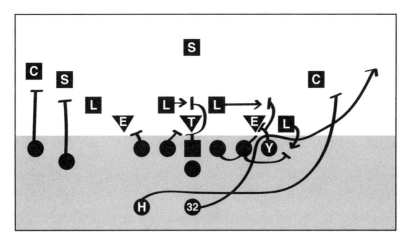

19. Franco Harris fullback trap. Under Hall of Fame head coach Chuck Noll, the Steelers' trapping game featuring Franco Harris (32) rose to unprecedented heights. As tight end Randy Grossman blocks down on Raiders defensive end John Matuszak, right tackle Gerry Mullins pulls and blocks outside linebacker Phil Villapiano. Right guard Jim Clack seals off inside linebacker Willie Hall, freeing Franco to flow to the outside behind the blocking of halfback Rocky Bleier. Image created by the author.

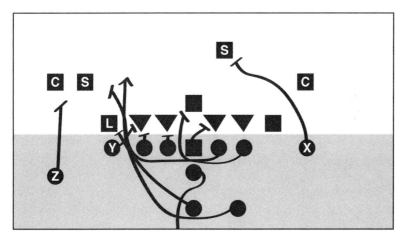

20. Raiders off-tackle play. A signature play for the Raiders under Hall of Fame coach John Madden was the sweep behind Hall of Fame left tackle Art Shell and Hall of Fame left guard Gene Upshaw. Shell and Hall of Fame tight end Dave Casper double-team Steelers defensive end Dwight White, Upshaw blocks Ernie Holmes, and Hall of Fame center Jim Otto angle blocks Joe Greene. Bullish fullback Marv Hubbard leads fleet halfback Clarence Davis into the Steelers' secondary. Image created by the author.

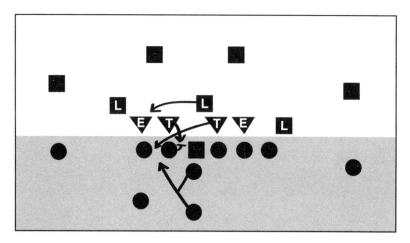

21. Steelers Stunt 4-3 defense. A staple of the Steel Curtain's success in the 1970s was its Stunt 4-3 alignment coached by defensive lieutenants George Perles and Bud Carson. Right tackle Ernie Holmes and left tackle Joe Greene angled on the nose of Raiders center Jim Otto and looped and stunted into the Oakland backfield. Hall of Fame middle linebacker Jack Lambert read the play and flowed to the ball carrier. Image created by the author.

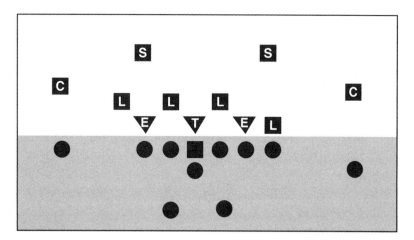

22. Oakland's "Orange" defense. Oakland's "Orange" defense was similar to the Oklahoma defense run in the 1950s by Sooners coach Bud Wilkinson. Because Oakland had more quality linebackers than defensive linemen in 1976, the 3-4 became the Raiders' base defense in the mid 1970s, and its success helped usher in the era of 3-4 fronts in the NFL. Image created by the author.

Lamonica was in his prime. He was the starter and one of the best quarterbacks in pro football. He was a great pure passer who threw a tight, perfect spiral almost every time. And the Mad Bomber delivered the deep ball as well as anyone who ever played.

Blanda was the veteran relief pitcher, a savvy former starter who had seen it all. Football to Blanda was like a chess game. He studied the game from the sidelines, saw how it was taking shape, and if called upon to go in knew exactly what he wanted to do. Blanda had a quick release and was the greatest competitor Madden had ever been around.

Stabler was the young understudy, a quarterback still in the developing stages but who kept his cool on the field as well as anyone Madden had ever seen. Snake was the same on Sunday game days as he was in Wednesday practices. Stabler didn't have a powerful arm, but he could throw long when needed and was extremely accurate on short and intermediate passes.

Madden's plan in those years was to start Lamonica, bring in Blanda if Daryle was hurt or the Raiders needed a lift, and go with Stabler if Daryle's injury turned out to be long term. Madden said having three guys like that at the same time was a "once-in-a-lifetime situation."

Stabler earned the starter's role for the 1972 season opener against the Steelers in Pittsburgh, but when the offense sputtered Lamonica rallied the Raiders with two touchdown passes. Oakland lost but Lamonica won, regaining his starter's role the rest of the way. Stabler relieved him in the late stages of the playoff loss in Pittsburgh, and when the Oakland offense failed to score a touchdown en route to a 1-2 start in 1973, Madden made the move.

The switch in starting quarterbacks was precipitated by Stabler's complaint to his coach concerning his lack of playing time. When Stabler simulated St. Louis quarterback Jim Hart and ran the scout team to perfection prior to a Week Four game against the Cardinals, Madden installed him as the starter. Not because Kenny complained, Madden said, but because he didn't give up and instead went out and won the position on the practice field. Stabler recalled Madden tossing him the playbook and letting him do what he wanted as long as the Raiders won.

Stabler knew it was his time. He respected Lamonica but was aware that when Daryle was in his prime, most defenses played man coverage and the Mad Bomber's arm gave the Raiders' offense a big advantage. By the time Stabler was ready to take over in '73, most teams had switched to zone coverage to ban the bomb. Stabler didn't have Lamonica's arm strength, but his strong suit was accuracy, and that gave him an advantage against zone defenses.

With Stabler installed as the starter, the Raiders beat the Cards and then the Colts. Against Baltimore the Snake threw for more than 300 yards and three touchdowns and broke Redskins legend Sammy Baugh's record for completion percentage by connecting on twenty-five of twenty-nine passes. Stabler finished the season as the second leading passer in the AFC.

Al Davis still favored the vertical game, but he couldn't complain about Stabler's success. With the Snake calling the shots, the Raiders went 74-25 in regular season games and 7-4 in the postseason and won their first Super Bowl. Oakland won 74 percent of its games and played in five straight conference championship games, turning Snake Stabler into a folk hero in Oakland. He was still the star, still the guy everyone looked up to, even his fellow Hall of Famers. Shell said that when Snake called a play, everyone in the huddle knew it was the right play. "Because if it wasn't the right play, he wouldn't have called it."

The Raiders' defense believed the same. Tatum thought Stabler the best quarterback in football and not just because he was his teammate. He saw Snake as the kind of quarterback who would look over a situation and remain cool despite pressure from the opposing defense. The Oakland defense knew Stabler would move the offense by taking whatever he could. If the running game was ineffective that day, Snake would take to the air. And if defenses doubled the outside receivers, Stabler would throw to the tight end. If it was a tough zone and receivers were covered, Snake would send a running back into the pass patterns.

It was enough to impress even the game's greatest quarterbacks, Green Bay legend Bart Starr for one. "I don't know what I can add to what has been said about Stabler so many times," Starr remarked.

Like Stabler, Starr was a former Crimson Tide quarterback, and he considered the Snake a superb passer who did an amazing job calling a game. Starr saw Stabler up close when Bart was coaching the Packers in 1976. He called Stabler a "thing of beauty" to watch. "He operates on you like a skilled surgeon," Starr said, "and cuts you up into little pieces."

Madden said Stabler had a great mind for football. "He always saw the big picture," Madden stated.

What Stabler saw of ABC's *Monday Night Football* broadcasting crew he didn't like. Frank Gifford was the play-by-man, a Hall of Fame player whose plain, low-key delivery perfectly complemented his more flamboyant broadcast partners—Howard Cosell and Alex Karras.

Cosell was cocksure, brassy. "Arrogant, pompous, obnoxious, vain, cruel, verbose, a showoff. There's no question that I'm all of those things," Cosell once said. In an era when most sports reporting involved unabashed adulation, Cosell provided a blustery counterpoint. His staccato voice, syntax, accent, and cadence became much copied. Cosell declared that he was "telling it like it is." Sportswriter Jimmy Cannon countered by pointing out that Cosell was a guy who "changed his name, put on a toupee, and tried to convince the world that he tells it like it is."

Karras, an all-pro defensive lineman with the Detroit Lions from 1958 to 1970, turned to acting and earned renown for his role in the 1974 western parody *Blazing Saddles*. He was hired by NBC to replace Fred Williamson and made a memorable comment when he joked that Otis Sistrunk hailed from the "University of Mars."

Stabler knew Monday-night football was a big thing. Most teams enjoyed playing on Monday night because it was still something new and different, and it was a chance for them to have the spotlight to themselves. Snake was aware that *Monday Night Football* could do a lot for a player, both ways. If Cosell said a player was good, people watching believed he was, even if he wasn't. The same went for someone Cosell knocked. Howard had that kind of influence. Stabler believed that what Cosell said on Monday-night broadcasts influenced sportswriters who didn't see teams play every week. Those same sportswriters vote for all-pro teams and might vote for a player based on what Howard had said during a telecast.

Stabler thought Cosell a front-runner, someone who said nice things about players who were doing well. Stabler believed that whichever team was going good was Howard's favorite. Snake knew football was entertainment and saw Howard as a showman. He was impressed by Cosell's near-total recall and saw it as part of his act. Howard, he said, seemed to think people turned on the game to see him instead of the teams. Cosell could rattle off information about players, Stabler said, but he didn't really know the game. "That telling-it-like-it-is crap," Stabler said, "isn't much if you don't know football."

Stabler had less of a problem with Gifford. An All-America at USC and Hall of Fame halfback and flanker with the New York Giants, Stabler knew Gifford could relate to what was happening on the field. He rarely knocked players, preferring instead to simply relate what was happening on the field. To Snake, Gifford and Cosell were a good combination; Frank confined his comments to the game, and Howard was showbiz.

Stabler didn't find Karras to be funny or informed. Snake would take exception to Karras's claim prior to a 1976 Monday-night game against Cincinnati that Oakland was not as interested in winning since they had wrapped up their division. The Raiders blew out the Bengals, and it was only later Stabler said that Karras gave Oakland any credit.

As ABC cameras showed sideline shots of Landry, Madden, and Blanda, the latter accompanied by actor and Raiders fan James Garner, Stabler and Staubach took center stage. Staubach led Dallas to an early 9–3 lead before Stabler countered with second-quarter scoring strikes to Biletnikoff and Charlie Smith. Leading 17–9 at halftime and wanting to rest Stabler for the playoff showdown with the Dolphins, Madden sent in Blanda, and the old master made it 24–9 in the third with a TD pass to Branch.

The Cowboys, playing for pride, sandwiched two Doug Dennison rushing TDs around a Blanda field goal, but Oakland outlasted Dallas 27–24.

The Steelers would have their own classic encounters with the

Cowboys, but before they reached that point Pittsburgh would first have to figure out its troubling situation at QB.

Just as the Raiders had done the season before, the '74 Steelers underwent a transformation at QB. While Oakland had gone from Lamonica to Stabler, the Steelers moved in the opposite direction in going with the gun-slinging Gilliam over Bradshaw.

Prior to the players' strike in '74, Gilliam was the No. 3 QB behind Bradshaw and Terry Hanratty. Gilliam did not take part in the players' strike and enjoyed a standout preseason, completing 65 percent of his passes and throwing for twelve TDs as the Steelers went 6-0.

Though he preferred a run-pass balance, Noll stayed with the hot hand. The Steelers' season started in turmoil when Noll named Gilliam the starter for the opener against Baltimore. Joe Willie Gillie, as he was known, became the first black quarterback to start and win an opening day game in the NFL. He was the pride of Jefferson Street in Nashville and, in three quarters against the Colts on that sun-drenched Sunday, threw for 257 yards and two touchdowns. One was a 54-yard strike to Swann, who was making his pro debut.

Jefferson Street Joe's performance prompted Pittsburgh vice president Art Rooney Jr. to declare him a throwback to the 1950s, to Bob Waterfield and Norm Van Brocklin throwing bombs to Crazy Legs Hirsch and Tom Fears. "He hits people's hands," Rooney Jr. said of Gilliam's marksmanship with the football.

As he had during the preseason, Gilliam started out slowly against a resolute Colt defense. He was 0 for 5 and was intercepted by safety Rick Volk late in the first quarter. Gilliam was 2 for 10 for 12 yards at that point, but Joe Willie Gillie wasn't worried. "I knew sooner or later I'd stop missing them and start hitting them," he said.

With Pittsburgh's offensive line providing more protection than the Secret Service, Jefferson Street Joe engineered a 99-yard drive highlighted by his deep strike to Swann. The next time Pittsburgh got the ball Gilliam needed only three plays to navigate 64 yards. His first pass went to Frank Lewis and covered 20 yards. His next was a 40-yarder to Swann. The third and final one was a looped 4-yarder to Lewis that upped Pittsburgh's lead to 16–0 at halftime.

Gilliam completed 9 of 11 passes for 151 yards in the second quarter alone, and it became evident that the Steelers' offense was being tailored for the kind of classic drop-back passing attack that Gilliam had excelled at since his college days. Joe Willie Gillie wasn't classic in form—he held the ball down low, à la Joe Willie Namath, and often threw off his wrong foot. Yet he made up for his maverick style with a delivery that was faster than most and nearly as lightning-quick as Broadway Joe's.

Jefferson Street Joe jolted defenses with bullet-like passes to veteran wide receivers Lewis and Ron Shanklin and a pair of spectacular rookies in Swann and Stallworth. The team also responded to Gilliam's bubbling spirit, and after six games the Steelers were 4-1-1. Still, the offense lacked balance. Gilliam winged what was then a team record 50 passes in one game and 198 in the six games he started.

Gilliam's fill-the-air-with-footballs mentality conflicted with Noll's preference for high-percentage football. After Pittsburgh beat Cleveland 20–16 win Week Six in Three Rivers Stadium, Gilliam's performance—5 for 18 for 78 yards—convinced Noll to reinstate Bradshaw for the next week's hosting of Atlanta on *Monday Night Football.* "I never lost my job," Bradshaw insisted. "There was just another guy who showed up with a hot hand. Noll never gave up on me. He just had to go with the guy who had the hot hand. I didn't like it. But I accepted it."

Harris, who had gone down with an injury in the Week Three loss to Oakland, returned to form and rushed for a then career-high 141 yards and one TD to spark a 24–17 win.

As Franco rumbled and the Steel Curtain raged, Pittsburgh took a 7-2-1 record into New Orleans for another nationally televised performance on Monday night. The Steelers stormed past Archie Manning and Company 28–7, and the game marked a turning point for Bradshaw. Though Terry ran for more yards than he threw (99-80), his handling of the team is what impressed players like center Ray Mansfield. "You could see the transformation of Terry after that game," said Mansfield. "It's like anything else. If you've got confidence in what someone can do, you're going to have confidence in what you are doing. Terry picked up something against the Saints and we could feel it."

Two weeks later, in a Sunday, December 8, game that marked the Steelers' final road outing of the regular season, Bradshaw's stock with his teammates rose even higher. Mansfield said if he had to pinpoint a time and place when the Steelers began to fully appreciate Bradshaw's leadership, it was the New England game. The Old Ranger said the Steelers had overlooked Houston and lost the week after the Saints' game, but Noll stuck with Terry for the New England game. "Terry really came of age in that game . . . just things he said and did," Mansfield remembered. "He had complete control of the game. He knew it and we knew it."

Mansfield said Bradshaw would go into the huddle and be in complete charge. There had been times Terry wasn't quite so sure of himself on the field, but that wasn't the case anymore.

Bradshaw's road to his starting role was a difficult one. Myron Cope said Bradshaw navigated a course through big-city media in a manner that reminded Cope of Dizzy Dean, the ace of the St. Louis Cardinals' colorful "Gashouse Gang" of the 1930s. Like Dean, Bradshaw was a country bumpkin but one blessed with a rocket-launching right arm that Cope opined could propel a ball so hard, it might chop cotton if thrown low through a field.

Just as Dean had a habit of saying whatever came to mind, Bradshaw's first press conference in Pittsburgh saw him step to the microphone at the posh Pittsburgh restaurant the LeMont and brashly declare, "I'm here to lead the Steelers to the NFL Championship."

Privately, the son of the South looked out at the glittering view of the downtown skyline from the Mount Washington section of Pittsburgh and wondered what he had gotten himself into by coming up north. "What," Bradshaw recalled wondering, "is going to happen to me in this place?"

Bradshaw's NFL career started slowly. Winning a starting role as a rookie, he had to learn on the job and completed just 38 percent of his passes and led the league in interceptions with twenty-four. Pittsburgh was primarily a ball-control team in Bradshaw's early seasons, the Steelers leaning on the legs of Harris and an outstanding trap-blocking offensive line.

When the opportunity arose, Bradshaw, the "Blond Bomber," showcased one of the strongest arms in the NFL and a deft deep touch. NFL head coach Weeb Ewbank said once that a lot of quarterbacks can throw long, but few can pass long. Bradshaw could pass long. He was also physically tough and was a big-play quarterback in big games.

Raiders safety Jack Tatum said Bradshaw had the ability to produce the big play, in part because of his overpowering physical abilities and the daring to make things happen.

George Allen thought the 6-foot-3, 215-pound Bradshaw the modern mold for a quarterback—tall and powerful. He compared Bradshaw to Unitas in that defenders would beat them up, but Bradshaw and Unitas would always have enough left to win. Tough and durable, Bradshaw took his punishment and still did his job.

Bradshaw buttressed his powerful arm with powerful legs; he was not only a stronger thrower than most but also a better runner, rushing for thirty-two career TDs. Whereas Unitas cut defenses up with short passes and then opened up with long bombs, Bradshaw's long passes loosened up defenses for the short tosses. Allen called Bradshaw the most accurate long thrower he'd ever seen. Bradshaw's accuracy allowed him to complete soft tosses as well as the deep bombs. He was as adept at feathering short passes as firing long ones.

Bradshaw's bumpkin routine sometimes caused opponents to question his intelligence. Dallas linebacker Thomas "Hollywood" Henderson stated prior to Super Bowl XIII, "Bradshaw couldn't spell cat if you spotted him the C and the T."

Kansas City's Len Dawson defended his fellow QB, declaring, "A lot of us would like to be so dumb to quarterback two Super Bowl teams."

Bradshaw would win two more Super Bowls, and opposing coaches would come to see him as having "street smarts," an instinct for doing the right thing.

Tatum thought the perfect quarterback would be one who combined Bradshaw's body with Stabler's mind. Terry, Tatum remarked, sometimes made up his mind too quickly and forced mistakes. Tatum feasted on Bradshaw's passes, with nearly one-third of the Assassin's thirty-seven career picks coming at the Blond Bomber's expense.

Tatum thought Terry had a tendency to rattle quickly and impulsively throw the ball up for grabs.

Tatum did note Bradshaw's coming of age, and it all started, as Mansfield said, in 1974. Bradshaw acknowledged that he felt terrible following the loss to Houston. He believed he had blown his opportunity to once again be the starter. But when Noll called Terry into his office he told him he was giving him another shot against New England.

Noll's decision caused a seismic switch in Bradshaw's thinking. The big thing was in knowing his coach had confidence in him. When Noll questioned what Bradshaw was doing, Terry was the type of person who was going to be bothered by that doubt. He needed to know Noll was behind him. "I think I grew up a lot that season," Bradshaw said.

Against New England Harris rushed for one score and 136 yards, and Bradshaw threw a third-quarter strike to Swann, whose diving catch turned out to be the winning TD in a 21–17 final, clinching Pittsburgh's second AFC Central Division title. It was a total team effort by the Steelers—the offense, defense, and special teams all producing points as Roy Gerela hit two field goals and L. C. Greenwood tackled Patriots QB Jim Plunkett in the end zone for a safety.

Pittsburgh put the finishing touches on a 10-3-1 regular-season record with a 27–3 win over Cincinnati the following Saturday. It marked the fifth time that season the Steel Curtain had held opposing offenses to seven points or fewer in a game.

Lambert solidified the middle of the Steel Curtain and became the third Steeler in six seasons to be named NFL Rookie of the Year. Count Dracula in Cleats was one of Pittsburgh's key additions along with halfback Rocky Bleier, who recovered from leg injuries suffered in Vietnam to become a starter; and Webster, the little-known lineman from Wisconsin who would become one of the great centers in NFL history.

From opening day Pittsburgh put together a campaign crammed with great plays: safety Glen Edwards's 50-yard interception return in Kansas City and Mel Blount's pick-six against Philadelphia; Andy Russell, the grand old man of the defense, blitzing Browns QB Mike Phipps off his feet; fellow outside 'backer Jack Ham pirating a Plun-

kett pass; Franco flowing through the Falcons' defense; Bleier showing he's more than a blocking back, following pulling guard Sam Davis
for crucial gains.

For the Steelers and Raiders, one challenge had ended. Another
was about to begin.

Up next: the NFL playoffs.

Jim Campbell: After the blush of the "Immaculate" 1972 season and the
disappointment of the Steelers' early exit from the 1973 postseason—
and to the Raiders, no less—I was optimistic about the upcoming
1974 NFL campaign.

It started with the draft. Before training camp started, it seemed
to me that the ball club had filled some needs without veering too
far from the team's philosophy of drafting "the best player available,
regardless of position." Lynn Swann seemed like a no-brainer.

And the more I heard, saw, and read about John Stallworth, he
appeared to be someone who could also help. I recall reading, from
my post in Canton at the Pro Football Hall of Fame, how Jack Lambert was tooling his old beater of a car over the Ohio and Pennsylvania turnpikes to study film and learn the Steelers' playbook. Since
Lambert starred at Kent State—only a Bradshaw's bomb throw from
the HOF—I was quite familiar with his intense and aggressive style
of play. To me "Jack Splat" was a slightly shorter version of the Baltimore Colts' Ted Hendricks. Both had been tabbed by enterprising
sportswriters as "the Mad Stork."

A little later in his career he really established himself as a force
and one who brooked no nonsense from anyone. Also a part of Pittsburgh folklore includes the tale that more than one harried mother
of an unruly child was able to elicit better behavior by simply saying
to the wayward youngster, "If you don't behave, I'm going to call Jack
Lambert." It is also said the threat had a very calming effect on the
obstreperous youth. Of course, it was this approach to things that had
Lambert's personal fan club hanging bedsheet signs from the Three
Rivers Stadium railings proclaiming "Lambert's Lunatics."

The one future Hall of Famer who escaped my attention longest was Mike Webster. Perhaps, because starting center Ray Mansfield was my "sideline buddy," I thought the pivot position was pretty well accounted for with him and another sideline chum, Jim Clack. As part of Dan Radakovich's interchangeable offensive linemen, Clack was now playing center and guard.

But once camp started Webster proved to reward the faith Chuck Noll and the scouting department had in his ability to handle defensive linemen, who were much heavier than the 230 pounds that Webster packed.

While living in Canton I still managed to make a few visits to Latrobe and the St. Vincent College training facility. Early on it was an interesting time. The players were on strike. As I recall only vet Joe Gilliam crossed the picket line. He was vying for more playing time as a backup quarterback. This gave the rookies free run of the camp and gave the coaches a vast amount of camp time to work with the draftees and undrafted free agents: fewer bodies, more individual coaching. As the season played out it became more and more obvious how much the extra work in the '74 training camp paid off.

Like earlier training camps, an unheralded rookie, or rookies, would catch the public's eye—after catching the local beat writers' eye. For me it was Webster. He possessed amazing strength. As I talked to some of the vets, once they got to camp, I knew why. Jon Kolb, by then a mainstay at left tackle, was one of the first Steelers to be labeled a "weight-room warrior." It was reported that Webster followed the former Oklahoma State Cowboy into the weight room "like a puppy dog." Well, Webster soon became a Great Dane. Like Kolb, he was able to bench-press 500 pounds. At the time this was an unheard-of amount. It may be worthwhile noting that this was before pro athletes in many sports were "juicin'." When other Steelers, especially linemen, saw what Kolb and Webster were doing, they too joined in.

Before leaving Clack, mention should be made of the annual "dress-offs" between the young lineman and John "Frenchy" Fuqua. A time was set aside after a midseason practice for the contest of sartorial splendor. Clack was more the preppy type. His contest outfit featured knickers, argyle socks, sporty shoes, a sweater vest, button-down shirt, bow tie, and natty cap. For this particular contest "the Count" eschewed his fabled platform shoes with the transparent heels, which contained live goldfish. The velvet cape and Three Musketeers hat with an ostrich plume were also left in Frenchy's walk-in closet. By normal Fuqua standards, his outfit this day was rather pedestrian. But the Frenchman didn't need much. In his own words, "I knew I had him as soon as I pulled on my red pantyhose."

The winner by near-unanimous decision of his peers: Fuqua. One enterprising Pittsburgh scribe asked Fuqua's significant other at the time, "Countess, what do you think of all this Count/Countess stuff?" She sighed and replied, "It gives me a headache."

The weight room wasn't the province of just the burly linemen and linebackers. Rocky Bleier quickly became a devotee of pumpin' iron. He really worked to rehab from his Vietnam War injuries, increasing his speed to a level higher than when he was a rookie in 1968. But the real work was on strength. After many sessions he was able to join the 500-Pound Club with Webster, Clack, Kolb, et al. The pumping of iron became a badge of honor with the Steelers.

Back to Webster. What he did on the practice field and what he did when he got a chance to play were impressive and only portended what was to unfold as a Hall of Fame career and as possibly the greatest center in pro football history.

As he did in all training camps, Noll took his time with the candidates—regardless of the likelihood of a player making the final Steelers' roster. I've seen him spend time with a free agent from an obscure Division III school who didn't have a snowball's chance of making the club, just as he would with a Swann, a Stallworth, a Webster, or a Lambert. Above all else Noll was a teacher. In the tradition of Paul Brown or Sid Gillman, Noll was interested in helping a young player be all he could be. Training camp was also a place to learn at the foot of the master, Jack Butler. It was great to pick up "nuggets" from Jack.

It was during the time that the Chicago College All-Star Game was still regarded as the start of the football season. Teams' top draft choices were selected to play and, unfortunately, miss several weeks of training camp while preparing to play the defending NFL champions. The risk of injury to a valued draftee and the loss of time eventually sounded the death knell for the game that in its heyday drew crowds of more than one hundred thousand to Soldier Field and was heralded as the start of football season.

Jack Ham was one of the rookies missing the Steelers' 1971 camp for the All-Star Game. Each evening a Steelers All-Star would call to Latrobe and report on the team's rookies. I happened to be at the Five O'Clock Club (a gathering of coaches and media after the afternoon practice) when Ham called in. He gave his report and hung up. Butler was in a talkative mood, which wasn't always the case. He speculated about the 215-pound rookie linebacker. I remember Jack saying, "I think he'll put on a few pounds and be able to stand the gaff of playing linebacker in the NFL. But if he doesn't, I can see him as a strong safety."

Not only was Ham able to stand the gaff, but he became what many—myself included—thought the best outside linebacker in the NFL. Surely, Lawrence Taylor has his advocates with his spectacular play, play that changed the way a NFL linebacker played the position. However, to me, Taylor was a "disrupter," one who caused havoc by rushing the passer. Taking nothing away from the Giants' Hall of Famer, Ham was much more effective in pass coverage and in never being caught out of position. Ham's thirty-two career interceptions are testimony to his coverage skills and his speed and quickness.

More than once, I heard fellow outside linebacker Andy Russell say, "Jack Ham is the fastest Steeler for 10 yards, and that includes running backs and wide receivers."

Here's another interesting take on Ham. In the early '70s I would attend the NFL Drafts in New York City's Essex House ballroom. This was before it became a television extravaganza. After Ham's rookie season I had a conversation with Raiders scout Roy Schleicher, the older brother of my old Penn State buddy Maurice Schleicher. Roy admitted a mistake in evaluating Ham. He said, "He played in the middle as a senior because of injuries to other 'backers. So, we evaluated him as a middle 'backer rather than outside 'backer. Even though he made All-America, we felt he was too light for the middle. Oh, if we just had projected him on the outside . . ."

When the St. Vincent's camp broke on August, fourteen rookies made the Steelers' final roster—the "Fab Four," of course. But also notable contributors such as Jimmy Allen, Rich Druschel, Reggie Garrett, Randy Grossman, Reggie Harrison, Marv Kellum, and Donnie "Torpedo" Shell. Shell, unheralded out of South Carolina State, especially benefited from the added attention and coaching available due to the absence of striking veterans in the early days of camp. Shell quickly became a feared safety during a fourteen-year career, and as one wag put it, "Donnie left more than one runner or receiver 'Shell shocked.'"

Because of the extra time the youngsters got in training camp sans veterans, Joe Gilliam got the bulk of the time at quarterback in the exhibition season, which saw the Steelers finish with a perfect 6-0 record. He completed well over 60 percent of his passes, many of them bombs, and averaged two touchdowns a game.

When the regular season opened "Jefferson Street Joe" was under center. He continued to fling the football in the early-season games. Some of this was predicated on Franco being somewhat hobbled, but some of it was also predicated on the way Gilliam thought the game should be played.

As Bradshaw rode the pines, rumors flew of his being traded or wanting to be traded. Brad wasn't too subtle about his desire to leave the Smokey City for the Golden West. One rumor had "Ozark Ike in Cleats" going to the San Francisco 49ers. Bradshaw did little to quell the rumors. After a practice, one in which Gilliam was taking most of the snaps, Brad could be heard whistling "California Here I Come."

Something told me that Jefferson Street Joe wasn't the answer, although I wasn't sure what the question was. Nevertheless, Noll stuck with the winning hand as the Raiders came swashbuckling into Three Rivers. I, like the Steelers, was about to learn a valuable lesson. Mine was: don't judge how a team is going to play by the way they line up before kickoff. As noted, one of my game-day duties was to line up both teams for pregame introductions. That day it was the Raiders' defense and the Steelers' offense.

There wasn't much, if any, whoopin' and hollerin', as the Raiders awaited the intros. "Businesslike" might have been a good description, but I mistook it for apathy. On the other hand, the Steelers were their usual confident selves. No jumping up and down, just a little impatience—"Let's get this battle started." I never said much when introducing the offensive Steelers, just a little idle chitchat. When it was the defense's turn for introductions, it was different. Almost every time I'd counsel Mel Blount or Dwight White, "Take no prisoners today." I'm not saying I had anything to do with how the Steel Curtain performed, but they usually put a lickin' on the opponent.

Well, it wasn't much of a battle. The Raiders sailed out of the downtown stadium proud possessors of a 17–0 shutout victory. I couldn't ever remember the Steelers having a "bagel" hung on them. Not much went right for the home team.

It was during this time that I lost one of my best sideline buddies— Bleier. Since 1970, my first year on the Steelers sideline, Rocky and I would stand fairly close together and watch the passing scene. In the early years we joked about "just getting enough seasons in to qualify for the NFL pension." It took five seasons to be vested.

Rocky played as a rookie in 1968. His time in Vietnam also gave him a year. Through the goodness of Art Rooney's heart, he was kept on the taxi squad in 1970. Many thought that when he made the regular-season roster in 1971, it was again Art Rooney interceding, but it was in the book as counting. By 1972 Bleier was making real progress; speed and strength both increased, and he was a true contributor on special teams. It was a very good year, 1973, Rocky getting his fifth year in.

By mid-1974 his strong and unselfish blocking led other teams to label him "a third guard." He was a starter, paired with Harris at running back. His trap blocks opened consistent holes for Franco and others to barge through.

One day I said to him, "Rocky, you got your five years and a pension. Is this your last year?" With a twinkle in his eye, he just said, "What do you think? This is fun." He went on to play six more productive years and finish his career as the fifth-leading Steelers rusher all time when he retired. A truly amazing career, especially consider-

ing the obstacles he had to overcome. Rocky went on to have a fine
career as a motivational speaker. Not only did he have an intriguing
story, but he also had a great voice and delivery with which to tell it.

Despite losing a defensive struggle to Houston at home, Bradshaw
seemed be riding the elevator to the top floor. After a 21–17 victory at
New England, before the final regular-season game versus Cincinnati,
Ray Mansfield, in one of our sideline pregame chats, told me, "Brad has
changed. He's as confident as he's ever been. Finally believes in himself, and the team really believes in him. It was the old, loosey-goosey,
let-'er-rip Bradshaw in the huddle. He became our leader on offense."

The Bengals game was a 27–3 cakewalk. It was also the game Noll
told me, "Jim, we're starting the 'kids' at wideout." Noll had seen me
standing in an alcove, not wanting to get run over by tons of Steelers
beef as the players charged out of the locker room to take the field. He
had started up the exit ramp but retraced his steps to inform me of the
change to the younger wide receivers. Swann and Stallworth showed
a glimpse of what was to come as they replaced Ronnie Shanklin and
Frank Lewis as starters. Stallworth gave an eye-opening performance—
six receptions for 105 yards and one touchdown.

The drafting of Stallworth was just another example of Noll's sterling character. Remember, back in 1972 he wanted to take University
of Houston running back Robert Newhouse with the Steelers first-
round pick. With an open mind, he listened to Art Rooney Jr.'s sales
pitch on Franco Harris and selected the Penn State runner, even though
Franco was more of a "gamer" than a practice player.

This time Noll, looking to upgrade the Steelers' receiving corps,
wanted to use the first-round choice in '74 to select Stallworth from
Alabama A&M. Knowledgeable Bill Nunn Jr. assured the head coach
that Stallworth would be around in a later round of the draft. Again,
Noll deferred. Again, the Steelers got their man, another Hall of Famer.
There was never any doubt who was in charge in Pittsburgh, but Noll
was never a my-way-or-the-highway guy.

As for Nunn, Noll told him when they first met in 1969, at Noll's
hiring, "You just find the athletes. It's up to us to turn them into NFL
football players." Nunn certainly kept his end of the bargain, as did

Noll. Earlier, when Nunn was scouting the historically black colleges to compile information for the Courier's Black All-America team, he tipped off the Los Angeles Rams on Deacon Jones of Mississippi Valley Vocational and the New York Giants on Roosevelt Brown of Morgan State. The fact that both are enshrined in Canton is testament to Nunn's astute eye for talent. Why did neither Jones nor Brown became a Steeler? Jones was an NFL rookie in 1961 and Brown a rookie in 1953. Nunn was not affiliated with the Steelers until hired on a part-time basis in 1967. It wasn't until Noll sensed his value in 1969 that he became a full-time scout.

Swann really impressed me with his skills and his nerve. Noll worked with all punt returners in camp, stressing "no fair catches." More than anyone else, Swann seemed to absorb Noll's teachings. In returning forty-one punts during his rookie season, one of which was a dazzling 69-yard touchdown, he never signaled for a fair catch.

There were times when he got hammered immediately, but he never flinched and always held on to the ball.

Gerry "Moon" Mullins (wasn't everyone named Mullins nicknamed "Moon" as homage to Frank Willard's popular comic strip?) was a blocking tight end at USC. However, as a Steeler he was projected as a tackle and guard and performed well at both positions. But in the romp over Cincy, he rechanneled his inner tight end and caught a 7-yard scoring pass from Bradshaw. Moon was undoubtedly responsible for many more Steelers touchdowns as a path-clearing offensive lineman.

6

Hard Road to the Big Easy

Some four decades have passed, yet the 1974 NFL playoffs remain historically important. Not only do they mark the end of the Dolphins' dynasty and the start of the Steelers' Super Bowl reign, they also stand as the final postseason prior to the beginning of the league's modern playoff system in which teams are rewarded for success in the regular season.

The 1974 postseason marked the last one in which home playoff games were awarded based on a rotation that saw sites alternated annually by division. Expansion in the 1960s had caused the NFL to go from two conferences to four divisions in 1967, and the AFL expanded its playoffs in 1969. Such is the reason the 1967 Green Bay Packers, who won the newly minted Central Division with a 9-4-1 record, were able to host the 11-1-2 Los Angeles Rams in the Western Conference Championship, and the 1968 Cleveland Browns (10-4) hosted both the Dallas Cowboys (12-2) and Baltimore Colts (13-1) in the Eastern Conference final and NFL title game, respectively.

Expansion is also the reason the 1969 Kansas City Chiefs won the fourth and final AFL-NFL Super Bowl, despite finishing second in the Western Division behind the Oakland Raiders. Had the AFL not expanded its playoff format from two to four teams for its final season, the Chiefs would not have qualified for the postseason.

Beginning with the AFL-NFL merger in 1970, the two leagues were realigned and a new playoff format instituted. The NFC and AFC had three divisions apiece, and the champions of each division qualified for the postseason along with the best second-place, or wild-card, team.

Anomalies remained, however, most notably in the case of the 1972 undefeated Dolphins, who played at Pittsburgh in the 1972 AFC Championship.

The seeding system started with the 1975 postseason, but had it started in 1974, the No. 3–seeded Steelers would have headed to No. 2 Miami to face the two-time reigning world champions, and the No. 1 Raiders would have hosted No. 4 Buffalo, the Eastern Division runner-up and wild-card team. Instead, the Raiders hosted Miami in a matchup of East-West winners on Saturday, December 21, while the Steelers battled the Bills in Pittsburgh the following day.

The playoffs kicked off on Saturday at 1:00 p.m. eastern standard time with CBS's coverage of an NFC game, Minnesota hosting St. Louis in Metropolitan Stadium. Conditions were typical of Bloomington, Minnesota, four days before Christmas—game-time temps in the high twenties and flurries falling from a pewter-gray sky.

Calling the game for CBS, sportscasters Brent Musburger, Irv Cross, and John Unitas breathed frost amid frigid surroundings as the Vikings took advantage of Cardinal miscues and rode a decisive 16-point third quarter to a 30–14 victory.

What took place amid an electric atmosphere in Oakland later that afternoon would prove epic, providing a national television audience with a "name game" that stands with other Raiders classics—*Heidi* Bowl, Immaculate Reception, Ghost to the Post, Holy Roller.

The Sea of Hands classic with Miami kicked off shortly after 4:00 p.m. eastern time and in spectacular fashion for the Dolphins. Starting with their ascendance in 1970 the Dolphins had developed a fanatical following. Play-by-play announcer Rick Weaver exhorted South Florida's football fans filling the Orange Bowl to "wave your hankies." Dol-fans delighted in the notion and took to waving thousands of white hankies every game.

Raider Nation responded. When the two-time defending Super

Bowl champions took the field in the cloud-shrouded Coliseum on December 21, they were greeted with thousands waving black handkerchiefs, jerseys, shirts, and even a woman's black nightie and panties.

As the silver-and-black-clad crowd of 53,023 settled into their seats and the last notes of NBC's iconic sports theme song featuring high energy, horn-led funk and Michael Brecker's saxophone solo were struck on millions of TV sets across the country, sportscaster Curt Gowdy, accompanied by color analysts Al DeRogatis and "Dandy" Don Meredith, made the stunning call:

"It's a short kick. It will be handled by Nat Moore, coming out to the 20, 25, 30. He's up to the 40. He's at the 50! Moore has run the opening kick-off back for a touchdown!"

Moore, a Miami rookie, plucked the ball from overcast skies at the Oakland Coliseum, veered left toward the Dolphin sideline, picked up a key blindside block from Jim Langer on Neal Colzie, and raced 89 yards to the end zone.

"Number 89," DeRogatis told surprised viewers, *"is about to go 89 yards!"*

"And," Meredith added, *"Coach John Madden is saying, 'Now, wait a minute. What is happening here?'"*

The Raiders' boss was more perplexed minutes later when Dolphin defensive back Dick Anderson picked off a Ken Stabler pass. The Raiders rose up to force a punt and prevent further damage, but damage had already been done to the Dolphins, all-star safety Jake Scott suffering a knee injury after colliding with linebacker Larry Ball on Anderson's interception return and being sidelined the rest of the afternoon.

Both Miami and Oakland were nicked up going in. The Dolphins were absent right linebacker Doug Swift; the Raiders were without right cornerback Willie Brown. Miami power back Larry Csonka was slowed by injuries, while backfield mate Mercury Morris, center Jim Langer, and defensive tackle Manny Fernandez were all hurting. Raiders receiver Fred Biletnikoff was likewise less than 100 percent, nursing bone chips in his left knee.

Despite the long list of injuries, this was the game many felt was the de facto championship. Dan Jenkins said as much in his playoff preview for *Sports Illustrated* when he wrote that the real Super Bowl would be played in the mud of Oakland on Saturday when the Raiders hosted the Dolphins. Miami and Oakland, Jenkins stated, brought to the playoffs the NFL's best in speed (Morris, Paul Warfield, Cliff Branch), in quarterbacking (Stabler, Bob Griese), and in genius (Don Shula, Al Davis).

Gamesmanship enveloped the contest early. The Raiders warned officials to watch Griese's bobbing of his head while barking signals in an effort to draw Oakland offside. Griese countered by accusing the Raiders of having twelve men in the defensive huddle prior to each play.

There were must-see matchups all over the field. When the Dolphins had the ball, Langer dueled all-pro tackle Otis Sistrunk. When Oakland went on offense, all-pro left tackle Art Shell lined up against fellow all-star Bill Stanfill, and all-time-great center Jim Otto took on Fernandez, the All-Pro who lined up opposite Otto when the Dolphins went to their famed "53" defense. Due to injuries, the "53," named for the uniform number of hybrid linebacker/defensive end Bob Matheson when he entered the game in passing situations, became on this day the "51," Ball becoming the hybrid in Miami's shifting fronts.

This playoff would prove to be one of the greatest games ever played, an almost continuous highlight film from start to finish. But both the Dolphins—dressed in their road white uniforms in aqua and orange trim—and the silver-and-black Raiders missed early opportunities to put points on the board.

Surprisingly, it was game breakers Warfield and Branch whose hands suddenly turned as cold and hard as those on a statue. Warfield dropped a touchdown pass in the end zone that would have made it 14–0, while Branch likewise saw a big-play pass bounce off his hands.

Oakland tied the game in the second quarter when halfback Charlie Smith got behind middle linebacker Nick Buoniconti and gathered in Stabler's pass for a 31-yard score. The TD was reminiscent of Smith's score against the Jets in the *Heidi* Bowl four years earlier.

Miami regained the lead with 1:01 left in the half, Garo Yepremian hitting a 33-yard field goal to make it 10–7 at the break.

The second half saw bright sunshine break through the clouds and the lead change hands five times. The Raiders struck first, Biletnikoff making a circus catch in the end zone as he reached out with his left arm along the right sideline and somehow kept his feet in bounds while fighting off blanket coverage from cornerback Tim Foley.

Griese found a wide-open Warfield for a 16-yard score to reclaim the lead, cornerback Nemiah Wilson falling down on the play. But Bubba Smith blocked Yepremian's PAT to keep the score at 16–14. Garo found balm for the block by booting a 46-yard field goal early in the fourth quarter.

Trailing 19–14 the Raiders responded. Stabler lofted a bomb to Branch, who made a great diving grab, got up and got away from reserve defensive backs Henry Stuckey and Charlie Babb to complete a spectacular 72-yard score.

Gowdy: *"Here's a deep one to Branch . . . He's got it and he scores! They're going crazy here at the Coliseum! This reminds me of the Christmas Day classic between Miami and Kansas City [in 1971], the greatest game I've ever broadcast."*

Replays showed that the ball hit the ground at the same time Branch hit the turf, but since official's reviews were not yet allowed, the catch was ruled legal. Seeking a fourth straight trip to the Super Bowl, Miami took over on its 32 with 4:37 remaining. Griese guided his champions 68 yards in four plays, the steamrolling Csonka grinding out hard yard after hard yard. The Dolphin drive reached pay dirt when rookie halfback Benny Malone high-stepped his way 23 yards to a touchdown, breaking four tackles en route to a 26–21 lead.

Gowdy: *"Malone outside. He's at the 20, still going . . . Touchdown! Miami has taken the lead back again!"*

Oakland got the ball with 2:08 to go, and Stabler went to work. Putting on a clinic of precision passing against pro football's premier zone defense, the Snake struck for gains of 6, 18, 20, and 4 yards as the Raiders went to a three-wide receiver offense. Frank Pitts, the former Kansas City Chief whose flanker reverses tormented Minnesota in Super Bowl IV, had a juggling first-down catch at the Miami 14, and Clarence Davis carried to the 8. Madden called his final time-out to talk things over, and when the Raiders returned to the field, Stabler called a pass play designed for Biletnikoff.

For Oakland and Miami their seasons had come down to one final play. This was their third postseason meeting in five years, Oakland winning a playoff in 1970 and the Dolphins evening the score with a victory in the AFC Championship in 1973. The rubber match lived up to everyone's expectations. On the ensuing play it exceeded them.

Gowdy: *"This is a classic playoff game . . . [Stabler] fading, looking. He's under the gun; he's caught; he throws. It is . . . Touchdown! Unbelievable! What a finish!"*

Stabler was pressured, but the Snake slithered free for an instant before being caught from behind by defensive end Vern Den Herder. As he was going down Stabler threw into triple coverage, into a "sea of hands" to Davis. Babb, Ball, and Mike Kolen surrounded the Raiders' halfback, who stuck his hands out and took the ball away from three Dolphin defenders before being shoved to the end zone turf.

Meredith: *"He caught it! . . . Clarence Davis, Number 28 in your program and today Number 1 in the hearts of Oakland!"*

Linebacker Phil Villapiano's interception sealed the deal on the Dolphins' final series and sent the Raiders to the AFC Championship Game for the second straight year.

Gowdy: *"You'll never see a game better than this one, ladies and gentlemen, I'm sure you'll agree . . . This one was just the way it was advertised."*

DeRogatis: *"It was maybe the greatest football game I've ever seen. Just incredible."*

Gowdy reminded his national television audience during the final minute of the broadcast that Madden had called the Raiders and Dolphins the two best teams in football:

"Some fans aren't going to be happy with Madden's statement, but he said, 'When the best meets the best, anything can happen.'"

Among those taking issue with Madden's statement was Pittsburgh coach Chuck Noll. Referencing Madden's remark, Noll would tell his Steelers that the best team in the NFL was in Pittsburgh's locker room.

While experts pondered the exciting matchup between Bills record-setting running back O. J. Simpson and his "Electric Company" offensive line—so named because they turned on the Juice—and the Steel Curtain, Pittsburgh fans had their own method for predicting victory. "We figured out scientifically without any precedence who's going to win the ball game," a stalwart Steelers fan in Three Rivers Stadium told NFL Films prior to kickoff. "The Steelers are going to win because they're hungry. They didn't have breakfast today. They've been waitin' for the Juice!"

Amid cold sunshine Simpson, outfitted in Buffalo's road uniform—royal blue pants with white and red trim, white jerseys with red and blue trim, and white helmets featuring a charging blue buffalo logo—was stood up by Jack Ham and Jack Lambert, hammered by Ham on another play to the cries of "Way to go, Jack Hammer!" by Steelers on the sidelines, stuffed by Dwight White and Mel Blount, gang-tackled by White and Lambert, and flipped heels over helmet by Ham, Lambert, White, and Glen Edwards.

Simpson, who set an NFL record by rushing for 2,003 yards in 1973, gained just 49 yards against the Steel Curtain. Still, Simpson's total would be more than the combined amount of Pittsburgh's next two opponents.

While the Steel Curtain squeezed the Juice, Pittsburgh's offense blew away the Bills, putting thirty-two points on the board and producing 438 yards. Bradshaw threw for 203 yards and one TD and provided inspired play throughout. On one occasion he sidestepped Buffalo defenders and found Franco Harris, one of seven different Steelers receivers to whom Terry completed passes.

Bradshaw spiraled passes through the bright skies to Rocky Bleier, John McMakin, Larry Brown, and Lynn Swann, the latter making a diving catch on a 35-yard pass and sliding on the Tartan Turf to the Bills' 5-yard line. Bradshaw even bootlegged and hurdled his own lineman—Jim Clack—in an effort to gain extra yards.

Bradshaw was not alone in having an awesome afternoon. Swann sprinted and high-stepped his way for a medium gain on a nifty reverse and accounted for 51 yards on a scoring drive, and Harris led all rushers with 74 yards and broke the game open in the second quarter by scoring an NFL record-tying three touchdowns in a span of 4:52.

With Jim Simpson and John Brodie calling the game on NBC-TV, the Steelers struck first, taking the opening kickoff and driving 51 yards to Roy Gerela's 21-yard field goal.

Steelers special teams faltered, however, and the Bills took their lone lead following a short punt by Bobby Walden that put Buffalo in good field position at its own 44. QB Joe Ferguson quickly marched his team 56 yards, the last 22 coming on a scoring strike to tight end Paul Seymour. It was the franchise's first playoff points since New Year's Day 1967. On that snowy afternoon in Buffalo the Bills were bidding to become the American Football League's first three-peat champion. But Buffalo bowed to Kansas City and missed the opportunity to represent the AFL against NFL champion Green Bay in the first Super Bowl.

Though Buffalo led 7–3 at the close of the first quarter, the Steelers wasted little time reclaiming the lead early in the second, engineering a 63-yard scoring drive highlighted by several key plays. On third and 10 Bradshaw, the strongest running QB in the NFL, rushed for 12 yards and a first down. Two plays later he rifled a pass through the thirty-three-degree cold to Bleier, the Rock rolling into Pittsburgh's gold-painted end zone.

On the Steelers' next series Harris capped a 66-yard drive by tunneling for a TD from a yard out. On the first play following the ensuing kickoff, Buffalo fullback Jim Braxton busted loose for a 30-yard run, but the ball was stripped free by Mike Wagner and recovered by Ham. Two completions by Bradshaw set up Harris's second score, a four-yard run over the right side.

Pittsburgh regained possession on its 46 and marched to Harris's third TD, a 1-yard run off the left side with sixteen seconds left in the first half. The Steelers' four touchdowns in the second quarter set an NFL playoff record.

Trailing 29–7 at the break, Buffalo trimmed its deficit in the third quarter when Simpson scored from the 3 on a pass from Ferguson. In the only postseason appearance of his Hall of Famer career, Simpson finished with 86 total yards and one TD. Gerela's 22-yard field goal in the fourth capped the scoring.

Three days before Christmas, the Steelers had sent the 48,321 in attendance home with an early present. Still ringing in their ears, along with assorted holiday tunes, were the calls of Steelers radio announcer Jack Fleming:

"Here's Bradshaw, out of the pocket, lots of time, firing downfield, and the ball is caught by Rocky Bleier in the end zone! Touchdown!"

"Here's the handoff to Swann on an end-around coming to the left, the 40, 45, 50, and into Buffalo territory!"

"Bradshaw gives it to Franco, dives through the middle. He's in for a touchdown! Franco Harris lumbering in like a big locomotive!

"Bradshaw back to throw; Bradshaw firing. Look out—there's Swann! Diving catch at the 5-yard line! A sensational grab!

"Here's Bradshaw giving it to Franco, driving off the right side into the end zone! Harris carries 4 yards for the touchdown!"

"Here's the give. Franco left side. Touchdown!"

Later that afternoon at the Los Angeles Coliseum, Pat Summerall, Tom Brookshier, and Bart Starr called the action on CBS as Rams linebacker Isiah Robertson returned a pick-six of Sonny Jurgensen 59 yards to clinch a 19–10 win over Washington. It was a fitting final flourish in a defensive struggle played out under sunny sixty-one-degree temps, and it gave LA its first postseason victory since its championship game win over Cleveland in 1951.

While the Rams and Vikings prepped for the NFC Championship and their first postseason meeting since their 1969 classic in the premerger NFL, the Steelers and Raiders readied to renew a playoff rivalry that was now in its third straight season.

Oakland was viewed as the favorite since it had beaten Pittsburgh two straight times by a combined 50–14 and had just ended the Dolphins' dynasty. The latter came in what Jenkins in his SI playoff preview called "Super Bowl 8 1/2" and convinced many experts that the Raiders were the heir apparent to Miami, which was eyeing a fourth straight Super Bowl trip. Still, the Steelers would have something to say about the line of succession.

Oakland led the league in points scored, and Stabler ranked second to Cincinnati's Ken Anderson among AFC QBs in pass efficiency.

The Raiders had dethroned the Dolphins the week before and were expected to down the Steelers, despite the fact that Pittsburgh's defense was the class of the conference and had surrendered the fewest points in the AFC.

Jenkins wrote that while the Steelers were the most physical of all the playoff teams, they had played the easiest schedule in the AFC, while Oakland owned the NFL's best record at 12-2 and might have gone undefeated had it not suffered a last-second loss at Buffalo in the season opener and had an emotional letdown against Denver.

Championship Sunday started with the Vikings welcoming the Rams to frost-covered Minnesota for a 1:00 p.m. EST kickoff on CBS. Blinding sunshine and a balmy—for Bloomington—game-time temperature of thirty-one degrees greeted the Rams and Vikings as Summerall, Brookshier, and Starr settled in to call the NFC Championship inside banner-bedecked Met Stadium.

Fran Tarkenton threw for one score, Dave Osborn plowed for another, and the Vikings benefited from a controversial illegal procedure call against the Rams that ultimately led to linebacker Wally Hilgenberg's end-zone interception. It was enough to give Minnesota a 14–10 victory as a throng of 48,444 roared its approval. The Vikings advanced to their second straight Super Bowl and third since the 1969 season.

In Oakland 53,800 crammed into the Coliseum for the 4:00 p.m. EST kickoff. Brilliant sunshine bathed the Bay Area as the NBC-TV broadcast crew of Gowdy, DeRo, and Dandy Don returned to the booth they had occupied the weekend before. Inside a stadium festooned with festive red, white, and blue bunting, the swirling, violent action on the bright-green field below featured the talents of no fewer than fifteen AFC Pro Bowlers that season and eighteen Pro Football Hall of Famers. Equally illustrious was the man calling the play-by-play, Curt Gowdy.

Native to Wyoming and nicknamed the "Cowboy," Gowdy's voice defined big-game network TV broadcasting in the 1960s and '70s. The quintessential generalist, Gowdy was NBC's number-one announcer for its coverage of the NFL, Major League Baseball, and NCAA men's basketball. The Cowboy called seven Super Bowls from 1967 to 1979, twelve Rose Bowls, ten straight World Series from 1966 to 1975 and thirteen overall, sixteen MLB All-Star Games, eight Olympics, and twenty-four collegiate men's basketball championships. ABC sought to lure him to its network to be the first play-by-plan announcer for its new *Monday Night Football* programming, but NBC refused to release Gowdy from his contract.

Unlike many of his contemporaries, Gowdy avoided catchphrases and hyperbolic signature calls, preferring instead to provide professional nonpartisan but colorful descriptions of games. The list of famous football games covered by the Cowboy is a lengthy one. It includes Super Bowls I and III and such classic encounters as the *Heidi* Game, the Christmas Day marathon between Miami and Kansas City, the Immaculate Reception, the Sea of Hands game, and the Ghost to the Post.

Plainspoken and low-key, Gowdy modeled his broadcasting style on Red Barber and Mel Allen. Gowdy's voice was warm and slightly gravelly, his style easy and unforced. Author John Updike described Gowdy as sounding like "everybody's favorite brother-in-law."

Gowdy was a fan favorite as well. Homemade signs reading "Howdy, Gowdy!" welcomed him to stadiums across the country. Small wonder since his voice, along with the distinctive, kettle drum–like tones of Charlie Jones, served as the soundtrack for the AFL in the 1960s and the AFC in the 1970s.

DeRo and Dandy Don were former all-pro players, DeRogatis a defensive lineman for the New York Giants in the early 1950s and Meredith a quarterback for the Dallas Cowboys in the 1960s. DeRogatis would serve as an NBC color commentator for NBC's coverage of pro and college football from 1966 to 1975 and did well enough to be pro football writer and historian Paul Zimmerman's choice as the all-time number-one color analyst. The *Boston Globe* called DeRogatis the prototype gentleman—generous, gracious, kind, and polite.

He began his broadcasting career in 1960 working with legendary Marty Glickman on Giants games on WNEW-AM. DeRo's ability to analyze why one play worked and another didn't enamored him with fans listening on radio and caught the attention of NBC executives, who hired him in 1966 and teamed him with Gowdy on televised sportscasts of AFL games.

DeRogatis avoided hyperbole and clichés in his analysis; he saw his role as one that was meant to enlighten more than entertain. He impressed national viewing audiences with an insight that often led him to correctly predict what would happen before it did. In the Super Bowl III pregame show, he stated that if the underdog Jets could run the ball successfully against Baltimore, New York could pull off a surprise victory. Matt Snell rushed for a then Super Bowl record 121 yards and one touchdown, and the Jets claimed one of the greatest upsets in sports history. Gowdy called it one of the most astute prognostications in sports history. In that same pregame analysis DeRogatis broke down for viewers Baltimore's complex zone defense, which Jets quarterback Joe Namath proceeded to pick apart with strategic passing. Two weeks earlier in the AFL Championship Game in Shea Stadium, DeRogatis anticipated a post pattern to Raiders receiver Warren Wells would work for a touchdown. Moments later, Wells was free in the Jets' end zone on a post, but quarterback Daryle Lamonica threw instead to fullback Hewritt Dixon, who was double-covered.

One year later DeRo also correctly predicted the Chiefs would defeat the favored Vikings in Super Bowl IV and saw almost before anyone else the rise of the Dolphins' dynasty in the early 1970s. In Super Bowl VII he spotlighted Miami receiver Howard Twilley, who almost on cue caught a touchdown pass from Bob Griese.

Meredith has the distinction of being both an original Dallas Cowboy and an original member of the *Monday Night Football* broadcasting crew. Meredith was acquired by Dallas in 1960 and hired by ABC in 1970. Dandy Don's country-boy humor and folksy sayings quickly captured the imagination of viewers at a time when *Monday Night Football* was must-see TV.

Meredith's signature saying was "Turn off the lights. The party's over," which he warbled in his Texas twang when the game's outcome was almost decided. Dandy Don was blessed with charm, wit, and personality, and he perfectly complemented his MNF partners, low-key Frank Gifford and bombastic Howard Cosell. Meredith provided a perfect foil for Cosell, the two men playing off each other's personality to the amusement of viewers.

Meredith stayed with ABC through 1973 before joining NBC's number-one NFL broadcast team of Gowdy and DeRogatis in 1974. What Meredith brought to the sportscast was one of the most colorful characters in NFL history. Meredith's family described him as "kind, warm and funny," and Cowboys owner Jerry Jones said, "Few men have contributed, both on the field and as a broadcaster, to the impact that the NFL currently has on our country, more than Don."

As Gowdy, DeRo, and Dandy Don called the action on the field, some remembered the Raiders' dominance of the Steelers in the 1973 postseason and 1974 regular season and expected another Oakland victory. Noll recalled the Raiders' running Pittsburgh's proud defense "off the field" and believed the Steelers may have left their game on the practice field in Palm Springs. But he didn't deny that Pittsburgh had been outplayed and even believed that fact may have helped the Steelers set a tone in the '74 title game. He also felt it worked to his team's advantage that everyone was conceding that Oakland would be the AFC's representative in Super Bowl IX.

The Raiders' defense had been suspect at times during the '74 season—it ranked twenty-first against the run—but it matched the Steel Curtain blow-for-blow in a bruising first half. Swann's muffed punt in the opening quarter was recovered by the Raiders on the Steelers' 41. Blount's deflection of a Stabler pass on third down blunted an Oakland opportunity, and the Raiders settled for a 40-yard field goal from George Blanda and a 3–0 lead.

When Harris complained to an official about extracurricular activity after being tackled by Jack Tatum and Dan Conners, Meredith was moved to comment.

Meredith: *"You saw Franco talking to an official . . . There's definitely no love lost between these two teams. Franco said before the game that the last time they played out here they were throwing dirt in his face. Whether it's true or not, I don't know, but at least Pittsburgh remembers that and they're out here on a mission."*

Gowdy: *"This is not a game. It's a crusade!"*

Stabler looked forward to the heightened intensity of the show-down with the Steel Curtain. To him, it was not only a physical chal-lenge but an intellectual one as well. To the Snake, calling plays was the most fun a quarterback could have. The game became a mental chess match between him and the middle linebacker, in this case Lam-bert. Snake called the plays by feel, remembering what had worked and what hadn't. Since Lambert called the Steelers' defensive align-ments, Stabler would put himself in Jack's place and guess what the rookie might be expecting in the situation they were in.

The physical matchups this day were violent, the mental chess match just as intense. Stabler thought the Steelers' defense in this title game was the most complex he had ever seen. Pittsburgh was mixing coverages on every play, confusing the wily Snake just long enough to put pressure on with rushes by Mad Dog White, Mean Joe, Fats Holmes, and Hollywood Bags. "[The front four] did not give you a lot of time," Stabler said. "They gave you a lot of hurry."

The California sun flaring on their polished black helmets, the Steel Curtain refused to surrender time or space; Raiders runners were limited to gains of 4 yards or less. When Stabler looked to throw, he had to deal with defensive coach Bud Carson's double-zone scheme that was the perfect system for a Steelers squad that specialized in strength and quickness. "We had that edge," Carson said. "We were doing something that people didn't understand."

While Carson had come up with the double zone, fellow defen-sive lieutenant George Perles had invented the famous "Stunt 4-3." Joe Greene, lined up at an angle on the center's nose, slanted and occu-pied two, sometimes three offensive, linemen. That freed up Holmes and particularly Lambert, the other two members of the Steel Cur-tain's inside triangle, to make tackles. Carson said the Stunt 4-3 allowed Lambert to play his game by taking advantage of his natural talents. "The Stunt 4-3 and the double zone," Carson said, "turned Pittsburgh from a loser into a big winner."

Steelers assistant coach Dick Hoak backed up Stabler's comment on the 1974 version of the Steel Curtain being the most complex defense he had ever seen. "They had no idea what was going on," Hoak said. He added that besides the strategic advantage, the Steelers were tough—"top players and intimidators," Hoak said.

Cornerback J. T. Thomas said a psychological profile of the Steel Curtain would reveal two parts—the left side and right side. The left side—Greene, L. C. Greenwood, Jack Ham, Mike Wagner, and Thomas himself—was quiet. The right side, Thomas stated, was noisier. A transition, a total change, took place when you got to Holmes, Lambert, White. Thomas called Lambert "bizarre, wild." Holmes's motive, Thomas said, was to hurt somebody. White was always talking, "bitching for sixty minutes," Thomas said, that everyone was holding him. White cursed out everyone's parenthood on the field. Only Andy Russell, said Thomas, seemed out of place on the right side. "But all those personalities working together," Thomas said, "was the key."

Pittsburgh's offense, meanwhile, threatened on three occasions to reach the Raiders' end zone but was turned away each time after getting inside the 10. Gerela shanked what should have been a chip-shot 20-yard field-goal attempt in the first quarter, but his 23-yarder in the second quarter tied the score at halftime.

DeRogatis: *"We're going to have a whale of a second half."*

The first half had ended with defensive fireworks, Wilson making an end-zone interception after Stallworth had slipped on the turf. Lambert, his white shirt and gold pants streaked with grass stains, followed by blocking a Blanda field-goal attempt in the final seconds. The Raiders went up 10–3 in the third when Stabler, connecting on four passes for 76 yards on the drive, found Branch from 38 yards out.

Gowdy: *"Stabler going to work now. They have to go to the air. They can't do it on the ground . . . A play-action fake. They're going deep to Branch . . . Touchdown!"*

The swift receiver struck time and again in the Steelers' secondary, eventually finishing the game with nine catches for 186 yards and a gaudy 20.7 average. On the touchdown Branch turned Blount inside out, faking him toward the middle of the field, and then the man Madden considered the fastest in football simply outran Blount to the end zone.

Meredith: *"He's been working on Blount, and this time he gets it."*

Gowdy: *"He's dynamite. When he comes out of the huddle, you start worrying about him."*

The aerial attack was the only offense Oakland managed against the Steel Curtain. Employing the Stunt 4-3 scheme with Greene or Holmes angled on Otto's nose, the Steelers shut down the Raiders' running game that had gashed them for 232 yards the previous December on the same Coliseum floor. This time Hubbard, Davis, Banaszak, and Stabler were held to a combined 29 yards on 21 carries, a startling 1.4 average for a squad that ranked second in the AFC with a per-game rush average of 168 yards.

Gowdy: *"[The Raiders] just can't get a running game going . . . They can't get outside, can't move inside . . . Just can't nudge them out of there on the ground."*

The Steelers stunted into the strength of the Oakland offense and stopped it with sheer muscle. Madden told reporters the Steel Curtain gave the Raiders nothing on the ground. He thought Oakland's passing game sufficient, but they couldn't get the run game going. "I can't remember," Madden said, "when our ground game was shut down that effectively."

Stopping the Raiders' running game, Russell said, was the key to the Steelers' defensive game plan. He credited Pittsburgh's coaches with providing an excellent scheme. The Stunt 4-3, Russell stated, was a defense the Raiders hadn't seen Pittsburgh use. The Steelers also stayed away from their "stack-over" scheme in which Greene lined up directly over the center. "Their preparation for that didn't help them any," Russell said. "They couldn't pull their guards as much as they like."

The focal point of the trench warfare could be found in its fulcrum: Mean Joe versus Double-O in the middle of the line. Both are Hall of Famers, but while Greene was at the peak of his career, Otto, the original Raider who had been with the club since its AFL founding back in 1960, was playing his final game. Mean Joe turned twenty-eight years old three months earlier; Double-O was a week shy of turning thirty-six. Physically, Otto was older than his years. Fifteen seasons of hand-fighting defensive linemen like "Big Cat" Ernie Ladd, "Earthquake" Hunt, Curley Culp, and Tom Sestak had taken a toll on "Mr. AFL."

By afternoon's end the furious nature of the private struggle between Greene and Otto was evidenced by the grass and dirt stains that streaked the white jersey and gold pants of Greene and Otto's black shirt and silver pants.

Madden had predicted in the pregame that the championship would be more wide open than Oakland's 17–0 victory in Pittsburgh in Week Three of the regular season. The Raiders' boss expected the rematch to be like the Miami playoff game, with more points being scored. But he thought the offensive outburst wouldn't occur until the second half. The first half, he opined, would be a physical battle and "things will happen in the second half."

The rugged Raiders defense shut out the Steelers in the third quarter and held high-powered Pittsburgh to just three points over seven periods dating back to their regular-season meeting. Oakland seemed on the verge of a victory that would finally shed its bridesmaid label.

At the start of the final quarter NBC cameras caught Al Davis, in his signature high-collared white jacket, anxiously chewing his finger nails as he studied the action on the field. "The ol' fingernail biter," Gowdy called him. "Lucky he has any fingers left."

Earlier NBC had shown Steelers owner Art Rooney wearing a dark hat and tan coat—game-time temp was fifty degrees—while watching the battle from an outdoor suite.

Branch's TD caused Blount to be benched in favor of Jimmy Allen; it also served to incense Pittsburgh's offense. Countering with an eight-play drive, the Steelers tied it just seconds into the fourth quarter when Harris, following a trap block by Gordon Gravelle on Art Thoms, found a lane from the 8 to finish a 61-yard march.

Gowdy: *"Touchdown! Franco Harris up the middle, and the Steelers are back in it!"*

DeRogatis: *"Boy, have they been powerful . . . That offensive line blowing off the ball."*

Minutes later Ham's second interception in the fourth quarter was snagged at the Raiders' 33 and returned to the 9. The title game was turning into the greatest single-game performance for a man Fran Tarkenton considered the finest outside linebacker he ever played against. Russell went further, calling Ham the best linebacker he ever saw.

Ham, like Harris, was a Penn State product, drafted out of the Nittany Lions' linebacker factory in 1971. Also, like Harris, Ham was quiet and unassuming. To him, football was a science and the field his laboratory. He played his position with cold detachment, focusing on his techniques and responsibilities.

Ham's scientific approach likely led to his ability to play so well in high-pressure games, particularly those involving the Raiders. Madden said that of all the outside linebackers he coached against, Ham was the best. "He had the best feet, the best footwork," Madden stated. "He was never out of position."

If the Raiders ran inside, Madden remarked, Ham would close down on the ball carrier. If Oakland ran outside, Ham would string it out and stop it. If Stabler tried to pass against the Steelers' zone, Ham would get back to his area. If the Snake tried to pass against Pittsburgh's man-for-man coverage, Ham would cover his man.

Ham preferred playing pass defense to run defense. He knows some people think of a linebacker only as a guy who can get to the right hole in a hurry and hit hard. To Ham, that's less than half of being a linebacker. At 6 feet 1, 212 pounds, Ham was smaller than some linebackers of his era, but he played like a defensive back in pass coverage. Russell noted that for five yards Ham was the fastest man on the Steelers, and that included receivers and running backs. Ham, Russell said, would come off the ball and explode into a player. When he retired from the Steelers following the 1976 season, Russell said one way in which his life would change is that he would have to pay for the privilege of watching Ham play linebacker. "You've got to do your job on pass coverage," Ham said, "or you're a liability."

Ham did his job so well it amazed his veteran teammates. Russell remembered sitting on the bench on the sideline and listening to Ham explaining a stock deal he was interested in. The Steelers had to suddenly take the field on defense, and on the first play Ham read the pass, took a perfect drop, deflected the ball with one hand, intercepted it with the other, was tackled, and flipped the ball to the referee. Ham then caught up with Russell on their way off the field. "Like I was telling you," Jack said, nonchalantly returning to their conversation, "it's a really good investment."

"It was," Russell recalled with amazement, "like nothing at all had happened."

"I was pretty aware out there," Ham said. "You can make a lot of plays if you're a split-second ahead of everybody."

Still, Ham downplayed his ability to make big plays, preferring instead to play consistent, error-free football. Ham's playmaking abilities did not go unnoticed. He played in eight straight Pro Bowls from 1973 to 1980 and was the NFL's Defensive Player of the Year in 1975.

Green Bay great Dave Robinson, a Hall of Fame outside linebacker, calls Ham one of the first of the smaller, quicker linebackers and a man who turned the position into a threat to be an interceptor.

Maxie Baughan, a star linebacker in the 1960s and '70s, thought Ham one of the more intelligent players to ever play the position. Ham, Baughan said, diagnosed plays to the point where offenses couldn't ever fool him.

Defensive mastermind George Allen said that Ham's intelligence, quickness, and toughness made up for the fact that he was small for a linebacker. Allen believed Ham could serve as a model for other linebackers. "He's played the position about as perfectly as possible," Allen said. "He blitzes at the right time and drops back at the right time."

Allen recalled a story that said that when Ham showed up at the Steelers' preseason practices after being drafted, he was so young looking Art Rooney Jr. informed him that deliveries were made at the side door. Ham may have looked young, but he earned a starting position his rookie season after picking off three passes in the preseason finale. Ham's two interceptions against Oakland in the title game made an impression on Allen, who called him a "big-play guy on a big-play team."

Noll agreed and at a celebrity roast staged once in Ham's honor asked, "How do you roast someone who is perfect?" Pittsburgh sportswriter Phil Musick considered Ham's play so artistic that it was football's version of the *Mona Lisa*.

Ham's second interception in the fourth quarter set up Bradshaw's buggy-whipping a six-yard scoring strike to Swann.

Gowdy: *"Bradshaw throws a slant for a touchdown to Lynn Swann! The rookie has been phenomenal the last three games and puts the Steelers out in front."*

Meredith: *"Nice throw. Nice catch!"*

Trailing 17–10 the Raiders were forced to play catch-up football. Stabler responded with two big completions to Branch that put Oakland at the 12 and in position to tie the game.

Gowdy: *"When Stabler goes to work, he's something . . . Big crowd on its feet now."*

The Raiders reached the 7 before third-down pressure by Holmes, White, Greene, and a blitzing Wagner forced the Snake to throw the ball away. Facing fourth and 4 the Raiders chipped away at their deficit with a 24-yard field goal by Blanda.

Gowdy: *"The lead has been narrowed . . . The big question will be, can Pittsburgh run off two or three first downs, use four or five minutes? It could be disastrous for Oakland."*

With time on its side Pittsburgh went into ground-and-pound mode. The Steelers survived near disaster when Bradshaw fumbled at the Oakland 46 and the loose ball looked to be covered by Raiders linebacker Gerald Irons. Bleier instead covered it for the Steelers, who gained a first down on the next play. Harris and Bleier then combined to run down the clock and the Raiders' defense. By game's end Harris had 111 yards on twenty-nine carries and Bleier 98 on eighteen.

DeRogatis: *"The effectiveness of this offense has really been the diversity of the offense, the way it's been run inside, outside, traps and the pitch, that quick toss . . ."*

Bradshaw said the Steelers' scheme was to run against the Raiders.

"We planned to run the ball," he said, "and our offensive line blew those guys out."

Fronted by reliable escorts in Mansfield, Mullins, and Clack, the

Steelers fired through the middle and swept the flanks, finishing with fifty carries and 224 yards of terra firma.

Oakland still had an opportunity to reclaim the lead late in the game. The Raiders were 51-10-3 at home since opening the Coliseum in 1966, the best record in football since '67. As the California sun began its descent, Oakland fans were wishing for another miracle like the one against Miami.

But cornerback J. T. Thomas, rebounding from a controversial defensive holding penalty the play before, came up with the Steelers' third interception of the rattled Snake—a floater caused by a blitzing Russell—and returned it 37 yards to the Raiders' 24. Thomas had been told by Russell in the huddle, "Don't let the officials intimidate you! Keep playing your aggressive game!" Two plays later Harris provided Pittsburgh's clinching T D with a 21-yard run to make it 24–13 with just fifty-two ticks left.

Gowdy: *"There goes Franco Harris! He scores and it is all over! The Steelers and the Vikings will play in the Super Bowl!"*

Noll, who had taken over as Steelers coach the same year Madden had assumed the reins of the Raiders called the win the culmination of what he had been working for. "We feel you win the big ones on basic fundamental football," Noll said, "and that's what we used."

While the Steelers celebrated, the Raiders were devastated in defeat. "It's tough to come this far and lose," Madden said. "We had the feeling everything was going our way. We had the best record in the N F L, we beat Miami and we were playing at home. You can't play a team like Pittsburgh and do just one thing. You have to mix the run with the pass and have confidence when you run. Winning means being the best on the field that day. We weren't the best today."

As to who would be the best—Pittsburgh or Minnesota—two weeks later on Super Sunday in Tulane Stadium, Madden proved prophetic. "It will be a defensive battle," he stated.

Indeed. Pittsburgh's Steel Curtain and Minnesota's Purple People Eaters are two of the more famous—and feared—defenses in football history, and they showed why on a cool, cloudy, windy afternoon in Super Bowl IX. With temperatures at forty-six degrees in New Orleans at kickoff, Super Bowl IX was played in the second-coldest outdoor temp for a Super Bowl, the coldest being the thirty-nine-degree Super Bowl VI that was played at the same site.

Since the AFC was designated as the visiting team, the Steelers wore their road white jerseys with gold trim on the sleeves and gold pants. The Vikings wore their purple jerseys and white pants. Pittsburgh had history on its side. Each of the four previous teams to defeat Oakland in AFL/AFC Championship Games went on to win the Super Bowl.

Defense outscored offense in the first half. During the regular season the Steelers had surrendered just 189 points, the lowest in the AFC, and the Vikings 195. Following a scoreless first quarter the Steelers secured a 2–0 lead when Tarkenton and Osborn misfired on a pitchout in the shadows of the Vikings' goalposts. As the Vikings' QB attempted to recover the loose ball he slid on the slick Poly Turf into his own end zone. Dwight White, who was not to be denied an opportunity to play in the big game and had literally pulled himself from a hospital bed where he was recovering from pleurisy, touched the downed Tarkenton for a safety.

White lived up to his "Mad Dog" moniker, the 6-foot-4, 255-pounder brutalizing ball carriers by bulling past blockers from his right-end position. A product of East Texas State, where he played linebacker, White played every game for the Steelers his first four years in the league.

White tore up his knee playing linebacker his first year in college. When he came back the next season, his coaches made a defensive end out of him. "I didn't know the basics of the position," White said, "so when the ball was snapped I'd just go crashing in there. Sometimes I'd make a play, sometimes I'd get killed." One of his coaches told him, "White, you play football just like some crazy mad dog." The nickname stuck.

Mad Dog rose to prominence in Super Bowl IX. He didn't know if he could even play on Super Sunday since he had spent the entire week before the game in the hospital. He wasn't listed in the Steelers' starting lineup and wasn't released from the hospital until the eve of the game. White had lost a lot of weight and hadn't worked out all week, and his doctor told him he wouldn't play against the Vikings.

White thought otherwise. "The good pro," he said, "does what he's not supposed to do."

White would do what he had to do to succeed. On the field Mad Dog could be as nasty as anyone who ever played. He could play wild, but he knew it took patience for him to concentrate. "The more control I have of myself," Mad Dog said, "the better I play."

White's teammate at quarterback played conservatively in his homecoming—the Louisiana-born Bradshaw threw just fourteen passes—so Pittsburgh pounded the Purple People Eaters with Harris and Bleier. In their most recent meeting in 1972, the Steelers manhandled Minnesota 23–10 in a late November game in Three Rivers Stadium. On that day Harris hauled the ball for 128 yards and one TD, and the Steelers slugged their way to 206 yards on the ground.

Pittsburgh's game plan was much the same on Super Sunday. Noll believed that the best way to handle Minnesota's penetrating rush by Alan Page, Carl Eller, Jim Marshall, and Doug Sutherland was to send Harris and Bleier through the defense on traps and draws. Noll's plan was similar to the famous "Feast or Famine" game plan designed by his former boss in San Diego, Sid Gillman, who used similar tactics to defeat the aggressive defense of the Boston Patriots in the 1963 AFL Championship Game. Noll was a San Diego assistant in that game, and Sid's strategy stayed with him.

A favored play in Pittsburgh's plan for the Vikings was P-10, a play in which Harris would start up the middle and then follow his instincts and flow toward the hole that was open.

With Bleier blasting past Page and Sutherland on inside traps and Harris slipping outside Marshall and Eller on sweeps, the Steelers upped their advantage to 9–0 in the third quarter on Franco's 9-yard run behind Jon Kolb and Gerry Mullins.

The Steelers' score was set up when Marv Kellum recovered Bill Brown's fumble on the second-half kickoff. Four plays later Harris swept left and scored standing up.

Fleming: *"Bradshaw giving it to Harris, getting a key block from Mullins, running to the left, turning the corner—he's in for a touchdown! Mullins pulling and blocking for Harris!"*

Pittsburgh's lead remained at nine points until early in the final quarter. Minnesota linebacker Matt Blair blocked Walden's punt, and Terry Brown recovered in the end zone with 10:33 to play. The Steelers scored the clinching TD on their next series.

With a 25 mph wind dropping the windchill temp to twenty-two degrees, Bradshaw converted a clutch third and 2 with a 30-yard completion to tight end Larry Brown. The Vikings claimed Brown fumbled on the tackle, but officials ruled him down. Harris and Bleier ran the ball from the Vikings' 28 to the 4. Converting another crucial third-down situation, Bradshaw rolled right, got a great block from Harris, and drilled the ball to Brown in the end zone.

Fleming: *"Bradshaw rolling right. Bradshaw gets a big block and fires into the end zone, complete for the touchdown!"*

Pittsburgh's twelve-play drive covered 66 yards, melted more than seven minutes off the game clock, and closed the scoring at 16–6 with 3:31 remaining. Wagner's pirating of a Tarkenton pass on Minnesota's next series sealed the Steelers' first Super Bowl win.

Fleming: *"Time has run out! The Steelers are Super Bowl champions!"*

With Lambert and Russell limping, reserve 'backers Toews and Ed Bradley stood in and stepped up, and the Steel Curtain surrendered a meager 17 yards rushing and 119 yards total, both Super Bowl records.

Amid the gloaming Pittsburgh punished Minnesota mercilessly, hammering Osborn and running star Chuck Foreman as much as they had Oakland runners in the AFC Championship. The Vikings and Raiders combined for 42 rushes and just 46 yards against a Pittsburgh defense performing at its peak.

The Steelers harassed Scramblin' Fran into three interceptions. Greene had a pick courtesy of a deflected pass by L. C. Greenwood. The 6-foot-6 gold-shoed Greenwood had three of the Steel Curtain's four deflections, prompting NFL commissioner Pete Rozelle's pun at the Vikings' expense in the following year's draft: "Minnesota passes, and L. C. Greenwood knocks it down."

The Steel Curtain's Stunt 4-3 confused the Vikings. Holmes and Greene took rush angles on future Hall of Fame center Mick Tingelhoff and either attacked him directly or looped and stunted in double-team action.

By game's end the Vikings had run just twelve plays in Pittsburgh territory, tying 1971 Miami for the second fewest in Super Bowl history. The fewest were Oakland's eleven plays in its Super Bowl II loss to Green Bay. The record stood until Super Bowl XXXV, when the history-making Ravens defense allowed the Giants to run just four plays in Baltimore territory.

Pittsburgh also confused the Purple Gang with misdirection running plays, as Harris and Bleier found gaping lanes behind the flow of pulling and trapping linemen. Harris earned MVP honors by running for a then Super Bowl record 158 yards—eclipsing the total set the year before by Csonka against these same Vikings in Super Bowl VIII—and the Steelers piled up 249 rushing yards on a staggering fifty-seven carries.

Harris's contributions proved crucial. Franco outgained the entire Minnesota offense 158–119. It had taken forty-two frustrating years, but Art Rooney's dream had finally been realized. The Steelers were champions, and their venerable owner was a lovable loser no more.

Returning to Pittsburgh, the Super Steelers were welcomed by thousands of fans. In a helicopter high above the joyous throng, a Pittsburgh announcer described the wild scene: "The downtown area just packed with people. What a big party shaping up down there. You should see the balloons and the signs—'Go, Terry, Go,' 'Defense, Defense,' 'We're No. 1!' A lot of excitement, you can see it, on the face of the city. From up here, it's about the most exciting thing I've seen since the parting of the Red Sea."

From the shattered Raiders' viewpoint, it was a parting of sweet sorrow.

Jim Campbell: O. J. Simpson still had the moves in his playoff showdown with the Steel Curtain, but it seemed that he was making most of them in the Bills backfield and was quickly hemmed in by quick and ill-humored Black and Gold defenders. On this day, Juice could squeeze out only 49 yards rushing. He did, though, take a touchdown pass from Joe Ferguson in the 32–14 Steelers victory. It was O.J.'s only postseason game in an eleven-year HOF career.

With the Bills shuffled off to Buffalo, the Raiders were next. What could we expect? Would it be a repeat of the shutout loss to Oakland earlier in the season or a continuation of Bradshaw, Harris, Greene, and Company rocking and rolling? We would see.

Like Chuck Noll, I thought the assessment of the game and the teams that were left standing was a little premature, if not misguided. I was well aware of the lopsided home loss and the fact that this game was on the West Coast, but I had seen too much—up close and personal—of the Steel Curtain, Franco, Bradshaw, et al. to be willing to concede.

With the front four—especially Joe Greene and Ernie Holmes angling in on Jim Otto and the guards—flexing its considerable muscle and Oakland's defense doing likewise, it was a hard-hitting, low-scoring first half. But in the third quarter, Stabler put together a drive that was capped by Cliff Branch's 38-yard scoring run and catch.

I was concerned. Mel Blount, for whom I had great respect, was being beaten by Branch like the proverbial drum. Blount would prove to be the prototypical cornerback for the era. He was big, fast, tough, and smart. With his long, lean build and his affinity for wearing a ten-gallon Stetson, he reminded me of one of the large number of cowboys who worked the West before and after the Civil War.

Steelers teammates called him "Supe," as in Superman. And usually he was. It was said that "two-thirds of the Earth's surface is covered with water; the rest by Mel Blount." More than one NFL wideout would think this opinion only a slight exaggeration.

Noll, also, had seen enough. In the second half, Supe was sitting and rookie corner Jimmy Allen had taken over. While the Raiders would still pile up passing yardage, the defense made it next to impossible for Oakland to gain any appreciable yardage via the overland route. Defensive coordinator Bud Carson, ably assisted by defensive line coach George Perles and linebacker coach Woody Widenhofer, forced the Raiders into being one-dimensional.

The Steelers' "Stunt 4-3" was something the Raiders hadn't expected, and it limited the Silver and Black attack to 29 yards rushing.

Pittsburgh flew home with a 24–13 AFC Championship Game victory, and thoughts immediately turned to Super Bowl IX, where the Steel Curtain would be pitted against Minnesota's highly touted Purple People Eaters—anchored by ends Jim Marshall and Carl Eller and tackle Alan Page.

After the thrashing of the Bills in the first round of the playoffs, I remember saying to Coach Noll, "Just two more to go." Chuck didn't give a verbal reply, but gave a quick nod and his thin-lipped Cheshire-cat grin. I was pumped that the Steelers were going to the Super Bowl. But I was even more pumped when Joe Gordon told me that there was a good chance I could go along.

Naturally, I was pleased for myself, but I was also pleased for the organization after all those years of futility. A small taste of honey with the Immaculate Reception in 1972, but four decades of frustration weighed heavily on the Steelers and the city of Pittsburgh.

I was especially happy for Mr. Rooney. Through thick and thin, mostly thin, he stuck with the franchise, listening to and reading about how "the Rooneys are too cheap to ever win" and "should be forced to sell the team." The Chief suffered in silence, and now he was a game away from silencing his long-standing critics. But the Steelers would need to win the game. The Vikings were more experienced—with two previous trips to "the ultimate game"—but had nothing to show for it.

Joe Gordon told me I could fly on the Steelers wives' charter down to New Orleans before the Super Bowl. The days before departure time seemed to move like months, but I boarded the Steelers' charter at Pittsburgh International and headed south with Steelers wives and other Steelers personnel. It was a bumpy ride, but hardly anyone noticed or cared. As we got closer to the Crescent City, the captain came on the intercom and assured us that "we're experiencing a little turbulence, but we'll be just fine."

I guess I was too psyched to realize that we were coming in "hot." The plane was really moving down the runway of what is now Louis Armstrong International Airport. The would-be Chuck Yeager used every inch of the runway, but he got us down in one piece. It was only the next day that I realized how lucky we were and how skilled our pilot was, when I picked up a copy of the *Times-Picayune* and read the headline: "Tornado Touches Down at Airport."

With a day to kill before kickoff, I went walking down Canal Street. The weather was one of those Chamber of Commerce–type days. Sunny, warm, nice breeze. It was during this outing that I stopped to "loaf" (a Pittsburgh term for "hanging out") with the Steelers fans who "brought the wagon." No ordinary car for them for the 1,100-mile trip from the 'Burgh. They were a jovial bunch and all thought that the "Stillers" would win the next day.

As great as Saturday was, Sunday was anything but. It was cold. It was raw. It was rainy. It was windy. Since the Louisiana Superdome wasn't finished, the game would be played in Tulane Stadium, a.k.a. the Sugar Bowl.

I recall the rain had stopped, but that was about the only good thing. Cold, raw, and windy were the order of the day. Planks were laid down to allow bus passengers to get into the stadium without getting their shoes soaked. Because it was assumed that New Orleans weather in January would be quite warm, many were attired in their finery instead of more practical and warm clothing. I was one of them. I don't recall specifically what I was wearing, but it wasn't nearly enough to ward off the elements.

Temperature at kickoff was a blustery forty-six degrees. It was the second-lowest temp for a Super Bowl. Games in northern cities such as Detroit and Pontiac, Michigan, and Minneapolis were in colder climes, but it didn't matter—those games were played in domed stadiums. Even the temp at kickoff at SB XLVIII at Met Life Stadium in East Rutherford, New Jersey, was forty-nine.

Walking into the stadium, it didn't take much of an imagination to think one might be back at Three Rivers Stadium. Black and gold colors were all over the place, and when the Steelers did something good, the roar of the crowd made it sound like a home game. It perplexes me when announcers say "The Steelers travel well," like half of Pittsburgh packs up and goes to road games. Not quite true. Sure, some of

the faithful do make the trek, but most of the "travels well" are people attracted to the excellence of the team or are Johnny-come-lately
fans, who gravitate to the latest winner. Given the Steelers' long history of excellence, their numbers have swelled over the years.

One of the big questions before the game was the status of defensive end Dwight White. "Mad Dog," suffering from pneumonia during
the week, was actually hospitalized. While the media were not like the
hordes covering the game now, there were inquiring minds in New
Orleans, and they wanted to know what would happen if White was
not available. Low-key as ever, Noll said simply, "We'll go with Steve
Furness." No further elaboration necessary—at least not from Noll.
Furness, a fifth-round draftee from the University of Rhode Island
in 1972, had already proved himself as an integral part of the Steelers'
defense. He was a "swing man," who could fill in at both defensive-
end slots and both defensive-tackle positions.

As it turned out, although Furness played significantly, White started
the game. He literally got out of a hospital bed to take the field. He
was weakened and underweight, but few, if any, ever played with more
determination and enthusiasm than the young East Texas State alum-
nus. While I personally had confidence in Furness, it was still reassur-
ing to see No. 78 take the field at the start of play. White would make
his presence felt as the game played out.

As we all expected with two dominating defenses (the Steelers led
the NFL in rush defense, pass defense, and total defense), the first
quarter was a struggle. Greene and Company kept Chuck Foreman
in check, and Fran Tarkenton managed only 20 yards passing. The
law (and order) firm of Page, Eller, and Marshall, supplemented by a
stingy secondary, gave up only 18 passing yards, but an encouraging
61 rushing yards—many by Franco Harris.

I had expected Sir Francis to take advantage of the less than 100 percent Dwight White, but he stubbornly ignored him and tried to throw
over L. C. Greenwood, who kept rejecting his passes as though he were
Wilt Chamberlain or Kareem Abdul-Jabbar in gold football cleats.

The second quarter was more of the same. Not much happened
until the Vikings were pinned deep in their own territory. A botched

handoff between Tark and Dave Osborn resulted in a loose ball in the end zone, and White touched Tark down for a safety. I can't say I was ecstatic or that I thought a 2–0 score would hold up as a final winning tally, but a lead was a lead. As I often said, when a basketball team I favored had a 2-point lead, "All we gotta do is play them evenly the rest of the way, and we win."

I got a sinking feeling when Minnesota recovered Rocky's fumble at the Pittsburgh 24, but two plays later Fred Cox, late of the University of Pittsburgh, missed a 39-yard field goal.

Very late in the second quarter, Tark threw deep to John Gilliam. Glen "Pine" (he was dubbed this by teammates "because he's as tough as a pine knot") Edwards smacked into the Vike's wide receiver with a force few could duplicate. Gilliam went down, the ball went up, and Mel Blount cleared the rebound—end of threat. The Steelers took their 2–0 lead into the locker room—the lowest score in Super Bowl history to that time.

Unlike halftimes at Three Rivers, I had nothing to do—except try to get warm. I was only semisuccessful. However, the halftime show took my mind off of the meteorological conditions—still in the mid-forties, still a windchill in the twenties. The outstanding Grambling State Marching Band, augmented by the Duke Ellington Orchestra, under the direction of Mercer Ellington, played "A Tribute to Duke," who had passed away in the spring of 1974.

The rain-slicked field was a factor as the second half got under way. The Steelers' kickoff was fumbled by Bill Brown and recovered by bomb-squader Marv Kellum. Bradshaw directed the ensuing drive that culminated in a 9-yard burst into the end zone by Franco, behind Gerry Mullins's block. Gerela's bonus point made it 9–6.

If trap plays were the Steelers' bread and butter, then misdirection was ham and Swiss. Bradshaw faked to Harris and stuck the ball in Bleier's gut as he ran right. Seventeen yards later Rocky had the first down, and the drive continued.

A key fourth-quarter play was a pass to Larry Brown down the left sideline. The strapping tight end, who would later move inside and become an All-Pro offensive tackle, caught the ball for a sizable gain.

At the end of the play the ball came loose. Minnesota recovered. Two officials initially ruled fumble, but head linesman Ed Marion, one of the most competent officials I worked with during my seven seasons on the sidelines, made a case for its being a completion. Although his day job was not that of a lawyer, Marion convinced his fellow stripers that it was indeed a legitimate reception and blown dead. There was no instant replay at the time, so Ed really had to stand by his convictions and do a first-class selling job. Even more relief was provided when Brown took a short pass from Bradshaw to push the score to 16–6.

Another crucial fourth quarter play also involved the officials—this time referee Bernie Ullman. Greenwood rejected a Tarkenton pass again. This time Tark got the rebound and hurled a 42-yard completion to Gilliam. Ullman correctly ruled, as stipulated in the official NFL rule book, that only one forward pass can be attempted per play. The throw to Gilliam, caught or not, was illegal.

Had I not known the team as well as I did, there were a couple of injuries that might have given me pause. Both outside linebacker Andy Russell and middle linebacker Jack Lambert were forced from the game. True to the "next-man-up" approach of Noll and his staff, a pair of youngsters stepped up—Loren Toews for Russell and Ed Bradley for Lambert—and didn't miss a beat. They blended seamlessly with the other nine Steelers stalwarts.

When the game ended the Steelers had their first of what would be multiple Vince Lombardi Trophies. I was jubilant. I noticed a phenomenon that occurred during cold-weather games at Three Rivers. As the scoreboard mounted in Pittsburgh's favor, the temperature seemed to rise. By the end of the special game in New Orleans that day, the chilliness and rawness of the day were all but forgotten.

A humble Art Rooney graciously accepted the Lombardi Trophy from a pleased Pete Rozelle, the commissioner. Unnoticed to many, an imposing figure of a man is standing behind Mr. Rooney. It is Joey Diven, a large (6-foot-5, 245-pound), slick-haired Irishman. Diven, by reputation, was acclaimed Pittsburgh's most devastating and successful street fighter. His heyday was the 1950s and '60s, but you still didn't want to mess with him. It was said that Joey roamed Oakland (a section of the city near the Pitt campus) on weekends looking for someone foolish enough to challenge him. Regardless of the era, Pitt football recruited some formidable young men from the mines and mills of western Pennsylvania. Legend has it that on one night Joey sent the entire starting Panthers backfield to the emergency room.

On the bus back to the Steelers' hotel, I shared a seat with Perles. I had one of the first copies of the game's play-by-play sheets. Perles asked to see them. He studied a while and exclaimed, "Hey! This isn't right!" I don't remember the specific play he questioned, but the Vikings' ground game was credited with some yards that Perles felt hadn't been earned. The outcome was that Minnesota's official rushing yardage was revised down to a skimpy 17 yards.

Just how limiting the Steelers' defense was is reflected in the rushing stats of Foreman, who had 18 yards on twelve attempts—one of which was a 12-yard run. Take that one carry out of the mix, and the formidable Foreman had 6 yards on eleven attempts—0.5 yards a carry. Osborn was held to minus 1 yard on eight carries.

At a postgame celebration I caught up with Noll. I said, "Guess we were right about 'just two more wins.'" He didn't respond verbally, but this time his grin was much wider as he gave that quick nod, his eyes smiling as much as his lips.

Russell and Mansfield, about the only holdovers from "the bad ol' days," possibly savored the victory more than their younger teammates. Mansfield speculated, "I bet the 'Burgh's in flames about now." Not quite, but I imagine the Iron City, Duquesne, and Rolling Rock were flowing like the Monongahela, Allegheny, and Ohio Rivers.

As with most Steelers victories of the time, winning Super Bowl IX can be attributed to a strong running game. Franco broke Larry Csonka's Super Bowl rushing record—set the year previously—when he rumbled for 158 yards. It earned him Most Valuable Player honors. Rocky carried his share of the load by racking up another 65 yards.

Pittsburgh, with its interchangeable parts on the offensive line, ran a trapping running game better than any NFL team. Helping further was Bleier's blocking. It was so proficient that more than one opponent referred to the 5-foot-10, 215-pounder as "their third guard." One now anonymous defensive lineman lamented, "Those Steelers, they start trappin' you as soon as you step off the team bus."

The nomenclature of the key trap play was Brown 93. It, literally, was part of the team's tapestry. As such a huge and elaborate fabric wall hanging covered an entire wall of the Three Rivers Stadium reception area. It was, in different fabrics and colors, an enlarged diagram of the play, complete with Xs and Os and dotted lines showing the blocking routes and the path the ball carrier should follow. So revered was Brown 93 that when the franchise moved headquarters from soon-to-be demolished Three Rivers Stadium to Heinz Field in 2001, the tapestry was carefully packed to make the short trip and unpacked and rehung when the new facility was operational. As famous as the Green Bay Packers' Power Sweep of the Vince Lombardi era was, Brown 93 was equally so.

Stripped of its mystical and mythical aura, Brown 93 was a simple inside trap play over center, with Franco carrying the ball. To a man, Steelers vouch for its being largely responsible for the 1974 team getting to and winning Super Bowl IX. The play was usually run from a strong-right formation (tight end on the right side)—left tackle Jon Kolb, left guard Jim Clack, center Ray Mansfield, right guard Gerry Mullins, right tackle Gordon Gravelle, and tight end Larry Brown. This line was lighter than most in the NFL by 10 pounds per man, but they were quick, nimble, athletic, and amazingly strong.

Bradshaw was under center, and Franco and Rocky were split-backs lined up behind the guard and tackle gaps. Bleier would start left drawing the right outside linebacker with him, blocking him if necessary. Bradshaw would hand off to Franco, who headed into the line over center. Kolb blocked the right defensive end; Clack went out on the middle linebacker or Mike man. Mansfield helped Mullins double-team the left defensive tackle and then released to get the strong-side linebacker.

Mullins continued to stick with the left defensive tackle. Gravelle would pull to the left and trap the right defensive tackle. If all blocks were executed and sustained, Franco, sometimes using the unsuspecting, striped-shirted umpire as an additional "blocker," would gain a sizable and valuable chunk of yardage. A complementary play could be run to the other side, with Rocky carrying the ball and Franco as the blocking back.

With the Super Bowl victory, just how precarious the season was is overlooked. No other Super Bowl winner ever started three quarterbacks—Gilliam, Hanratty, and Bradshaw—in a season, and all of this took place in the first eleven games. Little known is the fact that Joe Greene, the acknowledged leader of the team, was so frustrated after the 13–10 home loss to the Houston Oilers that he actually cleaned out his locker and virtually quit. Mean Joe thought the team had Super Bowl potential, but wasn't realizing it. Had not receivers coach Lionel Taylor caught up to him, Greene may well have left the squad. Taylor and Greene sat in Greene's car and hashed things out for quite some time. Greene let off steam and Taylor listened. Greene reconsidered, and the rest is history.

It should be noted that once the strike was settled and the veteran Steelers were back in camp, Noll adopted a mantra—"Whatever it takes." Through the ups and downs of the quarterback situation, injuries, bad bounces, and more, it was very evident as the final seconds ticked off the Tulane Stadium scoreboard clock that the team took those words to heart.

I didn't have that much direct contract with Steelers broadcaster Myron Cope. He was a local version of Howard Cosell—raspy voice, extensive vocabulary, and strong opinions. At home games I was on the sideline. For road games I chose television over radio. I did, however, hear many of Cope's WTAE Radio daily commentaries. His fingers-across-a-blackboard voice was embraced by Pittsburghers, and his humor and irony, as well as his insight, were appreciated by all.

Once the super season was over, Cope said of his role as color commentator, "This has been the perfect job for the perfect season. The Steelers took every kernel of corn off the cob."

One final Super Bowl IX note: Bruce Van Dyke was an excellent pulling guard for a half-dozen years with the Steelers—a vital contributor to the trapping plays, as well as counter plays. With the versatility of guards Mullins, Clack, and Sam Davis, the team traded him to Green Bay in 1973, where his college coach Dan Devine was taking over as head coach. In a rather unorthodox stipulation in the trade agreement, Van Dyke was to get a Super Bowl share if the Steelers were to win a Super Bowl. So like all Steelers on the '74 roster, he got a check for $15,000—the winner's share.

What would lie ahead for the Steelers? Part of the answer was hanging in the Steelers' locker room before they left Tulane Stadium. A sign read: "There are only two kinds of Super Bowl teams that no one remembers—those that lost, and those that win only one."

As the next season played out, Noll's players showed just how much they bought into it.

7

Seeing Stars

"From Soldier Field in Chicago, Illinois, it's the College All-Stars versus the National Football League champion Pittsburgh Steelers in the Forty-Second College Football All-Star Game...

"Hello, everybody. I'm Keith Jackson..."

ABC's famous play-by-play announcer was flanked by Hall of Famer Bud Wilkinson, who had played and coached in the College All-Star series, and Howard Cosell, whom Jackson introduced as the "stalwart of Monday Night NFL Football."

Dressed in MNF's iconic yellow blazers, Jackson, Wilkinson, and Cosell settled in the booth overlooking the playing field made slick by a pregame downpour.

Jackson noted that while the collegians would love to beat the professional champions, the mere thought of such an occurrence was enough to make the Steelers "dyspeptic." Wilkinson, who coached one of college football's great dynasties at the University of Oklahoma in the 1950s, put forth a case for such an upset.

The All-Stars, wearing the traditional white helmets, white pants, and bright blue jerseys with red stars on the shoulders, were fortunate to have USC legend John McKay as head coach, Wilkinson said. As rousing renditions of the USC and Notre Dame fight songs from the collegiate band on the field framed his comments on this August

1 night, Wilkinson opined that the collegians enjoyed an edge over Pittsburgh in special teams play.

Cosell scoffed at the notion. The Steelers, he stated, "are an awesome football team with a magnificent offensive and defensive balance."

In classic Cosell-speak, with halting pauses for dramatic emphasis, Howard proceeded to tell it like it is. "This is a super football team. They should be able to win about . . . as . . . they . . . please."

Cosell and Wilkinson were, in fact, both correct. The latter had been a player in the All-Stars' first win over the NFL champions in 1937, the collegians defeating Curly Lambeau's Green Bay Packers 6–0. The pros led the series 29-9-2 (the 1974 game was canceled due to the NFL player's strike), but as recently as 1971 the Super Bowl champion Baltimore Colts had only beat the collegians by 24–17. In 1969 Broadway Joe Namath and the New York Jets barely survived the Stars, 26–24. After the game a shaken Namath admitted that the collegians had "scared" him.

The All-Stars' most recent victory came in 1963 against Vince Lombardi and his two-time reigning NFL champion Green Bay Packers. The defeat mortified invincible Vince, who lamented that football fans would forever remember his Packers' embarrassing loss.

Played every August but one from 1934 to 1976, the College All-Star Game served as the traditional kickoff to the professional and college football campaigns. The game was the creation of former Chicago sports editor Arch Ward, who had also been the primary force behind Major League Baseball's All-Star Game. Both classics were conceived during the Great Depression as vehicles that would raise money as well as the spirits of a citizenry struggling to maintain hope and confidence.

Originally benefiting Chicago-area charities, the College All-Star Game was annually played at Soldier Field, the exceptions being 1943–44 when it was held at Northwestern University's Dyche Stadium in Evanston. The games featured pro and college legends, Hall of Famers, and even a future U.S. president. Gerald Ford, a University of Michigan graduate, was a member of the 1935 All-Star squad that bowed to the Chicago Bears, 5–0.

Ward, who founded the All-America Football Conference that served as direct competition to the NFL from 1946 to 1949, attempted to have the AAFC's champion Cleveland Browns meet the College All-Stars in August 1949. The NFL convinced—and some say strong-armed—the *Tribune* board to overrule Ward and continue the collegians' game with the establishment rather than with the rebels.

As NFL teams improved and integrated, the collegians' victories grew increasingly scarce. From 1950 to 1973 the All-Stars won just four of twenty-four games.

Steelers coach Chuck Noll was familiar with the ups and downs of the College All-Star Game, having played in it twice for the Browns. In 1955 the Browns dropped a 30–27 decision; in 1956 Cleveland exacted revenge with a 26–0 victory.

Wearing the white jerseys and gold pants they wore eight months earlier for Super Bowl IX in New Orleans, the Steelers' starting lineup for the game against the All-Stars was almost identical to the one they fielded against NFC champion Minnesota. The major differences were at wide receiver, where Frank Lewis and Ron Shanklin started for Lynn Swann and John Stallworth.

The collegians' starting lineup was impressive as well, and one of the interesting aspects of this annual classic was the opportunity it afforded fans to watch established pros go head-to-head with collegiate stars. In previous years that meant NFL coaching legends like George Halas opposing Frank Leahy of Notre Dame, Dallas's Tom Landry opposite Nebraska's Bob Devaney, Kansas City's Hank Stram versus Otto Graham, McKay meeting Miami's Don Shula.

It also meant the first on-field meeting of Cleveland superstar Jim Brown and future fellow Hall of Famer Dick Butkus, which took place in 1965. Dan Jenkins wrote in *Sports Illustrated* that the ferocious Butkus bounced Cleveland ball carriers, including Brown, "like toys." Brown, whose only other on-field meeting with Butkus came in the 1966 Pro Bowl, remembers the All-Star confrontation and calls Butkus one of the toughest men he ever played.

In 1975 the All-Star classic saw Jackson State running back Walter Payton fighting for yardage against Steelers defensive tackle Mean Joe

Greene on one play and eluding the grasp of middle linebacker Jack Lambert on another. It would be the first of just three on-field show-downs between Sweetness and the Steel Curtain, the Bears and Steelers meeting in the 1975 regular season and again in 1980.

California's Steve Bartkowski, the starting quarterback for the Stars and No. 1 draft choice of the Atlanta Falcons, put the collegians on top early. Bartkowski's 28-yard pass to Harvard's Pat McInally highlighted the Stars' statistical domination in the first quarter. Pittsburgh tied the score in the second quarter on Terry Bradshaw's 2-yard toss to tight end Randy Grossman. But the collegians took a 14–7 lead into halftime when Virgil Livers returned a Bobby Walden punt 88 yards for the score.

The Stars still led the Steelers by seven points entering the final fifteen minutes. Joe Gilliam, having replaced Bradshaw under center, tied the score with a 6-yard pass to Rocky Bleier. The Super Bowl champs secured the comeback win when Gilliam found Lewis for a 21-yard TD.

Among the interested observers were the Oakland Raiders, and it didn't take long for their No. 1 pick in the 1975 NFL Draft, cornerback Neal Colzie, to introduce himself to his future blood rivals. A star defender for Woody Hayes's reigning Big Ten champion Ohio State Buckeyes, Colzie was playing cornerback for McKay. An all-purpose talent who would excel for the Raiders as a record-setting rookie return specialist, Colzie was part of a draft class dominated by Dallas and its "Dirty Dozen" that included Randy White and Thomas Henderson.

NFL historians have compared the Cowboys' talent haul in '75 to the Steelers' epic draft in '74. Two products of Pittsburgh's '74 draft—middle linebacker Jack Lambert and wide receiver Lynn Swann—established themselves as stars as the Steelers set about to defend their title.

Lambert, a toothless, twig-legged terror, was named to the Pro Bowl for the first of nine straight seasons and evolved into one of the great linebackers in league history. Lambert was a link in a long line of great middle linebackers, following in the footsteps of Joe Schmidt, Sam Huff, Bill George, Ray Nitschke, Dick Butkus, Tommy Nobis, Nick Buoniconti, Willie Lanier, Mike Curtis, and Bill Bergey and proving a fearsome forerunner to Harry Carson, Mike Singletary, and Ray Lewis. Lambert bridged two eras, starting his career in the mid-1970s as a young contemporary of Lanier, Buoniconti, Bergey, and Curtis and ending it as an elder statesmen a decade later when Carson and Singletary were entering their dominant years in the mid-'80s.

What Lambert lacked in heft, he made up for in hate. He was so mean as a player, teammate Joe Greene said, Lambert didn't even like himself. Lambert's ferocious play led to his being nicknamed Jack the Ripper, and his fearsome, toothless visage became known as the Lambert Look.

His fellow greats at linebacker appreciated Lambert's persona. Former Philadelphia Eagle great Chuck Bednarik thought Lambert "ornery," and Nobis considered Jack "all-out intimidating." When Lambert hit a QB or running back, Nobis said, they know who hit them.

Fellow Steelers 'backer Andy Russell shared the same NFL fields with Nitschke, Butkus, Huff, and Nobis in the '60s and Buoniconti and Lanier in the '70s following the merger with the AFL. What set Lambert apart from some of the other all-time greats, Russell opined, was his ability to defend the pass. Lambert was comparable to Nitschke and Butkus against the run but not as impressive, Russell thought. But Andy believed Jack better against the pass than the other great middle 'backers.

Lambert drew a distinction between his style of play and that of his predecessors. Butkus and Nitschke, he said, stood in the middle of the defense and dared opposing blockers and ball carriers to try to knock them down. Because he weighed twenty to thirty pounds less than Nitschke or Butkus, Lambert said he played a style that suited him best. If he could run around a blocker to get to the ball carrier, Lambert would do it.

Lambert was the final cog in the Steel Curtain's construction. On a unit known for its physical play, Lambert may have been its hardest hitter. NFL Films rates him No. 8 all-time on its list of most feared tacklers. "I tackle as hard as I can," Lambert said at the time. "We're supposed to be intimidators."

Hall of Fame coach George Allen, who bossed the Chicago Bears'

"Monsters of the Midway" championship defense in 1963 and the Los Angeles Rams' legendary "Fearsome Foursome" of the late 1960s, thought Lambert one of the hardest hitters he had ever seen. "No one has hit much harder than Jack Lambert," Allen stated. "He has been a punishing player, mean and nasty, who has put a lot of players out of commission. He is tall, tough, quick, a good pass defender and great run defender."

Lambert's leading the team in tackles in each of his first eight seasons, including fourteen in a game against Cleveland in his rookie campaign, was a product of two things: Steelers strategy that angled Joe Greene and Ernie Holmes on the center's nose in a Stunt 4-3 alignment, designed to clog the middle of the line and allow Lambert to roam sideline to sideline free of blockers, and Jack's überaggressiveness. "Because of my size," Lambert said, "I have to be active and aggressive."

Lambert, Greene, and Holmes formed one of the great inside triangles in NFL history. It rivals the 1958–62 Giant trio of Huff–Rosey Grier–Dick Modzelewski; the 1960–62 Lions' Schmidt–Alex Karras–Roger Brown; the 1965–67 Packers' Nitschke–Henry Jordan–Ron Kostelnik; the 1968–72 Chiefs' Lanier–Culp–Buchanan; and 2000–2001 Ravens' Ray Lewis–Sam Adams–Tony Siragusa.

The Raiders respected Lambert, but some Oakland players considered him a product of Pittsburgh's system. Jack Tatum thought Lambert a "fair" linebacker at best and one not in the same company as Lanier. Lambert was said to be great, Tatum said, only because he played behind the best defensive line in the NFL.

By 1976 Lambert would earn the first of two NFL Defensive Player of the Year honors. In 1977 he was named a Steelers captain. Flanked by fellow future Pro Football Hall of Famer Jack Ham on the left and veteran all-pro Russell on the right, Lambert was the linchpin of a unit that Allen called "one of the greatest sets of linebackers ever."

From the start of the Super Bowl era one of the similarities shared by championship teams lay in the linebacker units. In Super Bowls I and II, the Packers dominated their AFL counterparts in part because of one of the great linebacker trios in history—Hall of Famers Nitschke and Dave Robinson and all-pro Lee Roy Caffey. The Kansas City Chiefs won Super Bowl IV with a similarly great unit featuring HOFers Lanier and Bobby Bell and all-pro Jim Lynch. The Baltimore Colts' trio of Curtis, Ray May, and HOFer Ted Hendricks helped win Super Bowl V. Dallas's Doomsday defense held Miami to a Super Bowl–low three points in Super Bowl VI, thanks in part to linebackers Lee Roy Jordan, Dave Edwards, and Chuck Howley. The Dolphins won Super Bowls VII and VIII with a linebacker unit fronted by HOFer Buoniconti.

George Allen called Lambert and Ham a "terrific combination" for the Steelers. What Ham did with intelligence, Allen said, Lambert did with instinct. Allen thought Lambert was a natural, a guy who loved to play, loved to hit, played with enormous enthusiasm, and took pride in playing hurt. Allen thought Lambert almost animalistic at times. "He snarls at you all the time," Allen said.

Deacon Jones, one of the greatest defensive ends ever, called the best linebackers some of the hardest men in the Show. There was no one on a football field, the Deacon said, tougher than the top linebackers. While Russell stated that it's impossible to rate the best linebacker corps of all time because defenses are constructed differently, NFL Films ranks the Lambert-Ham-Russell trio the second-best ever behind the New Orleans Saints' Dome Patrol (Rickey Jackson, Sam Mills, Vaughan Johnson, and Pat Swilling) of the late 1980s and early 1990s.

Lambert personified the frenzy felt by fans. But Russell said that the rock-'em-sock-'em image had little to do with why Lambert was so successful. He thought him a very smart and technically proficient player who could anticipate what was going to happen.

Lambert, Ham, and Russell combined for twenty-five Pro Bowl honors. Because they played in the 220-pound range, they were able to play a style of defense that other teams couldn't even imagine playing. While other famous linebacker corps like the 1985 Bears' trio of Mike Singletary, Wilber Marshall, and Otis Wilson targeted quarterbacks, Lambert, Ham, and Russell covered the quarterback's targets.

The Steel Curtain dominated its decade; Fran Tarkenton deems it the greatest defense he ever faced. Manning the middle was an overnight success who had come from nowhere to reach the top of his profession. In his senior year at Kent State Lambert was named a team captain. He was also voted Mid-America Conference Defensive Player of the Year and MVP of the Tangerine Bowl.

As good as Lambert was, Kent State was a small school and far from a football power like nearby Ohio State. Because he played beneath the NFL radar, Lambert's football future was in doubt. He spent Super Sunday in January 1974 in his dorm room debating whether he would watch Super Bowl VIII matching Miami and Minnesota. He couldn't have known he would be starting in the NFL's ultimate game the following January.

Drafted in the second round, Lambert spent summer weekends driving from Ohio to Pittsburgh to study game films. Learning the Steelers' system was key to Lambert making the squad. As it turned out, fate took a hand in Lambert's situation. The NFL players' strike gave Steelers coaches a chance to watch their rookies more closely, Lambert included, and the question mark from Kent State became the exclamation point in Pittsburgh's punishing defense.

When the veterans returned to camp, fate took a hand again when Henry Davis, the Steelers' starting middle linebacker the past two seasons, was injured. In Wally Pipp–Lou Gehrig fashion, Lambert stepped in for the injured Davis and started his first game as a pro, and by season's end the former unknown from a small college was voted Defensive Rookie of the Year and a member of the NFL's All-Rookie team. In the process the beanpole middle 'backer became the third Steeler in six seasons to claim Rookie of the Year honors.

Lambert was literally born to be a Steeler. He was born in 1952 on the same day—July 8—that the Steelers had been founded on by Art Rooney Sr. in 1933.

The 5-foot-10, 178-pound Swann shared similarities with Lambert in that both were undersize for their positions. But where Lambert was rough and rugged, Swann was as smooth and graceful as his surname suggests. As an eleven-year-old Little Leaguer, Swann made a seemingly impossible leap at the outfield fence to snag in the tip of his glove a ball that had already cleared the wall. The catch preserved a win for Swann's team, the Senators. It was the kind of levitating leap Lynn became famous for during his Hall of Fame career with the Steelers, most notably at the end of the '75 season. "Lynn Swann," Noll would say, "has a sixth sense to go for the football and catch it."

Swann's acrobatic catches, his ability to twist his body into S curves at the height of his leap, could be traced to his mother's insistence that his childhood be about more than sports. Born in Alcoa, Tennessee, Swann grew up in the San Francisco suburb of Foster City. His father worked the night shift at the nearby airport, and Lynn's mother spent nights giving him Bible lessons. He was taken to restaurants to learn how to dine out properly and took tap-dance lessons and ballet classes in order to appreciate the arts. Swann became a regular visitor to art galleries, ballet recitals, museums, and the theater.

Each time Swann soared to make a catch, his years of ballet training and long jumping were in evidence. In high school he claimed the California state championship with a long-jump distance of 25-41/2. Some speculate that Swann could have been an Olympian in track and field.

But football proved to be Swann's primary sport. He earned a scholarship to a private Catholic school, Serra. His brother, Calvin, older by a year, attended a public school, San Mateo High. In 1968 a football game between the two schools was billed as a grudge match between the Brothers Swann. The disputes at home the week of the game became so contentious Lynn moved in with his coach in the days leading up to kickoff. Both of the brothers played well, catching two touchdown passes apiece, and Serra won 57–33.

Swann enrolled at Southern Cal, excelled as a receiver and return specialist, and was named All-America in 1971. He was a standout performer in the 1973 Rose Bowl against Ohio State, hauling in six catches for 108 yards and one TD.

As a rookie with the Steelers he led the league in punt-return yardage and by season's end was sharing playing time with Shanklin. Because Pittsburgh's offense was run oriented in 1974, Swann had just eleven catches for two TDs in the twelve games he played. Still, the Steelers' brass saw so much in Swann, they dealt Shanklin to Detroit prior to the start of the '75 season. Pittsburgh receivers coach Lionel Taylor, a former AFL star, had a way of testing a player's concentration and reflexes. Taylor would hold a small tube and in the course of a conversation with the player drop the tube. Most players would make a desperate grab but miss catching the tube. Swann snagged it virtually every time.

Swann, however, very nearly didn't make it through the '74 season. A light snow was falling on Pittsburgh in the early-morning hours following the Steelers' Monday-night game in New Orleans. The snow turned to ice, and Swann, driving Franco home from the stadium, hit an ice patch and slid down a hill. Swann recalled doing the worst thing he could do—hitting the brakes. Swann's car didn't stop skidding until it was within inches of the guardrail. "I thought I was going to kill Franco and myself," Swann said.

Firmly entrenched as a starter in '75, Swann did not disappoint. Despite drawing double coverage on a consistent basis, Swann caught forty-nine passes for an AFC-best eleven TDs and earned the respect of cornerbacks around the NFL. Willie Alexander of the division-rival Houston Oilers said Swann wasn't the swiftest receiver in the league and didn't own Isaac Curtis–style speed. "But," Alexander added, Swann "always gets to the ball."

Swann got to the ball often enough to help Pittsburgh post a 12-2 record that was a team-best mark to that point. Steelers fans bedecked Three Rivers Stadium with banners praising the young star who wore No. 88: "Swannie, How we love ya!" Additional banners cited a new math for the Steel City masses when it came time to totaling up the big-play Bradshaw-to-Swann connections: "12 + 88 = 6!"

One of Swann's leading tormentors, Jack Tatum, considered Swann a superb athlete. He admired Swann's grace, quickness, and speed as well as the fact that Lynn could catch the ball like few, if any, receivers could. Tatum played against several Hall of Fame receivers, including Paul Warfield, whom Tatum held in the highest esteem. Tatum credited Swann for understanding that self-preservation is an important part of football. Tatum said he practiced it himself when it came to confronting Earl Campbell and Larry Csonka in the open field.

When Oakland played Pittsburgh in the rivalry years, Tatum said the Raiders' defensive focus was more on flanker John Stallworth. The reason was that Oakland's Soul Patrol saw Stallworth as a receiver more likely to stick his nose into the action.

Swann and Stallworth played together for nine seasons and soared to rarefied heights reserved for only the greatest receiving duos—Fred Biletnikoff and Cliff Branch, Jerry Rice and John Taylor/Terrell Owens, Dante Lavelli and Mac Speedie, Tom Fears and Elroy Hirsch, John Jefferson and Charlie Joiner, Don Maynard and George Sauer.

Because Pittsburgh was primarily a power running team for the first four years of their careers, Swann and Stallworth's numbers aren't as impressive as later duos like Buffalo's "K-Gun" combo of Andre Reed and James Lofton, Minnesota's Randy Moss and Cris Carter, or the tandem of Torry Holt and Isaac Bruce on the St. Louis Rams' "Greatest Show on Turf."

Still, it's impossible to watch Super Bowl highlights and not see Stallworth or Swann making miraculous, game-winning catches. In their prime Swann and Stallworth provided Pittsburgh a one-two punch rivaled only by the Raiders' Biletnikoff and Branch. To have Swann or Stallworth would have given the Steelers a go-to guy; to have both gave them one of the all-time-great receiving duos.

Mike Haynes, a Hall of Fame cornerback with the New England Patriots in the 1970s and with the Los Angeles Raiders in the 1980s, said he would have no trouble calling Swann and Stallworth the greatest duo. Their career numbers may not be as gaudy as some, but the magnitude of their catches led to four Lombardi Trophies. The duo referred to themselves as the "game breakers." They may not have gotten a lot of opportunities, but when Bradshaw threw to them, Swann and Stallworth believed they would make the big play and break the game open. Swann was named MVP of Super Bowl X; Stallworth holds postseason and Super Bowl receiving records .

As a fellow Hall of Famer, Cris Carter appreciates Swann's ability to play the game above the ground and Stallworth as the "Silent Assassin" who was integral to the Steelers' success.

Dynamic duo though they were, Swann and Stallworth had contrasting backgrounds, personalities, and styles. They competed with

and against one another. Swann and Stallworth both wanted playing time, and both wanted to be primary targets. Their backgrounds
could not have been more different—Swann starred for the 1972 USC
Trojans, one of the great teams in college football history; Stallworth
set receiving records for the much-smaller Alabama A&M. Both wore
No. 22 in college and when drafted by the Steelers in 1974 bonded as
the reserve receiving tandem. When Stallworth and Swann entered
the game, they went in together.

Swann became the Baryshnikov of the NFL. He also became the
target for the rival Raiders. When Tatum and George Atkinson learned
of Swann's studying ballet and dance, they believed he could be intimidated. "They went after him," Raiders linebacker Phil Villapiano said.

The Steelers saw what Tatum and Atkinson were doing, but Stallworth said there was never a point where Pittsburgh believed that
Swann was intimidated. "The Raiders thought they could intimidate
Lynn by hitting him," Stallworth said. "I never saw him not jump or
not reach as high as he could to catch the football. So if that was their
strategy, it didn't work." Still, Swann added, it didn't stop the Raiders from trying.

The Steelers started the season with a 37–0 win in sunny San Diego,
and after an upset loss to O. J. Simpson and Buffalo in Week Two, Pittsburgh put together eleven straight wins to claim a second consecutive
Central Division title. Bradshaw enjoyed his finest season to date, completing 58 percent of his passes and firing eighteen TDs. He became
at age twenty-seven Pittsburgh's all-time leading passer, and Steelers fans praised him with banners proclaiming "No Flaw Bradshaw!"

Franco Harris rushed for a then team-record 1,246 yards and ten
TDs. He highlighted a 31–17 victory over Cleveland on December 7
by becoming just the seventh runner in NFL history to rush for at
least 1,000 yards three times. Backfield mate Rocky Bleier enjoyed
a career day on October 26 with 163 yards rushing in a win at Green
Bay's historic Lambeau Field.

The Steelers' success spurred the fan base, which continued to celebrate the players with personal fan clubs. The most famous remained
Franco's Italian Army, begun by Al Vento and Tony Stagno in 1972.

Vento was the owner of the decades-old Vento's Pizza in East Liberty, and he and Stagno, another East Liberty business owner, assembled an "army" of fans to root for Harris, who is of Italian and African American descent. Franco's Italian Army wore World War II helmet liners to games, where they ate pasta in the stands and drank Italian wine from goblets.

Franco's Italian Army was founded at a pivotal time in Pittsburgh history, a time when racial tension was evident in East Liberty and surrounding areas. In 1974 *Pittsburgh Post-Gazette* writer Clarke Thomas noted that despite the racial disharmony of the time, Italians and blacks both belonged to Franco's Italian Army. Vento and Stagno attended charity events with Harris and recruited their most famous member by taking a flight to Palm Springs to meet with Frank Sinatra. Vento and Stagno brought along their own cheese, prosciutto, and wine to celebrate Sinatra's induction into the Army as a one-star general.

Greene was slowed by assorted injuries to his neck, back, and groin, but the Steel Curtain was still superb. Cornerback Mel Blount pirated a league-high eleven passes and was named Defensive MVP. Cincinnati (11-3) and Houston (10-4) put pressure on Pittsburgh, but the Steelers swept all six games in the strong Central Division and beat the Bengals and Oilers twice in the season's stretch run to take command of the race.

Jack Ham said that if you looked to create a cornerback, Blount would be the blueprint. Ham thought Blount the most incredible athlete he had ever seen. Because of Blount's size (6 feet 3, 205 pounds) and physicality, he played cornerback like a linebacker, allowing the Steelers to write off one opposing receiver every game. "Mel could handle anyone in the league," Ham stated.

Gifted with great physical assets, Blount played arguably the best bump-and-run in the NFL during a Hall of Fame career that spanned 1970–83. Tom Landry called Blount the strongest cornerback his Cowboys competed against.

Green Bay Packers cornerback Herb Adderley, who set the standard for the position in the mid-1960s, compared Blount to Detroit Lions great Dick "Night Train" Lane as far as intimidation and toughness.

Blount was durable, missing just one game in his career. Jack Butler, an All-Pro defensive back with Pittsburgh in the 1950s and later the head of the BLESTO scouting combine, said Blount was tall to be a corner but had the speed of the smaller guys.

Blount recognized great corners of the past but looked to take his game to a new level. "I didn't want to be second to anyone," he said. "I wanted to set the standards for my position."

Early in his career Blount struggled to stay on the field. He began his career returning kickoffs and was routinely beaten when playing cornerback. He considered quitting—"I thought about it a lot," he said—but concentrated on improving. Blount's breakout campaign came in 1972 when he wasn't beaten for a single score. He went on to intercept a Steelers record fifty-seven passes and was named All-Pro three times and played in five Pro Bowls.

Blount had legendary duels with Oakland speedster Cliff Branch. Mel used his long arms to try to jam the Raiders' receiver at the line of scrimmage and played bump-and-run with the smaller Branch as Cliff ran his patterns. If Branch got free, Blount used his great closing speed to try to prevent a big gain.

Blount's bump-and-run techniques became so dominant, he forced the NFL to outlaw the tactic in 1978 by instituting what became known as the "Mel Blount Rule." The new rule declared that defensive backs could no longer draw contact with receivers past five yards. Prior to that, defenders could punish receivers all over the field.

The Steelers took exception to the new rule, believing that Dolphins coach Don Shula, the head of the NFL's Competition Committee, was seeking to stalemate a Pittsburgh defense that pitched five shutouts in a nine-game stretch in 1976.

The Mel Blount Rule changed the face of football. It opened up the game and led to the making of the modern NFL. The Chargers' Air Coryell offense followed in 1979, the West Coast Offense in 1981, and Dan Marino's record-setting season in 1984. Marino and fellow quarterbacks Dan Fouts, Roger Staubach, Joe Montana, and John Elway made the most of the Mel Blount Rule and filled the air with footballs. Ironically, the Steelers were among those benefiting from the

Blount Rule, as Bradshaw, Swann, and Stallworth combined to help fuel the 1978 and '79 Super Bowl championship teams.

Blount, Lambert, and Swann proved emblematic of the Steelers' success story in the '70s. Thirty-four members of the Steelers' Super Bowl roster in January 1975 were original Pittsburgh draft choices. En route to repeating as division champs, the Steelers provided fans with some scintillating highlights: Lambert storming New York Jets star Joe Namath into the Shea Stadium infield dirt; Blount beating Billy "White Shoes" Johnson of Houston to the ball for an end-zone interception en route to becoming the first Steeler since "Bullet" Bill Dudley to lead the league in picks; Dwight White sacking Dan Pastorini in the Astrodome; Bradshaw taking the deepest drop in football and firing a 60-yard screamer to Swann over the Chiefs' Jim Marsalis; and Ray Mansfield, Jim Clack, Jon Kolb, Gerry Mullins, Gordon Gravelle, Mike Webster, and Sam Davis executing trap blocks that set Franco free.

Noll followed the same formula in building his offensive line as he did his defensive front. The Steelers' line was built through the college draft, the lone exception being Mansfield, the Ol' Ranger having been obtained from the Philadelphia Eagles in 1964.

Pittsburgh's offensive line benefited from a rotation aimed at keeping them fresh by alternating five players at three positions. Clack played left guard in the first and third quarters and shifted to right guard in the fourth. Mullins played right guard in the first and third quarters. Davis played left guard in the second and fourth quarters, while Webster played in the first and third. Kolb and Gravelle played the entire game at left and right tackle, respectively.

Steelers assistant coach Dan Radakovich said no one in the NFL in the mid-'70s alternated players as much as Pittsburgh did. The reason, Radakovich remarked, is that Pittsburgh's players were so close in talent, it was hard to pick one over the other. "If there is a wide difference then the guy who is better will play most of the time," he said. It wasn't that way with the Steelers, so they played them all. Radakovich, or "Bad Rad" as he was called, also altered the jerseys of Steelers linemen so that they were form-fitting. The jerseys not only fitted like a second skin and showed off the Steelers' muscle, the tight fit also prevented the opposition from grabbing Pittsburgh's linemen and moving them in one direction or another, a common practice with defenders.

Bad Rad's contributions to the Steelers included his helping convince Chuck Noll to draft Franco Harris out of Penn State. A native of western Pennsylvania, Radakovich had been an assistant coach at Penn State in charge of linebackers when the Nittany Lions were becoming known as "Linebacker U."

By the end of the regular season the '75 Steelers had won more games, scored more points, and surrendered fewer than any team in franchise history. One of Pittsburgh's more intriguing contests came on November 30 against Namath and the Jets in Shea Stadium. The *New York Times* previewed the game as appearing to be the "grossest mismatch in Jets' history."

But the *Times* also reported that Broadway Joe was looking sharp in midweek workouts. Joe Willie White Shoes and his receivers still had quick-strike capabilities that the *Times* stated were, on a good day, "probably as good as any in the league." If the Jets score quickly, the *Times* said, "it just might stun the Steelers enough to make it an interesting game."

Broadway Joe versus the Steel Curtain was a showdown worth watching. Following a scoreless first quarter, Namath drove the Jets into Steelers' territory. Looking to strike first, Broadway Joe tried to beat the Steel Curtain deep. His pass was intercepted at the goal line by Glen Edwards and returned 47 yards. The turnover set up the Steelers' first score, Roy Gerela's 26-yard field goal.

Namath, alias "Lord Fu Manchu," brought the Jets back on another drive. Again, his potential scoring pass was picked off, this time by Blount in the end zone. And again, Pittsburgh's defense paid off, Bradshaw finding Harris for a 44-yard scoring play. Blount intercepted Broadway Joe again in the third, and the turnover led to another Gerela field goal.

Trailing 20–0 in the fourth, Namath got New York on the board when he finally dented the Steel Curtain with a 6-yard strike to Jerome Barkum. Pittsburgh picked off four Namath passes and limited him to eight completions in twenty-one attempts.

While the Steelers dominated their division in '75, the Raiders romped through the West with an 11-3 record. The Chiefs had fallen from the heights scaled in 1971, the Broncos were two years away from their Orange Crush years, and the Chargers were four years away from flying the friendly skies of Air Coryell.

Oakland began the season in transition. The last of the original Raiders, "Double O," Jim Otto, the only All-AFL center ever, retired after fifteen seasons and was replaced by Dave Dalby. Oakland opened the season with a nationally televised Monday-night win over Miami. Two seasons before, the Raiders snapped the Dolphins' regular-season win streak at sixteen and overall win streak at eighteen games with a 12–7 decision. Oakland ended another Miami win streak in the '75 season opener, dealing the Dolphins a 31–21 defeat that snapped a run of consecutive victories in the Orange Bowl at thirty-one.

Because their baseball counterparts in the Coliseum—the three-time World Series champion A's—were in the playoffs for the fifth straight season, the Raiders played their first five games on the road. John Madden's outfit faced other challenges besides being road warriors. Otto's retirement and QB Kenny Stabler's knee strain hobbled the offense, but the Raiders' depth was readily apparent at running back, where Madden could call on Pete Banaszak, Mark van Eeghen, Clarence Davis, Jess Phillips, and Marv Hubbard. Sure-handed Fred Biletnikoff and speedy Cliff Branch complemented each other at wide receiver, and the offensive line featured a future Hall of Fame tandem on the left side in guard Gene Upshaw and tackle Art Shell.

Neal Colzie provided spark as a return specialist, the rookie leading the league in return yardage (655) and setting an NFL record in the process. The Raiders had another new recruit in veteran outside linebacker Ted Hendricks. Blanda and Ray Guy joined Colzie in sparking the special teams.

The elderly Blanda had more lives than Morris the Cat, another celebrity of the '70s. Blanda was thirty-one years old in 1958 when George Halas phased him out in Chicago. He was forty in 1967 when the Oilers let him go. In 1970 Blanda became a folk hero when, at the age of forty-three, he passed or kicked the Raiders to four final-minute victories and a last-second tie.

Redskins star Mark Moseley, the last of the straight-on kickers, called Blanda his hero. "He was a great athlete, a real competitor," Moseley said. "He had a mind of steel, he never got riled."

Over twenty-six seasons Blanda produced 2,002 points—more than 500 ahead of his closest pursuer—and all but 54 came via his square-toed shoe. During his record 340 games, Blanda booted more field goals (335) and extra points (942) than any man in pro football history. By the time he retired at the close of the '75 campaign, Blanda had played professionally in four decades and tied or owned sixteen regular-season records and twenty-one championship-game marks.

Allen thought Blanda one of the most remarkable athletes of all time. "He played until he was almost 50," Allen said. "He played quarterback until the last year or two of his career." That Blanda was past forty when he had perhaps his greatest season, the miraculous 1970 campaign, was, Allen said, "darn near unbelievable."

Blanda ranked at the time with Cleveland's Lou Groza and Kansas City's Jan Stenerud as the best placekickers in league history. Blanda hit field goals long and short and hit them consistently. More important, Blanda hit them under pressure. There may have been better pure kickers, but there was none better under pressure than Blanda. If the game was on the line, Allen, for one would rather have Blanda going for the winner than anyone.

Ray Guy gave the Raiders another all-time great on their special teams. He was the NFL's biggest weapon in the punting game since Kansas City's Jerrel Wilson. The Raiders made history in 1973 when they became the first pro team to select a full-time punter in the first round of the NFL Draft.

Guy was a game changer. An All-America at Southern Mississippi, he was the nation's leading punter in 1972, averaging 46.2 yards per punt and booming a 93-yarder against Mississippi. Guy's three-season average in college was 44.7 yards per kick. The strength in his skinny right leg was such that he had a 61-yard field goal against Utah State.

It didn't take long for Guy to establish himself as a field-position weapon along the lines of greats like Wilson, the Giants' Dave Jennings, Detroit's Yale Lary, Green Bay's Don Chandler, Chicago's Bobby Joe Green, and Cleveland's Horace Gillom.

Allen thought Guy set himself apart from other great punters. The reason was Guy's punting in the Raiders' big games and postseason contests. Guy was cool, quick, and consistently outstanding in the highly important special teams.

Guy averaged 42.4 yards per punt, and while others kicked it farther and some—like Lary—as high, Guy was the first to combine hang time with distance and placement. Mutual Radio sportscaster Al Wester noted during a Raiders-Steelers playoff game in 1973 that Guy once hung a punt for more than five seconds. "Can you imagine that?" Wester asked.

Guy's ability to scrape the sky with his kicks resulted in his ricocheting a punt off the overhead scoreboard that hangs 90 feet over the surface of the Superdome.

In 1975 Guy led the league in punting for the second straight season. He was impervious to pressure, showing no fear of charging defensive players hell-bent on blocking his punts. He would go five full seasons and 619 kicks without having a punt blocked. Highly durable, Guy played in 229 consecutive games and had just 3 punts blocked in 1,049 attempts.

Pro football historian Joe Horrigan considered Guy the first punter who could be said to have won games. He thought Guy combined power and placement, kicking high, long punts and putting the ball where he wanted.

Dave Jennings, a contemporary of Guy in the '70s, called Ray the first superstar punter. Guy, Jennings said, had the perfect style, kicking perfectly straight with the right leg on his follow-through going toward his face. Paul Maguire, the former NBC analyst and punter for the AFL's Buffalo Bills in the 1960s, took note of the great extension and power in Guy's leg. Sean Lendeta, the Giants' punter in their Super Bowl seasons in '86 and '90, said that while others owned better numbers, Guy consistently kicked it higher than anyone else and had very good distance on his punts.

A seven-time Pro Bowler and three-time Super Bowl champion, Guy became the first pure punter elected to the Pro Football Hall of Fame and just the second pure kicker along with Stenerud.

With a solid offense and a sometimes shaky defense, the '75 Raiders were not unlike their '74 edition. What wasn't shaky about the defense was the play of Tatum, a man nicknamed the "Assassin" for his hard hits. NFL Films ranks Tatum the sixth most feared tackler in league history. His hits are enshrined in lore and immortalized on film. He separated Sammy White from his helmet, wrecked Riley Odoms, had a violent collision with Earl Campbell, and crippled Daryl Stingley in one of the most controversial hits in NFL history. Chiefs Hall of Fame QB and longtime radio broadcaster Len Dawson called Tatum's hit on Campbell the "most vicious" he ever witnessed in all his decades of playing or covering pro football. Four months later, the Oilers traded for Tatum.

In 1975 Tatum earned Pro Bowl honors for the third consecutive season. He had the innate ability to explode through his targets. On one of the great secondary units of all time—the "Soul Patrol"—the Assassin was even more of an enforcer than Dr. Death, Skip Thomas.

Opponents didn't want to go across the middle, Atkinson said, because getting hit by Tatum was like getting hit by a truck. Raiders teammates thought Jack was devastating with his timing and angles of contact.

Raised in rough Passaic, New Jersey, Tatum didn't begin playing organized football until high school. At age fifteen he was one of just two sophomores on Passaic's varsity team. Originally a backup, Tatum took the field as a linebacker early in the season opener. Several plays later, Tatum delivered a crushing blow on the quarterback and knocked him cold. He then knocked out the second-string QB as well. As the game wore on, the opposition was down to lining up its tight end under center. Tatum was promoted to first string and put on the fast track to success.

As a senior he was named a high school All-America. He accepted a scholarship to Ohio State and was part of Hayes's celebrated "Super Sophomores" that won the national title in 1968. Hayes recruited

Tatum as a running back, but Jack kept sneaking over to the defense during practices and was eventually inserted at monster back at the request of assistant coach Lou Holtz. Tatum was First Team All-Big Ten from 1968 to 1970 and unanimous All-America in 1969–70. He was college football's best defensive player in 1970, and in his years starting for the Buckeyes Ohio State went 27-2 and just missed winning three straight national championships.

Tatum was a hammer. Hayes said Tatum could hit an opponent so hard, it would lift both feet off the ground. Because the Buckeyes always played him to the open side of the field, opponents chose to run away from Tatum.

The Raiders were a poor tackling team in 1971, and Madden insisted the team draft the best tacklers they could. Oakland selected Tatum with the nineteenth pick, and Madden said the Raiders never had another poor tackling season in Jack's nine years with the team. Tatum served notice by knocking out two tight ends for the Super Bowl champion Baltimore Colts in the 1971 College All-Star Game. Madden said Tatum's toughness rubbed off on the rest of the Raiders.

Tatum was more than a tough guy and tackling machine. The man who most embodied the merciless image of the outlaw Raiders pirated thirty passes, and his all-around play inspired future star safeties like Ronnie Lott.

Many remember Tatum's Raiders career, especially for two infamous plays. The first is the Immaculate Reception in a December playoff; the second is the hit on Stingley in a dreary August exhibition game.

Less remembered is the fourth quarter of a game against New Orleans his rookie season in which Tatum knocked out not only Saints receiver Danny Abramowicz but also teammate George Atkinson, a double knockout in a single collision. He got Atkinson a second time that season and also knocked out fellow defensive backs Willie Brown and Nemiah Wilson. In subsequent seasons Tatum twice sidelined Cleveland receiver Frank Pitts in the same game and ко'd Paul Warfield in a playoff game.

In Oakland's system the cornerbacks covered the wide receivers on most formations, and the strong safety almost always took the tight end. As a free safety Tatum didn't have anyone specifically to cover.

His job Tatum said, was to patrol the secondary "like a sheriff." He would position himself so that when the receiver would go for the ball, Tatum would go for the receiver.

As he gained experience Tatum learned to combine technique with power. He left opponents reeling from the force of his collision. Frenchy Fuqua was concussed, Colts tight end John Mackey was left writhing on the ground struggling to breathe, and Denver tight end Riley Odoms was likewise left gasping. "Damn, Tate," Odoms moaned. "You almost killed me."

If the Assassin almost killed Odoms, he nearly decapitated Minnesota wideout Sammy White in Super Bowl XI. Tatum drilled White so hard Sammy's helmet went flying in one direction, his chinstrap in another. Tatum stood over White, striking a pose that would become familiar to Mike Tyson's prostrate opponents in his prime.

Tatum patrolled the field like a guided missile, a warhead waiting to explode on enemy receivers. Wideouts became so wary, they sought to defuse him before he could strike. Eagles receiver Harold Carmichael once ran a decoy pattern in Tatum's territory and told the Assassin, "Hey man, I won't try blocking you today if you don't hit me." "Okay by me," Tatum replied. Under his breath, Tatum said, "My job's done."

The '75 campaign provided several Tatum highlights—delivering a forearm to the helmet of Baltimore receiver Glenn Doughty, flipping Colt Roger Carr, and chopping down Chiefs Morris LaGrand on a goal-line stand—as well as a season's worth of Silver and Black memories: Harold Hart's 101-yard kickoff return for a touchdown that clinched a classic matchup with Miami; Art Thoms corralling Colts quarterback Bert Jones for one of Oakland's six sacks in Baltimore; Otis Sistrunk leading a defensive rampage in sun-drenched San Diego; Blanda booting the winning field goal to beat the Redskins in the first overtime game in Raiders history, then following the same script in a win over Atlanta that gave Oakland an unprecedented eighth division title in nine years; Banaszak, the Raiders' most inspirational player in '75, blasting to three TDs against the Chiefs in the final game for a club record sixteen on the season and, in the same game, Blanda becoming the first player to score 2,000 career points.

In all '75 was another golden season for both the Silver and Black and the Black and Gold. Having established themselves as the top two teams in the AFC, Oakland and Pittsburgh prepared for another pulse-quickening postseason collision.

Jim Campbell: The feeling of euphoria following the Steelers' victory in Super Bowl IX was not something that wore off quickly. It was a first for the long-suffering Pittsburgh fans who had long wanted, felt entitled to, a Super Bowl championship, but had to settle for occasional successful seasons by the Pitt Panthers and World Series championships by the Pirates.

In a "football town," this was unacceptable. While the NFL was not the colossus that it is today, it was an important part of many Pittsburgh lives. A winning team was almost demanded. With the winning of SB IX, the masses were finally satisfied—to an extent. And this was very important. It came at a time when Pittsburghers weren't feeling too good about things. The city was transitioning from its long-held image as a steel town. The Steelers' success gave them something to grab onto.

On a personal level, the Steelers' success affected me also. I was only a part of the world champion Pittsburgh Steelers, but I was proud of the connection. I was looking forward to a continuation of the dynasty. I truly believed it was under way. As stated earlier, I felt that the Steelers were so young and potentially so good as a team that they could stay championship contenders for the foreseeable future.

It wasn't too long after the Vince Lombardi Trophy presentation—Pete Rozelle handing off to Mr. Rooney—that the 1975 draft was looming on the horizon. I was looking forward to the draft meeting, although unlike in earlier years I would not be attending in the ballroom of the New York Hilton at Rockefeller Center on January 28 and 29.

As in other years I felt a certain amount of optimism after the draft. Dave Brown, a really fine defensive back from Michigan, was the No. 1 pick. He was from Akron, Ohio, just up I-77 from Canton. I had followed his stellar Wolverine career. Most of the other names were relatively unknown to me—I was immersed in NFL football, not the collegiate game. But I had faith in the Steelers' scouting department and was satisfied that those drafted could help sustain the success. It turned out to be misplaced confidence. In the years prior to 1972, when the Steelers struggled, they were drafting early in each round. By 1975 they were mostly choosing last in each round. It was more a case of where and when the club drafted than any deficiency in the player personnel department.

Add to that the fact that the Steelers had what could be described as a pat lineup. In retrospect the '75 draft was a washout. Dave Brown stuck, but was gone the next year to the newly minted Seattle franchise in the expansion draft—he would have a long and successful year with the Seahawks.

One thing from this late-drafting era saved the newcomers' situation—an unheralded free agent always seemed to capture the imagination of training-camp observers. In 1975 this role was filled by John Banaszak, a Marine and defensive end from Eastern Michigan. Like Glen Edwards and Loren Toews, each of whom were the talk of their respective rookie camps. Banaszak was a contributor through the 1970s and early 1980s.

On the occasions that I visited St. Vincent College in Latrobe for the Steelers' training camp, there wasn't much of a buzz. Bradshaw was firmly established as the starting QB. Hanratty, who would take his offbeat personality to expansion Tampa Bay in 1976, was almost forgotten—he did not attempt a pass in 1975. Swann, especially, and Stallworth were slated to be the first-string wideouts. Basically, the Super Bowl IX starters were intact and ready to defend their world championship. Again, only the emergence of Banaszak, the ex-Leatherneck, was the only thing causing a stir in camp.

When it was time for Noll and his staff to finalize the 1975 regular-season roster, cutting down to forty-three players, it was a part of the game that the coach liked least. He knew it was the end of football careers for many of the young men. One of the cuts that affected me most was Preston Pearson, a serviceable running back in the building years who came into the league as a University of Illinois basketball player. Preston had an unorthodox running style. I called it "turkey hopping," a step here, a step there, and maybe an occasional 10- or 12-yard gain. Additionally, he was a threat—as he would prove at his next stop—as a receiver out of the backfield. Young runners Reggie Harrison and Mike Collier made Preston expendable.

At last the regular season was here. The team traveled to San Diego. I fondly remembered San Diego as the venue in 1972 as the place the Steelers shed their image as "lovable losers." The win clinched the Central Division title, the Steelers' first championship of any kind and the precursor to the "Immaculate Reception" game with the Raiders.

In San Diego the Steel Curtain proved to be stainless, shutting out the future Air Coryell, led by Flight Captain Dan Fouts, 37–0. To me, it seemed that the secondary, Mel Blount and his fellow marauders, had as much to do with pitching a shutout as the front four. As good as the defense looked against the Chargers, they looked equally as bad against the Buffalo Bills at home the next week. O. J. Simpson, at the peak of his considerable powers, shredded the Steel Curtain for 227 rushing yards. The 30–21 loss wasn't as close as it sounds.

This was the game where I saw Jack Ham make the only mistake I ever remember seeing him make. I'm sure there were others, but not many. This one was so costly that it's seared forever in my memory. It was a "student body right" sweep, the Juice being led by the Electric Company, and, boy, did they turn on the juice. Ham came across the line of scrimmage and got hooked inside—probably by tight end Paul Seymour. O.J. was still in the backfield, but I remember thinking to myself, "He's gone! There's nobody gonna catch him." I was right. Simpson blazed down the right sideline at Three Rivers as though he were running out a play at a USC dummy scrimmage—88 yards! After the game I was wondering, "Is this so-called Super Bowl hangover somewhat for real?" I think others were also wondering the same thing.

However, our fears proved to be groundless. In the next three games the defense hammered the Browns in Cleveland as well as Denver and Chicago at home. While limiting those three teams to a combined eighteen points, the Bradshaw-led offense racked up ninety-nine points of its own. On the field I saw several things happening. Bradshaw was gaining maturity and consistency on a weekly basis. Swann, especially, and Stallworth were working themselves into the offensive scheme of things. Frank Lewis was still getting occasional starts at wide receiver, but Stallworth was emerging as the first-stringer. Swann had pretty much nailed down his starting position.

It was fun watching "the kids," as Noll referred to them, develop. Randy Grossman was working his way into significant playing time at tight end, and this would make it easier for Larry "Bubba" Brown to transition from blocking tight end and occasional pass catcher to full-time offensive tackle, a new position at which he would excel.

Someone, probably the always-on-top-of-things Joe Gordon, pointed out at the end of the season that Swann made eleven catches as a rookie; in his second season he made eleven touchdown receptions.

Stallworth was also opening eyes. None were wider than mine when in the closing minutes of the game with the Oilers, a 24–17 victory, he caught a 21-yard touchdown pass from Brad that sealed the deal. What I remember about the catch is that Stallworth made it one-handed. His right hand was pinned down by the Houston defensive back, but he made the catch with only his left hand. I guess the back judge resorted to the old "no harm, no foul" theory, because nothing was called. Roy Gerela lined up for the PAT, and that was that.

Franco continued to rampage. Only O.J. had more rushing yards at this point—helped undoubtedly by Ham's once-in-a-lifetime mistake. By this time Franco was the primary beneficiary of Rocky Bleier's third guard–like blocking. As a lead blocker on the omnipresent Steelers trap plays, Rocky was devastating. He was over his Vietnam War wounds and regarded as the best blocking back in the NFL. As a change-of-pace runner, he also contributed to the Pittsburgh ground game. "Ground Chuck (Knox)" and "Ground and Pound" would come later in NFL lore, but nickname or no nickname, the Black and Gold running game was something to be feared—and then there were Bradshaw and his bevy of receivers. To my way of thinking, the Steelers were a complete offense, and then there was the Steel Curtain defense. The Steelers truly were a force with which to be reckoned, and few seemed up to the reckoning.

The season's log stood at 12-2, and Pittsburgh caught another case of playoff fever.

Of Ice and Men

For the first time since the Immaculate Reception, the NFL playoffs opened in Pittsburgh. At 1:00 p.m. Eastern Standard Time on Saturday, December 27, 1975, NBC-TV announcers Jim Simpson, John Brodie, and Don Meredith welcomed a national viewing audience to frigid Three Rivers Stadium.

A paid attendance of 49,557 bundled against a twenty-two-degree windchill to wave their new Terrible Towels, which debuted in this game courtesy of Steelers color announcer Myron Cope, and watch the No. 1–seeded Steelers take on the Baltimore Colts. Pittsburgh was the top seed for the first time in team history and thus would enjoy home-field advantage throughout the AFC playoffs under the new postseason rules.

The 1975 postseason was the first in which the NFL used a seeding system. The three division champions in the AFC and NFC owned the top three seeds, while the wild-card clubs had the fourth seeds. One old NFL rule the league did maintain was prohibiting teams from the same division meeting in the opening round of the playoffs. Had the rule not been in place, Pittsburgh would have hosted Cincinnati, the wild-card Bengals being the fourth seed. Oakland, the No. 2 seed, would have hosted Baltimore.

Instead, the Steelers faced the Colts in Saturday's playoff opener followed by the NFC game on CBS matching Eastern Division champion St. Louis and Western Division kings Los Angeles in the LA Coliseum.

Baltimore was making its first playoff appearance since 1971 and returned just a single starter—punter David Lee—from that defending Super Bowl champion squad. The Colts' resurgence from a 2-12 campaign in '74 was keyed by head man Ted Marchibroda and a revamped roster featuring Bert Jones, Lydell Mitchell, and Roger Carr.

The Colts' coaching staff included a young assistant named Bill Belichick. The impact of winning a division title, going to the playoffs, and facing the defending Super Bowl champions in his first season in the NFL left a lasting impact on Belichick. "We went to Pittsburgh for the playoffs and they had a great team," Belichick once told Boston-area columnist Mike Petraglia. "For my first year in the league, just seeing how good they were, they were so good on defense. Every guy was better than the next guy. From [Joe] Greene to [Jack] Lambert, that whole front four, and then the secondary. And offensively, the trapping scheme that they ran was very innovative."

Belichick said that when you're a young coach, you look at who does things in a way that you admire and want to emulate; you look at what you can take from a good program to help you as a coach. Noll's Steelers, he said, were one of those teams. "From the first year [in 1975]," Belichick said, "the Steelers had a very strong impact from the outside on my philosophy as a coach."

The Steelers' trapping scheme that Belichick admired was tailor-made for Franco Harris. The big fullback had vision and anticipation, and his strong suit was reading certain situations rather quickly. Pittsburgh's offensive line may have been undersized—though it did handle Minnesota's "Purple Gang" and the Dallas "Doomsday" defense when it counted—but their system of traps and counters allowed Harris to adjust and have the read he needed. "I would make the adjustment to what I had to do," Harris said.

The Baltimore-Pittsburgh matchup, the first since the 1974 season opener, was a collision between a Colt offense that ranked second in the NFL in scoring at 28.2 points per game and the Steel Curtain defense that ranked second in points allowed at 11.6. Baltimore wide receiver Glenn Doughty made like another famous poet laureate from the Charm City—Ogden Nash—and provided a pregame rhyme:

The Eastern Division title is all in the past
When we arrive in Pittsburgh we'll be cookin' with gas;
There's no question there'll be a lot at stake
But our oven will be set to shake and bake.

Taking the field in its white uniforms with blue trim, with the Colts' classic horseshoe logo on both sides of their helmet and equally classic UCLA-style shoulder loops on their jerseys, Baltimore believed it was destiny's darlings, the charmed team from the Charm City. Still, the Colts had to go through the Steelers and, like their previous encounter, won by Pittsburgh 30–0, the Steel Curtain was dominant again.

Joe Greene, nursing an injury, was replaced by Steve Furness in the starting lineup at left tackle, but the defense didn't miss a beat, scoring one touchdown, setting up two others, and sacking Colt quarterbacks five times. Middle linebacker Jack Lambert provided his own fire on this frosty day, personally preventing a Colt touchdown by standing up Mitchell at the 6-yard line and deflecting a pass on the following down. Baltimore managed but 154 yards of offense, 58 of which came on one late pass play.

The Steel Curtain set a tone on its first series. Defensive end Dwight White nearly decapitated Jones with a high tackle, and even though the Colts' QB scrambled away he ran into cornerback J. T. Thomas. Jones suffered an injured throwing arm on the play and was sidelined. Linebacker Jack Ham followed with an interception of backup Marty Domres, and Pittsburgh needed just four plays to drive 61 yards to the game's first score. Terry Bradshaw found Frank Lewis for 34 yards on first down, and three plays later Harris followed pulling guard Gerry Mullins for 8 yards and a 7–0 lead.

Jack Fleming made the call on the Steelers' WTAE Radio broadcast.
Fleming: *"Harris, trying to get blocking, cuts over the left side to score! Franco on a great run, the hole opened up by Gerry Mullins!"*
Cornerback Lloyd Mumphord's 58-yard interception return set

up the tying score in the second quarter, Domres delivering a 5-yard pass to a wide-open Doughty in the end zone.

Colts defensive coordinator Maxie Baughan, a former star linebacker for the Los Angeles Rams' "Fearsome Foursome" unit of the late 1960s, did a solid job in helping Baltimore hold Pittsburgh to one score in the first half. Just before the break, Mumphord upended a scrambling Bradshaw, and the Steelers' QB had to be helped from the field after suffering a sprained knee.

The Colts claimed a 10–7 lead early in the third when Nelson Munsey's fumble recovery set up Toni Linhart's field goal. The turning point for Pittsburgh came midway through the quarter when the Colts faced third and 9 from their own 20. Not willing to gamble, Domres called a running play to set up a punt. His strategy changed when Baltimore tackle David Taylor felt his hamstring snap and fell forward. The offside penalty pushed the Colts into a third and 14 and forced Domres to rethink his play call.

Looking to connect with Carr on an inside slant, Domres had his pass picked when Mel Blount, who led the league in interceptions, jumped the route and returned the ball to the Baltimore 7. Rocky Bleier slanted right and ran behind pulling guard Sam Davis to put Pittsburgh in front to stay.

On the radio Jack Fleming called it this way: *"Domres back to throw, and it is intercepted! Here comes Mel Blount! He goes down in a crowd at the 7-yard line . . . Carry by Rocky Bleier off the right side. He's in for a touchdown! Bleier gave it a great effort!"*

"A great play," Steelers coach Chuck Noll said of Blount's pick. "That was the one that turned it around."

Russell called it a "super play," and Ham thought it the best interception he had ever seen. "I just read the ball all the way and beat [Carr] back to it," said Blount, who was aided by Russell's refusing to let Carr release inside and forcing him wide off the line of scrimmage.

In the fourth quarter Harris, who blasted the Baltimore defense for a Three Rivers Stadium–record 153 rushing yards on twenty-seven carries, pounded to the 2. Bradshaw, gimpy but game, dove to his right behind Jim Clack and Gordon Gravelle to push Pittsburgh's lead to 21–10.

Fleming: *"Here's the sneak . . . Bradshaw goes over the right side, and he's in for the touchdown! You had the feeling he was going to do it himself, and he did!"*

Returning to the game, Jones connected with Doughty for a 58-yard play that carried to the 3. On the next play Ham hit Jones and forced a fumble. Russell scooped up the ball and, despite sore knees, returned it for an NFL-playoff record 93 yards for the final score in a 28–10 victory that sent the Steelers to a third straight title game.

Russell's return was the source of several humorous anecdotes. Ham said the thirty-four-year-old veteran ran so slow he couldn't tell if Andy was running for a touchdown or running out the clock. Teammate Ray Mansfield joked that NBC cut away to a commercial during Russell's long run and returned in time to see him score. *Sports Illustrated* called it the "longest, slowest touchdown ever witnessed."

Jokes aside, Russell's teammates had tremendous respect for him. Greene said that while some spoke of Russell being the third linebacker in the Steelers' great trio, Andy was really the first. Greene explained that Russell was there when Pittsburgh was the team everyone could beat. Russell was selected by the Steelers in the sixteenth round of the 1963 NFL Draft. A holdover from the Steelers' dark ages, Russell was a playmaker, picking off eighteen passes in his career. He was a good linebacker prior to Noll's arrival but a great one after that, Noll working with Russell on learning the fine points of his position. Russell then passed that teaching on to teammates.

Greene called Russell a "special teammate." Because Andy had experienced all of the bad things that happened with the Steelers, he could also share the kinds of things that were needed to be successful. Russell was the player who Greene said "brought the word"—Noll's coaching philosophy—to the locker room. Russell also helped bring new players along. Greene recalled Russell telling Ham and Lambert "what to do and where to be, telling them about formations and what to expect."

Russell's mentoring paid dividends, particularly in the playoff win over Baltimore when the defense had to come up big again and again. "We had a hell of a lot of pressure on our defense," Noll said, citing the Steelers' giving Baltimore both the ball and good field position. "They were on the field all day."

"Once we overcame ourselves," Mansfield said, "the rest was easy."

Through it all waved the gold-and-black Terrible Towels, the inspired brainchild of Cope. Working at the Steelers' flagship station WTAE Radio, Cope was approached in December 1975 by station general manager Ted Atkins and vice president for sales Larry Garrett to come up with a "gimmick" for the Steelers' home playoff game. "I'm not a gimmick guy," Cope responded.

Garrett reminded Cope that the latter's contract with the station ended in three months and that a Steelers' "gimmick" could warrant a raise. Cope quickly changed his mind. "I'm a gimmick guy," he said.

It was suggested that costume masks with Noll's "Whatever It Takes" motto be distributed to fans, but when it was learned that such a promotion would cost $25,000, the idea was dropped. Cope suggested something that was lightweight and portable.

Garrett suggested towels, and Cope seized upon the idea, calling it the Terrible Towel. He went on TV and radio and declared that the Terrible Towel was "poised to strike."

The Terrible Towel, Cope told listeners, could be used to clean their stadium seat, cover their head if it rained, and as a muffler for their hands when it got cold. Cope introduced the Terrible Towel on the 11:00 p.m. Sunday TV news, hurling them at the anchorman, weatherman, and floor director. Cope canvassed Steelers players and received resounding rejections.

"I think your idea stinks!" Ham told him, and Ernie Holmes remarked that he didn't want Cope to do this. Cope approached Bradshaw, who was reading the farm reports.

"How do you feel about the Terrible Towel?"

Bradshaw looked up. "Huh?" Cope checked Terry off as a yes. Myron made his way through the locker room, registering yes votes like a banana-republic dictator.

Heading for the door, he was stopped by Russell, whose features were formed in a scowl. "What's this crap about a towel?" Russell asked. "We're not a gimmick team."

Unfazed by the players' rejections, Cope told Atkins the Steelers were overwhelmingly in favor of the Terrible Towel. The day of the playoff the *Pittsburgh Post-Gazette* protested that Cope was turning Three Rivers Stadium into a tenement district, the inference being that in such places laundry was hung out to dry. Steelers fans didn't agree, and at the opening kickoff some thirty thousand Terrible Towels waved wildly throughout the stadium.

Cope said that on that December 27 the Terrible Towel burst into the world like a "bawling infant." Lisa Benz liked the favorable effects of the Terrible Towel so much she wrote Cope a lengthy letter describing its miraculous powers. The final verse focused on Russell's run:

> He ran ninety-three
> Like a bat out of hell,
> And no one could see
> How he rambled so well.
> "It was easy," said Andy
> And he flashed a crooked smile
> "I was snapped on the fanny
> By the Terrible Towel!"

Three years earlier tens of thousands of Miami fans waved white hankies during the heady days of the Dolphins' dynasty. Raiders fans followed in 1974 with black handkerchiefs, but the hankies of Miami and Oakland have not had the staying power of the Terrible Towel.

Since its inception Cope's creation has been credited with numerous on-field miracles. The list of opponents who disrespected the Terrible Towel and brought negative karma upon themselves and their team is a lengthy one:

Prior to a 1994 playoff game, Browns running back Ernest Byner stepped on the Terrible Towel and yelled, "We don't care about your Towel!" The Steelers won 29–9.

In 2005 Bengals receiver T. J. Houshmandzadeh wiped his cleats on the Terrible Towel, and Cincinnati's season ended with a 31–17 loss to Pittsburgh in the playoffs. The Bengals failed to return to the playoffs until Houshmandzadeh left the team.

In 2008 Ravens receiver Derrick Mason stomped on the Terrible Towel, and Baltimore was beaten by Pittsburgh three times that season, including in the AFC Championship Game.

Also in 2008 Jacksonville's mascot rubbed the Terrible Towel beneath his arms and on his buttocks. The Jaguars lost to the Steelers and dropped eight of their next eleven games.

That same season Tennessee players LenDale White and Keith Bulluck stepped on the Terrible Towel, and the Titans lost eight straight games, including a franchise-worst 59–0 loss to New England. Titans coach Jeff Fisher reversed the curse by having his players autograph the Towel and mail it to the Pittsburgh charity that now owns its trademark rights. Tennessee won its next five games.

In January 2009 the Cardinals mascot blew its nose on the Terrible Towel, and Arizona fell to Pittsburgh in the Super Bowl.

Later in 2009 Detroit's mascot tore the Terrible Towel, and the Lions lost to the Steelers.

In 2106 Washington punter Tress Way posted a video of his mother burning the Terrible Towel, and the Steelers routed the Redskins.

Also in 2016 Bengals RB Jeremy Hill ripped a Terrible Towel after scoring a TD. He was held to minus 1 yard on his next six carries and was forced to leave the field several times with injuries. Cincinnati lost and was eliminated from playoff contention that same day.

Fans who watched Russell's record-setting run and switched their television dials to CBS following the Steelers' win on NBC witnessed another postseason record, Los Angeles's Lawrence McCutcheon running for 202 yards on thirty-seven carries in a 35–23 win over St. Louis. Frank Glieber and Hank Stram were in the sun-streaked Los Angeles Coliseum to call the action, which featured a standout performance by Jack Youngblood, the Rams' defensive end, returning an interception for a touchdown, recording a sack of Cardinals quarterback Jim Hart, blocking an extra point, and forcing a fumble.

The next day, Sunday, December 28, started with an NFC playoff featuring Gary Bender and John Unitas on the call as No. 1 seed Minnesota welcomed wild-card Dallas to snow-ringed Metropolitan Stadium for the 1:00 p.m. kickoff on CBS.

With twenty-four seconds remaining Roger Staubach dropped back from the 50-yard line and heaved a desperation bomb—a Hail Mary, the deeply religious QB called the miracle pass—to Drew Pearson. Despite claims by the outraged Vikings that Pearson pushed off Nate Wright and was guilty of offensive pass interference against the Minnesota cornerback, the touchdown stood, and Dallas won 17–14. The stunning victory remains a storied part of NFL lore, and it introduced the term "Hail Mary pass" into football lexicon.

At 4:00 p.m. EST NBC's coverage of the Cincinnati-Oakland game began with Curt Gowdy and Al DeRogatis broadcasting from sun-soaked Oakland. The Coliseum was a sea of silver and black as a crowd of 53,039 looked to rouse the Raiders to a fast start.

"The Bengals are riding high right now and a lot of people don't give us a chance," Raiders running back Pete Banaszak said before the game. That Oakland was entering the playoffs with a low profile was good, Banaszak believed. In previous years, he stated, the experts blew smoke at the Raiders and told them how great they were. This time nobody was talking about Oakland. "Maybe that's justifiable," he reasoned. "But I know what we're capable of doing and so does everybody else on this team."

Quarterback Ken Stabler and the Oakland offense seemed unstoppable as it sped to an early advantage against Cincinnati's conference-leading pass defense. George Blanda kicked a 27-yard field goal to give the Raiders a 3–0 lead in the first quarter, and the Snake made it 10–0 in the second with a 9-yard strike to Mike Siani.

Lindsey Nelson, known for his Technicolor coats and equally colorful broadcasts of Notre Dame football and New York Mets baseball, made the call on the Mutual Radio network.

Nelson: *"Stabler drops back, guns it into the end zone . . . Mike Siani with the touchdown!"*

The Bengals, playing their final game under retiring legend Paul Brown, took to the emerald-green Coliseum grass in their road white uniforms with burnt orange and black trim that was strikingly similar to the uniforms Brown made famous when he founded the Cleveland Browns in the 1940s. Cincinnati made it 10–7 when Stan Fritts finished a 65-yard drive with a 1-yard run. The drive featured league-leading passer Ken Anderson's 28-yard hookup with wide receiver Charlie Joiner and a play-action pass to fullback Boobie Clark that carried to the 1.

Stabler, slowed by a knee strain all season, upped the ante with his second TD pass, an 8-yarder to tight end Bob Moore. The score was Oakland's third in five first-half possessions, and the Raiders would have had more had it not been for a missed field goal and blocked field goal.

Nelson: *"Fading back from the 8-yard line is Stabler, throws out into the left flat, and it is taken by his tight end for a touchdown!"*

Ahead 17–7 at halftime, Oakland's opening drive of the third quarter saw the Raiders march 35 yards in four plays and Banaszak blast in from the 6.

The score ignited a second-half slugfest. Back came the Bengals with a fourteen-play, 91-yard drive that ended with Lenvil Elliott scoring from the 6 on a triple-effort touchdown run that cut Cincinnati's deficit to 24–14. The Raiders rallied in the final quarter with a twelve-play marathon march. On third and goal and with three tight ends in the lineup, the Snake bit the Bengals with his third scoring pass, a 2-yarder to tight end Dave Casper.

Nelson: *"Stabler has the ball, and he throws to Dave Casper for the touchdown!"*

Just when it seemed like a Raiders rout, Ken Riley's 34-yard interception return swung momentum to the Bengals with 10:00 left. Two plays later Joiner beat Jack Tatum for a 25-yard TD, and the Bengals were making a fitting final stand for their legendary field boss.

Following Oakland's first punt, Cincinnati struck again. A brilliant call on second and 20 led to the game's longest gain, a 37-yard completion to Chip Myers. Anderson, who completed seventeen passes for 201 yards and two TDs despite constant pressure, brought the Bengals to within three points when he hit receiver Isaac Curtis, who went high into the air for a 14-yard score.

With 4:19 left defensive tackle Ron Carpenter recovered a Banaszak fumble on the Raiders' 37. On the Cincinnati sideline quarterbacks coach Bill Walsh had a special play that called for Anderson to keep the ball or pitch to running back Essex Johnson. It would have been the perfect call for that situation, but Walsh, citing the incredible pressure of the moment and the chaos that came from the intense noise from fans who seemed to be right on top of the field, didn't think of it and instead called for a pass play. What happened next helped convince Walsh to script his plays calls when he became head coach in San Francisco.

Nelson: *"Anderson retreats. He is sacked by Ted Hendricks! That's the fifth time the Oakland defense has sacked Ken Anderson today!"*

Hendricks, Oakland's outside linebacker who was called the "Mad Stork" for being tall and rangy and running the field with arms flapping, produced one of the game's biggest plays when he eluded the attempted block by Clark and sacked Anderson for an 8-yard loss to take the Bengals out of range of a tying field goal. Walsh learned from this and as 49ers coach years later devised a flexible pass-protection scheme that had guard John Ayers, rather than a running back, blocking another great blitzing linebacker, the Giants' Lawrence Taylor.

The Raiders got the ball but were forced to punt with fifty seconds remaining. Oakland got an excellent kick by Ray Guy, whose 48-yarder sailed into the Cincinnati end zone. Gowdy called Guy the best punter in the NFL.

"He kicks them deep," Gowdy said, "and he hoists them high."

Desperate to block the punt, the Bengals drew a flag when Brad Cousino and Jack Novak ran into Guy. The Raiders retained possession and ran out the clock, prompting the waving of thousands of black hankies in the Coliseum as the clock wound down in a 31–28 win.

Nelson: *"The clock is running . . . There's the gun! Oakland has defeated Cincinnati. Oakland will be playing Pittsburgh for the American Conference Championship!"*

The wild fourth quarter was typical of the fantastic finishes the Raiders had become famous for. "It seemed like we had things pretty well under control until the Riley interception and then things got a little tight," said head coach John Madden. "But after all, we weren't playing the Little Sisters of the Poor."

Hendricks starred for a defense that was without tackle Tony Cline, the Raiders' most versatile D-lineman. When Al Davis signed Hendricks the previous summer, he said the former Colt star and Super Bowl veteran "might help us win a game down the line that we normally might lose."

Hendricks had four sacks on Anderson, contributed four other solo stops, and also batted down a pass, blocked a punt, and applied continuous pressure to the pocket. "Al Davis went to considerable trouble to get Hendricks on his team," Brown said. "Today, it finally paid off for him."

The trade also paid off for Hendricks, who finally found a home with the Raiders. Selected in the second round of the 1969 NFL Draft by Baltimore, Hendricks helped the Colts win Super Bowl V and return to the AFC title game in 1971, but his off-the-field antics persuaded the Colts' conservative management to deal him to Green Bay in 1974. When Hendricks was a free agent the following year, Davis gave Green Bay a pair of first-round picks for the rights to sign the Pro Bowl linebacker.

Hendricks and the hard-playing, fast-living Raiders proved a perfect fit for both sides, and the Mad Stork flourished in his new surroundings. "Everywhere I've been I've been the screwball on the team," Hendricks said. "But here [with the Raiders] I'm just a normal guy."

The 6-foot-7 Hendricks made the most of his height, swatting down passes and altering countless others with his extraordinary wingspan. He excelled against the run and the pass and as an edge rusher in blitz packages. His strength and mobility allowed him to stuff runners seeking to get outside, and he used his quickness to cover tight ends and running backs in pass patterns.

Clothesline tackles were legal at the time, and Hendricks's size 37 sleeve was imprinted on many a ball carrier. His long arms also enabled him to intercept twenty-six passes in his career and recover sixteen fumbles. The Mad Stork is also credited with an unofficial NFL career record twenty-five blocks of extra points, field goals, and punts.

Green Bay Hall of Fame linebacker Dave Robinson thought Hendricks "something different." Because of Hendricks's height, Robinson said, he was one of the great kick blockers and was also hard to throw over. "He had a devil-may-care attitude," Robinson said. "He sacrificed his body."

Hendricks's loose, gangly frame was matched by a loose, garrulous attitude. He showed up for an October practice wearing a hollowed-out Halloween pumpkin mask with face bars carved into it; on another occasion he donned a World War II German helmet. He once charged onto the practice field in full uniform, riding a horse and using a traffic cone for a lance.

Recognizing that Hendricks was a fellow maverick—"Ted's elevator doesn't go all the way to the top," Madden remarked—the Raiders let him freelance. Some plays found him floating along the line of scrimmage, diagnosing plays according to down and distance and then blitzing when the situation called for it or backpedaling into pass coverage.

Oakland position coach Charlie Sumner said at least once every game Hendricks would make a play that the Raiders had no idea how he did it.

Opposing offenses rarely knew what the freelancing Mad Stork was going to do and found it difficult to game plan for him. George Allen considered Hendricks the most opportunistic player he had ever seen, someone who forced as many mistakes by opponents as anyone ever did and one who took advantage of mistakes as well as anyone.

Because Hendricks was so resourceful, offensive game plans sought to neutralize him. In that regard Hendricks was a forerunner to Lawrence Taylor, who wreaked havoc from his linebacker position and forced opponents to create special game plans. "That's the mark of a great player—that he requires special handling," said Allen, who felt that no Raider was better in big games than Hendricks.

Rams linebacker coach Fred Whittingham called Hendricks a dominating player: "LT [Lawrence Taylor] with less athletic ability," he said.

Hendricks was the first great outside linebacker who wasn't built in the traditional mold of a linebacker. Hendricks looked lanky but was strong and tough. He was an amazing athlete, and he changed the concept of what a linebacker has to be.

Hendricks's physique initially led NFL scouts to question whether he could play linebacker at his weight, but he never missed a game in fifteen years, played in eight Pro Bowls for three different teams, won four Super Bowls, and gained induction in the Pro Football Hall of Fame. Like Lambert, Hendricks thought it silly that his thin build was called into question. "If you're good," Hendricks said, "you're good."

Sunday, January 4, 1976, broke cold and overcast in Pittsburgh. Bundled against the elements, Al Davis was incensed when he inspected the Tartan Turf of Three Rivers Stadium in the morning hours. Wintry weather had left the playing field snow-swept and ice-covered, particularly along the sidelines. Steelers head groundskeeper Steve "Dirt" DiNardo and his crew had covered the field with a tarp, but DiNardo claimed that strong winds swirling inside the stadium overnight and in the early-morning hours had torn the tarp along the sideline areas, allowing ice crystals to form.

Davis disputed the claim and wasn't shy about hiding his disgust. He believed the tarp had been intentionally rolled back to slow the Raiders' speedy receivers and hamper their perimeter passing game. NFL commissioner Pete Rozelle tried to calm the Raiders' boss by claiming field conditions were the same for both teams.

Davis blew up. "Damn it, Pete," he snapped. "You don't even understand what you're saying!"

The conditions in question were created when an Arctic front swept through the upper Ohio Valley Saturday morning and deposited a half inch of precipitation. It started as rain due to the warmer air ahead of the front but changed to snow when the Arctic air arrived.

Along with the precipitation, there was a rapid decline in temperature. Saturday's high of forty degrees was recorded at 2:00 a.m., but by 5:00 p.m. the temperature had dropped to twenty-three degrees.

Madden inspected the field on Saturday and saw DiNardo and Company covering the turf with a canvas tarp. They put weights around the tarp's edges and then blew it up with hot air so it provided a makeshift tent while they painted the field underneath. Madden told DiNardo if the grounds crew kept the field in that condition, it would make for ideal playing conditions.

But as DiNardo later explained, overnight winds were brutal, gusting up to 25 mph and cracking the tarp in half. On Sunday morning, strong, cold air combined with a northwesterly flow led to the development of lake-effect snow showers and squalls. Surface temperatures continued to fall, the temperature plummeted to two degrees, and sustained winds of 15–20 mph dropped the windchill to minus ten.

When the canvas cover was removed, moisture from rain and snow crystallized and froze the field in certain spots, particularly outside the hash marks and in the back of the end zones since the tarp was sized to fit the field. DiNardo and his grounds crew melted the ice with steam machines and looked to squeeze the cold water from the field. With game-time temperatures at eighteen degrees and 18 mph winds buffeting the Steel City and dropping the windchill to minus twelve degrees, plans to make the field more playable failed miserably. DiNardo and his men took to chipping the ice with shovels but to little avail. By kickoff both sidelines were frozen solid.

Conspiracy theorists believe DiNardo turned the hose on the sidelines to help the Steelers' running game and hurt the Raiders' passing attack. Madden's plan was to use the Raiders' speed on outside rushes and sideline passes, particularly to game breaker Cliff Branch. Branch had burned Blount and the Steelers' secondary for nine catches and 186 yards and a touchdown in the 1974 AFC Championship.

Madden argued that Oakland's strategies would be rendered ineffective while Pittsburgh's plans to power through the middle and off-tackle would not be neutralized at all. DiNardo thought the complaints by the Raiders, who had lost the last five AFL/AFC Championship Games they had played in, sounded like a built-in excuse should they lose.

What ensued was Tarpgate or Icegate, a forerunner to the Patriots' Deflategate. Madden said when he saw DiNardo hosing down the sidelines, he rushed over and asked what the hell he was doing. Dirt's reply was matter-of-fact. "Melting the ice."

Madden was stunned by the surreal scene. "Here the field is frozen and they've got a hose out there and they're watering it down," he said.

"I'm standing there watching them and they're telling me they're trying to melt the ice! I said, 'Hey, it's so cold it's going to make more ice!'"

Dan Rooney laughed off the Raiders' claims. The Steelers, he said, couldn't run on ice any better than the Raiders. Often overlooked is that Pittsburgh boasted a deep passing game of its own. John Stallworth averaged 21.2 yards per catch, Frank Lewis 18.1, and Lynn Swann 15.9.

During Pittsburgh's time as the City of Champions, DiNardo was part of the grounds crew for seven World Series or Super Bowl champion teams. He started as a part-timer with the Pirates' grounds crew at Forbes Field in 1960, the year the Bucs won the World Series.

DiNardo was beloved by Pittsburgh players, coaches, and owners. In a city known for its larger-than-life sports personalities, the chunky, cigar-chomping DiNardo was as popular as Franco's Italian Army, Myron Cope, and Bob Prince. Steelers safety Mike Wagner said Dirt's fame eclipsed that of the players. A Korean War veteran, DiNardo was a demanding taskmaster who made certain Three Rivers Stadium was ready for play regardless of weather conditions. Wagner saw Dirt, with his long sideburns, tinted glasses, and baseball-style cap that bore a button reading "Sesame Street Kid," as a happy-go-lucky character with a larger-than-life personality. His good humor was infectious, and even Madden took a liking to Dirt. One of Madden's prized possessions is a jacket given him by the gregarious grounds crew chief. The jacket made Madden an honorary member of the Three Rivers Stadium crew.

The Rooneys thought DiNardo provided humorous moments amid even the most intense rivalry, and DiNardo was said to repay the Steelers by bending the rules. Steve's son, Carmen, worked for his father's grounds crew and said his father was a homer "all the way."

Rumors persisted that DiNardo ordered the gates behind the end zone facing the river to be opened on opponent's field-goal attempts so the swirling winds would wreak havoc with kicks. Dirt was also said to sweep snow from crucial spots on the Three Rivers turf.

And then there was Tarpgate.

Steelers radio announcer Jack Fleming said the frigid air and frozen field stirred memories of the famous Ice Bowl played between Dallas and Green Bay on New Year's Eve 1967. Raiders-Steelers is referred to as Ice Bowl II, and Gowdy and Meredith, the latter the Cowboys' QB on that memorable afternoon, referred to that iconic game during NBC's broadcast of the '75 AFC Championship.

Small chemical bodies called Sno-Flo were spread on the icy patches, but the players didn't like the feel of what one called "those little balls out there" crunching beneath their cleats. Jack Ham rubbed a white substance called Frost Guard on his hands before pulling on Wilson golf gloves. Ham learned of the procedure from 49ers tight end Ted Kwalick, who told Ham that men in the Coast Guard did the same. Wagner also wore gloves, marking the first time he and Ham used them in a game.

Mansfield tried to keep his hands from getting numb by licking his fingers so they would stick to the ball. But every time he did he tasted the Sno-Flo that was on the field.

Russell scoffed at his teammates' gloves but acknowledged that he had so many busted-up fingers that his knuckles were double-taped and thus a little warmer. Russell said his hands were so gnarled by years of football that he could barely pick up his helmet to go on the field.

To cope with the conditions, fourteen Steelers pulled on special Canadian football shoes with long, pointed cleats. The cleats were provided by trainer Tony Parisi, whose wife, Joan, aided the cause by sewing muffs on to the Steelers' black jerseys. The muffs were fleece-lined flaps that Pittsburgh's players could stuff their hands into to keep warm.

Jars of Firm-Grip, or Stickum as it was known, were available on the sidelines. Players put gobs of the goo on their socks for touchups when necessary. Stickum was of little use this day, however, since it froze and hardened when exposed to subzero temperatures.

The Raiders and Steelers were set for a 1:00 p.m. start on NBC, while Dallas–Los Angeles was scheduled for 4:00 p.m. on CBS. A trivia note was that each of the four starting QBs in the conference championships—Bradshaw and Stabler, Staubach and James Harris—wore No. 12. On NBC Gowdy, DeRogatis, and Meredith, decked out in hats, gloves, and heavy coats, welcomed a national viewing audience to frigid Pittsburgh.

Gowdy: *"The weather is favorable to no one, twenty-one-degree temperature here, twenty-mile-an-hour winds, and spots of the artificial surface are in frozen condition."*

Just as he had the year before when his team was an underdog in Oakland, Noll believed his Steelers to be the best team in football, even though Greene was suffering from a pinched nerve in his neck and a pulled groin muscle.

Holmes, Noll pointed out, was having a "hell of a season." Ditto White and Lambert. They could do two things in this situation, Noll said. They could say, "We lost Joe, so we better hang it up," or everybody could look for reasons to win. That's what the Steelers would do, Noll stated, because that was the mark of a championship club.

The Steelers spoke openly of the "spiritual and emotional uplift" they would receive from Mean Joe's appearance in the starting lineup. He had not started any of Pittsburgh's prior five games. But there he was at the start of the title game, removing his warm-up cape and heading onto the field. The scene jolted the Raiders. "We saw *Jaws* on our flight from the Coast," Madden said. "That shark reminded me of Mean Joe."

Noll was happy to talk about Greene and equally happy to talk about Stabler as well. Noll said the Snake, despite nursing a knee injury and wearing his special Knee-Stablerizer, looked fine against Cincinnati. Noll grinned. "We'll see how [Stabler's knee] feels in seventeen-degree weather."

Neither offense felt very good in a game dominated by bone-crunching hits and bone-chilling winds. Breathing clouds of steam, Oakland opened in a fury. Tatum picked off two Bradshaw passes in the first quarter. But the Raiders, bundled against the bitter weather and wearing long-sleeved thermal undershirts beneath their white jerseys, were unable to put up any early points against the combination of the Steel Curtain, shivering cold, and swirling gusts.

The Raiders responded with their own rugged defensive play. Swann was knocked cold by an Atkinson forearm late in the third quarter and was carried from the field by Greene, whose own injuries almost caused him to drop his concussed teammate. The photo of Greene carrying the injured Swann is an iconic scene from the '75 AFC Championship. Swann's severe concussion caused him to be wheeled from the field on a stretcher and hospitalized.

Tatum sidelined receiver Frank Lewis with a high, hard hit following a 43-yard catch and was himself hurt two plays later when hit by Harris and Swann following the first of the Assassin's two interceptions. Tatum was also injured when he recovered Swann's fumble following Atkinson's hit and was drilled while on the ground by Bleier and Mansfield. Moore left the game with a groin pull, and Ham was hurt after hitting the hard turf on a diving tackle attempt on Clarence Davis. In all seven players had to be helped from the field, and Bradshaw would spend the final minutes in the locker room nursing a head injury.

Gowdy: *"You've had some real hitting out there, as you usually do between the Raiders and the Steelers."*

The ice-coated field, ferocious hitting fueled by shared hatred, and the fact that the players were either bare-handed or wore gloves that were little more than mittens contributed to a combined thirteen turnovers and twelve punts. Gowdy proved prescient when he noted early in the first quarter that "in this cold weather, they're going to have frozen hands, and they're going to have to be sure as ball handlers."

The weather made handling the ball difficult, as players on both sides said it was the coldest game they every played in. The windchill temps did, in fact, make for the coldest game the Steelers played in prior to the 1977 Week Thirteen meeting with the Bengals in Cincinnati when it was minus seventeen. "We couldn't tell whether we had the ball in our hands or not," Pittsburgh returner Mike Collier said. Harris thought both defenses scraped and clawed in an effort to strip the ball.

The Steel Curtain stuffed the Raiders' running game, which Ham deemed key to the Steelers' game plan. "If we don't stop the Oakland run," he said, "we all get to watch the Super Bowl on TV because Stabler will be able to pick us apart."

Oakland's offensive plan was to avoid the middle of the field with their passes and work the sidelines. "But the sides were all ice," Stabler said, "and our receivers couldn't move well out there."

Wagner's diving interception and subsequent 20-yard return in the second quarter set up the Steelers' first scoring drive. Wagner nearly came to blows with Oakland players after being ridden into the Raiders' sideline by Marv Hubbard. On the next play Bradshaw spiraled a pass to Swann for 27 yards. The drive stalled, and Gerela drilled a 36-yard field goal for a 3–0 lead.

Bradshaw was beating the Raiders' rush, particularly that of Hendricks, by dropping deep in the pocket. Bradshaw's backpedal brought special comment by the NBC TV crew.

Gowdy: *"Bradshaw is setting up very deep. Hendricks is trying to get to him from the outside but can't reach him . . . He's setting up too deep."*

The Steelers noted that in Oakland's playoff win over Cincinnati, Hendricks had lined up against the weak side without a single Bengal opposite him. A guard or running back should have picked Hendricks up, but they never did.

Pittsburgh didn't figure to make that mistake, nor did the Steelers figure they would have many difficulties running against the Raiders' innovative 3-4 front. Mansfield believed it had to be weak against the run since all the Steelers would have to do is handle nose tackle Art Thoms. Handle Thoms, Mansfield figured, and Steelers runners could get 3, 4, 5 yards a crack.

Guard Sam Davis knew the Steelers couldn't cut-block Hendricks because the Mad Stork would simply step over them. Davis knew the Steelers' linemen also couldn't charge Hendricks because he would grab them with his long arms and throw them aside. The blocking scheme called for Pittsburgh's linemen to mirror Hendricks, play him like a basketball player, juke with him, stay with him. The Steelers would run to their strong right side, away from Hendricks.

As the chess match unfolded, both teams found themselves in constant adjustment. Pittsburgh's plans to run inside were ruined by Thoms, whom Mansfield said was "all over the damn place." When Oakland had the ball it showed immense respect for the injured Greene, and the Raiders ran just five plays to his side and managed only 9 yards. Ham said the Steelers succeeded in taking one side of the field completely away from Oakland. Forced to pass, Stabler sought to counter

Pittsburgh's furious pass rush with shorter drops, screens, and flare passes. The Raiders also muscled up and went to a two-tight end formation for power runs by Banaszak and Hubbard. The Steelers stiffened and took a 3–0 halftime lead into the locker room.

Noll thought the game featured the hardest hitting he'd seen all season, and the war of attrition continued through a scoreless third quarter marked by two big missed opportunities by Oakland. Jess Philips recovered Collier's fumbled punt, and the Raiders took over at the Pittsburgh 16. Stabler spun a short flare to Banaszak, who fumbled as he turned upfield. Lambert recovered, but Oakland got another opportunity when Tatum recovered Swann's fumble at midfield courtesy of Atkinson's hit.

Swann said Atkinson tackled him around the head and then "sandwiched" his head into the ice-covered turf, knocking him colder than the weather.

Davis fumbled when leveled by J. T. Thomas on a sweep right, and Lambert recovered again, this time at the Pittsburgh 30. The turnover set up Pittsburgh's first touchdown drive, a five-play, 70-yard march.

With snowflakes falling from a somber sky, a six-minute stretch in the fourth quarter suddenly produced three scores. Harris, who bruised his way to 79 yards on twenty-seven carries, picked up a crunching block by Stallworth on Tatum, skirted left end, bulled past cornerback Neal Colzie, and, negotiating the same snow-swept sideline the Raiders argued was all but impassable, outran Hendricks and Atkinson to the end zone for a 25-yard touchdown and a 10–0 lead.

Fleming: *"At the 25, with snowflakes falling again, Harris goes outside to the left, breaks a tackle. He's to the 20, down the sideline. He's going to go for a touchdown!"*

Harris said the play was an inside trap, but when he saw there was nothing there he headed outside. A hole opened courtesy of Stallworth, and Harris was able to tightrope the sideline for the score. "A hell of a block," Harris said of Stallworth's chain-reaction block. "They closed the trap so I just kept bouncing it to the outside."

On the Steelers' sideline, Bradshaw told Mansfield, "John threw a great block!"

"Kolb?"

"No," Bradshaw replied in a breath of frosty steam. "Stallworth."

In the NBC booth DeRogatis pointed out the importance of Stallworth's big block.

DeRogatis: *"Great block by Stallworth on Tatum . . . It's what shakes [Harris] loose!"*

Franco's score broke the ice, both literally and figuratively. The offenses sprang to life, but problems still remained. Clarence Davis had trouble holding onto the ball, dropping three passes in the deep freeze. The former Southern Cal star had ended the Dolphins' dynasty the season before with his famous "Sea of Hands" touchdown catch in the end zone—exercising a Miami vise, of sorts. But he called the title game in Pittsburgh the coldest weather he'd ever played in. His fingertips were numb, and there was no way, Davis stated, to keep warm.

Stabler switched his focus to Dave Casper, finding his second-year tight end on three straight passes. Russell thought the tension so thick he could cut it with a knife. The Snake ended the 60-yard march with a 14-yard scoring pass to Siani. The former baseball player was playing for the injured Biletnikoff, who was out with a sore knee.

Midway through the quarter Lambert, his gold pants spotted with blood, recovered his third fumble, this by Hubbard on a hit by Glen Edwards. Amid heavier snowfall Bradshaw kept the scoring flurry going by connecting with Stallworth for a 20-yard TD. The point-after failed when Walden fumbled the snap, and the score stuck at 16–7.

Fleming: *"Bradshaw back to pass. They're coming after him, gets away, and now he throws to the end zone . . . It is caught! Neal Colzie slipped and fell. Stallworth was open to make the catch on the far side of the end zone!"*

Colzie, the rookie defensive back who faced Pittsburgh in the College All-Star Game in the sultry summer, was run over by Harris on the previous Pittsburgh touchdown and then victimized by the icy conditions in the end zone, slipping and falling on Stallworth's score.

With Swann, the other half of the Steelers' dynamic duo sidelined with a concussion, Stallworth knew he had to perform. He did so, proving instrumental in two late touchdowns.

Players on both sides were suffering in the elements. Bradshaw was losing feeling in his fingers and eventually had to be helped from the field in the final two minutes after taking hard hits from linebackers Monte Johnson and Phil Villapiano. The Steel Curtain was hurting too. When it's late December, Dwight White said, when it's bitterly cold and everybody's banged up, people are playing hurt, the Steel Curtain would look into each other's faces in the huddle. Blood would be running from a teammate's nose and he would feel whipped, and another teammate would urge him on, telling him, "C'mon, babe, suck it up!"

"We were tough people," White said. "And we took great pride in being tough people. I took great pride from being from a smoky, dirty city. That was part of our personality. We're going to smoke your butt and dirty you up."

Breathing steam and spitting ice, battered and bloodied, the Steel Curtain would find a way to win. Huddled together, the Steelers' defenders—proud and mean but cold, hurting, and very nearly exhausted—presented a picture of heroism and gallantry.

Nearly out of time and hope, the Raiders regained possession at their 35 when Hendricks recovered a Franco fumble with ninety-one seconds remaining. The Steelers were trying to run out the clock, but the turnover, Pittsburgh's seventh of an eventual eight, restored Raiders hopes. The Snake drove to the Steelers' 24. On third down Madden made a tactical move that Ham considered brilliant. With twelve seconds left Blanda, playing in his tenth AFL/AFC Championship, booted his longest field goal of the year, a 41-yarder, for his two thousandth and final career points.

DeRogatis: *"Madden has done a remarkable job. He had no time to spare. It's almost like a basketball coach using up the clock in the closing minutes of a game, trying to take advantage of every possible second."*

Trailing 16–10, the Raiders sought another miracle finish.

DeRogatis: *"They remember the miraculous reception of Franco that happened here with the same two teams."*

Meredith: *"They figure anything can happen."*

Anything almost did. Casper covered Oakland's onside kick at the Raiders' 45, and the Snake was still capable of spitting venom. Holmes was so nervous, he was shaking. With seven seconds left

Stabler launched a 37-yard bomb to Branch, who made the catch at the Pittsburgh 15. But before Branch could get out of bounds, he was brought down by Blount as time expired.

Gowdy: *"It's over! The Raiders went down to the wire just as much as a team ever could . . . The Steelers again have won the American Football Conference Championship!"*

While Noll's Steelers sought to join Lombardi's Packers and Shula's Dolphins as the only teams to that point to win back-to-back Super Bowls, Madden's Raiders became the first team to lose three straight AFC title games. It was also Oakland's sixth straight loss in championship appearances dating to the AFL title game in 1968. "One more play was all we needed," Stabler said in the funereal locker room. "Why is it that time always runs out on us?"

The only thing wrong with the Raiders, Greene remarked, is that they were too good for their own good. "They've never been able to sneak up on anyone," Mean Joe said.

Madden thought the cold bad but the ice worse. The slick sledding made it tough for Raiders receivers, he said, because Oakland's routes required turning and cutting and working back to the ball. Branch, limited to two catches for 56 yards, said every time he faked, he slipped. The Steelers' secondary wasn't the problem, he stated. It was the field.

Noll did not disagree that the conditions played a big role. He called the weather "cold as hell" and said players couldn't do the things they normally did. But that made for a true test, he added, because it revealed character. Noll bristled when asked about the turnovers. "It wasn't sloppy," he said. "When you have hitting like that you have mistakes, no matter what the field's like."

The Steelers survived the Raiders for the third time in four straight playoff years and settled in to watch the CBS broadcast of the NFC title game, which saw the wild-card Cowboys upset the favored Rams 37–7 in the LA Coliseum.

The reigning champions headed south to sunny Miami for Super Bowl X. Unlike the previous January, when their meeting with Minnesota in New Orleans was played amid cold rain in Tulane Stadium, the showdown with Dallas would be held in the sun-splashed Orange Bowl.

For the second time in the '75 postseason the Steelers would be playing destiny's darlings. Like the Colts, the Cowboys were a Cinderella squad that defied the odds. Dallas is remembered as the first wild-card team to play in a Super Bowl, though the 1969 Kansas City Chiefs were technically a wild-card team, having finished as runners-up to the Raiders in the AFL's Western Division.

Super Bowl X isn't as historically significant as Super Bowls I or III, but it was the most exciting Super Bowl to that point. It was also the last NFL game played on the six-year-old Poly-Turf of the Orange Bowl, the Dolphins reverting to natural grass for the 1976 season.

The popular CBS television sports broadcasting tandem of Pat Summerall and Tom Brookshier, known also for their years working together on *This Week in Pro Football*, called the action for a national viewing audience of seventy million on Super Sunday. Coverage began with the iconic theme for *The NFL Today*—"Horizontal Hold" by Jack Trombey—and the trio of Brent Musburger, Irv Cross, and Phyllis George welcomed viewers to sunny South Florida. The theme of Super Bowl X was to celebrate America's bicentennial, and the Steelers and Cowboys were outfitted in their respective black and white jerseys bearing a bicentennial patch on the shoulder.

Cowboys hard-hitting safety Cliff Harris figured prominently in firing up Pittsburgh before and during the game. Prior to kickoff he took aim on the injured Swann. "I'm not going to hurt anyone intentionally," Harris said. "But getting hit again while he's running a pass route must be in the back of Swann's mind. I know it would be in the back of my mind."

Swann returned the verbal salvo. "I read what [Cliff] Harris said," he remarked. "He was trying to intimidate me. He said I'd be afraid out there. He needn't worry. He doesn't know Lynn Swann. He can't scare me or the team. I said to myself, 'The hell with it. I'm gonna play.'"

The stunned Steelers trailed 7–0 early. The Cowboys' complex offense confused the Steel Curtain; cameras caught a frustrated Fats Holmes furiously slamming his padded fist into the rock-hard Poly Turf of the Miami Orange Bowl. Pittsburgh was still down when Swann soared over Cowboys cornerback Mark Washington to make a leaping catch and tight-roped the sideline at the Dallas 16.

Bradshaw's DNA this day was bombs away, and his first pass impressed Summerall and Brookshier. CBS announcers were not accustomed to seeing the Steelers in person since Pittsburgh was an AFC team and its games were normally covered by NBC.

Summerall: *"Caught by Swann! A super catch!"*

Brookshier, a former Pro Bowl cornerback with the 1960 NFL champion Philadelphia Eagles, was effusive in his praise of Swann, Bradshaw, and the Pittsburgh passing game.

Brookshier: *"One of the great catches! Beautiful reception!"*

Swann's kangaroo catch set up Bradshaw's game-tying touchdown pass to Randy Grossman out of a special three-tight end set.

Fleming: *"Bradshaw rolls right. Wide-open Randy Grossman in the end zone!"*

Late in the half Swann eclipsed his previous superlative reception with one of the great plays in NFL history, a juggling, acrobatic catch that covered 53 yards.

Summerall: *"Bradshaw back. The blitz is on for Dallas. The Steelers pick it up ... Lynn Swann out there. What a catch by Swann!"*

Brookshier: *"He's made two incredible catches, and we're not at half-time yet!"*

With Dallas leading 10–7 in the third quarter, Cliff Harris mockingly patted Gerela on the helmet following a missed field goal and thanked Pittsburgh's placekicker for "helping" the Cowboys. Lambert, a blocker on special teams, took notice of Harris's actions and responded by grabbing the Dallas defensive star and tossing him to the turf.

Brookshier: *"Jack Lambert was after Cliff Harris ... Works him over."*

Summerall: *"Lambert's really hot, still mad at Cliff Harris!"*

"I felt he jumped up in Roy's face and that was uncalled for," Lambert said. "Someone had to do something about it. We were getting intimidated and we're supposed to be the intimidators. So I decided to do something. . . . I don't like the idea of people slapping our kicker or jumping up in his face and laughing when he misses a field goal. That stuff you don't need."

Greene said Lambert was the "guy who sparked us. When it wasn't going good for us . . . he spearheaded us. He made the three, four licks that got us going. You could just feel it."

Brookshier: *"Lambert may be biting people beneath the pile!"*

Staubach said Lambert's intensity, his screaming and hollering, intimidated the Cowboys. "Lambert and Swann," Staubach said, "were the instrumental players in that game."

Lambert played the rest of Super Bowl X in a barely controlled rage. His ferocity inspired the Steelers, who seized physical control of the game in the second half, bloodied Staubach with a Super Bowl–record seven sacks and turned the Cowboys' heralded shotgun into a popgun.

Brookshier: *"The Steelers' defense has turned on the entire club. A ferocious series. They really beat up on Dallas."*

L. C. Greenwood sacked Staubach four times for minus 29 yards, jolting Jolly Roger and jamming the Shotgun attack. For delighted Steelers fans, "Hollywood Bags" and his high-top, gold-colored cleats made for a colorful addition to the Dallas backfield.

Greenwood was drafted the same year as Greene, and the two men had parallel careers that saw them line up on the left side of the Steel Curtain next to each other their entire careers, win four Super Bowls together, and eventually retire together in 1981.

Greenwood's gold shoes were the product of happenstance rather than design. A severely sprained ankle suffered during the 1973 season led the Steelers' team doctor to declare Greenwood out for the next game. The only way Greenwood could play, the doctor said, was to wear high-top cleats. Greenwood agreed, and team trainer Tony Parisi, who had a friend who owned a shoe store in the Strip District, secured the black high-tops. Greenwood tried them on and found they fitted perfectly. Despite that, L.C. didn't like the look of his new footwear. "Tony," he exclaimed, "I can't wear these shoes, they're too ugly!"

Parisi offered to paint them white, but Greenwood declined; Joe Namath, he said, had already made white shoes famous.

Parisi said he could paint the shoes gold, and Greenwood, in a joking mood, said okay. Parisi did and placed the gold shoes in Greenwood's locker on game day. "They were the ugliest things," Greenwood said. "I thought, 'Wow. I can't wear these.'"

Greenwood wore them, reluctantly, but when the Steelers won, L.C. adorned them the following week as well. With his ankle healed, Greenwood returned to white cleats, and the Steelers lost their next game. Pittsburgh fans implored Greenwood to return to wearing his gold cleats. The shoes had become a good-luck charm for fans but something more for Greenwood.

A fifth-round selection out of Arkansas AM&N, Greenwood didn't arrive with the same notoriety as Greene. The 6-foot-6, 250-pound Greenwood quickly became a fixture at left defensive end and was soon recognized as one of the quickest linemen in the NFL. Greenwood had great pursuit, and his height and long arms made it difficult for quarterbacks to throw over him.

Greenwood, however, noticed that stadium public address announcers often made the call—"Joe Greene on the tackle"—when it was really L.C. on the stop. "I'd get up from the ground and look around and Joe wasn't there," Greenwood said.

Greenwood decided he would put his gold shoes to good use. Whenever he made a tackle he would roll over so his gold shoes were sticking high up in the air. "I noticed at that point that's when they realized I was on the field," he said. "It was, 'L. C. Greenwood on the tackle.'"

Even amid the mod, disco-oriented outfits of the 1970s, Greenwood, with his "Rec Specs" and gold shoes, had a flair for fashion. "He made gold shoes look pretty good out there," linemate John Banaszak said.

A product of Canton, Mississippi, Greenwood grew up watching his father working long, hard hours, going to the factory at six a.m., returning home at four, and then working around the house and in the garden until midnight. His father figured that L.C., as the oldest child in the family, should likewise put in long hours. "I had a good childhood," Greenwood said, "but I worked hard."

Greenwood's father worked him hard enough that he realized that playing football was better than working for a living. L.C. figured he could make enough money from football that he would never have to work that hard again. When he turned fourteen his father told him, "You're a big boy now. You've got to deal with life."

From that point on, whatever money L.C. got it was because he earned it. He went to work in a factory and started planning for a life in football.

Greenwood was a greyhound-quick pass rusher but played the run well enough to be named All-AFC five times and play in six Pro Bowls in his thirteen-year career. In 1971 he tied an NFL record for fumble recoveries with five.

Greenwood had natural strength as well as quickness. That good, strong, first-penetration step, he said, was how he got to the quarterback. Greenwood may have looked like a basketball player with his tall, lanky build, but he fared well enough against heavier opponents to lead the Steel Curtain in sacks six times.

While Greenwood brought the Cowboys' offense back to earth, Swann turned skywalker with levitating leaps and beat the Doomsday defense for the winning touchdown, a 64-yard score into the lengthening shadows on a play called "60 Flanker Post" that made it 21–10 in the fourth quarter.

Fleming: *"Bradshaw's back. He wants to throw. He fires the bomb! Lynn Swann going for it. Swann pulls it in for a touchdown!"*

Summerall: *"Sixty-four yards touchdown pass! Bradshaw to Lynn Swann!"*

Brookshier: *"That has to be one of the great passes in Super Bowl history!"*

Swann's four catches for 161 yards earned him MVP honors. Of the seven passes he was targeted for, Swann was on average 30 yards downfield, a Super Bowl record.

The Steelers had several heroes, including Lambert, who had fourteen tackles; Bradshaw, who was knocked groggy on his game-winning bomb but threw for two touchdowns; Harris, who had a game-high 82 yards rushing; Gerela, who kicked two clutch field goals in the second half; Greenwood, who recorded a Super Bowl record four sacks and a forced fumble; and Glen Edwards, who sealed the Steelers' win with an end-zone interception of Staubach's Hail Mary pass on the final play. "We did what we had to do," Greene told reporters amid the Steelers' celebration. "That is what this football team does. This is the best damn team in football."

Having defeated their two biggest rivals of the decade, the Raiders and Cowboys, in back-to-back championships and joining the Packers and Dolphins as two-time Super Bowl champions, the Steelers proved themselves to be one of the best damn teams in NFL history.

Jim Campbell: While driving in from Canton, I didn't quite know what to expect. The Baltimore Colts were formidable. Bert Jones was playing as well as most NFL QBs, Lydell Mitchell was a 1,000-yard rusher, and the defense was pretty stingy.

Arriving at Three Rivers, ambivalent might have been the best way to describe my feelings. What the Steelers had done up to this point was impressive, but the weather was a factor, and so were Jones and friends. My fears were soon realized. With weather a contributor, the Steelers' offense committed five turnovers. But Mel Blount did what he did eleven times in the regular season—intercept a pass. Things looked better when Rocky scored. And even better when Andy Russell gathered in a loose football. Things turned downright rosy when Russell recovered a Jack Ham–induced fumble at the Steelers' 7-yard line and started a painfully slow trek toward the Colts goal line 93 yards away. Some say his run was timed by a sundial; others thought it was the longest (in elapsed time) TD in NFL history.

However you want to describe it, it put the 28–10 verdict into the win column for Pittsburgh. I recall Andy, draped in a sideline cape, puffing into an oxygen mask, as the kickoff cover and offense subsequently took the field. The next day's papers photographically documented my recollections of Andy's ordeal. His mates good-naturedly ragged on him, but they knew the veteran linebacker had provided them with a key to victory.

As was usually the case, "the Old Ranger" (Ray Mansfield) had the best one-liner about his good buddy's long and tedious run. Said the veteran center, "NBC took time out to run a commercial as Andy was returning the fumble." Something overlooked—if Russell was that slow, how come no Colt caught him?

There was one other notable event at the game. Myron Cope, looking to counter Pirates announcer Bob Prince's lucky-green "weenie," came up with a talisman of his own—the Terrible Towel. It was a small gold towel that Steelers fans first waved at this game and has been a part of the Steelers ever since. No member of the Steelers' faithful would be caught without one.

Up next: the Oakland Raiders. As was custom, an AFC reception was held in the Allegheny Club at the stadium the night before. We attended, along with most of Pittsburgh's A-listers. Combining the sublime with the ridiculous, it was at this event that I met, in person for the first time, my boyhood idol, Stan Musial—and Mark Davis, Al's boy. Looking out of the floor-to-ceiling windows of the stadium club, I could hear the wind howling and see the rain pelting down. The wind was playing havoc with the canvas tarp that covered the Tartan Turf field. During the night the tarp would split. Unfortunately, or fortunately, depending on your individual allegiances, this led to the sidelines becoming iced over.

What this did, in the minds of the Raiders, was take away their deep passing game. Big Al (Davis) and Madden accused the Steelers' ground crew of purposely allowing the tarp to be rendered useless. Their way of thinking may go back to the days when the Raiders were suspected of purposely watering down the playing surface when the Raiders played at Frank Youell Field, which was basically a high school facility in Oakland.

Regardless, it was a frustrating game. Thirteen turnovers of all kinds by both teams—fumbles, inceptions, you name it. With three quarters in the book, only three points scored—by both teams. The 20 mph wind and the rain (sometimes snow flurries) played havoc, and all of this was exacerbated by twenty-degree temperatures. I recall being as cold as I ever was at a game—until the scoreboard began favoring the Steelers.

It was in the third quarter that a memorable play took place. Lynn Swann was running a crossing pattern in the middle of the Silver and Black defense. Bradshaw's pass was to the outside. Swann was completely out of the play—that is, to everyone but safety George Atkinson. From behind, Atkinson unloaded a forearm shiver that sent Swann to the turf like a rag doll. Swann stayed down as the play unfolded.

Apparently, the field judge and the back judge relied on a "harm, but no foul" theory. Atkinson wasn't flagged. As it became obvious that Swann was really hurt, I saw Joe Greene take matters in his own hands, literally. He ventured out on the field, scooped up his fallen comrade, and carried him to the Steelers' sideline. It wasn't easy for Joe. I could see he was losing his grip on the limp wideout.

Joe played several seasons with an arm that suffered nerve damage. It affected his play and affected his ability to carry the 185-pound Swann. He was quoted as saying, "I almost dropped Swannie." Swann spent the two nights in a Pittsburgh hospital after being diagnosed with a concussion. At this juncture the Steelers were up, 3–0, as a result of Mike Wagner's interception leading to Roy Gerela's 38-yard field goal. Lambert's fumble recovery, after Pete Banaszak caught a pass and headed upfield, led to Franco's eventual 25-yard scoring run to the outside. He was helped immensely by a block by Stallworth that took out two Raiders pursuers.

Stabler quickly got the Raiders on the board as I watched him complete three passes to tight end Dave Casper before capping the drive with a scoring pass to Mike Siani. Blanda's PAT closed the game to 10–7. Lambert, a fumble-recovery machine on the day, gathered in his third, which led to Stallworth's 20-yard score. The extra-point try looked something like an old Keystone Kops movie. Bobby Walden fumbled the snap, and kicker Gerela picked up the ball, took a few steps to the side, and attempted the all-but-forgotten dropkick. Not unexpectedly, it was no good. Who said the PAT was automatic?

Stabler began another drive, but with time running out, Oakland needed a touchdown and field goal to win—but not necessarily in that order. With eighteen seconds on the clock, Blanda kicked his longest field goal of the season—41 yards. Along with thousands at Three Rivers and perhaps millions across the country, I expected an onside kick. There were nine agonizingly long seconds left after Marv Hubbard recovered the kick for the Raiders. By this time I had drifted down toward the Steelers' goal line. The Raiders were out of time-outs, but Stabler was still the Snake. He connected with a 37-yard pass to speedy Cliff Branch at the 15. Blount made the tackle before

Branch could skitter out of bounds—about a scant yard from the boundary. The scoreboard clock showed 0:00. It also showed Pittsburgh 16, Oakland 10.

As he had the year before, Joe Gordon came through with tickets to the Super Bowl and other necessities. I was looking forward to the trip to Miami and Super Bowl X and soaking up some pregame sun. Unfortunately, it was cold by Florida standards—in the fifties.

Saturday night before the big game, there was a television extravaganza. I don't remember much about it except that O. J. Simpson was there. In the wings before the show, I introduced myself and mentioned his 88-yard dash against the Steelers the year before, saying, "I could tell when you were still in the Bills backfield that you were going all the way." He just smiled and said, "I could tell, too. Thanks, buddy."

The bus left pretty early for the stadium. I filed into the Orange Bowl, and although it wasn't well publicized, there was an added bonus to being at Super Bowl X: shooting for the Paramount Pictures feature film *Black Sunday* was taking place. The John Frankenheimer film was based on Thomas Harris's novel of the same name. Briefly, the plot by the Palestinian terror group Black September was to arm the ever-present Goodyear blimp with explosives and crash it into the Orange Bowl crowd. Bruce Dern was the psychotic blimp pilot; Robert Shaw was Israeli counterterrorist agent David Kabakov, who was charged with foiling the plot.

Film crews were visible on the sidelines before the game, as was Commissioner Pete Rozelle and Dolphins owner Joe Robbie (it's safe to say *Black Sunday* was the silver-screen debut for both Rozelle and Robbie). Knowing considerably about the plot, having read Harris's novel, it was an eerie feeling to see the ponderous airship come over the horizon of the Orange Bowl. Of course, nothing untoward happened, but it did instill a desire to see the film once it would be released in 1977.

Something else I noticed, since we were in America's bicentennial year, 1976, both teams sported appropriate two hundredth anniversary patches on their uniforms—the Steelers opted for displaying it on their left shoulder, the Cowboys on their left sleeve.

The status of Lynn Swann was on my mind. Sure, he would play, but how effective would he be after the brutal hit to the head by Atkinson? In Miami Swannie had been dropping numerous passes in practice, once he was cleared to play. It concerned him. And I couldn't help reflect on what was written earlier about assistant coach Dan "Bad Rad" Radakovich rolling his eyes when I asked about the diminutive wide receiver. To me, Rad's reaction was an indication that Swann's head may not be 100 percent in the game. I think the surrounding doubts caused Swann to enter the game with more resolve than had there not been a question of his physical and mental fitness to play the game.

I viewed the game with trepidation from the opening kickoff, which was an unusual play to say the least. Ex-Steeler Preston Pearson fielded Roy Gerela's kick at the 8-yard line, giving off to speedy, and as-of-yet-unheralded, rookie linebacker Thomas Henderson—the "Hollywood" nickname would come later—who ran up the sideline, right past the Steelers' bench to the Pittsburgh 44-yard line. Not a good way to open the game, I thought. In on the tackle, finally, was kicker Gerela, who injured his ribs stopping Henderson. This would be a factor later on. It turns out the Cowboys didn't think that highly of the Steelers' special-teams play, and Landry was talked into trying the reverse by Dallas special teams coach Mike Ditka. At the time, it seemed like a good idea.

The first quarter wasn't to the Steelers' liking. The usually reliable Mike Wagner got snookered on a 29-yard TD pass on a crossing pattern—Roger Staubach to Drew Pearson. However, I did feel better when Pittsburgh evened the score at 7–7. I felt better because the key play was a 32-yard reception by Swann over Dallas cornerback Mark Washington. To me, it showed Swann was Swann. I'm not sure how he did it, but he contorted his body in midair to catch a sideline pass, outjumped Washington, and somehow come down inbounds with the ball. No ill effects from the prior concussion, pure concentration and body control. Could those childhood ballet lessons have paid off? The play carried to the 16-yard line, and quickly Randy Grossman took a 7-yard touchdown pass from Bradshaw to make it 7–7.

Swann's next reception can only be described as a thing of beauty. As time was winding down in the first half, Bradshaw launched another pass in Swann's direction. The Blond Bomber's bazooka arm propelled the ball nearly 60 yards in the air. Swannie was engaged in another footrace with Washington. I saw them go up. I saw Washington tip the ball, and although I didn't believe my eyes at the time, I saw Swann stumble, concentrate on the ball, and clutch it to his chest as he hit the ground. I'm glad *Sports Illustrated* made it its cover shot, because I needed concrete proof that it actually happened and my eyes weren't playing tricks on me. Sad to say, the surreal catch didn't pan out. Gerela, undoubtedly hampered by cracked or broken ribs, missed a 36-yard field goal in the closing seconds. Of his spectacular catch, Swann shrugged it off by saying, "All I did was run under the ball."

Unlike Gerela, the Cowboys' Toni Fritsch made an earlier 36-yard field goal, and the Cowboys took a 10–7 lead into the Orange Bowl locker room. Those J. B. Stetson–hatted "Ca-boys" fans standing in the stairway with me were ecstatic. I was inwardly hoping Steeler Nation, a term not yet coined, would have the last—and best—laugh.

The third quarter turned from cat and mouse to more of a heavyweight match. When Gerela missed a 33-yard attempted field goal, Dallas safety Cliff Harris tapped the less than 100 percent kicker on the helmet twice, as if to say, "Way to go, buddy. You really helped us." Lambert grabbed the offending Cowboys safety and flung him to the turf, pointing his finger in Harris's face and saying, "That'll cool your [rear end]." It seemed to me to be a turning point. The Steelers apparently got their swagger back. In today's safety-first environment, Lambert may have been banished from the field of play or at least flagged for 15 yards. But no official reached for his yellow flag.

Despite a loud and noisy crowd, at times, early in the fourth quarter, I heard what was music to my ears—the dreaded or pleasing (depending on who's punting) "double thump," that is, the thump on the punter's, in this case Dallas's Mitch Hoops, foot connecting with the ball, followed by the thump of a special teamer's connecting with the punt shortly after leaving the punter's foot. That second thump was provided by reserve running back Reggie Harrison. The blocked punt resulted in a two-point safety for Pittsburgh. From the Steelers' sideline I sensed a shift in momentum in the final fifteen minutes.

It was in the second half that I had a feeling of déjà vu all over again, when Joe Greene left the field with a pulled groin. I recalled Chuck Noll saying before Super Bowl IX, subscribing to his "next-man-up" theory, saying, "If Dwight White [weakened by pneumonia] can't play, we'll go with Steve Furness." Greene out; Furness in. In less than a half of play, the combination defensive end and defensive tackle from University of Rhode Island was in on nine tackles—five solo—and registered a sack of Staubach.

Also during the fourth quarter, Gerela added two field goals—first a 36-yarder, then from 18 yards. It was a back-and-forth game for much of the final quarter, but with about 3:30 left a pivotal play occurred. Facing a third-and-4 situation, Bradshaw decided to cross up the Cowboys—remember, he called his own plays. With the Cowboys "red dogging" on an expected running play, Bradshaw threw deep to Swann. The future Hall of Fame receiver caught the ball in stride and scored. I'd put the length of the pass at 70 yards in the air.

The only downside, Bradshaw saw nothing of Swann's catch or the resulting jubilation. Harris and tackle Larry Cole arrived as Bradshaw was launching his bomb. Both made contact—Harris around Bradshaw's waist, Cole helmet to helmet with Bradshaw's jaw. Who knows how the play would be adjudicated today? Bottom line: no flag, six points. Gerela's PAT failed, but thanks to Harrison's safety, Pittsburgh still had a 21–10 lead.

After the kickoff Dallas began at its own 20-yard line with 3:00 to play. Staubach wasted no time, hitting Drew Pearson on a 30-yard pass over J. T. Thomas that carried to the Steelers' 43. With defensive coordinator Bud Carson deploying the Steelers in a so-called prevent defense, like many other NFL observers, I've always wondered just what it prevented. Staubach was able to move the Cowboys down the field rather rapidly. My heart sank when I saw Mel Blount stumble and free agent former Austin Peay basketball player Percy Howard make an end-zone catch for a 34-yard score. It would be the only catch of Howard's brief NFL career. Neither I nor anyone else expected anything but a Dallas onside kick. We were not disappointed.

The Steelers had the "good-hands people" ready for the short kick.

It came, and reliable Rocky Bleier smothered it at the Dallas 42. A look at the scoreboard clock showed 1:48 to play. With Terry Hanratty in for the woozy Bradshaw, the plan was to drain the clock with running plays, but three of them netted just a yard. Dallas had called a time-out after each run, and now it was fourth and 9. While Bobby Walden and the punting team didn't make a move to take the field, Hanratty and Noll conferred on the sideline. Noll undoubtedly recalled Walden's drop of the snap that set up the Cowboys' first score and how Cliff Harris and Bob Breunig had come close to blocking punts.

Those around me wondered what was going on. I must admit, I did too. Then I remembered a slogan I formulated several seasons before: "In Chuck We Trust."

I saw Hanratty return to the huddle and take quite a bit of time calling the play. What would it be? Would he go up to the line, use a hard count, and try to draw the Doomsday defense offside? Nope, they were going to go for it. In the huddle I was told by Bleier—a Golden Domer, like Hanratty—that the Rat shook his head and said, "All right, guys, here it is: 84 trap, on two." That was Bleier running off right tackle. The play gained 2 yards. The clocked stopped on the change of possession.

Dallas had the ball at its 39 with 1:22 to score the winning touchdown. Noll later said, "If a field goal could have tied the game I would have punted. . . . If we couldn't stop them, we didn't deserve to win. Our defense did exactly what I expected it to do."

The message I thought the unassuming future Hall of Fame coach was sending to Tom Landry and the Cowboys was "You're a great football team, but I like my defense's chances of stopping you."

Roger the Dodger scrambled to an 11-yard gain on the first Cowboys play. Connecting with ex-Steeler Preston Pearson for 12 yards, Captain Comeback had his team at Pittsburgh's 38. Preston cut back to the middle of the field, instead of stepping out of bounds, which would, of course, have stopped the clock. Captain America then gave me, and others, a thrill by throwing to the end zone. I was able to breathe normally again when I realized it was just to stop the clock and not a serious threat after finding no open receiver.

Next, Staubach tried to connect again with his secret weapon—
Howard. Although J. T. Thomas was somewhat out of position, it
seemed he may have obscured the former hoopster's vision sufficiently to cause the ball to fall harmlessly to the painted end-zone
turf. Three long and agonizing seconds left, Staubach, from shotgun
formation, pumped once and then let go a "Hail Mary"—remember,
he threw the first-ever such pass to Drew Pearson in the 1975 divisional playoff game in defeating the Vikings, 17–14. This Hail Mary
went unanswered. Instead of Drew Pearson catching the "prayer," it
was gathered in by Glen Edwards, the Steelers' free safety, much to
Pittsburgh's relief.

I'd like to poke holes in a myth-conception. It's been said by many
that the Steelers' first two Super Bowl victories were largely attribut-
able to Franco's running—he was voted MVP of Super Bowl IX—and
the Steel Curtain. Bradshaw was viewed as more or less a caretaker
or, what is now considered less than complimentary, as game manager. Those critics would concede that the Steelers' next two wins—
Super Bowls XIII and XIV—were Bradshaw driven.

I respectfully disagree with half of that myth—the second half.
Franco, valuable while chewing up clock, gained only 3.0 yards on
average on his twenty-seven carries; Bradshaw, helped immensely
by Swann's heroics, threw for 209 yards and two touchdowns. Of
course, the Steel Curtain was stellar also. The front four, especially
when needed most, pressured Staubach all afternoon. The linebacker
trio—Jack Ham and Andy Russell on the outside and Jack Lambert
in the middle—roamed the Orange Bowl turf. The defensive backfield, all of whom hit like linebackers, was very stingy with yards and
catches. It was during this time that ten of the Steelers' eleven defensive
starters were selected for Pro Bowls—only Ernie Holmes was passed
over, and his play certainly could have made it a unanimous situation.

If football is the ultimate team game, the '75 Steelers were the ultimate team.

9

Autumn Wind Is a Raider

NFL schedule makers indulged their sense of drama in the opening week of the 1976 season.

To kick off the campaign the league matched the AFC's championship finalists in 1974 and '75 in a 4:00 p.m. start in Oakland. The Steelers and Raiders were pro football's most successful teams over the two previous seasons, Oakland owning a 23-5 record that was a half game better than Pittsburgh's 22-5-1.

As soon as the schedule came out, Ken Stabler looked to see who the Raiders would play. "And there it was," he said. "Pittsburgh in the opening game."

On paper the rematch favored Pittsburgh. The Steelers were two-time defending Super Bowl champions; they had won four straight season openers, including a 34–28 victory over the Raiders to begin the '72 campaign, and had won their last previous two openers via shutouts.

Pittsburgh had started its preseason strong, earning a 24–0 storm-shortened win in July in the Chicago College All-Star Game.

Coached by recently retired Notre Dame legend Ara Parseghian, who was assisted by offensive mastermind Sid Gillman, the collegians fielded a lineup featuring future NFL starters in running back and two-time Heisman Trophy winner Archie Griffin, quarterback

Richard Todd, offensive guard Jackie Slater, and defensive linemen Dewey and Lee Roy Selmon.

Despite a downpour that drenched the area forty minutes prior to kickoff, a crowd of 52,895 flowed into Soldier Field. Las Vegas odds-makers installed the NFL champs as seventeen-point favorites, but Parseghian raised the stakes by telling reporters, "I'm not afraid to stick my neck out. When the whistle blows, the All-Americans will be ready for the Steelers."

Inside the dressing room Parseghian roused his college stars with a fiery speech. He told them they were on the verge of realizing their dream. Pointing to Griffin, Parseghian said, "You know how many men have won the Heisman Trophy two times? There's no one on Pittsburgh that's won the Heisman Trophy twice!"

Because the Steelers entered the game looking to sharpen their execution and avoid injuries, Joe Greene was surprised and angered when Jackie Slater cut-blocked him. "Hey, man, this is preseason," Greene snapped. "Stay off my knees."

Slater hit Greene on his legs again and was on the ground when he said the Steelers' star kicked across his face mask. Greene denies kicking Slater, stating that he only kicked at him—a warning shot across the bow.

Slater got the point and played the rest of the game straight up. Greene and Company held the collegians to 54 yards in the first half, and Pittsburgh led 24–0 with 1:22 left in the third quarter when a heavy rain rode in on a northern wind. Conditions worsened, and spectators stormed the field, body surfing on the slick artificial turf.

Referee Cal Lepore, fearing for the players' health, sent them to their locker rooms and awaited clear skies and the clearing of fans from the field. It was wishful thinking in both areas. The drenching rain persisted, and fans tore down the goalposts. At 11:01 p.m. the game was finally called, following consultation with NFL commissioner Pete Rozelle and a curtain, a Steel Curtain on this night, came down on the College All-Star Game. Chicago Tribune Charities discontinued the summer classic in 1977. The final tally for the Arch Ward spectacle predictably read in favor of the pros, 31-9-2.

While Pittsburgh had a recent history of starting strong, Oakland had won just one season opener since 1970. Entering the '76 season the Raiders were a team in transition. George Blanda lost his placekicking duties in the 1976 training camp and called it a career; it marked the second straight season a longtime Raiders legend had retired, center Jim Otto leaving following the loss to Pittsburgh in the January 1975 title game.

Head coach John Madden instituted another change in '76 when he altered the Raiders' base defense from a 4-3 to a 3-4. Oakland had used the 3-4 in previous years but as a mixer; they ran it at times en route to an AFL Championship in 1967. In Oakland's terminology the 3-4 was called the "Orange" defense, and its success was geared in part to linebacker Willie Hall, a 6-foot-2, 225-pound product of Southern Cal who had once been cut by the Raiders.

Jack Tatum believed the insertion of Hall in the starting lineup paid dividends in more ways than one. Not only did the Raiders' defense get big up front when they went to the 3-4, but they also got another great athlete on the field in the person of Willie Hall.

Tatum called Hall a great athlete who made great plays. "It seemed like he made at least one [big play] in every game," Tatum said, and Hall would make a very big play in the opener against the Steelers.

The problem for the Raiders was that when they played a 4-3, they had no place for Hall. Madden found the solution in the fact that Oakland didn't have a fourth defensive lineman who was as good as Hall.

There was something else weighing on the mind of Madden that did not have a quick fix. Speaking with Stabler, Madden lamented the fact that the Raiders had continually fallen short of returning to the Super Bowl. "We didn't get in because we lost to great teams," Madden said. Miami was a great team and manhandled the Raiders in the '73 AFC title game. Then Pittsburgh had great teams and beat Oakland in back-to-back title games. In each of the past three seasons the teams that defeated the Raiders went on to win the Super Bowl.

Stabler was succinct in his reply. "We're gonna win it all this year, John."

The Snake wasn't the only Oakland player feeling that way. Tatum found himself looking forward to this season more than any other. He, too, had the feeling this was the year the Raiders were going to win the Super Bowl. What was strange, Tatum said, was that everyone arrived in Oakland's camp feeling the same way.

The Raiders slugged their way through six preseason games that they knew didn't mean a damn thing. Their focus was on the Steelers, and how could it be otherwise? As Stabler said, how could Oakland forget what Pittsburgh had done to them in the past? How could the Raiders forget Franco's Immaculate Reception in 1972? How could they forget the frozen field in Pittsburgh in '75? Those were the kind of games Pittsburgh-Oakland slugfests had become famous for, games with controversy.

Raiders versus Steelers had become a hell of a rivalry, Stabler said. Even if they didn't clash in the regular season, they knew they would collide in the postseason. Oakland and Pittsburgh both knew they would have to beat the other to reach the Super Bowl.

The week of the opener, the Raiders got the game plan on Wednesday, and Stabler knew immediately that there were too many plays in it. Too many pass plays, he thought, since the Raiders were planning on running the ball. Oakland was pretty basic in its ground assault; the Raiders believed their offensive line could open up holes against any defense, including the famed Steel Curtain that Stabler knew was the best in football.

September 12 offered a sun-soaked, slightly breezy sixty-two-degree afternoon in Northern California for the Raiders' first home opener since 1969. Throughout the early 1970s the Raiders had to open on the road to accommodate their Coliseum cotenants, the A's, who were involved in the MLB playoffs every year from 1971 to 1975.

Curt Gowdy called the action for NBC TV:

"We're getting ready now . . . The season is under way here in Oakland!"

For all of the bad blood between Oakland and Pittsburgh, the game opened with a bit of levity. Raiders equipment man Dick Romansky painted expletives in large letters on the side of each football. When Steelers center Mike Webster went to snap the ball, he saw the expletive, thought it was aimed at the Steelers, and demanded a new ball.

The Pittsburgh papers reported after the game that the Raiders were such low-lifes that they went so far as to write obscenities on footballs to annoy the Steelers. Stabler, for one, remarked that it was purely accidental. "At least," he added, "that's what I was told."

What wasn't accidental was Oakland offensive guard George Buehler smearing Vaseline on his black-and-silver jersey. Playing right guard for the Raiders, Buehler would be battling Greene, who would be positioned at an angle between Buehler and center Dave Dalby in the Stunt 4-3 alignment. One of Greene's patented pass-rushing techniques was what the Raiders called the "Grab and Jerk." Greene would grab the guard's jersey, jerk him to one side, throw his other arm over the inside, and surge past him. Other defensive tackles tried the same maneuver, but none was as successful as Mean Joe.

Al Davis called Greene the most dominant player in the NFL in the mid-1970s, and Buehler, hearing Davis's words, would get geared up to face the Steelers' star. Buehler said that while he enjoyed playing against Greene, "I wouldn't want to do it every week." When Greene called Buehler one of the strongest blockers he faced, Buehler spent the following week wearing a big smile. By smearing his jersey with Vaseline, Buehler ensured that Greene would have a difficult time trying to use his grab-and-jerk technique.

True to its traditional season-opener form, Oakland struggled, while Pittsburgh picked up where it had left off in previous openers by pounding out a 28–14 fourth-quarter lead. The hitting amid the lush, green environs of the Oakland Coliseum was as fierce as it had been nine months earlier on the frozen Tartan Turf of Three Rivers Stadium.

Stabler thought it even more ferocious than their last meeting. George Atkinson's infamous "Hook" to the back of Lynn Swann's helmet hospitalized him with another concussion. Mel Blount picked up Raiders receiver Cliff Branch following a reception and dropped him on his helmeted head. Randy Grossman hit Tatum after the whistle, and the Raiders' safety responded by throwing the tight end to the grass and punching him. "The fact was," Stabler said, "the Raiders hated the Steelers and the Steelers hated the Raiders."

Despite the tremendous hitting, the offenses combined for a staggering 878 yards and fifty-nine points, the latter coming entirely over the game's final three quarters.

Oakland threatened early, but the Steel Curtain responded with Greene blocking a Fred Steinfort field-goal attempt and Glen Edwards picking off a Stabler pass in the end zone. Pittsburgh's lone entry into Raiders territory ended when a jarring hit by safety Charles Phillips freed the ball from Rocky Bleier and linebacker Monte Johnson recovered it.

The Snake struck in the second quarter. Relying on the Raiders' famous five-man receiver sets, Stabler found Branch and running backs Clarence Davis and Mark van Eeghen with completions that put the ball at the Pittsburgh 20. Stabler was sacked by Steve Furness and L. C. Greenwood but then hooked up with tight end Dave Casper along the left sideline for the 30-yard score and a 7–0 lead.

Gowdy: *"Stabler pump-faking. He hits Casper and ... he's in there for the touchdown! What a ropewalk he did down that sideline! He has the feet of a ballerina dancer!"*

Oakland's man-to-man coverage blunted Terry Bradshaw and the Pittsburgh passing game. The Steelers attempted a short field goal, but it was blocked. In the final minute of the half Bradshaw found Franco Harris down the middle for 39 yards. Two plays later Bleier blasted in from two yards out, and the rivals headed into the break tied at 7.

The third quarter was controlled by the punting game; the Raiders' Ray Guy averaged 44 yards on the afternoon with a long of 63, and the Steelers' Bobby Walden averaged 42 yards with a long of 56. Midway through the third Harris ripped off a 25-yard gain and then unexpectedly lateraled to wide receiver John Stallworth, who covered the final distance to complete a stunning score and give the Steelers a 14–7 edge.

Bradshaw began the fourth quarter with an 11-yard strike to rookie receiver Theo Bell to up Pittsburgh's advantage to two touchdowns. Raiders wide receiver Fred Biletnikoff said the team had the feeling that they could come back and catch the Steelers, and Biletnikoff played a pivotal role in the rally, his diving 21-yard touchdown catch capping a 67-yard drive.

Gowdy: *"What a grab by Biletnikoff! And the Raiders are back in it!"*

The Steelers struck back with a scoring march of their own, an 84-yard haul capped by Harris's 3-yard run with 6:43 remaining.

Gowdy: *"Harris in for the touchdown! Pittsburgh comes right back and roars 84 yards!"*

Like Ali and Frazier, who had pushed each other to the physical and emotional brink the previous October in the Thrilla in Manila, the Steelers and Raiders were heavyweights hammering each other with hellacious shots. Ahead 28–14, the Steel Curtain looked to land the decisive blow when Blount stepped in front of a Stabler pass on Oakland's first play from scrimmage following Franco's score. Set up inside the Raiders' 20-yard line with less than 6:00 remaining, the Steelers were staggered when Harris was hit by Johnson, fumbled the ball, and Johnson secured his second recovery. "We didn't play bad, we just kept breaking down," Tatum said. "When they got that big lead, we only had one aim left—get the ball for our offense."

From his own 25, Stabler started the series with a 15-yard delivery to Davis. Though the gain was wiped out by an illegal-motion penalty, Stabler came back with a completion to Casper that covered 21 yards. Flashing the form that had defeated the Dolphins in the "Sea of Hands" game two years earlier, the Snake found Casper again for 25 yards and Biletnikoff for 18. Pete Banaszak bulled for 11 yards, and Stabler connected with Casper in the back of the end zone to cut Oakland's deficit to 28–21 with 2:56 still remaining.

Tatum and defensive tackles Charles Philyaw and Dave Rowe combined to stop the Steelers on the next series. Warren Bankston, who formerly played for Pittsburgh, blocked Walden's punt, and Phillips, making his second big play of the day, returned the ball to the Steelers' 29. Three incomplete passes set up fourth and 10. Amid a deafening roar from Raiders fans, Stabler ducked away from Greene's thunderous rush and found Branch for a 27-yard gain to the 2-yard line. The Snake then sprinted to his left, getting a block from left guard Gene Upshaw on middle linebacker Jack Lambert to clear a path to the tying touchdown with 1:05 to play.

Bill King made the call on the Raiders' radio network:

"Stabler asks for quiet . . . First and goal on the 2 . . . Stabler rolling to the left. He could take it in. He tucks it under . . . Touchdown, Raiders!"

With overtime a seeming certainty, Bradshaw dropped back on first down. His pass was deflected by an onrushing Rowe and hauled in by the ubiquitous Hall, who returned it to the Steelers' 12. Banaszak carried twice to move the ball to the 4 with twenty-one ticks left. On third down and with eighteen seconds remaining, Steinfort sealed the stunning comeback with a 21-yard field goal that made it 31–28.

King: *"John Madden, on the sideline, after a momentary hesitation, shows some jubilance and exuberance!"*

The Raiders rallied past Pittsburgh by producing seventeen points in just 2:38 and denting the Steel Curtain for 440 yards.

"It was a fun game," said Stabler, who walked around the locker room after the game feeling as if he'd just won a championship. The Raiders had just beaten the team that had kept beating them in title games and had looked unbeatable on this day as well. But Oakland had come back and defeated the world champions. The win was so emotional and Stabler was so drained that he was in a daze afterward.

Tatum said the Raiders learned something in that game. If they worked harder than their opponent, they could play defense as well as anyone. "We all had that feeling," Tatum said, "and it got us going."

But the story of the '76 opener wasn't limited to what is remembered by Raider Nation as the Classic Comeback of '76; repercussions from this game would linger for years and reach all the way to the Supreme Court.

The Raiders rode the wave of momentum to an early winning streak; the Steelers would streak in the other direction and suffer four losses in their first five games. Injuries played a part in Pittsburgh's rough start, and it all began on a broken pass play in Oakland when on third and 5 at the Raiders' 44 with 1:24 left in the first half, a scrambling Bradshaw hit Harris for a short gain along the left sideline. Swann, the Most Valuable Player in Super Bowl X, was running across the field from the right side and was almost stopped at the Oakland 30 when he was belted to the Coliseum grass by Atkinson's blindside forearm blow to the back of the helmet. Swann, concussed by Atkinson in the previous January's conference championship and forced to spend days recovering in the hospital, was knocked out yet again.

Former Dallas Cowboys QB Don Meredith, doing color commentary on NBC-TV's national broadcast, offered a candid a review of the play:

"They're picking on Lynn. I don't think you're supposed to do that. Atkinson did another no-no—gave him a karate chop across the back of the neck."

Gowdy: *"You mean you're not supposed to take a guy's head off?"*

No penalty was called on the hit that forced Swann to be sidelined the next two games and prompted Steelers head coach Chuck Noll to pull no verbal punches in his postgame press conference. "There was a lot of discussion about putting a rule in against it this year," the Steelers' coach told reporters. "It wasn't done and the reason given was that, although it was illegal, no special rule was needed. There should've been a rule against slapping receivers years ago. Maybe they're waiting for somebody to get killed. They went after Swann again. People that sick shouldn't be allowed to play this game. Watching something like that clouds the hell out of what their offense did. It seems to come only from their defensive unit. Maybe that's a reflection on their coaching."

In his weekly press conference the following day in Pittsburgh, Noll pushed the envelope even further, referring to Atkinson as a "criminal element" who should be thrown out of the NFL. He said Atkinson's hit was done "with the intent to maim and not with football in mind. People like that should be kicked out of the game, or out of football.... There is a certain criminal element in every aspect of society. Apparently, we have it in the NFL, too."

Asked what he specifically saw on the play, Noll answered, "What I could see was that Swann had his back turned and somebody hit him in the back of the head and neck. That's why we have officials. That's why we have a league office."

A reporter reminded Noll that the Steelers had likewise been accused of dirty play, as in the previous year's Super Bowl against Dallas when cornerback Mel Blount was accused of breaking the ribs of Cowboys receiver Golden Richards. "We usually hit people straight on, nose-to-nose," Noll replied. "There's nothing wrong with hard-hitting football, but not when your back is turned. It's something that has to be straightened out. I don't think that's football. . . . We play football. We don't want to get involved with criminal actions."

Noll's comments, issued in a small room in the Steelers' offices on Monday, September 13, created a firestorm that engulfed the entire NFL. The Steelers' Dan Rooney sent an angry letter to NFL commissioner Pete Rozelle, one of many letters the league office in New York received from fans across the country who witnessed the game on NBC's national broadcast. Stating that he could not remember a more flagrant foul in his sixteen years as commissioner, Rozelle fined Atkinson $1,500. The commissioner also fined Noll $1,500 for violating league policy by speaking publicly against a player, Raiders safety Jack Tatum $750 for a different incident during the game, and Steelers defensive tackle Ernie Holmes $200 for another incident that occurred during the battle royale.

Now the Raiders got riled up, Atkinson defending his hit on Swann. "It was nothing intentional," he said. "The game is a contact sport. It might be different if we had flags in our pockets. I get knocked around; I've had concussions. I don't complain about it. I don't even think it was that severe a hit. The hit I gave him last year was worse."

Swann, for his part, said Atkinson's blow was illegal and "delivered with what seemed to be some type of malice. It's our contention it was basically criminal."

After he got news of his fine and Noll's comments, Atkinson responded, "This may be slander." On December 6 he slammed Noll and the Steelers with a $3 million libel and slander lawsuit, citing defamation of character. Atkinson also sued the *Oakland Tribune* after reporter Ed Levitt wrote, "Atkinson could have killed Swann instead of giving him a concussion. He could have been facing a murder rap."

A jury trial began on July 11, 1977, in U.S. District Court in San Francisco. The trial degenerated into the theater of the absurd. Swann, Atkinson, Noll, Madden, Rooney, Al Davis, Bradshaw, Harris, and Bleier took the stand in turn. High-profile lawyers represented the

Raiders and Steelers. Pittsburgh placed its fate in the hands of for-mer Patty Hearst lawyer James MacInnis; the Raiders retained Wil-lie Brown, an assemblyman from San Francisco who had spoken at the 1972 Democratic Convention and would be San Francisco's first African American mayor. Two years earlier, Brown had represented Atkinson against charges of embezzlement, larceny, and theft in the cashing of $3,000 worth of bank securities.

The eloquent MacInnis sought to convince the six-person jury that Atkinson was a dirty player. MacInnis looked to educate the jury of five women and one man not only on football and the NFL but also on the description of a "criminal," since that was the key word in ques-tion. He brandished a *Webster's Dictionary* to explain the definition of criminal, but Judge Samuel Conti, a no-nonsense jurist, ruled that the dictionary's description was hearsay since Noah Webster was not around to testify.

Conti's first ruling in the lawsuit was that Atkinson could seek only compensatory damages, not punitive. During the jury selection pro-cess he cautioned the pool that the trial could take place in two or three weeks rather than the assumed couple of days.

Noll was the first witness. Because he had been summoned by Atkinson's legal team, Conti allowed Noll to be treated as hostile. Dan Mason handled the examination and managed to back Noll into a figurative corner, no small feat since Noll was a former law student and his testimony was filled with keen observations along with some humor and sarcasm.

Mason: "Is there anybody else who constitutes 'Noll's criminals'?"

Noll: "The criminal element is made up of people who break the rules wantonly. I'd have to go back and review the films and find who fits into that category."

Mason: "Come up with another name, other than Atkinson."

Noll: "There have been people who played against us—Tatum."

Mason produced a projector and reels of films and showed the courtroom clips of Blount, Greene, and Glen Edwards engaging in violent hits.

Mason: "Shall I add those names to your list?"

Noll: "That's not my list. That's your list."

When Mason showed a play in which Blount hit Branch in the helmet with a forearm similar to Atkinson's hit on Swann, Noll was forced to admit the obvious.

"I think what Blount did was not right or correct. He was talked to after the game. We don't want that to happen. It was an act we do not approve of."

Noll made similar statements concerning plays involving Greene and Edwards.

Mason: "Let's add them to the list."

Noll: "Go ahead. You have the chalk."

Turning to what Noll had said to gain the fine levied against him by Rozelle, Mason asked, "Wasn't that a willful and wanton violation of the rules of the NFL constitution?"

Noll: "It was. Go put my name on your list."

On the plus side for Pittsburgh was the testimony of Rozelle and the NFL's supervisor of officials, Art McNally. The latter declared that Atkinson's attempt to injure Swann was deliberate and malicious and beyond the borderline play of the Steelers.

MacInnis painted the Raiders as bullies; the Raiders responded by calling the NFL the bully for what Davis and Company saw as the league's attempt to smear Atkinson. MacInnis countered that Atkinson's prior legal problems proved he didn't need any help in tarnishing his reputation. The back-and-forth verbal salvos grew increasingly emotional and ugly as the two sides traded barbs and insults and the league aired its dirty laundry.

William Oscar Johnson described the trial in *Sports Illustrated* as "a spectacle so bizarre, so beyond the realm of common sense and ordinary imagination that it might have been the creation of some mad comic production—a cross between Mel Brooks and the Marquis de Sade."

Closing arguments were spirited and spiteful. The case went to jury at 9:30 a.m. on July 22, and following almost two weeks of trial it took just four hours for the jury to issue a verdict of not guilty. The jury asked Conti the meaning of "actual malice," and the judge responded that in order to be defamation, Noll's statements about Atkinson had to "lower Atkinson in the estimation of the community, or to deter third persons from associating or dealing with him." Because Atkinson had been signing autographs throughout the trial, it was hard to convince the jury he had been defamed.

MacInnis called the vindication of Noll and the Steelers "a very good thing for football. It will put a stop to the kind of thing for which he criticized George Atkinson. As for George Atkinson, for whom we have nothing but good wishes, the verdict may be an indication of how he should play, and it may in the end make him a better and more glorious player."

Brown saw it differently. "The jury has substantially sanctioned Chuck Noll's right to use that term against anyone he deems it appropriate to do so," he said. "They should be ashamed of themselves. I don't understand how any citizens could sit back and let someone say someone is a criminal element without doing something about it."

Dan Rooney summed up the feelings of the Steelers following the end of the sordid trial. "It has been the most depressing experience of my life," he said, "but I'm happy."

Perhaps no one was happier than MacInnis's grandson. He walked away from the infamous "Criminal Element Case" with a football bearing the signature of Swann on one side and Atkinson on the other.

Noll and the Steelers won, but the damage was done. Blount, angry that he had been labeled by his head coach as part of the "criminal element" in the NFL, sued Noll on July 15 for $5 million in compensatory damages and $1 million in punitive damages. The All-Pro cornerback and Steelers Defensive MVP in 1975 also declared he would never again play for Noll. "There's no chance at all," Blount said, "that I'll play for the Steelers under Noll."

The situation was ultimately resolved and Blount dropped his lawsuit, but the trial would leave scars on the Steelers. Greene saw Atkinson's lawsuit as the Raiders' attempt to break up Noll and the Steelers. "I'll be inclined to think that the Oakland Raiders are using it as a wedge to turn us against Chuck," he said. "I'd rather settle any Raiders-

Steelers differences on the football field, but then again, I'm pretty old-fashioned. I don't think football matters belong in a courtroom."

The play of Blount and Atkinson reflected an era that was much more physical than the modern NFL. Raiders defensive backs Atkinson, Tatum (a.k.a. "Assassin"), Skip "Dr. Death" Thomas, and Willie Brown employed legal bump-and-run tactics before the ball was thrown. The Raiders' secondary, which huddled in a corner area of the locker room it proudly described as the "Ghetto," roughed up receivers with bone-rattling hits. Thomas, who was known to grant just two media interviews during his six-year NFL career, boasted in retirement that he put tape on the floor to warn reporters to stay clear of the Ghetto.

And if a reporter dared venture past the warning tape? "I'd dunk you in a trash can and spit on you," Dr. Death said. "The press knew better than to come down there [to the Ghetto]."

Out on the field receivers knew there was a similar price to pay when they ventured into territory inhabited by a Raiders secondary known as the Soul Patrol. With defenders nicknamed "Assassin" and "Dr. Death," the Soul Patrol's primary job was to strike fear in the hearts of those who thought themselves fearless.

The Soul Patrol's advice to enemy receivers: If your coach tells you to be tough and go catch a ball over the middle, don't believe him. If your quarterback throws you a pass over the middle, let it go because you're going to get hammered.

Highlights backed up the Soul Patrol's tough talk: Tatum separating Minnesota wideout Sammy White's head from his helmet; Tatum decking Pittsburgh's Frenchy Fuqua and Baltimore's Glenn Doughty; Tatum colliding with Houston's Earl Campbell and delivering a hard hit to Chicago's Walter Payton; Atkinson forearming Swann, Patriots tight end Russ Francis, and Chiefs tight end Walter White; Brown busting Bronco back Floyd Little and twisting the helmeted head of Green Bay's Eric Torkelson; Thomas tossing a Cleveland receiver to the dirt and flipping a Chiefs runner heels over helmet. "We didn't break any rules," Brown said. "But we sure did bend some."

The cornerback tandem of Thomas and Brown is considered one of the top ten in NFL history. Stabler called them terrific matchup corners. Thomas's nickname was thought by many to be a by-product of his hard hits; he was king of the now-outlawed clothesline tackle. But his moniker came from Raiders offensive tackle Bob "Boomer" Brown, who thought Thomas looked like the cartoon character Dr. Death.

Thomas pirated sixteen passes in a four-season span, including back-to-back years of six interceptions each. He would have had more if he hadn't developed a habit of knocking the ball down rather than intercepting it. Villapiano said he and his Raiders mates were always telling Thomas to "catch the ball!"

When Madden and his coaches told Thomas the same, Dr. Death responded in not-so-cryptic terms. "Pay me!"

As good as Thomas was, some considered him overrated. Miami receiver Nat Moore said Thomas was "average at best" as a cover corner. It was believed that in big spots, opposing teams would avoid Brown and throw in Thomas's direction.

No one considered Brown, a Hall of Famer who played tight end on a Grambling State squad that sent nine players to the pros, overrated at right cornerback. The 6-foot-1, 195-pound Brown was completely passed over in the college draft. Signed as a free agent by the Houston Oilers, Brown was converted to cornerback before being cut and picked up by the Denver Broncos in 1963. Inserted at cornerback, Brown developed into an AFL All-Star and Pro Bowl defender by his second season. His battles with AFL Western Division rival and superstar wide receiver Lance Alworth of the San Diego Chargers became so legendary that on Alworth's advice, Davis dealt for Brown in 1967. "He's the best," Alworth told Davis, referring to Brown. "No one's close."

Unlike his Soul Patrol partners, Brown was quiet and not given to trash-talking opponents. Still, his play on the field spoke volumes. Brown is credited with creating bump-and-run coverage that disrupted receivers' pass patterns and changing the way the cornerback position was played. He took his concept to Oakland, and Raiders defenders took pride in playing close man-to-man defense, hitting receivers, and staying stride for stride with them all the way down the field. NFL historian Joe Horrigan said Brown stuck to receivers like glue and never gave an inch. Herb Adderley, a Hall of Fame receiver for Green Bay and later Dallas, thought Brown had all the attributes of a great cover corner—quickness, straightaway speed, and good hands. Adderley said Brown also had the temperament to play on the perimeter.

Dick LeBeau, a defensive back for Detroit in the 1960s and later a defensive coordinator for the Steelers, called Brown a character player who refused to not play well. Brown played well enough to last sixteen seasons in the NFL and developed a long-term consistency unmatched among defensive backs. Coach George Allen, a defensive specialist, thought Brown had some of the flamboyance of Dick "Night Train" Lane in that he loved to gamble when going for interceptions and was an enthusiastic competitor.

Brown was a complete player who had fast feet, fast hands, and an acrobatic ability to twist and turn in midair. A strong tackler, Brown didn't mind the bumps and bruises that went with being a physical player. He could keep up with any receiver, and even when he momentarily lost position he had a knack for getting back into the play. Brown played with desire and confidence. He didn't believe any receiver could beat him, and few did. Raiders statistics showed that during one season, only ten passes had been completed on Brown over fourteen games.

Like his Steelers opposite Mel Blount, who also played right cornerback, Brown was partly responsible for an NFL rules change: the outlawing of bump-and-run coverage. Brown didn't miss a beat. Since the new NFL rule stated that contact could be made only within five yards of the line of scrimmage, Brown believed that was all he needed or wanted—one shot at the line of scrimmage.

Receivers who got past the line of scrimmage and caught the ball against the Raiders' secondary paid a price. Atkinson specialized in a tackling technique he called the "Hook." Now outlawed by the NFL, the Hook was a tactic that saw him deliver an arm around the neck or helmet of the receiver like a Soviet-era sickle and then drive him to the ground. The Hook was similar to the blow delivered by Kansas City's Fred "Hammer" Williamson in the 1960s. The Hammer once described it to reporters as a karate chop–like blow delivered per-

pendicular to Earth's axis. To locker-room buddies he bragged that
it was a "lethal mutha."

Nicknamed "Butch," Atkinson ranked among the toughest Raid-
ers. Listed at 6 feet he was actually closer to 5 feet 10, but it was said no
one had the courage to tell him. Atkinson was the Soul Patrol's leading trash-talker, but his actions spoke louder than words. He broke
Russ Francis's nose with a forearm smash. Paul Warfield, Hall of Fame
wideout for the Browns and Dolphins in the 1960s and '70s, said any
receiver who consistently went over the middle against Atkinson
and Tatum would eventually be carried from the field on a stretcher.
Atkinson owned blazing speed—he still holds the Raiders' record for
return yards in a game at 275—and was also strong enough to fight
through blocks and get to the ball carrier.

Like his Soul Patrol brothers, Atkinson was an intimidator, and he
teamed with Tatum to form arguably the most feared safety tandem in
NFL history. The Assassin physically paralyzed Patriots receiver Darryl
Stingley for life from the chest down on a play that also affected Jack
mentally for the remainder of his life. NFL lore includes the "Catch"
and the "Drive." Tatum's hit on Stingley is remembered as the "Hit."
Tatum was criticized for the play, but Patriots coach Chuck Fairbanks
said, "There wasn't anything at the time that was illegal about the play."

Tatum was the NFL's most terrorizing force since Dick Butkus.
In his first NFL game he tackled Colt tight ends John Mackey and
Tom Mitchell so hard that both left the game. Tatum weighed 205
pounds, but his incredibly hard hits made him, in effect, a linebacker
playing safety.

Tatum was also tough on the running game, taking on guards and
tackles to get to the ball carrier. In a Soul Patrol secondary filled with
intimidating players, the Assassin was the ultimate intimidator. The
Oakland organization saw Tatum as the standard-bearer for being a
Raider and an inspiration for playing the safety position.

Tatum said Oakland's opening-game win over Pittsburgh was
important because it set the stage for the rest of the season. The '76
season is still the greatest in Raiders history, the Silver and Black leaving the rest of the NFL black and blue.

Oakland followed its victory over rival Pittsburgh by beating another rival, Kansas City, the following Monday night. Stabler completed twenty-two passes in a 24–21 win, van Eeghen and Banaszak surged to sizable gains, and Raiders special teams shone brightly before another national viewing audience. The Raiders edged Houston 14–13 and then suffered a 48–17 loss at New England. It was the lone loss in Oakland's magnificent season.

The Raiders bounced back in Week Five with a 27–17 win in San Diego, setting the stage for a ten-game win streak that gave Oakland its fifth straight Western Division title. Key to Oakland's success was the defense's ability to overcome injuries. With defensive line starters Tony Cline, Horace Jones, and Art Thoms sidelined by injuries, Madden switched from a four-man front to a 3-4 scheme that featured All-Pro outside linebacker Ted Hendricks, the "Mad Stork." The result was that the Raiders surrendered fewer points than they had the previous season. Joining with Hendricks was free agent John Matuszak, who was signed after the opener and earned a starting slot at defensive end.

Stabler produced one of the great seasons of all time, posting a 103.7 passer rating that was sixth best in NFL history. Branch led the league in touchdown catches with twelve, and van Eeghen veered for 1,012 yards to become just the third running back in Raiders history to rush for more than 1,000 yards in a season.

There were highlights galore amid a 13-1 campaign that tied the 1967 squad of Daryle Lamonica–Jim Otto–Ben Davidson for the most victories in a season: Stabler finding Mike Siani for the winning score to silence Arrowhead Stadium; Neal Colzie's momentum-changing punt returns in sun-drenched San Diego; Villapiano's interception against Green Bay, sparking a point explosion that saw the Snake strike for three scores in just nine minutes; a fearsome pass rush that resulted in ten sacks of Denver QBs; Stabler and Branch burning the Bears defense in bitter cold in Chicago's Soldier Field; and Madden earning career win No. 80 as Otis Sistrunk and the defense roughed up Roman Gabriel and the Eagles.

The penultimate game of the regular season saw the Raiders hosting the Cincinnati Bengals in a nationally televised Monday-night game. The game had special meaning for the Steelers as well. Pittsburgh was 9-4 following a snow-bowl win in Cincinnati the week before, the Bengals were 9–3 and leading the AFC Central. A victory by Cincinnati would put them a game up on the Steelers with just one game remaining. The Raiders had clinched the West, and it was presumed by some that Madden might approach the matchup at less than full throttle. It was believed by observers that a Cincinnati win would actually aid the Raiders' cause, since it would all but eliminate the team proven to be Oakland's obstacle in three of the last four playoff years.

Since the Bengals would finish their regular season against the struggling New York Jets, Cincinnati's game against the Raiders was the one that would decide the division title. "We're going to try to will the Raiders to victory," Steelers linebacker Andy Russell told reporters. "We'll be the biggest bunch of cheerleaders the Oakland Raiders ever had."

Greene was less optimistic. "I'm going to watch the ball game but I'm ready to go south," he said, referring to his home in Texas. "I think Oakland is going to play to win but they have nothing to lose or gain and I just can't see them beating Cincinnati under those conditions."

Swann was rooting for, and against, both teams. "I hope they beat each other to a pulp," he said, "and Cincinnati loses."

Madden approached the game in the same manner as one of his mentors, the late Vince Lombardi, did when Green Bay headed to Los Angeles late in the 1967 season, having already clinched its Central Division title. The Packers had little to play for but pride and were facing a Rams squad that needed to win to keep pace with Baltimore in the Coastal Division race. NFL Films cameras captured Lombardi telling his team prior to the opening kickoff they could do "a great deal" for the prestige of their sport by going all out to win.

Madden likely implored his Raiders to do the same prior to facing the Bengals. The Raiders responded, overcoming a brief 6–0 deficit courtesy of a Ken Anderson 40-yard TD, with four Stabler scoring passes in a 35–20 final. The Snake found Casper twice for touchdowns and also connected with Branch and Biletnikoff. Banaszak bolted into the end zone from a yard out, and Oakland had helped the hated Steelers secure a postseason berth.

Pittsburgh's path to the playoffs was nowhere near as smooth as that of the Raiders. The Steelers sought to become the first team in the Super Bowl era to win three straight Super Bowls. Lombardi's Packers had won three straight championships during their decade of dominance, but the first title in their three-peat came in 1965 and preceded Super Bowl I by a year.

Don Shula's Dolphins were denied a possible third consecutive Super Bowl title by the Raiders in 1974. Now it was Noll's Steelers who had the chance to make history.

The Steelers struggled early, losing four of their first five games—including a prime-time Monday-night matchup in Minnesota—and lost Bradshaw to injury in Week Five in Cleveland after the QB was flipped heels over helmet by Browns defensive end Joe "Turkey" Jones.

With its offense crippled, the Steel Curtain stepped to the fore in Week Six. From 1972 to 1979 Pittsburgh would rank in the top ten in total defense every season and in the top three six times. It also ranked first or second in scoring defense in five of those eight seasons. But the '76 season stands as the Steel Curtain's zenith.

After surrendering an average of twenty-two points per game in the first five games, including thirty-one to Oakland and thirty to New England, proud Pittsburgh began punishing opponents in historic fashion. The turnaround began in Week Six with a 23–6 win at home versus Cincinnati. The game was notable for a sideline brawl between Lambert and Bengals middle linebacker Jim LeClair, who had belted backup QB Mike Kruczek out of bounds. The late hit incensed Lambert, who ran the length of the sideline to hammer LeClair.

The Steelers followed with a 27–0 jolting of the Giants in East Rutherford, New Jersey, the first of three straight shutout wins. The following Sunday was Halloween, and Pittsburgh allowed San Diego no tricks or treats in a 23–0 final. The Steelers finally got above .500 the next week in Kansas City with a 45–0 crushing of the Chiefs.

The Steel Curtain's streak of consecutive scoreless quarters reached fifteen in a 14–3 mauling of Miami. Pittsburgh would not permit a touchdown in twenty-two straight quarters or in eight of its last nine games, an astounding display of dominating defense. Houston managed to score sixteen in Week Eleven, but Pittsburgh doubled that output to post its sixth straight win.

The signature game of the Steelers' season came in Week Twelve in Cincinnati. Pittsburgh was riding a six-game win streak that had started with a victory over Cincinnati on October 17. Still, the Steelers trailed 3–0 at halftime in a game played beneath overcast but dry skies. Not surprising, since the '76 Bengals may be the best Cincinnati team to not make the playoffs. The Bengals won nine of their first eleven games, and six of their players made the Pro Bowl.

When the Steelers and Bengals took to Riverfront Stadium's synthetic field for the third quarter, the skies were dark, the temperature was twenty-six degrees, and a blinding blizzard had dumped three inches of snow on the AstroTurf.

While this was a game the Bengals wanted to win, it was a game the Steelers had to win. One more loss and Pittsburgh's dreams of a trip to sunny Pasadena and a Super Bowl three-peat would be over.

Injuries were a big reason for Pittsburgh's precarious position—Bradshaw, Swann, and Holmes had all missed playing time—but one Steelers club official blamed it on the players' overconfidence, a belief that they could win anytime they felt like it.

Art Rooney Sr. offered no excuses for the Steelers' dire straits. "If we're left out of it after today," he said, chewing on his cigar prior to kickoff, "we've got nobody to blame. No bad calls or bad breaks. We did it to ourselves."

The Steelers' self-inflicted wounds continued throughout much of the snowy early-evening hours. A crowd of 55,142, many dressed in the Bengals' bright orange, roared as a blizzard, broken plays, penalties, sacks, turnovers, and a blocked field goal combined with the Cincinnati defense to stall the Steelers every time they seemed poised to score.

It wasn't until late in the third quarter that the Steelers got the break they needed. Following a Pittsburgh punt, Clark sledded for seven yards but fumbled, and the loose ball was recovered—fittingly enough on this snow-swept day—by a player named White, Dwight White.

Taking over at the Cincinnati 25, Kruczek found Swann through the swirling snow for 14 yards. Bleier ran behind Davis and skated across the Astro rink for seven more yards—Rocky rushed for a game-best 97 yards—and Franco finished the mini-drive by veering right and plowing through the blizzard for the final four yards.

Pittsburgh led 7–3 and looked to score more, but Cincinnati stopped Kruczek's sneak on fourth and 1 near the goal line. With the clock winding down and the snow picking up, Anderson completed clutch passes to Curtis and Bruce Coslet. His bomb to Curtis disappeared in the blizzard before reappearing in Curtis's hands. With ninety seconds left Anderson drove the Bengals to the Steelers' 24.

In their two previous games the Bengals had claimed stunning last-second wins over Houston and Kansas City. Could Cincinnati complete the trifecta? By now the snow was so heavy that Steelers safety Mike Wagner couldn't even see Anderson in the pocket. Neither could Wagner see the ball in the air until it was halfway to the receiver. Anderson dropped back and, with his cleats slipping on the slick white turf, threw deep to Chip Myers in the end zone. Cornerback J. T. Thomas got his right hand up and knocked the ball away, and for the sixth time in seven games the Steelers' stingy defense had not surrendered a touchdown.

With the season saved, one Pittsburgh player looked ahead to Cincinnati's Monday-night matchup with Oakland. "Now we need the good Lord and the Oakland Raiders. What a combination that is!"

The final two weeks of the season saw the Steel Curtain cap its campaign by recording a shutout of Tampa Bay (42–0) to move into a tie for first and then Houston (21–0) to clinch the Central crown. Registering five shutouts in its final nine games and yielding just 28 total points, an average of 3.1 per game, Pittsburgh put together one of the greatest stretches of sustained excellence in NFL history.

Five years earlier WTAE had sponsored a contest to find a suitable moniker for the Steelers' defense. Drawing on Winston Churchill's "Iron Curtain" nickname for Joseph Stalin's Soviet Union and combining it with Pittsburgh's steel industry, Gregory Kronz's "Steel Curtain" was selected as the winner.

Never was it more apt than in a '76 season that stands with the 1966 Green Bay Packers, 1969 Kansas City Chiefs, 1972 Dolphins, 1985 Chicago Bears, 1991 Philadelphia Eagles, 2000 Baltimore Ravens, 2013 Seattle Seahawks, and 2015 Denver Broncos as among the best of the Super Bowl era.

Pittsburgh's nine straight victories during its run to a fourth division title in five years weren't just about defense. Kruczek went 6-0 as the starting QB, and Harris (1,128) and Bleier (1,036) joined Larry Csonka and Mercury Morris from the 1972 Dolphins as the only backfield tandem to that point in NFL history to surpass 1,000 yards rushing in the same season.

Against the Bengals in Three Rivers Stadium, Kruczek handed off to Harris forty-one times, an NFL record at the time. With that a blueprint for victory was established. Harris led the league in rushing TDs with fourteen and Pittsburgh's ground attack paced the NFL.

Harris's success was not unexpected, but Bleier was a different story. He personified this unattributed quote: "As long as you keep moving forward, you'll reach the finish line." The Appleton, Wisconsin, native was a key contributor to Parseghian's national champion Notre Dame team in 1966 and played in the famous 10–10 tie at Michigan State. Selected by the Steelers in the sixteenth round of the 1968 draft, Bleier had three games remaining in his rookie preseason when he was drafted again, this time by the United States Army. "I was still looking ahead to playing for the Steelers when I got back home," Bleier said. "I thought about that as much as I ever thought about anything when I first arrived in Vietnam."

Bleier never questioned why the United States was involved in Southeast Asia or why he was sent to Vietnam. He never thought about being killed or being shot or shooting someone. By May 1969 Bleier was in Chu Lai, South Vietnam, as a member of the 196th American Division's Light Infantry Brigade. In August he was on patrol in Heip Duc, heading for a clearing to be picked up by a helicopter when heavy machine-gun fire killed the soldier next to Bleier and caused everyone else to take cover in a rice paddy. Seeing where the enemy fire was coming from, Bleier began crawling toward the machine-gun nest to take it out with a rifle grenade. Just before Bleier fired he took enemy fire in return, a bullet tearing into his left thigh and ripping out a chunk of flesh. "I was about to fire," he said, "when someone yelled, 'Rocky!' and I felt a twinge in my leg as if someone threw a rock and hit me."

Bleier looked down and saw his own blood. As his squad sought to make its way toward the clearing, Bleier saw a grenade land a few feet from him. He was lying on his side and saw the grenade bounce in his direction. Bleier had a hurried thought: Jump with the roll of the grenade or go the opposite way? He wanted to get rid of it, and he strained to grab the grenade. "Before I could grab it," he said, "the thing exploded."

It exploded into Bleier's foot. He blacked out, and for the next four hours his squad was pinned down by enemy fire. It was early evening before Bleier and his squad were rescued by helicopters, but it wasn't until midnight that Rocky received the proper medical care. Some twelve hours elapsed since he had been shot in the left thigh and had part of his right foot blown off. Infections set in, and doctors considered amputating part of his right leg.

Awarded a Purple Heart, Bronze Star, and two campaign ribbons, Bleier returned to Pittsburgh and worked tirelessly to reward Art Rooney for the faith the Steelers' owner showed in him when others wanted to give up on the wounded warrior. The Fighting Irish product showed a fighting spirit, building his body in the weight room and regaining his running ability with miles of road work.

When he returned to Pittsburgh in 1970 Bleier was a shadow of the player he had been; he couldn't run without experiencing pain, had no feel for running, and couldn't cut or change direction. His foot swelled, and the pain was excruciating. Bleier underwent additional surgery to repair the damage to his leg, and his indomitable belief in himself paid off. He spent the 1970 season on injured reserve and made the squad in 1971 at the urging of Dan Rooney. "Why not put Bleier on the injured reserve list?" he asked Noll, who was prepared to cut Bleier from the team. "He needs surgery on that damaged foot. Let him get the foot repaired, have a chance to restore his strength, and then see what happens."

Bleier had a second operation, spent three weeks in the hospital, and went back to work. "The club gave me the opportunity to correct my foot problems," he sad, "but I also had to prove that I could be part of the team." Bleier made up his mind that he didn't want to feel like he was being kept around because someone felt sorry for him.

Bleier earned a role as a wedge buster on special teams. He suffered a setback in '72 when he endured a hamstring injury that nearly ended his career. He continued his conditioning and made the special teams in '73. He did so well that Mutual Radio sportscaster Al Wester commented during a game against the Raiders that Bleier must be leading the league in special-teams tackles. Bleier broke through in 1974, cracking the starting lineup as a blocking black. In '75 he posted a career-rushing day against Green Bay. The '76 season was Bleier's best, as he accounted for 1,330 yards rushing and receiving.

Just as few believed Bleier would ever become a 1,000-yard back, just as few expected fellow Wisconsin native Mike Webster to have the Hall of Fame career he would after taking over as Steelers center in 1976. Selected by the Steelers in the fifth round of the 1974 draft, Webster spent two seasons backing up starter Ray Mansfield in the middle of the Steelers' offensive line. Greene recalled Webster's early years in Pittsburgh when still-maturing Mike had the daunting task of dealing with Ernie Holmes in training camps and intersquad scrimmages. "Ernie, quite frankly, was killing him," Greene said.

It all changed one day when Holmes tried to move Webster and couldn't. Arrowhead Ernie tried again on the next play, and the result was the same. When Greene asked Holmes what was wrong, Fats shrugged. "He's gotten a little stronger," Holmes said.

Greene didn't believe the undersize center had gotten *that* much stronger. "Let me have him," Greene said.

Mean Joe tried to move the man who would become known as Iron Mike. "Nothing happened," Greene said.

Webster would go on to play more games than anyone in Steelers history and more consecutive games than anyone who played for Pittsburgh. Jim Ringo, a Hall of Fame center for Lombardi's Packers in the 1960s, thought Webster a smart, tough player who had a lot of durability. Iron Mike played in 177 consecutive games and in one stretch didn't miss a play for six seasons. Fred Hoaglin, who played center for the Cleveland Browns' playoff teams of the 1960s and '70s, called Webster "one of the great ones."

Tatum said that if he had a football team, he would have Webster as his center. Mike had the size, intelligence, and raw strength to ward off any lineman in the league. Webster excelled at recognizing defenses and making the appropriate line call and was known to turn around on occasion and suggest an audible to Bradshaw.

Like Bleier, Webster was a self-made man who built himself up through a rigorous weight-training regimen that left his arms thick as hams. It was Webster who created the modern look of NFL linemen— bulky arms bared to the elements via cutoff sleeves on their jerseys. When the Steelers' offense broke its huddle, it was Webster who was the center of attention, in more ways than one.

Greene knew that one of the things Mike loved to do was to emerge onto the field on cold days with short sleeves. In Webster's mind his bare arms intimidated opponents who didn't want to deal with cold weather. Dermontti Dawson, who succeeded Webster as a Hall of Fame center with the Steelers, said the sight of Mike Webster on a cold, snowy winter day taking the playing field in short sleeves symbolized the strength and toughness of the '70s Steelers.

Despite the huge arms of Webster and left tackle Jon Kolb, the line that included left guard Sam Davis, right guard Jim Clack, and right tackle Gerry Mullins was physically smaller than other offensive lines of its era. The reason was that while Pittsburgh prided itself on its strength, it preferred quicker, sleeker linemen who could fire out quickly and cut-block while executing the Steelers' intricate trapping schemes. "The trapping scheme that they ran was very innovative," recalled Bill Belichick, who coached against the Steelers as a young assistant with the Baltimore Colts. "Coach [Tom] Landry had some of that in Dallas but certainly not to the extent that Pittsburgh had it."

The success of the Steelers' celebrated ground game, NFL writer Paul Zimmerman opined, helped the '76 Steelers become the greatest in team history. Lambert was named the NFL's Defensive MVP, and ten of the eleven starters on the Steel Curtain were named to the Pro Bowl. The lone starter not named was Holmes, whom Dr. Z declared to be the most feared member of the famed defense.

With Bradshaw back in the starting lineup, with the ground game among the greatest ever, and the Steel Curtain at its peak and ranked first in the league (237.4 yards per game allowed), Pittsburgh was making its push for a historic season.

So too was an Oakland outfit that was seeking the NFL's first sixteen-win season.

With another confrontation looming, the NFL held its breath in anticipation of a fifth-straight Steelers-Raiders rendezvous.

Jim Campbell: Like all inhabitants of Steeler Nation, I was excited about the start of the coming season. It was America's bicentennial year, and the Steelers were looking to become the first NFL team to win three Super Bowls consecutively.

The Steelers were maturing into a truly great team. The Steel Curtain was steeling itself with even greater ferocity. Bradshaw seemed to be progressing as a passer and leader. Swann and Stallworth were continuing to keep defensive coordinators up at night. The light and interchangeable offensive line, effective as ever, was trapping unsuspecting opponents with a certain cold-bloodedness, allowing Franco to continue to be a free-range running back.

I made a few trips to the St. Vincent training camp and was impressed with what I saw. Joe Greene—if anyone was entitled to rest on his laurels, it was the Mean One—was as involved and enthusiastic as any Steelers player. Noll was as low-key as ever, but also coaching and teaching as always. It seemed to me that the Steelers were riding the crest of a "title" wave and like the gutsy surfers of those giant waves of the famed Bonzai Pipeline, the team was going to ride it for all it was worth.

As it had since 1934, football season got under way with the College All-Star Game in Chicago. In the beginning the game was more advantageous for the pros, as the NFL was struggling to get a foothold versus the college game. And the game gave the pros an avenue to accomplish this. As the 1970s dawned, the channel was changed.

The NFL was riding high. Teams were reluctant to send their high-drafted rookies away for the three weeks of All-Star camp, and players' agents weren't thrilled with the possibility of their "meal tickets" getting injured. Fan enthusiasm was also down. Attendance at the '76 game was announced as 54,895, which included 5,000 navy recruits from nearby Great Lakes Naval Training Station used to form a human American flag. Still a good number of fans, but not much compared to 1947, when a game attracted 105,840 paying customers to venerable Soldier Field on Chicago's lakefront.

A hard rain fell before kickoff but had passed before the game got under way. The Steelers were safely ahead when the rains came back with a vengeance at the 1:22 mark of the third quarter. Little did I know when Commissioner Pete Rozelle mercifully called off the game that it would be the end of a series that had raised millions of dollars for charity.

The regular season was upon us. As the NFL schedule makers so often did in those days, the opening weekend saw a rematch of play-off rivals—especially if the previously played game was close and hard fought. At the start of 1976 a Steelers-Raiders rematch qualified. It began as a low-scoring, but extremely hard-hitting, game. The hitting was ferocious. It was what you'd expect from two teams who just plain didn't like each other and played to the echo of the whistle—and sometimes a little beyond.

There was a little "déjà vu" in this game, courtesy of George Atkinson. With the action on the other side of the field, Atkinson clobbered Swann from behind with a karate chop to the neck, just as he did in the previous year's playoff game. Swann was down for the count and spent time in a Bay Area hospital. It was after this game that Noll issued his infamous "criminal element" statement that is discussed more fully above, along with the subsequent libel suit.

I gave the Raiders considerable admiration late in the season when they went all out against the Bengals in a Monday-night game that could have made the Steelers' playoff run more difficult—if not impossible— had the Raiders mailed it in.

To me, the loss to the Browns was particularly devastating. Joe

"Turkey" Jones, a lanky defensive end who specialized in rushing the passer, picked up Bradshaw and executed a classic pro wrestling "piledriver" move, planting Brad headfirst into the Municipal Stadium turf. Since Cleveland was less than an hour away from Canton, I made the game in person and was outraged by Jones's move.

Years later I saw Turkey as a baggage handler at BWI Airport in the Washington DC area. It was all I could do to keep myself from giving Jones an impromptu lecture on "the care and feeding and ethical treatment of NFL quarterbacks."

As the season drew to a close, I felt as though a space for a third Vince Lombardi Trophy should probably be made in the Steelers' Three Rivers Stadium offices. The defense, later dubbed the "best ever" by no less an authority than Jack Lambert, seemed able to cope successfully with anything anyone could throw—or run—at them. It was a unit that had at one time or another ten of the eleven starters as Pro Bowl selections. Simply stated: no one did it better.

Despite the late-season cold, it was a pleasure to drive in to Three Rivers and watch the Steelers dominate in the manner in which they did. Bud Carson, George Perles, and Woody Widenhofer were masterful in prepping their defenders.

One of the most unsung members of the Steelers dynasty is equipment manager Tony Parisi. The Niagara Falls, Ontario, native would seem an unlikely hero of the dynastic Steelers of the 1970s, but he indeed was, and on several occasions. Tony, after a typical Canadian youth's journey in amateur hockey, finally ended up in Pittsburgh as the goalkeeper of the Pittsburgh Hornets of the minor league American Hockey League. The league folded in 1965, and Tony needed a job. As he had so often in the past, Art Rooney took in a looking-for-work person. In the early days of the franchise, it was speculated that this was the way the Steelers acquired several nondescript coaches. It was even said that the only way the Chief could recoup loans made to one coach to cover the coach's penchant for betting on slow horses was to keep him on as head coach.

Joe Gordon was another Hornet benefiting from the Rooney largesse when he was hired as Steelers publicity director after the Hornet's demise. Tony took his new assignment seriously—as did Joe Gordon. Tony brought an innovative style to his job, one that included members of his family, as it turned out. As one responsible for all aspects of equipping the Steelers, Tony paid close attention to the forecast before each game.

Knowing that the weather for the 1972 Steelers-Raiders playoff game would be cold and inhospitable, Tony had his wife sew fleece-lined pockets to the fronts of Steelers jerseys to keep the players' hands warm. As a sideline worker that day, I could only wish Mrs. Parisi had done something similar for me. Until Franco's "miracle," I was as cold and uncomfortable as I was at any late-season Steelers game.

About the time the Steelers were beginning their Super Bowl run, Parisi was responsible for another trend-setting innovation—jerseys with no excess fabric for opposing linemen to latch onto. The Steelers' offensive line, especially, had jerseys that looked as though they were painted on—not a wrinkle, not a gap. Skin tight, particularly the arms. By this time, most football jerseys were of the short-sleeved variety. The weight-room warriors—Kolb, Clack, Webster—looked especially "ripped." Their bulging biceps were the original NFL "gun show." That's what other teams noticed.

I remember a postgame conversation after a Steelers victory over the Chiefs in 1975 between opposing centers Jim Clack and Jack Rudnay. Rudnay was struck by the Steelers' look, saying, "Hey, you guys look awesome with those tight sleeves. What pipes!" (the term for upper arms at that time). Clack just said, "Thanks," and smiled knowingly. While Rudnay and others thought there was some ostentatiousness to the tailored look, Clack and the Steelers knew it was more than fashion. The form-fitting jerseys (now for better or for worse an NFL-wide trend) gave defenders very little to grab hold of in the trenches and elsewhere. It didn't hurt that adding a little Vaseline to the jerseys in the shoulder-pad area—perhaps a page taken from the Raiders' playbook—provided even less of a grip.

All of this was possible because the ever-dedicated Parisi had his mother-in-law actually tailor the appropriate jerseys. That and add-

ing some double-sided tape kept the jersey and shoulder pads perfectly flat and gap free.

Before Super Bowl IX Tony called on his Canadian heritage to give
the Steelers a decided advantage over the Minnesota Vikings at cold
and damp Tulane Stadium. While it was to be the first Super Bowl
played in the Superdome, union trouble and construction delays, as
well as cost overruns, necessitated the old Sugar Bowl as the Super
Bowl venue.

Knowing what the weather was going to be like and what the resulting field conditions would be, he imported many pairs of shoes with
longer cleats from north of the border for the Steelers to cope with
the soggy Tulane Stadium turf. To say the Steelers "stood a little taller
than the Vikings" that day is not an exaggeration. When the footing
got a little dicey, the Steelers did quite nicely.

After Dan "Bad Rad" Radakovich rejoined the Steelers as offensive-
line coach, one of his unorthodox techniques was to have the offensive
linemen make their first move a stiff "punch" right under the shoulder pads of an opposing defender. It was a great technique, but one
that wasn't too kindly to the hands of the Steelers' offensive linemen.
While "Radical Rad" might not have been that concerned, I can tell you
that Kolb, Mullins, Mansfield, Webster, Sam Davis, Clack, and Gordon Gravelle were. At first they tried taping their hands like a boxer,
something that future surgeon and future Hall of Famer Danny Fortmann of the Chicago Bears did in the 1940s, for protection.

It might have helped Fortmann save his hands for his postplaying
practice of medicine, but in the "bigger, faster, stronger" NFL of the
seventies, it wasn't enough. Something more was needed. Enter Parisi,
equipment man extraordinaire, once again. Tony began supplying the
O-linemen with Everlast (a name that had been known in boxing cir-
cles since the turn of the twentieth century) gloves that boxers used
while working out on the heavy bag. The trend caught on league-wide
eventually, and before long a whole new industry sprang forth for specialized gloves, not only the padded linemen's gloves, but also lighter
gloves for receivers, which became "tackified," and even lighter gloves

for quarterbacks. Somewhere, someone should have been cutting a royalty check, payable to Anthony A. Parisi.

When I first began to work the sidelines on game days in 1970, it didn't take me long to realize that NFL officials were really "class" people. By 1976 my opinion had not changed. If anything, it was reinforced and amplified. Not every fan was aware that before a person could be considered as an NFL official there was another requirement to qualify beside just working enough games and working them well. A potential game official needed to have outside employment—a "day job," if you will—that was substantial enough that his earnings met a certain level. Back in the early 1970s, it was $50,000 annually. This was done to ensure that the officials remained above reproach.

It is only my opinion, but one shared by others, that "full-time refs" are not the answer to whatever officiating woes the NFL has today—and there are some woes. What would full-timers do all week? Would the lawyers and physicians and business owners be willing to give up their other lucrative careers? Think about it.

After getting the first call from Joe Gordon, I learned that my assignment would include working with game officials. I was to get the specific penalty calls, what the infraction was, and who was the player committing it. Then before the next play started have the info, via walkie-talkie, relayed to the press box in order for public address announcer Ray Downey to inform those in attendance what just took place. Time was somewhat of the essence.

My first season, 1970, was the first season of a fully integrated AFL-NFL schedule—all, of course, under the "shield" of the NFL. The old AFL teams, plus the Steelers, Browns, and Colts, formed the new American Football Conference. The NFC was composed of the remaining original NFL teams. Officiating crews were also integrated—a mix of old AFL officials and old NFL officials. The men of the AFL traded their red-orange striped shirts for the more traditional black and white stripes of the NFL.

What became evident to me early on was that it would take a while for the crews to get acclimated. There were subtle differences in the rules of the leagues and the way penalties were seen and called. Perhaps this is why a "mixed" crew was somewhat reluctant and hesitant in calling a game. To me, it seemed as though there were occasions when one official was hesitant to throw a flag for fear of looking incompetent in the eyes of the other officials.

It is possibly only my imagination, but the former AFL officials seemed to defer to the NFL officials, waiting for the officials of the older established league to flag the play. The NFL established "refs" (a term many use to indicate any official, regardless of which of the seven individual positions of which the official may be a member) were legendary—Tommy Bell, Red "First Dow-w-w-w-w-n" Cashion, Pat Haggarty, Norm Schacter, Bernie Ullman, and Jim Tunney. So, it was only natural that the new kids on the block would let them make the call. All well and good, but I thought there were a significant number of calls that just didn't get made. However, it didn't take but a few weeks before the old AFL officials began to assert themselves.

AFL referees who assimilated quickly and seamlessly in becoming authority figures in their own right included Ben Dreith, Jack Reader, and John McDonough. Of the thirty-four officials working in the old AFL in 1969, thirty-two were folded into the NFL in 1970. Notably, officials working at positions other than referee included Leo Miles, Al Sabato, Tony Veteri (whose son Tony Jr. is currently an NFL official), and Bob Wortman, who is the only person to work a Super Bowl and an NCAA Championship Game.

Jerry Markbreit, for years the only "zebra" to have worked four Super Bowls, was a highly regarded Big Ten referee for a decade. Because the NFL never had a first-year man join the league as a referee, Markbreit's first year was as a line judge, a position he worked long ago, if ever. A responsibility of a line judge was to "wind the clock" at the "ready for play," thus allowing the official scoreboard clock operator, in the case of the Steelers a fine gentleman named Lou Rossi, to start the clock.

More than once during Markbreit's first season, I'd hear Lou remind, "Jerry, gimme the signal." Markbreit, long removed from any position other than referee, would respond with an "Oops" and then properly signal Rossi. The clock would then start. The next season Markbreit was advanced to referee and became one of the most respected in the NFL.

My sideline duties would seemed to have eased a bit in 1973 when NFL refs were first miked, that is, if said microphone worked. They didn't always, so I was still needed as a backup. Commissioner Rozelle's theory was to make it more fan friendly. He reasoned that if the fans at home got specific penalty information, then those at the stadium were entitled to the same information. After a season of experimentation, the referees' microphones worked much better, and my Sundays became a little less stressful.

Once, when I was still calling penalties up to the PA announcer, Cincinnati middle linebacker Bill Bergey came up to me and said, "I heard you passing along the name of our lineman [I think it was guard Pat Matson] who was called for holding. That's pretty negative and you shouldn't do it."

I looked up at the burly Bengal and replied, "Perhaps, but you better take that up with Commissioner Rozelle. He's the one who implemented the procedure." I'm not sure Bergey was satisfied with my answer, but it did end our sideline discussion.

An example of the classiness of NFL officials is the time I didn't agree with a call that went against the Steelers. I expressed my displeasure with the call in no uncertain terms. Head linesman Ed Marion, instead of running me off the sideline, said very philosophically, "You know, it's pretty tough keeping things moving smoothly out on the field. When we catch heat from the sidelines, it makes it even harder." I was sufficiently chastened by the lecture, and as best as I can recall I kept my opinions to myself.

10

California Dreamin'

When it came to the AFC's wild West, the autumn wind was indeed a Raider, pillaging just for fun, knocking the Chiefs, Chargers, and Broncos around and upside down and laughing when Oakland won. And the Raiders won often. In 1976 Oakland became the first team to win thirteen regular-season games in two separate seasons, having done it in '67 as well.

The playoffs, however, had been anything but a laughing matter for John Madden and Company. Far too often to suit Raiders fans, the Silver and Black had been left black and blue by the Jets, Chiefs, Colts, Dolphins, and Steelers when it mattered most. It all added up to a hugely disappointing 1-6 record in AFL/AFC Championship Games dating to 1967 and an overall mark of 7-8 in postseason games in that span.

The Raiders had replaced the Dallas Cowboys as the team that couldn't win the big one, next year's champions. Following disheartening defeats to Green Bay, Cleveland, and Baltimore in the postseason, Tom Landry's 'Boys scaled the summit in 1971. Madden's Raiders were looking to do the same in '76 as they sought the organization's third straight AFC title game appearance and eighth since handling Houston in the 1967 AFL Championship.

The playoffs got under way on Saturday, December 18, with Minnesota hosting Washington in a 1:00 p.m. kickoff on CBS. The Redskins and Vikings, two teams who had combined to represent the NFC in three straight Super Bowls from 1972 to 1974, met amid frozen sunshine and a twenty-five-degree windchill temperature in Metropolitan Stadium.

Champions of the NFC's black-and-blue Central Division for the fourth straight year and eighth time in nine seasons, the Vikings wasted little time taking it to wild-card Washington. With Vin Scully and Paul Hornung calling the action on CBS-TV, Fran Tarkenton's passing and Chuck Foreman's running led to leads of 14–3 in the first quarter and 21–3 at halftime. The Vikings' vaunted defense limited Larry Brown, Billy Kilmer, and the Redskins to just two Mark Moseley field goals through the first three quarters, and Tarkenton and Foreman produced two more touchdowns in the third in an eventual 35–20 final.

The nation's football fans then switched their television dials to NBC, which had its broadcast tandem of Curt Gowdy and John Brodie in the sun-filled, comparatively warm Oakland Coliseum for the Raiders' hosting of Eastern Division runner-up New England. Raiders fans held signs imploring the Western Division champions to "Remember 48–17," the final score in Oakland's only loss in '76, a Week Four decision in New England that wrecked the Raiders' chances of matching Miami's perfect season in '72.

Fronted by former University of Oklahoma coach Chuck Fairbanks, the Patriots followed in the footsteps of the 1974 Baltimore Colts by becoming the latest Cinderella squad from the AFC East. Embodying the spirit of '76, the Patriots became destiny's darlings in the bicentennial year by fashioning an 11-3 record following a 3-11 finish the season before.

The biggest trade in Patriots history to that point saw New England send quarterback Jim Plunkett to San Francisco for QB Tom Owen and four draft choices. In his second year Steve Grogan settled in as New England's number-one signal caller and with production from young players stunned the Steelers and romped past the Raiders in consecutive games. By season's end New England owned victories over each of the other three AFC playoff teams; the bicentennial was indeed a good year to be a Patriot.

Fairbanks, who helped popularize the college-style 3-4 defense in the NFL and earned Coach of the Year honors in '76, was a major reason for the meteoric rise of the former Pat-sies. So too, was Grogan, a Kansas State product who proved himself in his first full season as an NFL starter, and cornerback Mike Haynes, the Defensive Rookie of the Year who finished second in interceptions and punt-return average. Johnson, Sam "Bam" Cunningham, and Don Calhoun helped power a Patriots attack that led the league in yards per rush and ranked second in scoring. Hamilton and nose guard Ray "Sugar Bear" Hamilton were key contributors to a defense that ranked first with fifty takeaways.

New England battled Baltimore for supremacy in the AFC East all season. Winning their final six games, the Patriots clinched the wild-card berth and punched their ticket to Oakland. It was the franchise's first postseason appearance since the 1963 AFL Championship and just its third overall, the Patriots having beaten Buffalo on a snow-covered War Memorial Field in the '63 Eastern Division playoff game. That victory set up the Patriots' previous trip out west for a postseason contest, but it proved disastrous, a 51–10 victory by a San Diego Chargers squad that ranks among the AFL's best and was the first AFL champion to invite comparison to the NFL.

The Patriots' return visit to the West Coast for postseason play proved much more competitive, and controversial, as penalties played an important part in the game.

Raiders return man Neal Colzie opened the door for an early scoring opportunity for Oakland when he took a punt into Patriots territory with a 24-yard return to the New England 46. A Ray Guy punt pinned the Patriots at their own 14, but Grogan guided New England 86 yards thanks in part to a pair of clutch third-down conversions. The first was a highlight-reel one-handed catch by tight end Russ Francis on third and 7, the second a 24-yard catch by wideout Darryl Stingley. Johnson capped the marathon march with a 1-yard touchdown run.

The Raiders retaliated on their next series. Ken Stabler connected with Fred Biletnikoff for 22 yards and Cliff Branch for 17. With 1:14 left in the opening quarter, Errol Mann's 40-yard field goal cut Oakland's deficit to 7–3, and the Raiders took their first lead late in the half.

With 2:30 remaining in the second quarter Skip Thomas picked off a pass from Francis on a trick play deep in the Raiders' red zone and returned it 18 yards to the Oakland 24. Stabler rode herd on a drive that covered 76 yards, the last 31 coming via a one-handed circus catch by Biletnikoff in the end zone with less than a minute remaining.

Tony Roberts, who would become a legendary play-by-play announcer for Notre Dame football, provided the call on the Mutual Sports Radio Network:

"A touchdown catch by Biletnikoff, and the Oakland Raiders have gone ahead for the first time in this game . . . and it all started with that intercepted pass by Alonzo 'Skip' Thomas."

Trailing 10–7, New England—wearing its road white uniforms trimmed in Americana red and blue and AFL helmet designs featuring a 1776-style Patriot in a tricornered hat hiking a football—rallied to take control with fourteen unanswered points in the third quarter.

Down 21–10, the Raiders were staring at yet another playoff defeat. Stabler authored a 70-yard scoring march that saw the Snake go five-for-five on pass attempts, including a 17-yard hookup with Biletnikoff on the final play of the third quarter. Mark van Eeghen made it 21–17 with a 1-yard run.

Roberts: *"Stabler wants it quiet . . . Touchdown . . . Van Eeghen got the call!"*

Roberts's broadcast partner Tom Pagna, a former Notre Dame offensive backfield coach under Ara Parseghian from 1964 to 1974, credited the right side of the Raiders' line.

Pagna: *"You've really got to credit George Buehler, the right guard, and John Vella, the right tackle . . . They fired off the line."*

With the sun setting on both the Coliseum and Oakland's season, New England drove toward the clinching score late in the game. At the Raiders' 28 Grogan appeared to have picked up a crucial first down on a QB sneak, but the play was nullified by an illegal-motion penalty on Cunningham. The penalty proved costly. Oakland's defense slammed Bam on a draw play, and Fairbanks gambled by going for a 50-yard field-goal attempt rather than punting and pinning the Raiders deep. The kick fell just short, and the Raiders had the ball and 4:15 on the scoreboard clock to work yet another miracle.

Given new life, Stabler marched the Raiders 68 yards, thanks in part to a pair of clutch catches and two big penalties. Branch had a 12-yard reception and tight end Dave Casper a 21-yard catch to put Oakland on the Patriots' 28. Stabler was sacked for an 8-yard loss on the next play by tackle Mel Lunsford and then fired incomplete on second down.

On third and 18 the Snake threw incomplete, but the Raiders were handed what many still believe was a holiday gift when referee Ben Dreith hit Hamilton with a roughing-the-passer penalty for striking Stabler's helmet with his right hand. The disputed play, one of the most controversial in NFL history, put the Raiders at the Patriots' 13 with fifty-seven seconds remaining and would prove as controversial as New England QB Tom Brady's apparent fumble in the "Tuck Rule Game" against the Raiders amid the snow-swept confines of New England's Foxboro Stadium in the 2001 AFC divisional playoff game.

Oakland's fans see the "Tuck Rule Game" as the "Snow Job Game." Just as Raider Nation believes it was robbed in 2001, Patriots fans believe the game-changing call on Hamilton's hit on Stabler in '76 stole an opportunity to win a Super Bowl.

Roberts: *"Stabler was hit just as he released the football. There's a penalty marker on the play . . . against Ray Hamilton."*

Pagna: *"That's an awful big call at this point in the game. He's putting a ferocious rush on. He probably hit Stabler after Stabler threw the ball."*

The roughing-the-passer penalty helped keep the Raiders' drive alive. Haynes said it cost the Patriots their composure and allowed the Raiders to drive toward the winning TD. A personal-foul penalty on safety Prentice McCray gave Oakland first and goal at the 1. With 53,050 fans standing and roaring, the Snake faked a handoff to Pete Banaszak, rolled left, and, following the blocking of pulling guard Gene Upshaw, dove into the end zone with fourteen seconds remaining.

Roberts: *"Penalties certainly have played a big part in this game . . . Second down, goal to go, at the 1-yard line . . . Here's Stabler rolling. He's got a touchdown!"*

Pagna: *"When they talk about this play, they're going to talk about one block . . . Gene Upshaw pulled out and made the long block on the cornerback . . . A great block."*

Raiders radio voice Bill King provided an equally dramatic call:

"Stabler rolling to the left. He's gonna go . . . runs it in . . . Touchdown, Oakland!"

With New England's playoff hopes going up in smoke—literally, since someone had thrown a smoke bomb on the Coliseum field—Raiders linebacker Monte Johnson secured the dramatic 24–21 comeback win with an interception on the game's final play.

New England defensive end Julius Adams noted the twenty-one combined penalties and declared it "one of the worst-called games I have ever seen in my life." Fairbanks was a bit more diplomatic but wondered aloud about the controversial call on Hamilton. "I just hope they were right," he said. "It looked to me like Hamilton hit the ball first. If he did deflect the ball it was an incorrect call."

Haynes thought it a terrible call that changed the momentum of the game. What isn't noted or remembered about this controversial play is that officials missed Raiders receiver Carl Garrett being illegally belted out of bounds by defensive backs Dick Conn and Willie Germany while running a deep route.

Linebacker Phil Villapiano acknowledged that the Patriots had the Raiders on the ropes all afternoon. New England, he said, probably had a right beating Oakland that day. The roughing penalty wasn't often made in that rugged era, Villapiano acknowledged. Still, he was happy it was called or else the Raiders, he said, likely don't reach the Super Bowl.

Madden took exception at reporters' questions regarding penalties. "If you could sit there and say the officials turned that game around with penalties at the end, you were wasting your time," he said. "There was some great football out there."

There was more great football the following afternoon in Baltimore's Memorial Stadium, almost all of it provided by the Pittsburgh Steelers.

The Colts entered the game as Beasts of the East, having won their third straight Eastern Division title. It didn't come easy. The Colts' campaign had a chaotic beginning, the team losing four of its six exhibition games and prompting owner Bob Irsay to proclaim in the locker room, "I've got to make some changes."

After Irsay criticized players and head man Ted Marchibroda, the latter resigned amid a power struggle with Irsay and general manager Joe Thomas just prior to the season opener. "I can't tolerate this kind of interference," Marchibroda stated.

Several assistants threatened to follow Marchibroda out the door. On September 6 QB Bert Jones read a statement from the team, declaring that Irsay and Thomas "have completely destroyed this team." Thomas and Irsay made peace with their embattled field boss.

Winning eight of their first nine games, the Colts sprinted to another division title. Jones threw for 3,104 yards and twenty-four TD passes. Wide receiver Roger Carr was a favorite target, a deep threat who led the league in receiving yards, while versatile running back Lydell Mitchell ranked second in the conference in rushing and third in receiving. Kicker Toni Linhart led the league with 109 points. The Colts' high-octane offense paced the conference, but the Baltimore defense was susceptible in spots, as Pittsburgh would prove quickly in its playoff matchup.

Because churches had influence in the city since the 1885 Baltimore Catechism, they requested that the Colts and Orioles not start their games until 2:00 p.m. so as not to interfere with church attendance.

Jim Simpson and John Brodie handled the broadcast for NBC-TV. The Colts' hopes of avenging a postseason loss to the Steelers the previous year dimmed just four plays into the game when QB Terry Bradshaw caught the Colts in double coverage on receiver Lynn Swann. Looking deep for his other wideout, Bradshaw whistled a bullet through the thirty-six-degree temps for Frank Lewis. The sudden 76-yard strike gave Pittsburgh a lead it never relinquished.

Roberts, fresh from the Raiders' playoff win the day before, made the call on Mutual Network Radio:

"A bright, sunny day here in Baltimore . . . Bradshaw back to throw, looking, throwing long upfield. He's got Frank Lewis . . . Touchdown!"

Steelers head coach Chuck Noll believed Baltimore's secondary was vulnerable, but even Bradshaw was shocked that Noll, a man described by Pittsburgh's press as "Coach Conservative," would send Lewis on a fly pattern so early in the game. "Never since I've been here have we ever opened up with a bomb," Bradshaw beamed.

Roy Gerela's extra-point attempt was wide left, but he followed with a 45-yard field goal for a 9–0 advantage, quieting a holiday crowd of 60,020.

Jones rallied the Colts late in the first quarter, capping a 69-yard drive with a 17-yard TD connection with Carr. The TD was the first the Steelers had surrendered in the opening quarter all season, and it brought the big Baltimore crowd alive. It was made possible when Jones stood tall in the face of a furious rush by Steelers defensive tackle Ernie Holmes.

Roberts: *"Bert Jones got knocked flat by Ernie Holmes, but a diving catch by Roger Carr and a touchdown for the Colts!"*

It was just the third TD surrendered by the Steel Curtain in their last ten games and only the fifth passing TD they allowed all season.

The two-time defending Super Bowl champions sealed the deal by scoring on three of their next four series. Theo Bell's 60-yard kickoff return set up reserve back Reggie Harrison's 1-yard TD run out of a triple tight-end formation. Bradshaw's 29-yard TD pass to Swann, who had five receptions on the afternoon, capped a drive covering 54 yards and made it 23–7.

Executing its trademark trapping game to near perfection, Pittsburgh's offensive line pried open cracks in the Colts' defense, and Steelers backs burst to daylight. "We couldn't stop them," Marchibroda said.

One of the leaders of Pittsburgh's line was left tackle Jon Kolb, who was largely underrated outside the Steel City but was a man who helped personify Pittsburgh's power. A fourth-round draft choice in 1969 out of Oklahoma State, Kolb was not only the strongest Steeler but also the strongest player in the NFL, as evidenced by his bench-pressing 550 pounds. The 6-foot-2, 262-pound Kolb was self-motivated; along with lifting weights, he played basketball to improve his footwork and quickness. He also watched game films tirelessly. When people would ask if he ever tired of watching film Kolb would tell them, "That's my job. I want to better myself game after game."

As the left tackle Kolb was critical when it came to protecting Bradshaw's blind side from blitzes and edge rushers. He worked to correct his pass blocking, eliminating the little step backward he had been taking that was costing him a fraction of a second. Kolb also learned he was tipping Steelers plays by leaning slightly backward in his stance instead of forward. "There are so many things to learn," Kolb said. "The offensive line is the position where you have to learn the most." People could point to a player and say he's a natural running back, Kolb said, but there are no natural offensive linemen.

Growing up in Ponca City, Oklahoma, Kolb was undersize and wondered if he could even make his high school football team. He weighed 120 pounds and didn't earn a uniform his freshman year. Kolb bought weights and took a job in a dairy so he could drink a lot of milk, at least a gallon per day. He packed on 30 pounds his sophomore year and made the football team. By his senior season Kolb weighed 210.

Tragedy nearly struck Kolb in 1973 when, while working his 326-acre farm outside of Pittsburgh, he noticed smoke billowing from his two-story farmhouse where his one-year-old son and four-year-old niece were sleeping. Kolb sprinted 100 yards across the field to find the first floor destroyed. He ran around the house several times to find another opening. Kolb climbed onto the roof, kicked in the window, and rescued his son and niece.

Pittsburgh's offense needed no rescuing against the Colts, but it got a helping hand from free safety Glen Edwards, whose interception set up the Steelers' final score of the half, a 25-yard field goal by Gerela that put Pittsburgh up 26–7. The Steelers upped their advantage to 33–7 in the fourth when Bradshaw and Swann worked their magic formula—12 + 88 = 6—for the second time on the afternoon, this one covering 11 yards.

The Colts countered with a 1-yard scoring run by Roosevelt Leaks—the first rushing TD allowed by the Steel Curtain in ten games—before Pittsburgh put the finishing touches on its fifth straight postseason win with a 9-yard run by Harrison that closed the scoring at 40–14.

Pittsburgh did not play a perfect game. The Steelers were penalized twelve times, they dropped passes, and Harrison fumbled the ball away at the Baltimore 2, but their dominance was reflected in the final stats, Pittsburgh outgaining Baltimore 526–170. "Five hundred and twenty-six yards? In a playoff game?" an incredulous Bradshaw asked. "That's phenomenal."

The infantry of Harrison, Franco Harris, and Frenchy Fuqua churned over the winter-brown field in the Baltimore Dirt Bowl—a field so barren of grass it was dubbed Astro-Rock—for a combined 225 yards. Harris ground out 132 yards, 122 in the decisive first half, before Baltimore's Joe Ehrmann bruised Franco's ribs with 10:22 remaining in the third quarter. Bleier was injured in the first quarter, suffering a sprained toe, and left following just one carry.

The Steel Curtain continued its physical play, picking up where it left off in the regular season when it blanked five of its final eight opponents. The Colts' offense, ranked first in the AFC, was held to just 170 yards, including 71 on the ground.

Offensively, the Steelers' big star was Bradshaw, who missed six games with injuries but showed no rust and completed fourteen of eighteen passes for 264 yards and three TDs. "That's the best Terry's been in a long time," Noll told reporters.

"You saw a Super Bowl club out there today," said Marchibroda, who then offered a prediction. "Pittsburgh," he opined, "has two more games to play."

Fortunately for all concerned, the Steelers helped empty the stadium in time to avoid a disaster. Some ten to twenty minutes following the final gun a single-engine Piper Cherokee plane piloted by Donald Kroner buzzed the stadium several times before crashing into the nearly deserted upper deck overlooking the south end zone.

The NFC playoff that followed in Dallas on that Sunday afternoon was much more competitive. CBS's Pat Summerall and Tom Brookshier were on the call as the Los Angeles Rams horned in on the Dallas dynasty and corralled the Cowboys 14–12.

The conference championships had a familiar feel—the Steelers and Raiders were colliding in the AFC final for the third straight season and in the playoffs for the fifth consecutive year; the Vikings and Rams were meeting in the NFC Championship Game for the second time in three years and third time in the postseason since 1969. Minnesota and LA would also go on to face one another in 1977 in the famous "Mud Bowl" and again in '78.

Pittsburgh and Oakland advancing to the championship game for the third straight year marked the first time since Cleveland and Detroit went helmet-to-helmet from 1952 to 1954 that the same two teams met in back-to-back-to-back championship games. It has happened just once since, Dallas and San Francisco squaring off in NFC Championship Games in 1992–94.

Championship Sunday on December 26, 1976, began at 12:30 p.m. EST with *The NFL Today* on CBS, hosted by Brent Musburger, Irv Cross, Phyllis George, Jimmy "the Greek" Snyder, and Jack Whitaker. The intro included the classic theme music "Horizontal Hold" by Jack Trombey. Summerall and Brookshier handled the call on TV as the Vikings welcomed the Rams to frigid Metropolitan Stadium, where temperatures hovered in the teens.

Special teams and defense became the deciding factors in a 24–13 final that sent the Vikings to the Super Bowl for the third time in four years and fourth time in eight seasons. In so doing Bud Grant's squad became the first team to qualify for four Super Bowls.

The sounding of the final gun in the frost-covered Met meant millions of TV dials clicked to NBC for the renewal of the Steelers-Raiders rivalry in the AFC title game in the sun-soaked Oakland Coliseum. A sax solo by Michael Brecker flowed over a video montage of players suiting up in the locker room spliced with game action. Gowdy and Meredith were in the TV booth, Bill King in the Raiders' radio booth, and Myron Cope on the Steelers' broadcast.

King and Cope were as much a part of their respective team's personas as "Just win, baby!" and Terrible Towels.

King, a native of Bloomington, Illinois, was greatly aided by pro sports' westward expansion in the late 1950s and early 1960s. He began his broadcasting career while stationed in the Mariana Islands following World War II. He later referred to himself as the Robin Williams of

Guam, referring to the actor's popular portrayal of Adrian Cronauer in the 1987 movie *Good Morning, Vietnam*. From the Armed Forces Radio Network King returned home to Illinois and began his professional career in Pekin, calling high school basketball and football games and Minor League Baseball. He gravitated to calling basketball games at Bradley University in Peoria and football and basketball for the University of Nebraska.

King's career took a dramatic turn in 1958 when he heeded Horace Greeley's advice to "Go west" and accepted a position with radio station KSFO in San Francisco. It was a right place–right time scenario for King, who took advantage of the baseball Giants' cross-country move from New York to San Francisco. King worked with broadcast legends Lon Simmons and Russ Hodges on the San Francisco Giants' broadcasting team and went on to call University of California sports, including football and the 1959 national championship basketball team, which allowed him to work in concert with another legend, head coach Pete Newell.

Well versed in the classics, King would sprinkle references to F. Scott Fitzgerald and Aristotle into his play-by-play accounts. He was a Renaissance man whose trademarks included a Van Dyke beard and handlebar mustache, an unmistakable voice, and signature calls "Holy Toledo!" and "Touchdown, Raiders!" Of the former, King considered it better to shout "Holy Toledo!" into the mic rather than "Holy s—t!" King enjoyed opera and ballet and like Raiders owner Al Davis studied history; in King's case it was a leaning toward Russian history. He also enjoyed the sea and in his spare time took his two-mast sailboat, *Varuna*, on long trips.

King's career with the Raiders began in 1966 and lasted until 1995, when a dispute with Davis ended King's tenure with the team. By then the Sausalito resident had become one of the leading men in the Golden West's golden age of sports broadcasters. At the same time King was calling Raiders games, Simmons and Hodges were with the Giants, Vin Scully with the Dodgers, Chick Hearn the Lakers, and Dick Enberg the Rams and UCLA men's basketball.

From 1962 to 1985, King called Golden State Warriors games, and there is debate as to whether he or Hearn was a better basketball broadcaster. Some believed King's passion—he is believed to be the only professional broadcaster to cost his team a technical foul, which happened when he used an expletive in referencing a referee's call he disputed—preparation, thoroughness, and word play made him a sportscaster without peer.

King's big break with the Warriors had come via his association with Warriors owner Franklin Mieuli. When the club moved west from Philadelphia in 1962, Mieuli hired King after having worked with him on Giant baseball broadcasts.

King would join the Oakland A's broadcast team in 1981 and remained with them through 2005, marking the longest tenure with the franchise since they first started broadcasting their games in 1938 when they were Connie Mack's Philadelphia Athletics.

But it was King's association with the Raiders that most endeared him to Bay Area fans. Davis, however, was initially skeptical of the slightly built King when the two first met in the Raiders' training camp in 1966.

"You've got to be kidding me!" Davis exclaimed when King was hired to call Raiders games in the American Football League. "What could this little fella know about football?"

King succeeded in impressing not only Davis but also what would become Raider Nation. His calls of classic games and moments are a huge part of Raiders legend. In 1970 King's call of George Blanda's weekly wonders on the football field captured the imagination of millions:

"Gorge Blanda has just been elected king of the world!"

In 1978 King called the ending to the Raiders' "Holy Roller" win over San Diego:

"Casper has recovered in the end zone! . . . The Oakland Raiders have scored on the most zany, unbelievable, absolutely impossible dream of a play! Madden is on the field. He wants to know if it's real. They said yes, get your big butt out of here! He does! There's nothing real in the world anymore! The Raiders have won the football game! This one will be relived . . . forever!"

King's calls will be relived forever, as will the words and deeds of the Steelers' sportscaster occupying a radio booth not far from King in the Oakland Coliseum. Cope was not the wordsmith King was—Myron was a color analyst, Bill a play-by-play announcer—but his contributions to Steelers history are as indelible as King's are to the Raiders.

Cope was a Steelers broadcaster for thirty-five years, the longest tenure of any sportscaster with an NFL team, and like King, Myron was known for his distinctive voice. In the case of Cope, who was born in Pittsburgh, his voice had a instantly identifiable "Pittsburgh English" that branded him a "Yinzer." The word refers to speakers of Pittsburgh English using the second-person plural pronoun "yinz." Popular among Scots-Irish, Polish, and Pennsylvania German, yinz is a self-deprecating dialect that became a badge of honor to blue-collar workers in western Pennsylvania.

Cope's brand of yinz was uttered in uniquely nasal tones and an idiosyncratic speech pattern. Like King, Cope got excited when broadcasting games, and he too had his share of catchphrases, his most popular being the Yiddish phrase "yoi!" Cope's comic phrases also included "okel-dokel" (for "okey-dokey") and "mmm-hah!"

He was fond of providing nicknames for some—the division rival Cincinnati Bengals became the Bungles; multitalented Kordell Stewart was called "Slash" because he was a passer/runner/receiver—and popularizing others. In the case of the latter, hard-hitting Jack Lambert was "Jack Splat" and wide-body running back Jerome Bettis the "Bus."

Cope's career with the Steelers began in 1970, two years after he had begun doing daily sports commentaries on WTAE-AM Radio in Pittsburgh. Steelers officials noted Cope's strong Pittsburgh accent and teamed him with Jack Fleming in the broadcast booth.

Fleming, a native of Morgantown, West Virginia, had begun his broadcasting career while recuperating at Ashford Military Hospital. He had flown twenty-three combat missions while serving as a U.S. Air Force navigator during World War II.

Fleming had been in the Steelers' broadcast booth since 1965. Cope's arrival five years later coincided with the Steelers' emergence as the Team of the Seventies. Cope helped popularize the term "Immaculate

Reception" following the 1972 playoff against Oakland and the "Terrible Towel" prior to the 1975 playoff versus Baltimore. He was also instrumental in Frank Sinatra's induction into Franco's "Italian Army."

Cope was an accomplished journalist by the time he reached the Steelers. By age twenty-two he was writing for the *Pittsburgh Post-Gazette* and then became a freelance writer, with articles appearing in *Sports Illustrated* and the *Saturday Evening Post*. In 1963 he profiled young Cassius Clay, soon to be heavyweight champion Muhammad Ali, for a piece that earned Cope the E. P. Dutton Prize for "Best Magazine Sportswriting in the Nation."

As Cope, Fleming, King, Gowdy, hundreds of media, and thousands of fans settled into the sold-out Oakland Coliseum for the AFC Championship Game, emotions were running high on all sides.

Joe Greene said what happened to Swann in Oakland at the start of the season was still fresh in the Steelers' collective memory. "If anything like that happens again," Mean Joe warned, "I'll come off the bench myself. We can play any kind of game [the Raiders] want to play."

Madden noted the hype surrounding what many expected would be a bloodbath. "I have the feeling that the game's been forgotten," he said. "It's being treated like World War III."

Amid fifty-two-degree weather, Gowdy opened NBC-TV's broadcast in inimitable fashion:

"And a very happy holiday season from NBC Sports to all of you across America . . . We have some side effects coming into this game. Number one, they're calling this the 'Super Brawl.' There's a feud between these two teams, no doubt about it . . . Injuries are going to be a big part of the game. The Raiders are almost completely healthy . . . It's a different story for Pittsburgh. Franco Harris, with bad ribs, will not start . . ."

Harris (bruised ribs) and Bleier (sprained big toe) were in uniform but unavailable due to injuries suffered the week before in Baltimore, so Noll used a three-tight end offense that utilized Larry Brown, Bennie Cunningham, and Randy Grossman fronting lone running back Reggie Harrison. In long yardage situations the Steelers went to a three-wideout look featuring Lynn Swann, John Stallworth, and Frank Lewis along with either Harrison or Frenchy Fuqua. With Fuqua playing with a sore calf and backup Jack Deloplaine having suffered a broken leg earlier in the season, Harrison was the Steelers' lone healthy running back. "They can do without me," Bleier said, "but it'd be tough without the big man [Harris]."

Greene called the chance of Franco playing "damn near impossible." "Broken ribs are kind of hard to suck up," he said. "Even if they're not broken, a bad bruise makes it very difficult to breathe."

Madden said the Raiders knew Deloplaine was out, and when they kept hearing during the week that Franco, Rocky, and Frenchy weren't practicing, the Raiders adjusted their defense. "We started working against a four-end offense," said Madden. "Tight ends, wide receivers—what difference does it make? There are only so many combinations you can use."

Six years later Redskins coach Joe Gibbs would win a Super Bowl with an Ace-back offense featuring John Riggins. But Noll's one-back offense in '76 was unique for the time.

The game marked the final one for Steelers linebacker Andy Russell and referee Tommy Bell. Russell was capping a career in which he never missed a game at the high school, college, or NFL level.

Bell, a veteran of fifteen seasons in the NFL, was long regarded as one of the league's most respected referees. Arriving in the NFL in 1963 from college football's Southeast Conference, Bell was named referee his first year and held the title for the remainder of his career. He was the referee for the 1966 and 1969 NFL Championship Games, Super Bowl III, and Super Bowl VII. In the final minutes of the Jets' famous victory over the Colts in January 1969, the diminutive Bell drew himself up to his full 5-foot-7 frame and told Baltimore, "Now, men, let's go out like champions."

Bell was also the lone NFL representative to stand up to Broadway Joe Namath that afternoon in the Orange Bowl. "You know, you fellows are doing a pretty good job, even if you are NFL officials." "Don't compliment me, Joe," Bell replied. "My team is still losing."

A Lexington, Kentucky, lawyer on weekdays, Bell literally whistled while he worked and strove for utter anonymity. If pro football fans knew who Tommy Bell is, he said in 1969, chances are he did something wrong. Bell did few things wrong and would be the last NFL rookie to referee a crew until Brad Allen in 2014. Because the 1976 postseason would be Bell's last as referee, NFL commissioner Pete Rozelle gave him the option of working the AFC Championship or Super Bowl. Bell barely hesitated, opting for the Pittsburgh-Oakland rematch.

Bell's decision to choose a conference championship over a Super Bowl showed the importance of pro football's most heated turf war. Just three months before Noll had called out Oakland defenders and coaches for the Raiders' rough treatment of Swann.

Al Davis didn't take Noll's charges lying down. "The Steelers started all this, but their coach was smart enough to turn it around on us," he said. "[Noll] was smart. He made us look like the villains, but you don't think the Steelers got where they are by playing nice, soft football, do you? Be assured, they didn't get to the Super Bowl the last two years by being nice fellows."

Davis also responded to Greene's statement that he would play any kind of game Oakland desired. "Greene is trying to become the Muhammad Ali of pro football," Davis said. "I'm sure we've got many players willing to meet Joe halfway and get it straightened out before the game. When Greene made those statements, one of our new defensive linemen asked if he could challenge Greene before the game. We've got a lot of guys who could handle him. I'm not so sure Tatum couldn't do it himself."

Fans and media ate up the charges and countercharges. One reporter compared Raiders defensive backs to "Attica's all-star intramural team."

By the time Bell brought the team captains to midfield for the pre-game coin toss, the intensity on both sides was as high as the bright-blue skies. Before the day was done, Swann and Tatum would square off in a shoving match, Atkinson would assault Swann with words rather than blows, and Oakland offensive tackle John Vella and Lambert would throw punches at one another. Yet this was a far more civil war than its predecessors in this rivalry. "They didn't come to fight and we didn't either," Stabler said. "I'd get knocked down and I'd tell whoever knocked me over, 'Nice play.' And then I'd complete a pass and they'd say, 'Good throw.'"

Meredith and Gowdy took note and mentioned it on their broadcast.

Meredith: *"They're being awful nice to each other early in the ball game, helping each other up, patting each other on the shoulder . . ."*

Gowdy: *"Where's the bloodbath? They've both played very cleanly."*

That the Raiders and their fans were hungry for victory was evident by a banner carried by some shaggy-haired members of the Coliseum crowd: "Raider Menu—Swann Soup, Franco Dog, Terry Aki."

Errol Mann's 39-yard field goal gave Oakland a 3–0 lead in the first quarter and was set up by an injury to Steelers center Mike Webster. When Webster went to the sideline, backup center Ray Mansfield came on, and the result was a slow exchange that allowed Oakland's Hubie Ginn to partially block Bobby Walden's punt and gain a short field.

Gowdy: *"There's Bobby Walden. He's been in this situation hundreds of times . . . Look out! They nearly had the punt blocked! A short kick, a 19-yard punt by Walden . . ."*

A Steelers offense that averaged 212 yards in its last eight games but was without Harris and Bleier managed just 8 yards and zero first downs in the opening quarter. In the second quarter linebacker Willie Hall intercepted Bradshaw's pass that bounced off the hands of Fuqua and returned it to the 1. Three plays later Clarence Davis drove in to make it 10–0.

King: *"Stabler gives to Clarence Davis. He dives . . . Touchdown, Raiders!"*

With less than ten minutes remaining in the half, the Steelers' offense, which had not yet completed a pass, clanked into gear. Bradshaw found Lewis for 11 yards, Stallworth for 18, and Swann for 30. The latter cut through the Soul Patrol's territory and carried to the 7. A face-mask penalty on Villapiano moved the ball to the 3. Ray Pinney took the field as an additional tackle for Pittsburgh, and the 5-foot-11, 218-pound Harrison rumbled right and followed the pulling block of Sam Davis to slice Oakland's lead.

Gowdy: *"Touchdown, Pittsburgh! And the Steelers come back!"*

With kicker Roy Gerela suffering from a pulled groin, Mansfield booted the extra point to make it 10–7. As time was running out in the half, the Raiders reached the Pittsburgh 8, and Oakland went to its own

three-tight-end offense. Stabler's pass was incomplete, but a holding penalty on Pittsburgh cornerback J. T. Thomas put the ball at the 2. On the
next play tight end Warren Bankston was wide open in the left half of the
end zone, and Stabler floated a pass for an easy score and a 17–7 lead.

King: *"Stabler play-fakes, drops back. Here comes the rush. He gets
rid of it to Bankston . . . Touchdown, Raiders!"*

One person who can't be overlooked in Oakland's dominance was
Casper. The former Notre Dame star enjoyed a breakout season in '76
when he emerged as a full-time starter and caught fifty-three passes
for 691 yards and a career-high ten TDs. He earned the first of four-
straight Pro Bowl and All-Pro honors.

Meredith said if he was ever in a bar brawl he would want Casper on
his side. Gowdy remarked that Casper "did it all" for a tight end—he
could catch the deep ball as well as short passes and sideline throws.

Nicknamed "Big Ox" and "Ghost," the 6-foot-4, 240-pound Casper
provided a power-blocking third tackle, a position he played at Notre
Dame before converting to tight end.

Casper's contribution to the Raiders' win was significant. He caught
just one pass for 5 yards and lost 13 on a tight-end reverse, but he saved
Oakland from an early turnover when he wrestled the ball away from
Lambert, denying the Steelers early momentum near midfield. In the
second quarter Casper fought off Russell and then used his left arm
to hook Lambert and spring Davis free for a 17-yard gain on a touchdown drive.

Lambert played well for Pittsburgh—"Lambert is all over the field!"
Gowdy proclaimed—but Oakland's offensive line was shredding the
Steel Curtain:

Gowdy: *"They are ripping some holes in that Steelers front four! Those
tackles and guards just eating them up!"*

Their silver-and-black uniforms smeared with grass and dirt, Vella,
George Buehler, Dave Dalby, Art Shell, and Gene Upshaw paved a
path for an assortment of sweeps, traps, line bucks, and off-tackle runs
that gashed the Steelers for 100 yards rushing in the first half alone.
Two years prior in the 1974 title game the Steel Curtain had surrendered just 29 yards to Raiders runners the entire game.

With van Eeghen and Banaszak pounding away, Oakland secured its Super Bowl berth with a twelve-play, 63-yard drive late in the third quarter. Key plays included a 28-yard pass to Branch, a 7-yard toss to Bankston on fourth and 1, and Stabler's 5-yard play-action pass to Banaszak to make it 24–7.

King: *"Stabler back. Here comes the blitz by Ham. He throws . . . Touchdown, Raiders! Ham's blitz levels Stabler, and Stabler is down. Madden is on the field . . . Madden is absolutely furious Stabler was allowed to be leveled like that."*

The Snake was flattened by Ham, who came in high and hard, so hard Ham knocked a cap off Stabler's tooth. An angry Madden rushed onto the field to complain to officials while Stabler stayed down, but no penalty was assessed. As the final seconds ticked away, Raiders fans stormed the Coliseum floor to celebrate.

King: *"The Super Bowl really exists for the Oakland Raiders! All along they've been thinking it was somebody's crazy illusion!"*

Meredith made the point that while Pittsburgh's offense was hobbled, the Steel Curtain was healthy and the Raiders still took it to them. "Even though they couldn't run on us we weren't supposed to be able to run on them," Stabler said. "But we did. That was what finally decided it."

Madden agreed. ""Winning the way we did was right. After going 13 and 1, then 14 and 1—beating Cincinnati to get those people (the Steelers) in here. I know Franco and Rocky didn't play. But it wouldn't have made any difference."

Madden and his wife, Virginia, had just celebrated their seventeenth wedding anniversary. He had told her he would take her anywhere she wanted to go. Following the win over the Steelers, Pasadena—the site of Super Bowl XI—seemed the perfect destination for the Maddens.

The win was such an emotional one for the Raiders that the veteran Banaszak, who joined the team in 1966, found himself smiling one moment, crying the next.

The Steelers were emotional as well, but their emotion was an anger fueled by having to play their biggest game minus a pair of 1,000-yard runners. "I'd play 'em again tomorrow," Lambert said. "Just give me a few beers, a couple of hours of sleep, and I'll be out there at 1 p.m. tomorrow."

"Nobody feels like fighting a war without weapons," Noll said, but Greene offered a different perspective. "There's no doubt about it, Oakland won the game," said Greene. "We're a good team, but they were better today."

The Raiders headed to Pasadena to meet a Minnesota team that had been handled in its three prior Super Bowls by Kansas City, Miami, and Pittsburgh. Despite the addition of defensive mastermind Buddy Ryan to Bud Grant's coaching staff, the Vikings were underdogs.

AFC champions had dominated Super Sunday, winning four straight showdowns with NFC titlists and six of the previous seven. The Raiders were favored by four points, but those who looked a little further saw physical mismatches all over the field, most notably on the left side of the Oakland O-line, where the 6-foot-5, 265-pound Shell would take on 6-foot-4, 248-pound Jim Marshall and the 6-foot-5, 255-pound Upshaw would go against the 6-foot-4, 245-pound Page.

When the Raiders went on defense, 6-foot-7, 280-pound nose tackle Dave Rowe would face Viking center Mick Tingelhoff (6 feet 2, 237 pounds). Oakland's secondary also looked too rugged and physical for Viking wideouts Ahmad Rashad and Sammy White.

Story lines abounded. Stabler's twenty-seven TD passes were the most in the NFL since 1969 and his 67 percent completion rate the highest since Sammy Baugh during the war years; Tarkenton had thrown for more yards and touchdowns than any QB in history. Foreman and Branch, arguably the two most dangerous big-play threats in pro football, were sharing the same field for the first time. Guy had never had a punt blocked in his four-year NFL career, while the Vikings had blocked fifteen kicks during the season.

Pete Banaszak, who played in Oakland's previous Super Bowl, acknowledged that he had been "a little scared" at the prospect of facing the fearsome Packers back in January 1968. He had seen Green Bay QB Bart Starr on the field before the game and had an urge to trade football cards with him. Banaszak wasn't scared this time around, even though he knew the Vikings were good and that they were frustrated from reaching the Super Bowl before and not winning it. For either Madden or his coaching opposite, Bud Grant, this Super Bowl would be a big win. "A very big win," Banaszak emphasized, "the biggest."

Super Sunday dawned clear and sunny, and an audience of 100,421, a Super Bowl record to that point, crowded into the famous Rose Bowl in Pasadena. The broadcast audience was estimated at 125 million. Held on January 9, this was the earliest Super Bowl played during the calendar year. To avoid playoff games on Christmas Day, the NFL had moved up the start of its regular season. Super Bowl XI would be the last to finish under daylight and also the last to feature two classic straight-on kickers in Errol Mann and Fred Cox.

Minnesota's famed Purple People Eaters entered the game as the NFC's best defense, having surrendered just 176 points during the regular season. The Raiders planned to emphasize the run game, following a game plan similar to the ones employed by the Chiefs, Dolphins, and Steelers against the Vikings. The latter two had used more than fifty running plays, the Chiefs forty-two. "When you've got the horses you ride them," Stabler said. "We're not a fancy team. We just line up and try to knock you out of there. Nobody's better at it than those two guys [Shell and Upshaw]."

From the NBC-TV broadcast booth Gowdy highlighted the decisive battle in the trenches on Oakland's opening series.

Gowdy: *"Oakland likes to run behind Shell and Upshaw. They like to go to their left . . . Minnesota is hard to run outside on . . . A lot of years in that front line, forty-seven years' experience in the front four of the Vikings."*

Amid near-perfect fifty-eight-degree temperatures, Oakland took the opening kickoff and used eight plays to go from its 34 to the Minnesota 11. Mann's 29-yard field goal hit the left upright, but the Raiders' confidence was exemplified by Stabler's comment to Madden. "Don't worry," the Snake told his coach. "There's more where that came from."

Late in the opening quarter Guy suffered the first blocked punt of his pro career. Minnesota's Fred McNeil blocked the ball and returned it to the 3 before being stopped by Guy.

Gowdy: *"They said nobody could block Ray Guy's punts, and the Vikings have done it."*

Owning an opportunity to take their first lead in a Super Bowl, the Vikings, outfitted in their deep-purple jerseys, turned it over two plays later, running back Brent McClanahan fumbling and linebacker Willie Hall, a truck driver prior to the season, recovering.

King: *"Tarkenton gives to McClanahan. Stonewalled! There may have been a fumble . . . Oakland recovers! Holy Toledo!"*

Their white jerseys and silver helmets dazzling in the Pasadena sun, the Raiders drove 90 yards in twelve plays and Mann's 24-yard field goal gave Oakland a 3–0 lead early in the second quarter. On its next series Oakland marched 64 yards in ten plays, and Stabler capped the series with a 1-yard TD pass to Casper, who was wide open in the end zone.

King: *"Stabler back to pass, a quick throw to the end zone. Touchdown, Raiders! Jascha Heifetz never played a violin with more dexterity than Kenny Stabler is playing the Minnesota Viking defense!"*

Neal Colzie's 25-yard punt return set up the Raiders' next score, Banaszak blasting in from the 1 to make it 16–0 at the half.

King: *"Handoff to Banaszak. He powers over . . . Touchdown, Raiders!"*

Both Oakland touchdowns had been set up by Biletnikoff, the slick, Stickum-smeared receiver who earned the Super Bowl MVP Award after hauling in four catches for 79 yards. Three of his receptions set up touchdowns, and Biletnikoff made it two straight years that the Super Bowl's best player was a wide receiver, Swann having won the MVP the year before.

Biletnikoff was blessed with what Madden simply called "hands." "'Hands' are more than a gift for catching the ball," Madden said. "The true definition of 'hands' in football is where both hands work as one. No matter where the receiver is, how off balance he might be, it's both hands going for the ball as though they were one. I learned that from watching Freddy."

Madden said Biletnikoff could catch anything he could touch. Biletnikoff's productivity did not come by accident. While some receivers would catch fifteen or twenty passes in practice, Biletnikoff would catch a hundred. Fellow great receiver Paul Warfield, a contemporary of Biletnikoff's, said Freddy probably had the best hands of any receiver he's seen in the modern era.

Biletnikoff inherited his gift in part from his father, who used his hands to become a national Amateur Athletic Union boxing champion. Born in Erie, Pennsylvania, Biletnikoff flourished at Florida State University, setting Seminole marks for receptions, touchdowns, and points scored. He was named All-America in 1964 when his fifty-seven receptions ranked fourth in the nation. Al Davis drafted Biletnikoff in the second round in 1965 and outbid Detroit during the AFL-NFL signing wars.

Biletnikoff would go on to be a Hall of Famer, but his career did not start with a bang. He dropped five passes in his first game as a rookie, a preseason date with Denver in Salt Lake City. Biletnikoff did catch an 80-yard touchdown pass, but he spent the postgame bus ride sitting alone, staring at his hands and pondering the differences between pro and college ball.

At FSU he had played against defenses where all he had to do was run straight downfield, cut in or out, and be in the clear. In the AFL Biletnikoff found out quickly that to get open he had to beat defensive backs who were very good. "I tended to get so hung up trying to beat my man," he said, "I had trouble catching the ball."

His worrisome attitude never left Biletnikoff during his fourteen-year career. Before games he smoked cigarettes, drank coffee, and then vomited. When Fred lost his pregame meal in the locker room, the Raiders knew he was ready to play.

Biletnikoff also readied himself by studying the skill of pass receiving as if it were an applied science. A dedicated practice player, he spent every training camp breaking down his pass patterns into a series of individual moves. Biletnikoff then practiced each step until it was in stride and smooth. He perfected his routes, particularly the comeback pattern. He brought variations into his routes and over the years created what one observer described as a rhythm of acceleration, body control, and momentum.

Biletnikoff not only studied his patterns but also studied opposing cornerbacks to learn their reactions to a given route. "Running a pattern is not as easy as it looks," Biletnikoff said. "Unless you've worked hard on the difficult steps in a route, it gets awkward when you try it in a game."

Biletnikoff was at his best in big games. Wearing his silver-colored No. 25, and with his cheekbones streaked with eye-black grease and his forearms taped to appear gauntlet-like, Biletnikoff beat the best cornerbacks of his era with an awesome array of routes and was enough of a technician and tactician to find the openings in the best zone defenses of his day. Competitive and skillful, he flowed fearlessly through thickets of defenders with fluid moves and a change of pace and used unerring hands to bring the ball into his body. "He could make a great, difficult catch in a key game," Warfield said. Stabler agreed. "In big games," he said, Biletnikoff "made more clutch catches than any receiver in the league."

Biletnikoff retired ranking first all-time in postseason receptions and receiving yards. He hauled in 589 passes from 1965 to 1978 and rivaled Raymond Berry of Baltimore as the best possession receiver in pro football history to that point.

Biletnikoff broke both records and rules. His Oakland outfit was in constant violation of NFL commissioner Pete Rozelle's uniform code. Biletnikoff rolled his silver uniform pants above his bony knees, an infraction allowed by what was later said to be a bogus claim by a doctor that Fred had a skin infection; grew his blond hair long enough to flow from the back of his helmet; and covered parts of his taped forearms and calves with streaks of Stickum.

Stabler said that once Biletnikoff caught a pass, the ball was no longer usable. "Jim Otto would go to the line to snap the ball for the next play, but he wouldn't touch the ball until they gave him a new one."

Snake said Freddy would tape his forearms and then spray Stickum on them. He would then apply Stickum on his socks and jersey.

Biletnikoff wore no knee or thigh pads, and his shoulder pads were so small they resembled those worn by quarterbacks. He is the last NFL player to wear the flared-sides suspension helmet and was one of the last nonkickers to wear a single-bar face mask.

Despite his lack of padded protection, Biletnikoff was as durable as he was dedicated. From 1968 to 1974 he did not miss a single regular-season game. In that 98-game span he had 367 catches, an average of nearly 4 per game, and scored 52 touchdowns for a total of 312 points.

To Stabler, Biletnikoff was simply the greatest pass receiver of all time. "He caught almost six hundred passes," Snake said, "and I think he caught half of them standing on his head." The greatest thing about Biletnikoff, Stabler said, was his consistency.

Biletnikoff and the Raiders were consistently dominant in 1976, and their dominance on Super Sunday was evident in the early going. Through the first thirty minutes of play Oakland outgained Minnesota 288–86 and owned sixteen first downs to the Vikings' four.

Mann's 40-yard field goal in the third upped the Raiders' advantage to 19–0 before the Vikings finally scored on Tarkenton's 8-yard pass to White. In the fourth quarter Biletnikoff's 48-yard catch-and-run led to Banaszak bolting in from the 2. Willie Brown picked off a Tarkenton pass and, churning over the emerald-green turf, returned it a Super Bowl–record 75 yards for a 32–7 lead.

King: *"Willie Brown . . . He's going all the way! Touchdown, Raiders!"*

En route to a 32–14 victory, the Raiders set a Super Bowl record with 429 total yards, breaking the mark of 358 set by Green Bay in Super Bowl I. But for a pair of missed extra points by Mann, Oakland would have set a then Super Bowl mark for points scored, eclipsing the thirty-three scored by the Packers against the Raiders in Super Bowl II. Davis ran for a career-best 137 yards on sixteen carries, and Marshall was completely shut out in tackles despite having numerous plays run his way. By game's end the Raiders had run fifty-two times for 266 yards and two TDs.

The exclamation point on Oakland's overwhelming win was provided by Tatum. The Raiders' safety hit White so hard on a pass over the middle that the receiver's purple helmet flew off. The battered White also had his helmet stripped by Skip Thomas.

In the final minutes the heated passions of the old NFL-AFL rivalry resurfaced. Gowdy, who broadcast AFL games for ABC and then NBC, reminded viewers that AFL/AFC teams were claiming their fifth straight Super Bowl title and seventh in eight years. Meredith, the Cowboys QB during the NFL-AFL war years and a man who was broadcasting his final game for NBC before returning to ABC's *Monday Night Football*, pointed out that three of those Super Bowls were won by former NFL teams Baltimore and Pittsburgh.

"Different players!" Gowdy countered. Meredith defused the situation with his down-home humor.

California had become the home of champions, the A's winning three straight World Series from 1972 to 1974, the Golden State Warriors the NBA title in 1975, and the Raiders the Super Bowl in '76. All that was left in the end was the countdown of the Super Bowl's final seconds.

King: *"There's the gun sounding the end of the game! John Madden goes on the shoulders of his players!"*

In 1976 the autumn wind, and the winter wind, was indeed, a Raider.

Jim Campbell: The Steelers were off to Baltimore to play the Colts in the divisional round. As good as I felt about the state of the Steelers, Bert Jones still scared me significantly. I had a lot of confidence in Pittsburgh, but Jones was playing as well as anyone in the NFL at that time. In more than one discussion I had with other NFL folks, we concluded that if you were starting a new franchise, Jones would be the player you would select first. He was that good.

The Steelers cruised to a 40–14 victory. There were several things I didn't know, or simply missed, that would have grave consequences in the near future. Franco and Rocky were both injured in the game. Harris's ribs were severely bruised, and Bleier's toe was hurting enough to prevent him from playing in the championship game.

This left only Frenchy Fuqua, now primarily a backup, and Harrison, primarily a special teamer, to carry the load versus Oakland. Something also bizarre was the small plane that crashed into the stands at Baltimore's Memorial Stadium. Fortunately, the stands were virtually empty, and the pilot was uninjured. Always ready with a quote, Mansfield opined, "I thought it was a kamikaze from Oakland."

I had no idea of the seriousness of the injuries to Harris and Bleier or that Fuqua was not 100 percent physically. I was blithely unaware of the physical state of the Steelers.

Because of the Raiders sterling 13-1 record (the Steelers were 10-4), Oakland would be the host of the AFC Championship Game. After the way the Steelers dismantled the Colts the week before, I wasn't much worried.

True, the Steelers would have to contend with the rabid Raiders fans—especially those who called the Black Hole (end-zone sections 104–7 of Oakland–Alameda County Stadium) home. Some of those fans, mostly a hybrid of Darth Vader and the Hell's Angels, took up to two hours to get in costume. There is a heavy dose of painted and spiked shoulder pads, military and football helmets, silver and black face paint, and anything else that lends itself to a sinister look. One would think that black and silver were the only colors of the spectrum—if indeed, they are colors. The denizens have even designed an official-looking logo, complete with skull and crossbones, declaring themselves "football's most notorious fans." They even evolved to the point where they have for sale T-shirts, caps, hoodies, and the like.

The several hundred fans had their own house rules. First and foremost, "don't even think about wearing another team's jersey—especially the 49ers." Gonzo journalist Hunter S. Thompson had this to say about fans in the Black Hole: "Beyond doubt the sleaziest and rudest and most sinister mob of thugs and whackos ever assembled in such numbers." One visiting player once remarked, perhaps only half-jokingly, "I couldn't believe all the moustaches and tattoos—and that was just the women."

Mention was made of the injuries to Franco Harris and Rocky Bleier, but I didn't take it that seriously, that is, until I saw the presentation of the REA (Railway Express Agency) NFL Man of the Year Award. Much to my pleasure, Franco was the recipient of the handsome bronze trophy. I was aware of this beforehand, because the Hall of Fame was involved in conducting the voting. As the award was made to Franco, curiously he was standing beside the bronze football player and made no attempt to lift it for a photo opportunity. At forty pounds it was simply too heavy for the All-Pro running back to hoist with his damaged ribs.

Still, I wasn't too concerned. Maybe it was because I thought back to

Chuck Noll's mantra of "Whatever it takes." Franco's 1,000-plus yards would be missed, and I wasn't quite sure how much Rocky would or could contribute, but I had an almost blind faith in what Noll could come up with as a game plan. I found out quite early on that the plan would include all three tight ends and the one healthy running back, Reggie Harrison. Perhaps deluding myself, I thought that would get the job done. Also, the Steelers had beaten the Raiders in three of four previous playoff games.

The Black and Gold fell behind 10–0, before Harrison plunged for a touchdown and Mansfield (subbing for Gerela, who suffered a groin pull in the Colts game) made the PAT to make it a 10–7 game.

Warren Bankston, an ex-Steeler acquired by the Raiders, scored for the Silver and Black, and the halftime score jumped up to 17–7. I convinced myself that Franco was really able to play but was held out until the second half, so that Oakland could not make any halftime adjustments. Yet Franco appeared at the start of the third quarter on the sideline wearing a cape—looking much like the anonymous player depicted by the bronze trophy he was unable to lift before the game.

I thought, "The Steel Curtain is still intact, and Pittsburgh still has a chance." Although the defense gave up only a third-quarter touchdown and shut down the Silver and Black attack in the fourth, the game was essentially over not too long after the opening kickoff. Not only was the offense severely handicapped, but the Steel Curtain also suffered some serious dents and dings.

After the way the Steelers ended the regular season, and the way they throttled the Colts, it was especially disappointing to the Steelers how the championship game went.

When the "criminal element" lawsuit got under way, Noll was "forced" to admit that certain Steelers could be considered part of the criminal element—namely, Mel Blount. Blount took offense to Noll's depiction of his style of play and filed suit against the head coach and his employers. Ruffled feathers were smoothed, and Blount was back at his familiar cornerback spot, set to burnish his already impressive résumé.

My game-day association with the Steelers was about to end, when

I took a position with NFL Properties (the merchandising and publishing arm of the league) in Los Angeles. I would miss being around what I considered the classiest franchise in the NFL, but I left with several indelible impressions. None more vivid than just how much character the whole organization had—from Mr. Rooney and Chuck Noll to Joe Greene and the more insignificant special teamers.

Members of the Lombardi-era Packers, after winning multiple championships (both NFL and Super Bowls), often cited "love" as a vital component of their success. For example, "We win because of the love we have for each other."

I don't profess to know much about psychology, but I can tell you that the Steelers of the time I spent on the sidelines had a tremendous amount of respect and admiration for each other. Perhaps "harmony" would be a better word than "love." There was not a bad apple or a clubhouse lawyer in the bunch. To a man (once Noll got the roster to where he wanted it), everyone got along. No friction. No animosity. No jealousy. Noll, early in his tenure, took care of that.

The best example is when he got rid of any player who was a distraction. In 1970 that would have been All-Pro wide receiver Roy Jefferson, who had led the NFL in receiving yards a couple of years earlier. When Jefferson, despite his considerable talent, became a detriment to Noll's vision of the team, he was shipped to Noll's old team, the Baltimore Colts. Another rabble-rouser, a pretty good defensive back named John Rowser, found himself in Denver after the 1973 season.

A great example of team harmony is illustrated by how in the early days of the Super Bowl dynasty there was no sniping at the offense by the defense, which was disproportionately responsible for the team's success. This was in contrast to the New York Football Giants of the late 1950s and early 1960s, when the defense would leave the field after a stop and tell the oncoming offense, "Try to hold 'em." How Joe Greene took a young and confidence-challenged Terry Bradshaw under his wing in the early years speaks volumes of the "all for one, one for all" spirit that went a long way in making the Steelers what they were in the seventies.

Much of the franchise's success could also be attributed to the businesslike way Dan Rooney shaped the front office. While the Chief sometimes let his emotional attachment get in the way of business decisions, Dan did not. He did not lack his father's empathy for people, but he based his decisions on what was good for the Steelers. It's hard to argue with the results.

Steelers folklore has it that some of Mr. Rooney's coaches were more racetrack buddies than football coaches. Their won-lost records would indicate that to be true. It was said that one coach was kept on because his coaching salary was the only way the Chief could recoup the loans made to the coach to cover the coach's penchant for betting on slow horses.

Another benefit of working the sidelines in Pittsburgh was to get to know and see how some of the legendary photographers of the era worked. Walter Iooss Jr., Heinz Kluetmeier, Neil Leifer, John Iacono, Manny Rubio, Tony Tomsic, Vernon Biever, John Biever, Malcolm Emmons, and Dick Raphael all became acquaintances, if not friends. I recall a conversation between Tony Tomsic and Franco Harris in which the photographer said, "Franco, you're a tough one to get on film. I study runners and can anticipate what their next moves may be, and that allows me to focus on where you might be and what you might do. But you have no set way of running. No way can I anticipate what your next move will be. I just point my camera in your direction and hope for the best." Franco just smiled something of a *Mona Lisa* smile.

It was fun to watch a play unfold and hear the buzz-click of the legendary photogs' motor-drive Nikons, which at the time were the choice of practically all the first-rate photographers. It was a while later after Cannon made a deal with the NFL that included free equipment for the photographers that one would see a significant number of Cannons on the sidelines.

Something else that was interesting to see was how the sidelines became more crowded. In the 1970s there was still some open space on an NFL sideline. At least once I noticed a young society-type lady, dressed to the nines, along the sideline with her Kodak Instamatic in hand. My guess was she was probably a friend of a writer who had wrangled a field photo pass for her from an unknowing Steelers front-office type. In those days, it was something that could be done.

Epilogue

Hot War Turns Cold

The most ferocious and violent postseason rivalry in the history of North American sports ended with the 1976 AFC Championship Game. Coming as it did on the day after Christmas, perhaps it did signify, at least as far as the Steelers and Raiders were concerned, peace on earth.

Oakland and Pittsburgh played once more in the 1970s, the Raiders earning a 16–7 decision at Three Rivers Stadium in Week Two of the 1977 regular season. Errol Mann field goals of 21, 40, and 41 yards in the second quarter gave Oakland a 9–0 lead at halftime, and Mark van Eeghen ran it in from 8 yards out in the third for a 16–0 advantage. The Steelers answered in the fourth with a 43-yard TD from Terry Bradshaw to tight end Bennie Cunningham.

Bradshaw threw for 268 yards in the loss; his Hall of Fame opposite, Ken Stabler, had 107 passing yards in the win. Pittsburgh outgained Oakland 369–247, but the Raiders won the turnover battle 5–0 and had interceptions by Willie Brown, Charlie Phillips, and Jack Tatum.

Pittsburgh's 9-5 record was its worst since 1971, but it still won its fourth straight Central Division Championship and fifth in six seasons. The Steelers would go on to extend their dominance in the division and in pro football with Super Bowl titles in 1978 and '79.

Oakland finished 11-3 and for the first time since 1971 failed to win the West, the Silver and Black surrendering the crown to the celebrated Orange Crush of the Denver Broncos. The Raiders returned to the AFC Championship thanks to another classic encounter—a thrilling double-overtime victory over Bert Jones and Company in the Baltimore Dirt Bowl made possible in part by Dave Casper's "Ghost to the Post" grab on an unseasonably warm Christmas Eve.

Playing without injured defensive stars George Atkinson and Phil Villapiano, Oakland was looking to claim its first road playoff victory. The Colts, Eastern Division champions for the third straight season, were seeking the franchise's first postseason win since Johnny Unitas, Mike Curtis, Tom Matte, Bubba Smith, et al. beat Cleveland in muddy Municipal Stadium on December 26, 1971.

The Raiders had in their repertoire a pass called "91 In," which called for the two outside receivers to run "in" patterns and the tight end to run a deep post. It was the job of the tight end, in this case Casper, to clear out the deep middle while the outside receivers came inside. Oakland assistant coach Tom Flores, who would replace Madden following the latter's retirement at the end of the 1978 season, noticed that the Colts' safety had been sneaking up when the Raiders ran "91 In." He told Stabler prior to calling the play late in the fourth quarter, "On '91 In' take a peek at Ghost to the Post."

With just over two minutes remaining and the Raiders trailing 31–28, Stabler faded to pass amid the roar of 60,763 fans, planted his back foot, pump-faked, and fired deep just before Baltimore defensive end John Dutton reached him. Looking like Willie Mays making his famous over-the-shoulder catch of Vic Wertz's bomb in the 1954 World Series, Casper looked up, saw the ball, adjusted his path, and split two defenders as he made a spectacular running grab.

Casper said later he didn't think he had caught a pass on that pattern all season. "I did some maneuvers to set [cornerback Nelson Munsey] up and I faked an out and went underneath him to the post and I had him going the wrong way and I was open," Casper stated. "Because I was late, Snake had already thrown the ball, guessing where I was going to go. When I looked up over my shoulder, I took one look and said, 'The ball isn't going where I'm going.'"

Colts outside linebacker Stan White called it the play of the day.

"Stabler just threw it up for gabs," White said, "and Casper made a superb adjustment."

The Ghost's grab set up Mann's tying field goal with twenty-six seconds left. In the second overtime Stabler's 10-yard touchdown pass to Casper clinched a 37–31 win that took three hours and fifty minutes from start to finish. Decades later the "Ghost to the Post" remains one of the top ten name games in NFL history, ranking with other Raiders classics—the Immaculate Reception, Holy Roller, and *Heidi*.

Legendary sportswriter John Steadman of the *Baltimore Sun* summed up the epic, which started in early-afternoon sunlight and ended in evening darkness, as "Truly a classic . . . a football masterpiece that will long be admired by those who played and those who witnessed. Put it away in a book of football keepsake and remember it as a game that neither team lost . . . but only one could win."

Denver's defeat of Pittsburgh later that same afternoon in the Mile High City was less artistic. In the second quarter Mean Joe Greene decked Broncos guard Paul Howard with a right uppercut to the solar plexus that venerable sportswriter Cooper Rollow, who was covering the game for the *Chicago Tribune*, called "better than any punch Muhammad Ali has delivered in the last two years." Howard was on the ground for several minutes. After receiving first aid Howard had to be helped off the field, though he later returned to the game. As the two teams headed to their respective locker rooms at halftime, cameras caught Broncos boss Red Miller angrily complaining to Steelers defensive-line coach George Perles about the rough play.

In the aftermath of a 34–21 loss, Greene, who also delivered a blow to the ribs of center Mike Montler, agreed it was a cheap shot against Howard. But the man named by head coach Chuck Noll Pittsburgh's defensive captain for the 1977 season suggested he had to take the law into his own hands. Even though it was Christmas Eve and the season of giving, Greene didn't appreciate being dealt what he said were illegal tactics. "My job is to get to the man with the ball," Greene said. "If the man in front of me is impeding me illegally and the officials are not calling it a foul . . . then I have to do something about it. Believe me—those punches I threw at Howard and then at center

Mike Montler were retaliatory reactions. You can put them in the category of defending one's self. And believe me, I take more than I dish
out. I was playing football, taking care of myself. I'm not sorry it happened. I'm a gentleman in this game all the way down the damn line."

Pete Rozelle fined Greene $5,000 for punching Howard, the NFL
commissioner still a little touchy over Mean Joe's threat earlier that
season to knock down some officials and "cleat 'em in the spine."

Greene had a prior history with Howard. During a 35–35 tie in Denver in 1974, Howard charged Greene with kicking him in the groin so
hard it ripped open his scrotum. No fines were assessed because then
Broncos coach John Ralston reviewed the game films and withdrew
Howard's charge after finding no evidence of Greene kicking Howard.

Denver's disputed 20–17 victory over division rival Oakland—just
the fourth time in NFL-AFL history that teams from the same division
met for the championship (Oakland–Kansas City 1969, Baltimore-
Miami 1971, Dallas-Washington 1972)—was made possible by head
linesman Ed Marion's controversial call on Broncos running back
Rob Lytle's fumble.

One play prior to Jon Keyworth's 1-yard touchdown run in the third
quarter, Lytle lost the ball when he was jarred in midair by Tatum as
he sailed over a pile of humanity toward the goal line. Oakland nose
tackle Mike McCoy recovered the fumble and began lumbering toward
the Denver end zone with nothing but green permafrost in front of
him. Marion, however, declared it Denver football, believing Lytle's
forward progress was stopped prior to the fumble. To add insult to
injury, officials hit Oakland with an unsportsmanlike conduct penalty for arguing the momentum-changing missed call, and the Broncos scored on the next play to take a 14–3 lead en route to an eventual
three-point victory.

NBC cameras clearly showed Lytle fumbling upon being hit by
Tatum and McCoy recovering for the Raiders. Play-by-play announcer
Dick Enberg told viewers "obviously the fumble occurred before Lytle
hit the ground and apparently in that mass of humanity the officials
did not see it."

The Lytle fumble ranks as one of the most controversial missed calls in postseason play in NFL history. The noncall helped the Orange Crush trump the Silver and Black on championship Sunday, but had the NFL used instant replay in 1977 the Raiders might have returned to the Super Bowl, where they would have had the opportunity to defend their world title against the Dallas Cowboys. Since they had met in just one official game prior to 1977, an Oakland-Dallas Super Bowl would have generated significant interest. Instead, Super Bowl XII saw Dallas destroy Denver 27–10 in a game that wasn't even as close as the lopsided score.

Just as they had jockeyed for position atop the pro football world for five straight memorable seasons, the Steelers and Raiders continued to take turns hoisting the Vince Lombardi Trophy presented to each season's Super Bowl champion. The Steelers secured their legacy as the Team of the Seventies with titles in 1978 and '79; the Raiders returned to claim the crown in 1980 and '83, the latter coming after they had left Oakland in favor of Los Angeles and defeated Pittsburgh in the playoffs.

From 1974 to 1980, the Steelers and Raiders combined to win six Super Bowls in seven years. Oakland's 1980 season included a thrilling 45–34 shoot-out win over the Steelers in Three Rivers Stadium on a Monday night in mid-October.

By then many of the principals had changed. Madden had retired and been replaced by Flores; Stabler and Tatum headed to Houston and were replaced by Jim Plunkett and Burgess Owens, respectively. Reggie Kinlaw, Dave Browning, Matt Millen, Bob Nelson, Rod Martin, Lester Hayes, Dwayne O'Steen, Mike Davis, Bob Chandler, Raymond Chester, Kenny King, and Chris Bahr were the faces of the Raiders now, not Dave Rowe, Otis Sistrunk, Villapiano, Monte Johnson, Willie Hall, Willie Brown, Atkinson, Fred Biletnikoff, Casper, Clarence Davis, and Mann.

On the Steelers' side, Steve Furness and John Banaszak started where Ernie Holmes and Dwight White had before, and Jim Smith, Ted Petersen, Ray Pinney, Tyrone McGriff, Matt Bahr, and Craig Colquitt were in the lineup for John Stallworth, Jon Kolb, Sam Davis, Gerry Mullins, Roy Gerela, and Bobby Walden.

The Raiders rode their Monday-night comeback victory in Pittsburgh to their second Super Bowl title in four seasons. On December 7, 1981, Oakland outgunned Pittsburgh again, this time by 30–27 in the Coliseum. On New Year's Day 1984 the Raiders, now in Los Angeles, used a Marcus Allen–inspired 38–10 playoff romp over the Steelers as the springboard to a third world championship. Powered by Frank Pollard and Walter Abercrombie, Pittsburgh reversed the trend on December 16, 1984, defeating the defending Super Bowl champs 13–7 and costing them home-field advantage in the following week's wild-card playoff game against Seattle. The Raiders' reign ended in the Kingdome, 13–7.

The Steelers' victory over the Raiders allowed them to edge Cincinnati for a second straight division title. Two weeks later the Steelers stunned the Broncos 24–17 in Mile High Stadium. Pittsburgh's upset win prevented the much-anticipated AFC Championship duel between Denver's John Elway and Miami's Dan Marino.

The Steelers, who had dealt Joe Montana and the 49ers their lone loss of the season, a 20–17 October surprise in San Francisco's Candlestick Park, were fire-bombed by Marino, a Pittsburgh product whom the Steelers had passed on in the draft. The 45–28 loss in the Miami Orange Bowl kept the Steelers, the Team of the Seventies, from a rematch with the 49ers, the Team of the Eighties, in the Super Bowl. Also lost was a Chuck Noll versus Bill Walsh matchup that would have had two of the game's greatest coaches on opposing sidelines on Super Sunday.

Following their 1984 meeting, Steelers-Raiders games grew increasingly infrequent, and the two franchises didn't face each other again until September 1990. By then their rivalry was a fading echo, but at their peak in the seventies Pittsburgh and Oakland were the premier pro football teams of their era, and their rivalry ranks among the greatest in sports history.

Yankees–Red Sox, Rangers-Flyers, Ohio State–Michigan football, Duke–North Carolina men's basketball, Ali-Frazier, Palmer-Nicklaus, and Borg-McEnroe have all served to capture the imagination. So, too, have the Raiders' wars out west with division rivals Kansas City,

San Diego, and Denver as well as their East Coast–West Coast battles with Joe Namath's Jets. The Steelers have likewise feuded with Central Division neighbors Cincinnati, Cleveland, Houston, and, most recently, the Baltimore Ravens, as well as colliding with the Cowboys in three memorable Super Bowls.

Still, Steelers-Raiders stands alone in its intensity. NFL rules were changed because of the brutally physical Oakland and Pittsburgh teams of the seventies. Their games became so violent that the highest law in the land, the United States Supreme Court, was required to restore some sense of civility.

The impact of the "Mel Blount Rule" remains to this day. The 1977 NFL season was the last to see not a single receiver amass at least 1,000 yards receiving. NFL secondaries, particularly those in Pittsburgh and Oakland, were so smothering that the '77 season was the first since 1957 in which the league's leading receiver had fewer than 900 yards, Dallas's Drew Pearson topping the NFL with 870.

The 1978 season and the combination of the Mel Blount Rule and the expansion to a sixteen-game regular season changed forever the way pro football is played. The Mel Blount Rule gave free rein to receivers and gave rise to record-breaking quarterbacks from Dan Fouts, Joe Montana, and Dan Marino to Peyton Manning, Tom Brady, and Aaron Rodgers.

The excellence of defensive football played in the '70s still resonates. Bill Belichick, one of the greatest defensive masterminds in NFL history, has paid tribute to Pittsburgh's famed Steel Curtain. "The best thing the Steelers did with their Steel Curtain defense is that they just dominated with their front," Belichick said.

Whereas the '85 Bears dominated with blitzing linebackers Mike Singletary, Otis Wilson, and Wilber Marshall, the Steel Curtain was able to put pressure on the QB with its front four. Tackles Joe Greene and Ernie Holmes would key the opposing center, and whichever direction the center went, the opposite tackle—Mean Joe or Arrowhead Ernie—would penetrate into the line of scrimmage. "This was the thing that the Steelers were so good at," said Belichick. "They were able to execute these stunts on the move, Hall of Famers like Mean Joe

Greene. It was tough [for offenses to deal with], just too much pressure. That's what they did a great job of on a very consistent basis."

Because they are nondivisional foes and because they are situated on opposite sides of the country, the rivalry between the Steelers and Raiders doesn't boast the longevity of NFL blood feuds like Green Bay–Chicago or Philadelphia–New York.

Yet the fact remains that for five years, Steelers versus Raiders was the greatest, most intense, most physical, and most talent-laden rivalry in sports history. An astounding twenty-two future Pro Football Hall of Fame players and coaches took the field for those Raiders-Steelers wars; include the front office personnel, and the number of those enshrined in Canton climbs to twenty-six. No other rivalry in any sport can match that level of greatness.

That number may grow if Cliff Branch and L. C. Greenwood gain induction, as many believe they should. Branch was a game changer, a man who proved that speed kills. "He's a Hall of Famer, period," Mike Ditka said. "What he contributed to the Oakland Raiders was unbelievable."

Fred Biletnikoff said that the way Branch played overshadowed a lot of Hall of Famers. Ronnie Lott said that even great receivers like Lynn Swann, Steve Largent, John Stallworth, and Art Monk didn't have what Branch had. "When you were in front of him," Lott said of Branch, "there was fear there."

The fear factor forced Hall of Fame defenders like Kenny Easley to give Branch a large cushion of space, as much as 12–15 yards. And even that, Easley stated, wasn't enough.

Mel Blount stated that the Steel Curtain knew it had to game-plan for No. 21. "If you didn't," Blount added, "you were going to go home a loser."

Blount said that Branch changed the way the game was played, leading other teams to look for wide receivers with speed.

Joe Greene agreed. "When he was going against our best guy [Blount], he could light it up from anywhere on the field."

Branch lit up in big games as well, raising his level of play in a way that impressed old rivals like Blount. "The stage never got too big for him," Blount said. "That's what great players are all about. They rise to the occasion and separate themselves from the pack."

Greenwood rose to the occasion as well, playing on the Steelers' four Super Bowl championship teams in the 1970s and earning berths on the Super Bowl's silver anniversary team. Greenwood's unique combination of speed and strength allowed him to dominate from his left end position.

L.C. was a six-time Pro Bowl selection and a two-time All-Pro choice. He was named All-AFC six times and led the Steel Curtain in sacks five times. In his career Greenwood amassed 73.5 sacks.

Fittingly, the ten games played between the Steelers and Raiders from 1972 to 1976 resulted in a 5-5 split. Pittsburgh led 2–1 in conference championships and 3–2 in the postseason; Oakland owned a 3–2 advantage in the regular season.

Add in the play that NFL Films and pro football fans rank as the single greatest in league history—Franco's Immaculate Reception—and it's clear that Steelers versus Raiders circa 1970s stands alone in sports history. It was a rivalry so great, even the nation's most iconic singer—Frank Sinatra—enlisted in Franco's Italian Army.

It was Pittsburgh's gold Terrible Towel versus Oakland's black hankies, Franco's Italian Army and Gerela's Gorillas versus Raider Nation, Myron Cope's nasally "DoubleYoi!" and Bill King's gravelly "Touchdown, Raiders!"

It was Pittsburgh defensive tackle "Mean" Joe Greene angled on Oakland center and fellow Hall of Famer Jim Otto, "Double O," in the Steel Curtain's celebrated "Stunt 4-3" scheme. It was Steelers QB Terry Bradshaw, matching up with Snake Stabler, a man his opposite in style and strategy.

It was Steelers receivers John Stallworth and Lynn Swann, the latter a man as graceful as his surname suggests, running patterns in the dark recesses of Oakland's Soul Patrol.

It was Greenwood's gold high-tops and Biletnikoff's gooey Stickum.

It was Steelers coach Chuck Noll, his fires well banked, against Raiders coach John Madden, who wore his emotions on his sleeves. It was Al Davis gnawing his fingernails and Art Rooney Sr. chewing the end of his ever-present cigar.

These were more than morality plays; they were coastal wars carried out, fittingly enough, on the grass at the Coliseum in Oakland and on the Tartan Turf of Three Rivers Stadium.

Finally, it was Franco Harris starting it all with his miraculous shoestring catch of a deflected pass against the Raiders in the 1972 AFC playoffs. Was it deflected by Tatum, which the Steelers and their supporters continue to claim and which would have made it a legal catch, or did it carom off Franco's teammate Frenchy Fuqua, which under the rules in 1972 would have rendered it illegal? "It doesn't go away," Madden said, "so there's never been any closure."

Two days after the Immaculate Reception, on Christmas Day, Myron Cope obtained from WTAE's newsroom the film of Franco's catch from one of the station's cameramen. Running the film at regular speed made it impossible to determine whether the ball had hit Tatum, Fuqua, or both. So Cope ran it through a viewing device that allowed him to review the play frame by frame at what he said was a "snail's pace."

No doubt about it, Cope stated. Bradshaw's pass struck Tatum on the right shoulder pad, and the force with which it was thrown, combined with Tatum rushing in to make the play—"I thought I might have a chance for the ball, until [Fuqua] got in front of me," Tatum said—caused the ball to ricochet several yards back and into the reaching hands of Harris.

Steelers radio announcer Jack Fleming proceeded to call the most famous play in pro football history:

"It's caught out of the air! The ball is pulled in by Franco Harris! Harris is going for a touchdown for Pittsburgh! Harris is going . . . Five seconds left on the clock. Franco Harris pulled in the football. I don't even know where he came from!"

Regardless of where Franco came from on that most famous play in football history, where Harris, the Steelers, the Raiders, the NFL, and the sports world ended up was a place no sports rivalry had been before and hasn't been since.

Hell, with the lid off.